BASEBALL HISTORY
FROM OUTSIDE
THE LINES

A READER

EDITED BY

JOHN E. DREIFORT

UNIVERSITY OF NEBRASKA PRESS

LINCOLN AND LONDON

Acknowledgments for the use of previously
published material appear on pages 347–48,
which constitute an extension of the copyright page.
© 2001 by the University of Nebraska Press
Manufactured in the United States of America
Library of Congress Cataloging-in-Publication Data
Baseball history from outside the lines: a reader / edited by John E. Dreifort.
p. cm.
Includes bibliographical references and index.
ISBN 0-8032-6587-5 (pbk. : alk. paper)
1. Baseball—History. I. Dreifort, John E.
GV862.5 .B39   2001
796.357'0973—dc21   00-061540

To my parents
To my father, who taught me how to play catch
To my mother, who indulged my fantasies

Contents

Illustrations

Editor's Introduction

During the past few years, while offering a popular college course on the history of baseball, I have learned that while there are several fine single volume surveys of the history of the game, there are few scholarly materials to complement such texts. Yet during the past couple of decades a rich new body of baseball literature has been published that provides fresh and exciting insight into the nature, evolution, and impact of the national pastime. Thus was born the notion to produce a supplemental anthology that would for the first time gather into one volume some of the best recent historical literature about the game. My first impulse was to suggest such a project to Benjamin Rader, who has written the best single volume history of the game. In a neat trick of reversing the tables, however, he suggested that while such an anthology was needed, I should do it. Moreover, he proceeded to send me materials that he had already collected for such a project. Boxed into a corner by his generosity, I had no recourse but to proceed with this work.

Such a collection of essays, I believe, should be directed not only to classroom students, but also to the general audience who are students and enthusiasts of the game. Indeed, many of the students who take classes in the history of baseball are not history majors but enthusiasts who are keenly interested in the history of baseball. As Larry Gerlach has written, "Baseball history . . . represents a rare intersection of academic and public interests." Here then was an opportunity to provide important scholarly perspectives on various issues of importance in the American past that have generally remained outside the purview of most students of the game. Consequently, this book is intended to serve not only as a supplement to surveys in the field. It is also designed as a stand-alone volume that will pique the interest and satisfy the curiosity of baseball's general reading public, who may not have considered either the game's impact outside of the field of play or the effect of external influences on the game.

These essays, drawn from scholarly journals and appropriate mono-graphs, cover the gamut of baseball history and provide a sampling of the best recent writing about the historical development of the game. However, their perspective is from "outside the lines." Some of the essays are the products of tightly focused research, while others are based on broadly conceived interpretation. My intent is to provide a selection that provides a chronological flow emphasizing the historical growth and development of the sport. The anthology is also designed to complement the framework of narrative histories of the game by permitting a deeper treatment of fewer topics. Many readers will be familiar with the various events, people, and feats described herein, but they will be asked to view them through the analytical eye of a scholar. Within that broad organization a series of topics that range broadly in scope and time frame are explored. My goal is to provide the reader with a sense of the richness of the history of the game, as well as the depth of insight and freshness of analysis that can be brought to its study. My purpose is not merely to describe developments in the game's past, but to assess what impact they had or how they reflected the period in which they occurred. In the course of such reading, a student may also develop a better appreciation for the broader American society and culture.

As with any anthology of this nature, one can debate the merits of the essays selected—indeed, there was always one more piece that appeared to deserve inclusion. My criteria for inclusion in the volume were several. First and foremost was the goal of incorporating the best and most important or fascinating recent scholarship based on extensive archival research and critical analysis. Just as importantly, however, essays selected are written in an eminently readable fashion, free of arcane academic jargon. As historian Doris Kearns Goodwin has proved in her recent baseball memoir, the terms "readability" and "scholarly" are not necessarily exclusive. In this way, I anticipate that the volume will be appreciated and understood by students and general readers alike. My hope is that they will be encouraged to read further in the field.

Second, the essays are primarily drawn from the work done by scholars during the last two decades of the millennium. This decision was based on the fact that it has been largely during that period that the history of baseball has achieved respectability as a field of historical inquiry. The outpouring of scholarly pieces during the last twenty years has brought great insight and prominence to the field. For most of its existence, the study of baseball has been relegated to the "academic bush leagues" by the professional historical community. Those professional scholars who undertook more than an occasional foray into the field risked loss of credibility among their peers. One suspects that there existed a sense that anything that could be so much fun must not be serious academic material. Little respected by intellectuals and largely left to sports columnists and well-intentioned enthusiasts, much of the writing about the sport tended to focus upon its myths, heroes, climactic moments, and anecdotes. In a self-fulfilling prophesy, therefore, the writing about the sport was viewed by serious scholars as interesting but superficial. This began to change as a result of the domestic turmoil of the 1960s and 1970s, which gave rise to increased interest in American social and cultural history within the professional historical community. An increased willingness to work with the tools and approaches of other disciplines such as anthropology, sociology, economics, and psychology, among others, brought an interdisciplinary perspective to the historical study of a variety of interesting and important new fields of inquiry, including baseball. Although skeptics continued to abound, serious scholars began to recognize that baseball, along with sport history generally, was an important ingredient in understanding the American character and the nation's past. New organizations such as the North American Society for Sport History and the Society for American Baseball Research (SABR) were established. Conferences and panels organized around baseball-related topics cropped up around the country. Articles and essays appeared in the most respected scholarly journals such as the *American Historical Review* and *Journal of American History.* In the past decade many of the most venerable and respected academic presses have published important books on baseball subjects. All of these developments now make it possible to draw upon a wealth of significant scholarly pieces for such a collection as this.

Lastly, I have attempted to include essays that sample and display the broad range and scope of issues that have confronted the game, as well as the society of which it is a part. Not only are some of the game's heroes discussed, but also its villains—the game's achievements as well as its disgraces. Indeed, it has been said that history consists of many stories, so the essays that are included also examine such diverse topics as demographics, communities, social mobility, race and ethnicity, business and player-management relations, local amateurs, women, and foreign players. All of the selections present distinct points of view and interpretation in an effort to shed additional light on areas of baseball's historical experience that are often overlooked or underappreciated. In the end my intent is to immerse readers in the subject and to deepen their understanding of the game as well as its complex relationship to America's past—putting flesh on the bare bones of historical fact, while simultaneously encouraging critical thinking about the past. Inevitably, perhaps, more questions than answers will be generated about the game and its history. That is as it should be, for it is the critical judgment and analysis that underlie all historical research that make the retelling and rethinking worthwhile and make such a foray into the history of America's "pastime" enjoyable and exciting. In the end I hope that additional insight will be offered to the wider audience about what it is that historians do.

The volume has been divided into four parts. The first three are organized chronologically to offer insight into baseball and American society at various stages of history and to complement the fine narratives that detail the history of the game. Nevertheless, several of the essays cut across neat, but often artificial, historical divisions. The eras chosen for this volume are distinguished by characteristics that set them apart, or they are divided by events that are clearly turning points. World War I, the Black Sox scandal, and the subsequent arrival of Babe Ruth were among those turning points for the game's structure, play, and popularity. Similarly, World War II, followed by Jackie Robinson's integration of professional baseball, marked a departure that profoundly changed the game.

At the same time, there are threads that run through each section and connect each period. Although the later sections of the book tend to focus on the professional game, the role of amateur and semiprofessional baseball has a place in each of the eras, especially in the first three decades (covered in the first part), when the game was almost entirely amateur. Additionally, another thread is provided by an essay in each section devoted to the African American experience in baseball.

The selections in part 1 provide readers with perspectives about baseball's antecedents and its development during its formative years until the game ultimately established its place in American life as "The National Pastime." The essays assess the underlying causes of the game's diffusion throughout the country and analyze the reasons that the nation developed a passion for the game. They confront the game's relationship with larger social and cultural moods, as well as the dynamic political and economic changes of the nineteenth century.

One can debate the designation of part 2 as the "Golden Era" because there were many who did not enjoy the benefits associated with such a label. Players remained subservient to and victims of owners' whims. Blacks remained barred from participation in the major leagues. Moreover, the Great Depression caused financial hardship for much of the baseball world, as it did for society at large. Nevertheless, the era that roughly incorporates the years between the end of World War I and the end of World War II was far more important than one simply embellished by nostalgia. Perhaps because it was a period when too much history happened in too short a time, dynamic forces and fundamental structural changes occurred in American society that eventually engulfed baseball. Not only did the game provide a welcome respite from the grimness and dislocations of the Depression era, but it also generated a revolution of its own in the way in which the game was played. It produced a galaxy of epic heroes whose accomplishments and fame immortalized them among the century's greatest athletic legends. Although a relatively short period in the history of the game, that era had an impact far beyond its time. It served as a bridge between the old "deadball era" and the "modern game" and set the stage for subsequent changes that would influence the course of the game for the rest of the century.

The postwar era discussed by the essays in part 3 saw professional baseball become truly a "national game" for the first time in its existence. Integration of the major leagues in 1947 opened up the game to a large segment of the population hitherto excluded. With the availability of improved transportation systems, the game grew and moved with the population— from city to suburbs, east to west, north to south. Major league franchises relocated to the West Coast and to the south. League expansion began to fill the spaces in between, so that the number of "major league cities" nearly doubled. Night games made baseball available to working class segments of the population. Television brought baseball into the homes of millions who had never seen a major league game, eventually stimulating their desire to see the game in person. Even the franchises themselves were no longer the private fiefdoms of a handful of baseball lords. Communities and local governments assumed large financial stakes in the teams, wealthy large multinational corporations assumed faceless control, and media empires vied for broadcast rights. Players became empowered through their union and drew additional national attention to the game. All of these interest groups had a direct interest in broadening the game's national base.

The fact that the opening game of the 2000 season took place between the Chicago Cubs and the New York Mets—in Tokyo—attests to the basis for part 4, "The International Game." Despite the early efforts of Albert Spalding to spread the game overseas, baseball had remained confined to the Western Hemisphere, with an outpost in Japan. But during the last couple of decades of the twentieth century the game exploded internationally. It became an Olympic sport, where the American contingent found itself regularly bested by teams from Cuba and Japan and severely challenged by Canadian and Korean entries. Traditionally strong professional leagues in the Caribbean found new rivals for players from new leagues in Australia, Taiwan, Italy, and Holland. Although playing at an admittedly low level, amateur and professional teams could be found even in such distant places as Israel, France, Russia, and Poland, among others. And in youth baseball, American teams found themselves challenged and often beaten by teams from Taiwan, the Philippines, and Puerto Rico, which attested to the building of an infrastructural base in those countries that will eventually allow them to compete at a high level in the professional game. It was not uncommon for major league teams to field multinational teams made up of Asians and Hispanics, as well as Australians and Canadians. Many other international players were knocking on the door in the minor leagues. In light of such developments, it is not difficult to imagine that not too far into the twenty-first century the new frontier of major league expansion will be overseas, where new-found wealth and leisure time among burgeoning populations will provide attractive markets for America's game.

In their original form the collected essays included significant scholarly apparatus, important documentation, and references. In the interest of space, such notes have been excluded for the purposes of this anthology, but the reader is encouraged to refer to the Source Acknowledgments to find and explore the original readings for additional insights.

While surveying the state of the history of baseball in his fine essay "Not Quite Ready for Prime Time," historian Larry Gerlach has admonished, "Whoever would write the history of baseball had better know the dynamics and nuances of the game." Although I am one of those historians whom he reproaches for pausing in their professional pursuits for "a cup of coffee" in the field of baseball history, I believe that I bring to the endeavor an enduring commitment to the game and knowledge of its subtleties far beyond most rookies in the field. I have played it, coached it, taught it, and spent a lifetime watching and studying it. As the father of a professional major league baseball player, I also have served as occasional agent, part-time financial adviser, and full-time sport psychologist. I also happen to be a trained historian. To those who know my past and present avocation, as well as professional vocation, and have encouraged me in this new scholarly direction, especially Benjamin Rader, Hal Rothman, and Douglas Bendell, I give my profound thanks. I thank my colleagues in the Department of History at Wichita State University who put up with my transgressions, and I am appreciative of the valuable assistance of the interlibrary loan service of the university's Ablah Library. I am indebted to my colleague Peter T. Zoller for once again lending me the benefit of his keen editorial eye and thoughtful perspectives. To Gerald Loper and the Faculty Support

Committee at Wichita State University, I give my appreciation for the funding that made possible the release time to see this project through to completion. I am grateful to Michael T. Kelly for the use of illustrations from his private collection. Most of all, however, I give thanks to my wife Carol for allowing me to indulge in my fantasy and to my sons, Todd and Darren, for keeping me in the game and on the edge of my seat for the past twenty years.

PART 1: THE NATIONAL PASTIME

WARREN GOLDSTEIN

1. The Base Ball Fraternity

Recent students of the history of baseball have become fascinated with the game's antecedents and its relationship with American society, from its earliest formative years to its phenomenal rise to popularity and respectability as America's national pastime. The history of the organized game begins in the 1840s, when, as a social consequence of the industrialization and urbanization of the nation, several factors combined to encourage the rise of team sports for participants as well as for spectators. During the relatively short period of three decades prior to the emergence of the professional game in the late 1860s, there developed an amateur game led by the young clerks and artisans of the country's bustling major East Coast cities. Energetic enough to challenge established rituals, innovative enough to create new forms of participation, and prosperous enough to engage in leisure pursuits, these like-minded young men established voluntary associations, or social clubs, and called themselves members of the "base ball fraternity."

Warren Goldstein provides interesting insights into the origins and membership of these formal social clubs, whose activities extended well beyond the game itself. In doing so, he places the game and its adherents squarely in the mainstream of mid-nineteenth-century social and cultural forces. The game's simplicity, low cost, individual participation within the larger group, and the period's notions of fair play all appealed to the cultural and social proclivities of a dynamic urban-industrial America. It is important to know who played the game in order to understand better how the game came to achieve such popularity as the national pastime and how it related to larger social and cultural developments of the young nation. Additionally, it is instructive to understand how the notions of work and play developed a harmonious relationship in the minds of participants and spectators of the period, a relationship that increased and perhaps justified the game's popularity.

RITES OF PLAY

The men who played early baseball considered themselves members of "the base ball fraternity," a fraternity organized around the baseball club. Although the language of the baseball club is still used today, even with respect to professional teams, it has been obsolete for a century. The earliest baseball organizations were genuine social clubs, in which baseball playing was an important but far from the only activity. As one club constitution put it, "the objects of the Club shall be to 'improve, foster and perpetuate the American game of Base Ball,' and advance morally, socially, and physically, the interests of its members."

Baseball clubs had much in common with other male fraternal organizations in antebellum America. They were governed by constitutions, by-laws, and officers. Members paid dues and met regularly, either in their "club rooms" (usually located in a hotel or tavern) or on the playing field. Membership ranged from a dozen to more than two hundred. Depending on the number of members, clubs designated a "first nine" (the nine best players), a "second nine," and sometimes a "third nine." Most also had what was known as a "muffin nine," comprising the club's worst players.

Competition between clubs during these years was quite formal. Although most clubs had regular "practice games," not all clubs played matches, and some played many more than others. Players and the press distinguished between "practice games," "friendly games," and "social games," on the one hand, and more competitive "matches" or "match-games," on the other. In order to arrange a match, a club first issued a written challenge to the club it wished to play; the challenged club then decided whether to accept the challenge. Matches could consist of a single game, but a club usually challenged another to a "home-and-home" series, best two out of three games.

The captains of the opposing nines would agree on a mutually acceptable umpire, the press would be notified of the upcoming match, and occasionally the games would be advertised. Some matches were played for special prizes, but prizes were usually awarded only in large tournaments. The prize for victory in most matches was the game ball. At the end of the game, a spokesman for the losing club would present the ball to the winner with a short speech, to which a representative of the winning club would respond in kind. The ball was then retired, inscribed with the date and the score, and put in the winners' trophy case, usually located in their clubroom.

Presentation of the ball did not end the affair. Throughout the 1850s and much of the 1860s, a match game was followed by a meal hosted by the "home" club, commonly at a local tavern, restaurant, or hotel. The festivities, which included toasts, speeches, and songs, sometimes lasted well into the night. These postgame social activities were mentioned in game stories, and from time to time they received detailed coverage. The fraternity kept track of the best hosts. A game with the Atlantic Club, for example, appears to have guaranteed its opponents (who were usually its victims) the "well-known hospitality" of this Brooklyn club. Such hospitality frequently included alcohol. At a match between the Atlantics and Eckfords in 1862, a third club provided a "fine collation including champagne." And an informal game a month later "was concluded in true base ball fashion, cheers and 'tigers' being exchanged in a hearty and earnest manner, and the 'lager and segars' were also hospitably dispensed." The *Clipper* observed good-naturedly of a game in 1860 that a "keg of lager" may have contributed to the apparent inability of the players to remember the score.

When clubs traveled to a neighboring city or town, as many did once or twice a season, they were always entertained by the host club. The further they traveled, the more extravagant their treatment. Arriving in Baltimore at 4:00 A.M. for a match later that day, the Brooklyn Excelsiors were met by a committee of their hosts, the Baltimore Excelsiors,

> by whom they were escorted to Guy's Monument House, where all sat down to a splendid breakfast. . . . During the morning they were escorted in carriages to the various places of interest throughout the city, every attention it was possible to bestow upon them being given them by the gentlemanly members of the Baltimore Excelsiors. Indeed from the time of their arrival to their departure not a cent's expense were they allowed to incur, and whenever they desired to visit any place, carriages were at once placed at their disposal; in fact, nothing that the most generous hospitality could suggest, or yield, was wanting to make their time pass agreeably, and in this respect the Baltimoreans were most successful and victorious, taking the palm from every previous occasion the Excelsiors have hitherto enjoyed.

About an hour before the time appointed for the commencement of the game, the Brooklyn party were escorted to Holliday street, where a city car, gaily decked with flags, and drawn by four horses, was in readiness to take them to the ground.

The game itself was lopsided, as the "masters of the game" from Brooklyn crushed their hosts, 51 to 6, but no one seemed to care. What mattered was the evening's entertainment:

> . . . the company, to the number of fifty and more, sat down to a most sumptuous entertainment. . . . After full justice had been done the good things there spread before them, and the appetites created by the exercise in the field had made things rapidly disappear, Dr. Hawks, President of the Baltimore club, in a few appropriate remarks welcomed the Excelsiors, and closed by toasting them as the Champion club of the United States. . . . Dr. Jones, of the Brooklyn Excelsiors, ably responded to the toast in his usual eloquent style, but begged to be excused from receiving the compliment of the "champion club," and closed by offering as a sentiment, "the Excelsior club of Baltimore," which was responded to most heartily by three times three from the Brooklyn boys. Other toasts followed. . . . And so the time passed, until . . . evidence of the dawn's appearance.

After spending the rest of the day sightseeing, the Excelsiors departed for Philadelphia, where they easily defeated a "picked nine," or allstar team, and enjoyed similar festivities.

Combining their baseball with other forms of socializing during the season, clubs stayed active through the winter months as well, even when they played no baseball at all. In fact, the early 1860s equivalent of the hot-stove league consisted of the numerous social events of the prominent New York and Brooklyn clubs: balls, suppers, hops, promenades, skating parties, "soirees," and the like. Each club seems to have had an annual ball, an occasion for a different kind of performance, but still a performance, and one that engaged no small amount of competitive spirit.

At the second annual ball of the Eckford Club of Brooklyn, for example, the ballroom was "elegantly and profusely decorated with an abundance of bunting," along with the colors of a dozen area clubs. Frank Pidgeon, the "veteran captain" of the club's first nine, displayed his prowess on the dance floor, "officiat[ing] at the head of the floor managers in regular Parisian style." Press coverage was as enthusiastic as if the Eckfords had just hosted a major tournament. "It affords us sincere pleasure to chronicle the entire and perfect success of the Eckford's second annual reunion," the story went on, "and we hope that the club and their 'troop of friends' will long live to arrange and indulge in the joys of many similar festive occasions."

Members of baseball clubs were proud of their ability to attract women both to observe their baseball skill and to participate in their social events. Fearful that their sport would be dismissed as "boys' play," they were especially happy to draw women to undeniably adult social occasions. The press, in turn, was eager for evidence of this sort. The *Clipper* observed that the Eckfords had "long been noted for the number of ladies who assemble upon their grounds, as spectators of their playing." If "the full attendance at last winter's re-union" was any indication, at their balls, too, "their fair friends always assemble in unusual numbers." Similarly, the winter social calendar of the Bowdoin Base Ball Club of Boston was a tribute to the club's members, who "gave evidence," according to the *Clipper*, "that they were as much at the 'home base' in the ball room, with the ladies, as on the ball grounds with their friendly opponents." The rites of play extended from the ballfield to the ballroom, structuring the life of the baseball club.

"Hard Work and Victory"

That baseball club members participated in a wide range of social activities off the field did not mean that they failed to take their baseball seriously. On the contrary, players and commentators alike understood that first-rate baseball play depended on frequent practice, mastery of one or two positions by each player, and a disciplined cooperation on the ballfield. Baseball reporters stressed the advantages of regular practice, and commonly attributed victory or defeat to practice or indolence.

After being thrashed by the Knickerbockers, for example, the Empire Club earned little sympathy: the losers "gave evidence of a want of practice altogether, and like all who go into matches without due practice, merit the defeat they sustained." A *Clipper* reporter scolded the Atlantics for their "relaxed state of discipline" and advised them of "the necessity of their at once introducing a prompt reform in this respect, by giving more attention to the practice requisite to insure success." Noting that a Philadelphia club's members were "working like beavers" to prepare for matches in New York, another reporter asked rhetorically, "What are our Clubs . . . doing? Simply nothing." On the other hand, when the Star Club overwhelmed the New York Gothams 41 to 16, *Wilkes' Spirit of the Times* noted this "practical and striking illustration of the advantages of continuous and regular practice." Because the Stars had begun practice on April 1, by mid-May they were "a unit, each backing each other up, in every and all positions, like clock-work." A victory for the Gothams, who had not practiced all season, "would be strange, indeed."

Skill was only rarely connected to "natural talent" or "innate ability." The play of the Athletics in 1865 was "a practical and pertinent illustration of the efficacy of constant and steady *practice*: for to it almost solely are the Athletics indebted for a large proportion of their success and fame." In the Excelsiors' case, two defeats in 1863 "roused them up" the next season, not to acquire better players but "to the knowledge of the facts that a better organization of their first nine and more practice are necessary to insure that success the reputation of the Club and the well-known individual skill of its members deserve." Similarly, "superior muscle" may have helped the Harvard freshmen defeat the Brown sophomores in 1863, but the *Providence Journal* emphasized the "longer and more thorough training of the Harvard boys." Even a very bad ditty dedicated to the Columbia Base Ball Club of Bordentown, New Jersey, advised matter-of-factly in its closing stanza: "Practice, then, and when you play, / You'll be sure to win the day."

But practice alone was not enough. Baseball commentators had a more sophisticated approach to training very early in the history of top-level competitive baseball. Clubs, they urged, should practice so as to concentrate on the skill of the first nine by playing the "first nine against the field"— that is, the starting lineup against everybody else. That way the best players would get used to each other and to their set positions. Most of the contenders for the informal championship of these years appear to have taken this advice to heart. In early May 1865, for example, the Atlantics drew a thousand spectators (on a Monday afternoon) to watch the first of a series of "instructional games between the first nine and the field."

These methods had important consequences. First, a focus on the most skillful players made practices one-sided; other players had less chance to develop their skill or simply to play the game with their fellow club members. In this light, club social activities and post-game entertainments take on additional significance: they helped maintain the allegiance and participation of members who played little or not at all.

Second, this kind of practice contributed to the growing specialization of ballplayers as adepts at one or two positions. Failure to promote such specialization exposed a contending club to serious criticism. In one 1860s game the players' "positions were, as usual, different to those the majority of the same players had before occupied." It was "entirely out of the question," the reporter continued, "to suppose that special excellence in playing any one point of the game can be obtained unless the players, appointed to the position, permanently occupy it. A first base player, for instance, should be known as a first base player only, and the same as regards the other bases, the pitcher, catcher, and short field [shortstop]." An account of a match for the championship of Massachusetts in 1859 made a similar point: "It was evident to everyone present, that the distinguishing features of these Clubs were their admirable discipline and training, each player having his place, and being perfectly at home in it. Our city clubs would do well to imitate their country friends in this particular."

Finally, good baseball playing demanded a high degree of cooperation among the players as well as individual skill. Consistent success depended on players' familiarity with each other's style of play. The play of the Eckfords in a "grand match" in 1860, for example, made it "unnecessary to offer any comment; they are in a most perfect state of practice, and . . . enter the field and play as a unit. An exhibition of their Nine's playing is worth going some distance to look at, and we regard it as about the perfection of base ball playing."

What is striking about these commentaries from baseball's early years is that they employed almost exclusively the language of work: discipline, training, skill, specialization. By and large, such language was appropriate. The better New York and Brooklyn clubs practiced three times weekly, while the 1865 Philadelphia Athletics practiced four days a week. Increasingly during these years, particularly on competitive clubs, players did specialize at one or two positions. And without a doubt, the most successful nines owed their victories to practice, acquired skill, and highly coordinated play.

Neither reporters nor players tried to insulate their game from the language or ideology of work. A club just organizing in 1860 announced that it had begun practice, and would soon "be most happy to meet in the field any challenging club, when they will strive to render themselves worthy of their motto, 'Hard Work and Victory.' " The club motto is particularly arresting. No hint of frivolity or casualness, no suggestion of fun, and no appeal to health disturbed the terrain it claimed. And although that terrain was physically outside the workplace—it was, as a matter of fact, in the Elysian Fields of Hoboken, New Jersey—it was in other ways quite close to it. Nor was this club alone. Members of the Fulton Club could be found every Monday "hard at work" on their grounds in Hoboken. Members of that Philadelphia club, it will be recalled, were "working like beavers" to prepare for a match in 1863.

The language of work was used to describe the play of individual games as well. The Putnams, for example, "were slow in getting down to their work" in a game against the Eckfords, and found themselves eight runs behind after three innings. Teams that had fallen behind in a game and were trying to catch up were often described as going "into their work." Exhorting his team to make up a four-run deficit, the captain of the Atlantics urged his players: "Stop fooling, boys, and go into your work."

Reporters, in other words, showed little interest in the experience of "true sport" or "pure play." When they praised or criticized particular players and clubs, they appealed not to a concept or realm of leisure and play but rather to the standards of the workplace—a workplace in which craftsmen still exercised considerable collective autonomy over the pace and organization of their labor. By evaluating baseball play in the language of work, reporters were not breaking new ground. Their readers were not surprised to see the language of productive labor used to describe baseball playing. (In fact, some of the same language was used to describe prizefighting.) The language never heard or read was the language of "pure" play or "pure" recreation. The concept of pure recreation was only beginning to be created at this time. The development of play and leisure as a separate sphere of activity was largely a product of the latter half of the century, as we shall see.

PLAYERS AND WORKERS
The experience of baseball play in the mid–nineteenth century was not very far removed from the experience of work, especially from the world and culture of the urban workplace. Some clubs were based in specific shops or workplaces, such as the prominent Eckford Club of Brooklyn, which drew its members and players from the shipwrights and mechanics of the Henry Eckford shipyards. Other clubs appear to have been grounded in certain trades or occupations. The Baltic, Jefferson, and Atlantic clubs of the late 1850s were based in the food trades, which seem to have contributed disproportionately large numbers of baseball players. Clerks were also well represented in the ballplaying fraternity, perhaps especially in Washington DC, where government clerks filled the membership rolls of the local clubs.

In any attempt, then, to generalize about the composition of the fraternity as a whole, we must keep in mind that certain clubs were centered in particular trades, workplaces, or neighborhoods. Nevertheless, there is still value in looking at the general membership. In New York and Brooklyn, where we have the most extensive data on ballplayers' occupations, patterns were relatively stable between 1855 and 1870. Roughly one in five club members during this time belonged to a highly ranked occupation (a profession or a "high white collar" position); about a third were skilled craftsmen; while a little less than half (between 44 and 48 percent) were "low white collar or proprietors." There were so few unskilled workers that their significance lay mainly in their scarcity. In any given year, between 75 and 80 percent of the baseball fraternity could be found in occupations running from journeymen and clerks to master craftsmen and small shopkeepers. When we focus on the most active ballplayers during this period, as opposed to overall membership and occasional ballplayers, we find fully 90 percent of these men in the middle groupings. The absolute numbers of ballplayers begin to get rather small, so statistical breakdowns have less meaning, but it does seem that, especially in Brooklyn, it was skilled craftsmen who dominated the game on the playing field.

In Chicago, where the baseball fad reached its height in the latter half of the 1860s, bookkeepers and clerks appear to have substantially outnumbered skilled and unskilled workers on club nines. Nevertheless, as in New York and Brooklyn, the middle occupational groupings continued to account for roughly three quarters of active club players. In New Jersey during the late 1850s, skilled workers outnumbered clerks and small proprietors on the ballfield; combined, these two groups made up a little more than 60 percent of the total.

Baseball clubs represented in the National Association of Base Ball Players were at the center of the baseball fraternity and received most of the press coverage. These were the clubs that played the most, sponsored the most postseason social events, and furnished the most skillfully played exhibitions of the sport. But the sporting weeklies would also publish brief notices of other games when correspondents provided them, for many men played the newly popular game without belonging to a club. Baseball nines (or teams)—as distinct from baseball clubs—seem to have formed wherever men came together in organized groups: workplaces, voluntary associations, military organizations, colleges. The most fertile sources of baseball nines were volunteer fire companies and workplaces. Workers in the printing trades in particular—pressmen, compositors, engravers, and typographers—appear to have been the most active nonclub players.

Among those whose matches were reported in the press were the compositors and pressmen of the *New York Daily Times*, the Oceana Hose 36 and the Lafayette Engine Co. No. 19, Hose Company No. 55 and Engine Company No. 34. Engravers of the American Bank-Note Company frequently played their counterparts at the National Bank-Note Company. Very few of these nines ever joined the National Association. Evidently the relatively new ballplaying fraternity had less appeal than the preexisting fraternity of the firehouse or workplace.

Typographers received extensive press coverage from their journalistic brethren, and were understood as a distinct category of ballplayer. "Base Ball in Rochester among the Typos," read a typical headline to an 1860 report of a match game between "nine valiant men from *The Express* office" and their opposite numbers from the *Union.* By 1866 printers were playing each other at the "Typographical Grounds" in Brooklyn. Not coincidentally, printing was one of the better organized trades in the 1850s and 1860s, and the National Typographical Union's Local 6 of New York was the strongest local in the union. These skilled workers had craft traditions, rituals, and fraternal activities that went back a good many years. Apparently preferring occupational homogeneity on the ballfield, "typographical base-ballers" rarely played matches with nines outside their trade. More typical was the 1866 match in which two clubs of "typos" played for the championship of the trade in Philadelphia.

The baseball fraternity, then, was something of a mixture of classes, neither exclusively a middle-class nor a working-class sport. That is not to say that the fraternity was a democratic melting pot, in which men from all walks of life could rub off their class distinctions in competition on the diamond. This view—a staple of baseball ideology in the early twentieth century—was no more true of baseball's eary years than of any other. The game was born into a particular social context, and distinct class and cultural elements of that context nurtured the game in its infancy. Artisans and clerks, for instance, accounted for most of the players on workplace nines. Of the skilled craftsmen represented in the baseball world, a disproportionate number came from trades that had so far escaped the complete industrialization and restructuring into "sweated" workplaces characteristic of furniture, clothing, and shoe manufacturing in antebellum New York.

Printers—compositors, pressmen, typographers—were relatively well paid among skilled workers in New York, and maintained a sense of pride in their craft. The Eckford shipbuilders included relatively prosperous master craftsmen as well as journeymen in a trade that, at least in New York, was still governed substantially by artisans themselves. And among the food trades, butchers in particular managed to retain an unusual amount of control over Manhattan's principal markets and, as a result, over the pace and conditions of their work. We know less about the clerks and shopkeepers who joined baseball clubs, though there is evidence that the food trades supplied a number of baseball's small proprietors and some indication that clerks in dry goods firms, as well as in New York City government, played quite a bit of baseball.

That so many of baseball's best players were skilled craftsmen, men who, depending on their trade, still retained significant control over their work rhythms, helps to explain how players could have given so much time to baseball practice. (So does the early closing time of the food markets.) Many historians of the game have suggested casually that baseball must have been a middle-class sport because players had to take time off from work, but this description fits relatively few of the fraternity's best and most active players.

CULTURAL ANTECEDENTS

Baseball's demographic profile provides the background for understanding the culture into which the game was born. The new pastime's cultural antecedents lay in the swirling street life and frequently boisterous amusements of the urban (particularly New York) lower classes in the four decades before the Civil War. Fueled by extraordinary urban growth and massive immigration from abroad, shaped by technological innovation and the transformation of artisanal production, riven by sexual segregation, political factionalism, and nativism, the urban working-class popular culture of these years had a richness and density that historians have been mining for more than a decade without exhausting. Tracing the origins of this world lies beyond the scope of this book; nor is it possible to do justice to its multifariousness in a few paragraphs. A quick look at some of its distinctive institutions will serve.

In New York's Bowery were concentrated theaters and sideshows, brothels and oyster houses, saloons and gambling houses, markets and dance halls. Patronizing these institutions, working in them, or making their headquarters at them were members of volunteer fire companies, street gangs, political organizations and factions, and volunteer military companies. The degree of overlapping membership among these characteristic plebeian groups will never be known precisely, but undoubtedly it was substantial.

They shared a number of important qualities: they placed great importance on the integrity of their particular group, which possessed very clear boundaries of occupation, political faction, neighborhood, ethnic group, or some other measure of membership; they were frequently engaged in a physical rivalry with similar groups, whether through ritualistic competitions, spontaneous defense of honor, or drunken brawling; they shared a history of original "respectability," a quality they had lost by the late 1830s or early 1840s; each group served as an arena in which working-class men experienced and demonstrated "cultural autonomy and manly independence."

Commentators have remarked on the resemblances between fire-company competitions and team sports, but the sport with the closest ties to antebellum working-class culture was prizefighting. Saloonkeepers promoted boxing matches, and fighters made their headquarters in chosen bars. Boxers were recruited by fire companies and by political machines, and frequently belonged to New York's street gangs. During the heyday of this culture, baseball was literally unheard of.

By the late 1850s, however, the urban landscape had changed. The volunteer fire companies had fallen into such disrepute that many cities across the country were replacing them with professional forces. But before they disappeared from New York, volunteer firemen took up baseball, providing a kind of cultural bridge between this new sport and the earlier, more rough-and-tumble world of working-class leisure. Their baseball activities received less press attention than typographers', but the firemen clearly contributed a great deal more to the emerging culture of organized baseball. The New York Mutuals, for example, one of baseball's leading clubs into the 1870s, were founded in 1857 by Mutual Hook and Ladder Company No. 1.

Most striking are the cultural similarities between the two institutions. First, the names of early baseball clubs and fire companies were virtually indistinguishable. Names of fire companies tended to cluster around place names and nicknames (Buckeye, Missouri, Knickerbocker, Atlantic [Avenue]); Indian names (in New England); patriotic names (Washington, Franklin, Liberty, Union, Lafayette); names referring to water (Neptune, Oceana, Cascade); and names suggesting admirable qualities (Invincible, Perseverance, Alert, Friendship, Good Intent). A few New York companies conjured up more flamboyant images: the Black Joke, Red Rovers, Honey Bees, and Shad Bellies. Baseball clubs followed almost identical patterns in choosing their names, and to a remarkable extent seem simply to have copied the firemen. Water references naturally held less attraction for baseball clubs, which compensated by reaching into the heavens (Stars, Constellation, Satellite, Meteor) and into the classical past (Olympic, Minerva, Neptune, Sparta). Ballplayers chose Indian names more frequently (Powhattan, Pocahontas, Mohawk), and occasionally named their clubs after trades or workplaces (Typographical, Eckford, Henry Eckford, Fulton Market, Chestnut Street Theatre). If not all baseball club names had antecedents in fire companies, nearly all fire-company names were picked up by baseball clubs.

Patterns of baseball sociability closely parallelled those of the volunteer fire companies. The following description will sound familiar:

Firemen turned out in full regalia for the ceremony known as "visiting," . . . in which one fire department would play host to other fire companies for a few days. . . . A typical visit began with a triumphal departure from the engine house, bands playing and banners (presented "on behalf of the female friends of the company") waving, and a march through the city to the rail yards or docks. . . . On arriving, the visitors would be met by a delegation of firemen from the host city, and paraded to their quarters. . . . The next few days would be spent in a round of receptions, processions, trials of equipment, and endless collations ("wine and toasts passing freely around").

The postgame socializing enjoyed by baseball clubs was clearly modeled on that of the fire companies, even to the kind of food preferred at the dinners. "Chowder suppers," were characteristic of both institutions. Similarly, the annual fireman's ball preceded the annual balls of the early baseball clubs by several decades. The proceeds of the 1858 Brooklyn–New York all-star matches—the first time spectators paid to see a baseball game—were donated to the firemen's fund for widows and orphans. The Elysian Fields, where the Knickerbockers rented their grounds, were hosts to a full range of working-class leisure activities at this time, from fireman's parades and chowder suppers to union meetings.

Politicians' interest in baseball equaled their efforts to organize the fire companies and prizefighters only toward the end of the century. William Marcy Tweed, however, was more foresighted than most. A member of the Mutual Hook and Ladder Company, he later served as a longtime director of the New York Mutuals baseball club as well. The Mutuals' close links to Tammany Hall eventually brought the club into serious disrepute.

When baseball clubs gathered on the ballfield for a match, their players wore uniforms based on those of the firemen. Their belts were all but identical; the most visible resemblances between the two were their distinctive shirt fronts. Both wore rectangular or shield-shaped double-breasted panels, on which were carried the insignia of the club or company. Peck & Snyder, the premier sporting goods retailer in New York City, advertised firemen's belts and shirt fronts along with its line of baseball clothing. Whole firemen's uniforms were displayed next to the uniforms of baseball players.

Volunteer military companies, which survived until the Civil War, also provided important cultural antecedents for the baseball fraternity. One historian has even gone so far as to call the volunteer militia "the first national pastime in the Middle West." Like firemen and ballplayers, militia members wore distinctive uniforms (in fact, their uniforms were far gaudier than those of their ballplaying or fire-fighting counterparts), undertook elaborate "visits" between cities, held annual balls, engaged in public display and competition, and came in for public disapproval when such competitions degenerated into drunken melees.

However much baseball drew on previous traditions of workingclass leisure, its exhibitions were considerably less violent, less drunken, and on the whole less raucous than its cultural predecessors'. Baseball clubs included more middle-class members than fire companies, men who frequently held leadership positions within their clubs. Perhaps the combination of skilled workers and a complex team sport put a premium on a kind of self-disciplined cooperation ill-suited to the more expressive style of prize-fights or fire-company competitions. Baseball seems to have appealed to the more "respectable" members of the working class. Early baseball reporting emphasized the game's respectability as much as its character as skilled work.

Men of the middle classes responded to the appeal of respectable sport. For if middle-class members of the baseball fraternity offered their clubs little in the way of first-rate baseball skill, they contributed much to baseball culture. Most obviously, perhaps, the extended—and expensive—socializing between clubs could not have been paid for out of club dues, which ranged from $2 to $5 a year. Wealthier members clearly subsidized such activities.

It was not only their interest in flowery toasts and "splendid chowders" that drew middle-class men into the baseball fraternity. The Victorian middle-class attitude toward sport and physical recreation had begun to shift in the 1840s and 1850s, a development with important consequences for the history of all American sports. Although historians debate the precise causes of this change, it appears to have been linked to concerns about the growth of cities and sedentary occupations, a Protestant moral code emphasizing individual self-control, and a growing faith in social progress. Increasingly during these years, according to Elliott Gorn, these Victorian ideals were seen as realizable through physical education and respectable sport.

So the new concern for physical health led many men to embrace fresh air, exercise, and "manly sports" in the 1850s. The sporting press was full of articles about the benefits of exercise and all kinds of outdoor sports. Particularly during the late 1850s and early 1860s, baseball was defended, praised, and advertised as a "healthful recreation"—in Henry Chadwick's words, an "invigorating exercise and manly pastime."

Finally, middle-class club members brought to their baseball playing and and socializing the characteristic Victorian fear of unregulated passion and concern for self-control. This central component of American middle-class and respectable working-class culture has been insufficiently appreciated by students of American baseball. Early baseball players are usually pictured as priggish "gentlemen" whose "quaint" notions of "genteel sportsmanship" and "fair play"were quickly (and rightly) outgrown by the more "realistic" and competitive masses.

Although this view is exaggerated, it is not unfounded. Baseball was straddling a cultural boundary during those years, a position it has never managed entirely to escape. The game appealed simultaneously to the culture of the urban streets—a culture that was losing some of its principal institutions by the late 1850s—and to the respectable and newly vigorous culture of middle-class Victorian men. Participants in the baseball fraternity would find these two cultures difficult to reconcile.

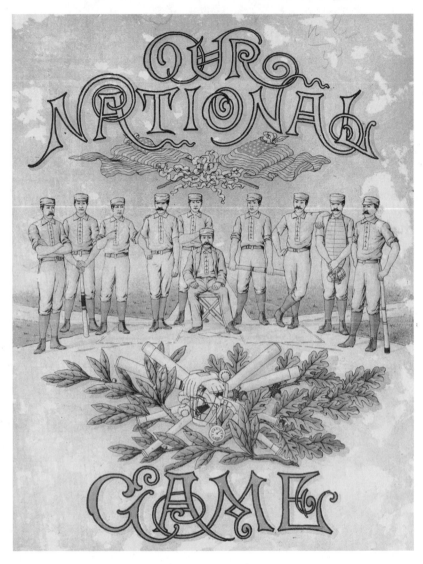

Cover illustration of *Our National Game* (Liebenroth Von Auw & Co., 1887). Private collection.

RONALD STORY

2. The Country of the Young: The Meaning of Baseball in Early American Culture

The transformation of the game of baseball from a relatively genteel social diversion among a comparatively limited segment of America's urban middle class around the mid–nineteenth century to a serious undertaking for substantial numbers of young American men has been studied widely. In the aftermath of the Civil War a baseball mania swept the country. The game quickly became the dominant summer pastime in villages, small towns, and rural whistle stops throughout the United States. Baseball became the favorite topic of wintertime arguments around the hot stoves of the country's general stores as the game emerged from the East Coast cities to capture the interest and imagination of America's rural and small town communities. It became a national rather than a regional craze. In the process it sealed the fate of cricket, which was still widely thought of as England's game, a view that London's pro-Confederate sympathies during the Civil War did little to change.

All of this we know. What has been more difficult to ascertain and assess are the underlying causes of this phenomenon. Was it the simplicity of the game for those who sought to learn it as opposed to the apparent complexity of cricket? Was it the speed with which the games could be completed? Or was it the relatively inexpensive nature of the game? Perhaps other, more subtle and deep-seated forces may have been at work. Was the geometry of the game more in tune with the biorhythms of the seasons? Was there a symbiotic relationship between the game and larger social and

cultural moods of the period? Did it not foster important qualities
of courage, self-discipline, and social solidarity? Was it the game's
delightful balance between physical prowess and mental agility? Or
perhaps the Civil War's influence on the spread of the game was of
paramount importance, as veterans returned home spreading the
game that they had learned from their comrades. Indeed, baseball
may have been seen as a remedy for that natural postwar boredom
and loss of camaraderie that they had experienced in the military.
It also provided a salve for the sectional divisions that had severely
wounded the nation.

Ronald Story explores some additional, tentative answers as to
why baseball, as one sport among many, came to capture the passions
of the nation during the period from 1875 through the 1880s. His
arguments, based on an analogy of the youth movements of the
twentieth century, provide an interesting and thought-provoking
insight into the adolescent emotional needs of the period and how
they became the cultural base upon which baseball rested.

We know we love it above all others. But why do we? Or rather, since
it started a long time ago, why *did* we? Why *baseball* and not some
other sport? Or *no* sport? And why baseball with such passionate single-
mindedness rather than as one sport among many? How did this come to be?

We can find some tentative answers, I believe, by looking closely at
the period when baseball truly began to sweep the country: the years
from about 1875 to 1895. Because it was the 1880s (as we'll call them for
brevity's sake), with their gaudy promotionalism, kaleidoscopic franchise
and league formation, spring training and transcontinental and international barnstorming treks, expanded seasons, city and world series, tobacco
cards, product endorsements, knothole gangs, booster clubs, flamboyant
daredevil players and weekly baseball newspapers—it was in the '80s that
baseball became what can only be described as a mass cultural movement,
a large-scale, passionate American affair on the scale and intensity of other
mass movements such as revivalism or temperance, and capable, therefore,
of creating a bedrock of players and "cranks" on which promoters and
sponsors would build.

A mass cultural movement of this kind cannot be accounted for, it seems
to me, the way most baseball historians have tried to account for it, by
reference to, for example, working-class occupations or Irish ethnicity, or
to the masculine subculture or railroad-based entertainment industry, or to
promotionalism and sponsorship. These were all significant, the Irish factor

particularly so. But they do not explain why the groups, the subculture, the entertainment moguls, and the politicians gravitated so powerfully to baseball rather than to something else. Nor, most importantly, do they explain the intensity and passion, the sudden breathless sweep, of the late 19th century's involvement with the game.

Baseball became so enormously popular in the 1880s for one reason: men loved it. And they loved it, I would argue, because they played it when they were young. Our concentration on the men's clubs and professional teams has misled us. The fact is that for every club or professional player we can identify from the late 1860s to the early 1880s, there were almost certainly a hundred nonprofessional players on organized teams and a thousand on unorganized ad hoc ones, almost all of them boys or young men between the ages of 10 and 20. It was the coming of age during the late 1870s and '80s of these thousands of youthful players that produced the huge critical mass of players, spectators and followers on which the mass baseball movement rested.

Love and passion—strong but appropriate words. Because these boys and young men not only played baseball but played it in the face of adult disinterest and disapproval. This is one of the most important differences between the 19th- and 20th-century games. Nineteenth-century adults did not really want their adolescent sons playing baseball. Stories abound of 19th-century fathers tracking down sons and whipping them off the ball field, of mothers throwing iron pots and boiling water at team organizers, of tempestuous quarrels over ball playing instead of chores and serious work. Nor, except for a handful of colleges, did schools sponsor baseball teams; and when school teams did appear, it was the students themselves who organized the teams.

So baseball was not only a mass movement, it was a youth movement, fomented in the face of disapproving authority. It was not only a counterpart to 19th-century revivalism and temperance, it was a precursor to 20th century movies and rock and roll. And it left an equally indelible impression.

Mass movements, and mass youth movements especially, arise because they satisfy deep-seated emotional needs among their adherents. Baseball must have been no different. The question, then, that finally addresses the meaning of baseball in early America, and the reason for its fabulous later popularity, is simply this: What needs did this era's adolescent male population have that baseball seemed able to satisfy so powerfully?

First some basics. Baseball was an outdoor activity for the hot months of the year. Nineteenth-century houses were places of work and basic bodily functions, with poor ventilation and lighting and, until the mid-1880s, no window screens. In summer, a house was "a place to get out of," as were most school buildings and places of work. And houses were crowded, commonly holding eight or more persons in a few small rooms. Front porches and steps were important living and socializing spaces in hot weather. But many houses had the main porch in the rear, and anyway, step and porch activities had to be fairly restrained. That left the streets and vacant lots and fields. Baseball flourished more than "saloon" games such as cards, darts or billiards partly because it gave exuberant young males something exciting and vigorous to do outdoors at a time when staying indoors was agony.

Early baseball was also aggressively physical. It was simple to learn and unlike, say, cricket, easy enough to play to accommodate a range of ages and skills. But the same thing that made the game relatively easy to play—underhand pitching and lenient ball-strike rules—insured lots of hitting and thus lots of fielding and base running, too. There were, therefore, endless bursts of action and limitless quick sprinting with very little dead time in between. And even though agility, speed and reflexes mattered, so did muscle—the capacity to throw the ball swiftly and hit it powerfully.

Baseball, in other words, was a superb outlet for the energies of boisterous young males in a way that languid pursuits—fishing or the saloon games or backyard games such as horseshoes or marbles—were not. Baseball's intensely competitive nature, even in the most casual contests, also led ball players to develop and hone their skills—to exert, that is, even more physical energy and on a more sustained basis. The sport probably never produced enough exertion to trigger the state of ecstasy reported by modern track stars and mountaineers. But the combination of physical exertion and competitive tension could produce tremendous exhilaration, something that even experienced young players called "joy."

This physical side of baseball, the premium it placed on strength, speed, and agility, is especially significant in view of the conditions in the country during the years when it became popular. Nineteenth-century America was nothing if not rough, and although the ball field was not the boxing ring, a reputation for baseball excellence carried over in other areas, lending status to players in a brawling era that held physical prowess and "grit" in high regard.

Ball players' pride in their skill, toughness, and physiques must have been acute in the 1860s and '70s because so many men were visibly unfit—frail, disabled, or both. The frail consisted in great measure of Irish immigrants and their offspring, who bore the twin burdens of the potato famine and its aftermath and the harsh poverty of unskilled laborers. Some Irish were, of course, rugged specimens, but many others were not. Their arrival in

America lowered the country's average height and held urban life expectancy to under 45. And with this residue of hunger and poverty went the damage of the Civil War. Limbless veterans inhabited every town and city for years after Appomattox, multiplying prosthesis shops as well as pension relief.

Paul Longmore argues that the disabled have been a negative reference group for other Americans just as blacks have been for whites. We define ourselves by what we are not—disabled, black, feminine, and so forth. Conscious of these frail, damaged men, their haler counterparts reacted typically: to display their health and wholeness, they rushed to play a physically demanding, highly visible sport—baseball.

Lastly but perhaps not least, baseball had some sexual significance. Anthropologists have speculated about the phallic symbolism of the ubiquitous bat. But the bat seems no more suggestive than other sporting implements—guns, fishing poles, cricket bats, lacrosse or hockey sticks— and the sport itself no more sexually freighted than games such as football, basketball, or soccer where players "penetrate" the goal with the ball. Yet baseball must have had a sexual dimension. Its players were almost exclusively young males with high testosterone levels and strong sexual urges that did not simply vanish because the sport was all-male. Promoters, in fact, took great pains to stress the game's "manly" and "masculine" qualities, and journalists took careful note of the number of women among the spectators and whether they were young, attractive, and single.

It was, in fact, not the bat but the player that had sexual import, particularly at higher levels where players wore tight-fitting, sometimes colorful, even red, uniforms. Opportunities for male physical display were rare in this era. Ordinary clothing did not enhance distinctive masculine features— broad shoulders, powerful chest, strong thigh and calf—and few activities gave adolescents and young men an opportunity for aggressively physical, therefore implicitly sexual, behavior that everyone, including women, could see. This may have appealed especially to our young Irishmen. Ireland had a heritage of separation, almost segregation, by gender, and the Famine migrants brought this legacy with them to America strengthened by the Great Hunger and reinforced by same-sex schooling. Irish boys had limited occasions to meet girls and gain facility at courtship, and most native-born Americans had it no easier. All-male sports allowed young Irishmen to send sexual signals while remaining safely apart. In this, baseball was a godsend, and not for the Irish alone.

Unfortunately, the basics, interesting as they are, don't really explain baseball's staggering popularity because there were other physical outdoor alternatives that might have satisfied these needs. Walking contests were leading spectator events in the mid–19th century but never captivated the country's youth as baseball did. Young men would watch walkers but only sporadically walk themselves, so an ardent mass following never developed. Important boxing matches drew throngs well into the 20th century, and boxing clubs attracted immigrant members and political patronage. Every 19th-century boy had to know how to fight with his hands or take a licking at every corner, and boxing as a sport with commonly accepted rules attracted zealous young participants. Yet neither walking nor fighting swept youthful America save on exceptional occasions when hordes would show up to see who was "fastest" and "toughest."

And there were others. The kicking and/or tackling game of football had been known since colonial times, got frequently touted by the mid-century sporting press as a cool weather sport, and had scattered "clubs" of its own. But it made little headway even after important collegiate matches began; "Irish" football, a soccer-like game played in the 1850s, did no better. Lacrosse, introduced here and there in the 1860s, made even fewer waves, while gymnastics, again widely known, remained almost exclusively a German pastime. Even cricket, which had a significant following before the Civil War, ultimately fared badly.

The question thus recurs. What emotional needs did the young males of this era have that were not met so well by these others sports but that baseball could, and did, meet singularly well? There were, let me suggest, three such needs, intertwined, but nonetheless distinctive: comradeship, recognition, and order.

Twentieth-century studies indicate that young Americans prefer team sports to individual sports while Europeans and Japanese incline to the opposite. This American preference first manifested itself in the 1860s and '70s, when baseball began to outstrip boxing, footracing, gymnastics and other individualistic physical activities. The young men's clubs that sponsored the earliest organized baseball teams were, in fact, highly "clubbish" affairs even off the field, placing great emphasis on dinners and fetes, and while such fraternal clubbishness declined with the spread of professionalism its aura may have lingered into the '70s.

But far more crucial, similar feelings flowed from the field of play. Not only did "teams"—aggregates of individuals—contest for victory, but the victory itself seemed to require actual "teamwork," a constant working together to blend disparate talents. Warren Goldstein suggests that early artisan players brought this stress on "victory through teamwork" with them from the shop floor and thereby imbued the sport with their particular mode of competitive labor excellence. But the game itself generated "team spirit," too. Teams that won with consistency needed several good players, not just one; even though only one player batted at a time, no one player, however talented, could carry a team. Winning was an inherently collective enterprise, inherently engendering solidarity. So, for that matter, was losing.

Far more than today, moreover, 19th-century teams at every level of play used what Bill James calls a "long sequence" offense, scoring by stringing small things together (two singles, two errors, and a single for three runs) rather than by doing fewer, but bigger things (double, single, home run). Historically, long-sequence offenses seem to produce more teamwork and team solidarity than short-sequence offenses because they force players to rely more on one another, thereby producing greater esprit de corps. And this playing-field esprit was intensified by the comradeship of the "bench"—teammates sitting or standing together when their "side" was batting, swapping vulgarities in the summer heat, shouting support in unison, enjoying male closeness.

The collective bonds produced by interdependence, joint contributions, and shared fate were different from the fraternalism of the early baseball clubs. Club members came together on the basis of common interests and attributes to play ball, or at least jointly sponsor ball playing. Teammates, by contrast, felt bound emotionally because they played together. But this esprit then spilled over the boundaries of the ball field to produce an intense camaraderie off it, too—at the adolescent level a tighter neighborhood or ethnic or "street" feeling, at the older level "the boys" singing on the train or in the hotel lobby, seeing new sights together, challenging all comers. The sociability of the club thus fused with the spirit of the team. "We played for love and excitement," they said. "We were a band of brothers, carrying everything before us."

Why did the young males of this era find this dimension of the sport so compelling? Why was the fraternal impulse so powerful among the period's young males? Undoubtedly in part because the rate of urbanization was so high. Urban populations were doubling every 10 years, propelled by a steady migration from country to city. This migration was disorienting under the best of circumstances. Massive war mobilization and demobilization and still more massive immigration, particularly from Famine Ireland, made it especially so. Nor did merely settling in the city mean the moving was over, because the population constantly churned so that boys would often live in three neighborhoods and attend four schools by the age of 15.

Young urbanites of this generation were highly likely, in other words, to have been born elsewhere or to have had parents born elsewhere and therefore to have experienced a dearth of conventional significant others—

cousins, grandparents and the like and, even more, familiar faces from their own age cohort. Nineteenth-century boys were perpetual "new kids" in town, "green as the verdant prairies," nervous about going outside lest they "be spoken to by someone not a member of the family." Boys created and recreated their own communities all through the 19th century, forming Tom Sawyerish "gangs," shaping streets and blocks into play areas and turfs, finding school "chums." Young men, encountering unfamiliar social landscapes, did much the same with fire companies, reading groups, political clubs and other voluntary associations. But it was not easy for so "scattered" a people to do. Therefore the opportunity to participate in a sport such as baseball, to "break into those crude games of ball," which seemed to create instantaneous community, was irresistible.

Other sports developed facsimiles of this comradely ethos. Racing and fighting exuded a pungent masculine clubbishness, as did early cricket. But they did so almost exclusively at the adult level, where gambling, drinking, and politics helped create the atmosphere, and almost exclusively as spectacle, the comradely ambience deriving from the shared excitement of observing and celebrating, with the contestants' arena more or less delineated from the spectators. Baseball engendered this clubbish aura, too; but it also generated a sense of solidarity among its participants, drew its players together as they played, in a way that fighting and running could not. Further, the dynamic of "the bench" helped produce a sense of comradeship not only by drawing together the players as they played but, as game pictures show, by blurring the line that separated participants and spectators, and rolling players, bench and crowd together into an emotionally unified whole.

But baseball meant more than comradeship. It also, to a degree unique among team sports, meant individual recognition. Lacrosse, soccer, and later basketball and hockey enabled individual players to stand out, chiefly by handling or scoring with the ball. But these sports did not guarantee every player a chance to gain recognition; and particularly at lower skill levels and among youthful players where baseball took strongest root, a handful of players, even a single player, could not only dominate a game but virtually monopolize the ball, leaving other players few ways to excel or even participate.

One player could influence a baseball game, too, especially pitchers; and some positions—pitcher, catcher, first base—got more action than others. But baseball's entire defensive and offensive configuration had individualis-tic overtones. Each player bore a title corresponding to a specific position— third baseman, rightfielder, and so on; each player bore responsibility for the area indicated by his title; each player himself defended it—caught balls thrown or hit to or through it—alone, out in the open, without aid or hindrance. Some positions had more action than others, but the ball came to every position sooner or later, usually pretty often in the early, high-scoring games. When it did, a single, visibly isolated player had to handle it.

Similarly on offense: A team's players took the offensive in serial fashion, one at a time in prearranged order, for approximately the same length of time—each batter until he reached base or made an out, each team until it made three outs, the game to last until teams made 27 outs or it got dark. Baseball's fundamental structure, that is, guaranteed that every player would have exactly the same offensive opportunity as every other player; that his opportunity would come automatically, without competition or combat for the opportunity; and that in the course of these high-scoring games, teams would bat through their lineups frequently, so that individual opportunities would recur just as frequently.

The offensive structure had other implications, too. By sending one batter to the plate at a time, baseball made every player the team standard-bearer, a personification of the whole team with all eyes on him, teammates' included—a limelight opportunity that the game guaranteed not just occasionally, but frequently during each game. And the rapidity with which teams wheeled their batters to and from the plate insured that offensive players not hitting or on base would keep focused on the field because their turn would soon come again. The sport's structure, rules, and inherent dynamic gave every player an equal chance to play the role of team champion in the offensive spotlight; and it gave him a captive audience while he was there.

Baseball thus brought recognition to its participants by scattering them defensively and bringing them quickly and serially to bat. Early newspaper coverage and the notational formulas devised to summarize the game accentuated these patterns. Organizing a team in the spring meant, among other things, submitting a roster—nine players plus an extra or two, all with their positions—to the press along with an appeal for opponents and sometimes the address of the club's headquarters or captain. Midwestern papers of the 1870s normally published only the rosters of the better young adult teams, but by 1880 they were publishing the rosters of adolescent teams as well. Playing serious baseball was often the best, if not the only way for boys to see their names in print—visible testimony to their individual as well as group identity. Once the season's games began, the papers sometimes announced impending contests by giving the starting lineups, printing players' positions along with their spot in the batting order, hence doubling the individual recognition. At the professional and semiprofessional levels and for big collegiate and city championship matches, papers that would occasionally include a box score consisting of times at bat, runs scored, and some fielding information along with the written account, thereby tripling the recognition factor.

Numbers mean immortality, argues Bill James. Baseball players will live in a way that football or lacrosse players cannot; a player's numbers, compiled from the evidence of the box score, guarantee it. For young players of the 1870s and early '80s, far below the professional level where statistics most mattered, it was not so much the cumulative record of the boxes that counted, although boys may have kept rough track of their own numbers and perceived their games partly through the borrowed lenses of the professional box scores—conceptualized their participation, in other words, according to the portrait of individualized collectivity suggested by the boxes. It was rather that rosters and lineups, and box scores later, publicly acknowledged players' existence not only as *belonging* persons but as *persons*.

Why did the era's young males yearn for recognition? A simple answer is that they resembled young men in most places at most times. The literature of the 18th and 19th centuries is filled with "young men from the provinces" seeking fortune and fame—a little recognition in the world's urban centers. Nineteenth-century Americans were no different, though many already lived in cities. They merely had more immediate models than Robinson Crusoe: the older ball players on display at the nearest grounds of whom they "made heroes" and "dreamed of imitating." They even dreamed of becoming heroes themselves.

For baseball, while a collective endeavor, was collective partly in the sense that the sum of a series of individual actions constitutes a collectivity. A team achievement was a statistical construct, the rolling together of many small components. Recognition was comradeship transposed. You were accepted, wanted, for what you yourself, with our own distinctive strengths and idiosyncrasies, could accomplish for your mates. When you failed, then that, too, the downside of responsibility, was glaringly evident. The inherent properties of the game guaranteed it.

Nineteenth-century boys may have felt the need for recognition with a special urgency. As family historians are beginning to show, mid-19th-century fathers, both immigrant and native-born, commonly related to their sons in two ways: by neglect, if farmers or wage workers; by domination and control, if artisans or clerks. Life, after all, was an ordeal. Security and status as well as survival spurred long hours at work or politics. Long hours meant long stretches when the father was not present, leaving children to feel ignored and neglected—not "recognized" as having value. What they got, instead, was regulated—rigidly directed as to daily regimen, as to schooling, as to fealty, behavior, work. Fathers did what they believed necessary under the alternatively tantalizing and ominous circumstances of the 19th-century world. Sons experienced it differently.

Were nineteenth-century mothers different? Ball players, like everyone else, remembered their mothers as "friends" and "supporters," full of compassion and concern, and maybe they were. But the typical household was large, with four, five, or more children to make demands on mother's attention and energy. Housework itself was arduous. And consider this: nearly half the total time that a boy might live in his parents' home, his mother was either pregnant or in postpartum recuperation, growing weaker, in many cases, with each pregnancy. Whatever the memories, it hardly seems possible that mothers had much in the way of surplus attention to bestow on a needy son or of surplus energy for meeting the innumerable emotional demands of a bursting household.

A speculation might be in order in this connection with the Irish and baseball. In the "stem" system of Irish families, a single son, usually the eldest, traditionally received what there was by way of patrimony and therefore what existed of concentrated, undivided attention. Favored, usually eldest, sons lived longest at home, got the most advantageous schooling, were introduced earliest to potential patrons or employers. Younger sons—the vast majority of sons—got packed off to work or school. So they sought recognition where they could find it: on the ball field.

Comradeship. Recognition. But also order. Allen Guttmann observes that whereas most team sports—soccer, hockey, rugby, basketball, polo, football, lacrosse—oscillate between the two poles, baseball is circular in its fundamental configuration and flow. This is true because, unlike other sports, where a team scores by moving the ball forward across a line or through a space that the opposing team defends, baseball players score without the ball, which is driven away from the offensive action, thereby enabling an individual player to touch the four points of a square (diamond) for a "run." Guttmann speculates that baseball's rounding of the square perhaps touches fundamental biorhythms related to the transit of the seasons and, by extension, the rhythms of the agricultural world. If so, he reasons, baseball may have served as a mechanism for easing the great transition from rural to urban life that has characterized the U.S.

Guttmann is almost surely right that there was something significant about the geometry and configurations of the game. Before the Civil War, players of ball-and-bat games had three more or less distinct ways to lay out a playing ground. One way was for cricket, with bowler and batsman occupying positions determined by the location of the wicket that the bowler aimed at and the batsman protected; batsmen scored by running along a line to the bowler's area and back. The field itself was oval, extending in every direction to a boundary laid round the outer limits. With "fair" territory defined in this way as anywhere inside the oval, which is to say everywhere, cricket had no fixed defensive posts, and players assumed a sometimes bewildering variety of positions according to their captain's orders.

Another was for baseball New England style, or "town ball,' as it was first called. Here the striker stood halfway between home and 1st, then ran to touch markers at the four corners of the square to score before being hit by a thrown ball. The position of the batter meant, however, that there was no good way to demark "fair" from "foul" territory. If lines were drawn along the home–3rd base line and the 1st–2nd line, the field became a rectangle reaching outward from the home–1st line towards the "out" (now left) field, leaving a narrow confining space where crowded fielders jockeyed and jostled for room. As a result, baseball New England style reverted to the cricket mode, a limitless space extending in all directions where players occupied uncertain spots depending on whim, circumstances, or a captain's will. Moreover, with no out-of-bounds there was no particular reason to touch bases in order and, therefore, no need for base paths to control a runner's movement, producing a game that was even more random and willful—disorderly—than cricket. This square-within-an-ovoid New England baseball lasted until the late 1850s when the angular "diamond" New York game supplanted it. When baseball flourished after 1865, it was in this New York form, which then helped it pass cricket in people's affections and thus become *the* model for the sport.

So there was clearly something important about the diamond formed by placing the batter at home plate. In this New York game, three of the right angles formed by lines intersecting the fourth point ("home") were out of bounds. Balls batted there were foul, no good except in a few special instances, and so did not need defending. This definition of "inbounds" as the space inside the single 90-degree arc formed by the diamond thus combined with the four bases of the diamond to determine the logical distribution of defenders—namely, in a double arc, a four-position configuration around the outer limits of the "infield" and a thinner, three-man arc beyond that. And as noted in connection with the recognition factor, from this logical configuration of defenders (fielders), came with equal logic the conventions of fixed and separate positions, each with a name, each name associated with a special space.

Baseball's rules, in other words, and the defensive logic that flowed from the geometry of its diamond-shaped infield, gave its participants fixed defensive positions within discrete spaces. Once the rules and logic became clear, moreover, virtually the same was true for ad hoc contests between odd numbers of players on narrow streets or rooftops or other expanded or smallish areas lacking true squares or a limitless widening of the "fair" angle. The discrete spacing held even under these conditions because of what players had to do to score—touch all bases consecutively without the ball—and how the field was conceived—as a rapidly spreading 90-degree fair territory. Meanwhile, batters who struck the ball had to move along the sides of the square and there only. Baseball, that is, imposed order on its players by sending them to specific areas of the field on defense and down rigidly delimited paths on offense. And it did so automatically by its rules and regulations.

Here is a primary difference between baseball and Guttmann's oscillating sports. In the latter, players' movements were more random and willful, players' paths and spaces less inviolate. There was greater opportunity for conflict, including physical collision, and less clarity of individual opportunity and objective. Sometimes collision was inherent, as with rugby or Irish or collegiate football; or players could perform tasks with little knowledge of how plays developed, again as in football but also sometimes in lacrosse or soccer. Order—the setting of boundaries, trajectories, and responsibilities—could be found in all these sports, but it was a partial order and one largely imposed by a captain's, coach's, or manager's authority. None had baseball's fixity of position, hence inviolability of person, and delineation of pathways, hence clarity of trajectory. Moreover, baseball controlled space and people *automatically*. The rest did so, *if* they did so, by means of external authority.

And observers knew this right away. Baseball was a game "whose regulations are calculated to prevent the ill-feelings engendered by other games." It was a "nonviolent" sport, with "splendid order" and "control," the "most organized of all sports being played." Renderings of 19th-century games commonly show the players separated on the field, fixed in distinct spaces, poised for action yet scattered and detached, moving down the narrow paths of the base lines. They stand forth amid the representations of boisterous and uncontrolled 19th-century groups, all but frozen in worlds of their own spaces, detached from the welter of ordinary urban life.

Yet the question, as before, is not only what baseball offered—in this case order—but why young men thirsted for it. And explanations lie readily at hand in the period's disorderly, destabilizing mobility and insubordination, particularly as evinced in the brawling cities and experienced by boys in the city streets. Besides seeing their fathers move from job to job, their families from neighborhood to neighborhood, themselves from school to school and boss to boss, males born in the 1850s and 1860s lived through war mobilization and massive waves of immigration, sharp financial panic and deep economic depression, ravenous fires and bitter labor disputes. And disorder's handmaid was raw violence: crime waves, a raucous saloon culture, political combat, turf battles, gang fights.

These young men were tough, made no mistake. The fought continuously to prove and protect themselves, and for thrills. But even the toughest young men, Robert Coles shows, need respite, "time out," if they can find it without losing face, and the not-so-tough-beneath-the-surface majority need it especially. Lacking adult authority figures to furnish safety and sanctuary, in the 1860s and '70s they found their own: on the ball field.

Richard Sennett argues that in the absence of powerful overarching institutions—a standing army, a national church, a corporate economy, a rigorous system of national schooling—a chief 19th-century refuge from danger and disorder was the family. But this is not wholly persuasive for our period. Consider the household from the standpoint of a boy growing up there: perpetually crowded with little room for consolation or order; the mother distracted, fatigued, "sick" with childbirth; the father remote, often absent, but when at home severe and critical and a conveyor, too, of the angry social and political passions of the world outside, a bearer sometimes of its physical wounds, always of its anxieties.

We may surmise, then, as follows. Young males of this generation needed security and order—breathing space, respite—in a world where violence and chaos seemed the norm. But families, which might have been a refuge, were often microcosms of the outside world, fecund sources of their own forms of unhappiness and insecurity; schools and gangs helped but brought uncertainties of their own. Still needing security, young men sought it where they could, especially in the surrogate family ambience of team sports. And of the available team sports, baseball, after the adoption of New York rules, served best. It constrained willfulness and assault better, and ordered space better, and it did so automatically and spontaneously, without adult aid or intervention.

This was, finally, an encompassing national movement because all of America was in turmoil in the 1860s and '70s. And baseball, which carried the seeds of security and control, of comradeship and recognition, within itself, was there to scatter them in identical ways all across the country. Because adolescent boys of that generation needed them, baseball became their salvation and their love. And they never forgot it. In partial payment, they made it the American game.

STEVEN A. RIESS

3. Professional Baseball and Social Mobility

By the turn of the twentieth century professional baseball had achieved a new level of maturity, stability, and respectability as an American sporting institution. Baseball's mythical origins as being uniquely American were actively fostered, and a bevy of popular national heroes, anointed with colorful nicknames like "King" Kelly, "Cap" Anson, and "Wee Willy" Keeler, ignited popular enthusiasm and imitation. Franchise stability had been established, and a division of baseball into two major leagues, the American and the National, neared creation. Such changes would provide organizational order and structure for a half century. The basic rules of the modern game had been firmly established. The return of prosperity after the depression-riddled 1890s augured well for the financial health and popularity of the game. Indeed, baseball reflected the Progressive Era of which it was a part. With the return of optimism and confidence, America's game was passionately embraced by young men throughout the country.

Steven A. Riess, a perceptive analyst of the game's social dimensions, seeks to determine who actually played the game at the professional level. In doing so, he challenges the myths and conventional wisdom accepted by contemporaries as well as historians that baseball served as a valuable avenue for upward social mobility for poor and uneducated young men. By amassing impressive data, Riess studies the class, ethnic, and regional backgrounds of professional players during the first couple of decades of the new century. Moreover, he examines the sources of the game's new-found respectability. A conspicuously improved status for professional players significantly influenced the class and ethnic makeup of the talent pool available to the game, its growing fan base, and the livelihoods of players upon their retirement from the game. Despite the realities of the game, its myths continued to emphasize the long-held beliefs about the game's role in promoting individualism, democracy, and meritorious advancement in American society.

Professional sports in America, along with the church, crime, entertainment, and politics, have long been regarded as valuable alternate avenues of upward mobility for poor and uneducated, but talented and ambitious young men. Contemporaries and historians have both assumed that sport was an area of American life where youths made it on their own, regardless of social background. Unfortunately, historians have conducted little empirical research to test whether sports have actually been an important source of social mobility. This article shows that professional baseball, the national pastime, was greatly overrated as a source of upward mobility during the Progressive Era when the game was at its unchallenged height.

By 1900, baseball was already known as the "old ball game." It had been a professional sport since the 1860s when the increasing demand for victory led baseball teams to recruit better players, regardless of their social status. These recruits were attracted by a variety of inducements—gifts, a good job, or even cash. The first all-salaried team was the Cincinnati Red Stockings of 1869, organized by businessman Aaron Champion to bring national recognition to his city. These athletes, previously artisans, clerks, or cricket players, were paid from $600 to $2,000. By 1871 there were enough all-professional teams to encourage the creation of the National Association of Professional Base Ball Players. This player-oriented league led a shaky existence during its five-year life. Among its many problems were high salaries and roster instability. Players "revolved" or jumped from one team to another, depending on the best offer. Average annual salaries were between $1,300 and $1,600, with stars getting up to $2,500, twice the earnings of artisans and four times the wages of all non-farm employees.

The Association was supplanted by the National League in 1876. The new league sought to put baseball on a sound financial footing. One major step was to make players subordinate to management through the reserve clause (1879), which permanently bound the athlete to his contracting team, although the club could sell, trade, or release him whenever it chose.

The NL's success encouraged the development of other professional leagues, most notably the American Association (1882–1891), which quickly achieved recognition as a major league.

High wages comprised the main expense of club owners, who tried to reduce their costs by cutting salaries and regulating the labor supply. A $2,000 maximum salary was established by the magnates, but this understanding was repeatedly evaded by under-the-table payments to stars to keep them loyal. In 1887, for example, the fabled Michael (King) Kelly signed a $2,000 contract with Boston and received another $3,000 when he sold a photograph of himself to the club owner. Salaries rose substantially in 1890 because of competition from the new Players' League, a cooperative venture of players and capitalists who were to share all profits. However, the Players' League collapsed at the end of the season after several of its owners were coopted by the National League, which sold them shares in certain teams. The NL and the AA then merged before the 1892 season to form a single twelve team National League. This further weakened the players' bargaining position and magnates took advantage of their strength to introduce a strictly adhered to $2,400 salary limit. Deflated salaries became the norm for the rest of the decade. When the NL dropped four franchises after the 1899 season, the players were left in an even weaker position. Suddenly one-third of the major leaguers were unemployed and the remaining men were put in a perilous situation.

Little is known about the early major leagues, but it seems likely that they were either artisans or low level white-collar workers of WASP, Irish, or German origin. National Association players whose birthplaces are known were overwhelmingly native-born (93.6 percent). The few successful immigrants were mainly assimilated Englishmen, who readily adapted their cricket skills to the American bat and ball game. Eighty-four percent of the known American-born were from cities (2,500 inhabitants), mainly Philadelphia, Brooklyn, Baltimore, and New York—the early centers of amateur baseball. These professionals fared poorly upon retirement from baseball since 35.6 percent of the big leaguers active between 1871 and 1882 ended up with blue-collar jobs.

Despite their relatively high wages, ballplayers were poorly regarded by the respectable classes, who categorized them with actors and boxers. The *New York Times* asserted that "in every point of view, he [the ballplayer] is an eminently undesirable person, and he ought to be . . . completely suppressed." There was strong prejudice against the professional players for their supposedly lower-class, Irish origins, whereas high prestige was reserved for the amateurs who could afford to play for fun. It was bad enough that professionals played for pay, but even worse, they did anything necessary to win, like cheating or yelling at opponents to unnerve them. Rowdy behavior on and off the field did not help. Players drank immoderately, fought with other players, umpires, and even fans, and mingled with nefarious characters. For instance, in 1877 a gambler induced four Louisville men to fix several late season games. It was no wonder that middle-class parents discouraged their sons from entering this occupation, regardless of the attractive pay scale.

The status of major leaguers improved markedly around the turn of the century. One reason was the improved status of professional baseball itself. Although public opinion had been somewhat ambivalent about professional baseball in the nineteenth century, it was universally accepted as a great game by the early 1900s. The sport's popularity was reflected by the doubling of major league attendance between 1901 and 1909 and the proliferation of minor leagues throughout the country. Baseball's respectability was reflected in its middle-class spectatorship and by laudatory articles in prestigious middle-class periodicals such as *American Magazine, Collier's,* and *Scribner's,* which praised the national pastime as the epitome of the American way of life.

Early major leaguers detested their low social standing and tried on their own to improve the status of their occupation. They were led first in the 1880s by John Montgomery Ward, a Giants star and a practicing attorney. In 1885, Ward organized the first players' union, the Brotherhood, which was instrumental in establishing the Players' League. Two other short-lived unions were started in 1900 and 1912. Their goals were greater security, higher wages, and a better image, which they sought by encouraging all players to behave well.

However, poor conduct continued to plague the sport. Certain major leaguers like Arthur (Bugs) Raymond and George (Rube) Waddell were well known for their intemperance and generally dissolute behavior. In contrast to such negative role models were ethical heroes like the college-bred Christy Mathewson, who seemed to certify that traditional values and beliefs in hard work, morality, and rugged individualism still worked in the impersonal urban world of the early 1900s.

Management also tried to raise the status of baseball and the ballplayers. Connie Mack and John J. McGraw, team managers, required their men to wear business suits on road trips and tried to accommodate them in the finest hotels, where they had previously been unwelcome, all of which helped their players gain middle-class respectability. Mack made another important move by vigorously recruiting college players. He felt that they were excellent athletes who learned quickly, responded well to orders, would set a model of proper conduct for less sophisticated players, and would improve the status of professional baseball. Star college athletes had previously avoided professional baseball because of its low status and brutish reputation. But Mack believed that collegians would be attracted if they could be shown that a baseball career promised respectability, high wages, fame, and a suitable lifestyle.

Along with the higher status of the sport, baseball's substantially improved salary scale attracted a better class of men. Wages rose noticeably after 1901 because of competition from the new American League, which doubled the number of big league positions. A bidding war ensued as the AL tried to justify its claim to major league status. Typical salaries increased by as much as 50 percent to a range of $1,200 to $4,000, putting ballplayers into the upper middle-class income bracket. Rookies generally started at about $1,200 and could look forward to annual raises if they played well. By 1904, such New York stars as Jack Chesbro, Joe (Ironman) McGinnity, and Mathewson were all paid over $5,000. Six years later there were ten men earning over $10,000, topped by Honus Wagner, the superstar shortstop of the Pittsburgh Pirates, who earned $18,000. The average wage in 1910 was over $3,000, making baseball an attractive occupation for men from all social backgrounds.

Salaries continued to escalate in the next decade, especially after the rise of the Federal League, which in 1914 sought recognition as a new major league. The new association created more jobs and the competition drove up wages for all players. The most heated bidding was for stars like Detroit's Ty Cobb, who re-signed with the Tigers in 1915 for $20,000, but lesser lights also benefited. Ray Fisher, the Yankee pitcher, earned $3,000 in 1913, but a year later negotiated a three-year contract worth $20,000. By 1923 the median salary was $5,000 and that increased to over $7,500 within six years. As a comparison, professors in 1929 were earning $3,056, dentists, $4,267, doctors, $5,224, and lawyers, $5,534.

Players who wanted to supplement their wages could do so by working during the long off season. At the very least, players usually participated in some post-season baseball games. The more famous players went on barnstorming tours through the hinterlands. In large cities where there were two teams intra-city series were staged. In Chicago, players for the Cubs and Sox could earn several hundred dollars for a week's effort, not much less than the shares of competitors in the World Series. Star players had many lucrative opportunities; they were recruited by businessmen to endorse products and theatrical promoters sought such men as John McGraw to appear in baseball skits on their vaudeville circuits.

The typical big leaguer did not have such lucrative and glamorous opportunities. But many were satisfied with their high wages and did little outside of hunting and fishing. Slightly more than half of those active during the off season were white-collar workers or students, about 25 percent were manual workers, and fewer than 20 percent were farmers. Nearly half of the white-collar men owned their own companies, where they tried to capitalize on their fame to secure customers, but these ventures had a high failure rate, typical of most small businesses. Their billiard parlors, cafes, and taverns failed because some players were simply poor businessmen, but also because it was difficult to operate any enterprise when the proprietor was away much of the time. The other white-collar players, who worked as salesmen or real estate agents, were able to take advantage of the improved prestige of their occupation to obtain jobs which required direct public contact.

The combination of the improved status of the sport and the occupation of ballplayer, the attractive salaries, and the opportunities to take advantage of their fame attracted a higher class of men to professional baseball. Players were not coming primarily from lower-class backgrounds as contemporaries believed, but from lower middle- and middle-class families. Of the major leaguers active between 1900 and 1919, 44.6 percent had fathers in non-manual labor, 20.9 percent had fathers who were farmers, and 34.4 percent had fathers in manual labor. These figures are far more impressive than the occupation distribution for all male Americans in 1910 (see Table 1). Whereas nearly half of that group (45.4 percent) were either semiskilled or unskilled, merely one tenth (10.7 percent) of the players' fathers worked at the least prestigious jobs.

The improved status of ballplayers was reflected by the women whom they married. The public image, popularized by the media and by Ring Lardner's short stories, was that players married "fast women" in the mold of the show girls that Michael Donlin, Richard (Rube) Marquard, and George (Babe) Ruth married. But in reality, players usually married respectable, well-educated women. Over three tenths of the wives of major leaguers who were active between 1900 and 1919 had continued their education beyond high school. One fifth of the wives of noncollege men and nearly seven tenths of the wives of college men had attended college. Although these figures may be exaggerated, the dimension of the numbers is so high as to indicate that the professional ballplayer was now more favored as a potential spouse.

Table 1. Fathers' Occupation of Major Leaguers Active 1900–1919 Compared to All U.S. Males

OCCUPATION	U.S. MALES, 1910 (%)	PLAYERS' FATHERS (%)
Professionals	3.1%	10.2%
Proprietary—Farm	19.9	20.9
—Others	7.9	27.0
Clerks	9.2	7.4
Skilled	14.5	23.7
Semiskilled	11.2	7.4
Unskilled—Farm	14.0	0.0
—Others	20.2	3.3
Total	100.0%	99.9%[a]

Source: Joseph Kahl, *The American Class Structure* (New York, 1957), 265; Questionnaire study data.
[a] Error due to rounding off.

The player's individual level of education was one more measure of the high status of the major leaguers. At least three quarters had attended high school and a quarter (25.8 percent) had attended college, compared to under 5 percent of the college-age population in 1910. These college men were not necessarily scholars, but might have been recruited by their college coaches. In return they received scholarships, had easy course loads, and high paying jobs. Many of these mercenaries spent their summers playing baseball for compensation under a pseudonym; becoming a full-time professional was seen as a natural outlet for their talents. Most college-trained professionals never graduated (although a surprisingly high proportion did), but the time spent on campus probably provided all of them with a broadening experience. The large proportion of college men in professional baseball further reflected the players' improved social origins, since college men were normally drawn from the higher social groups. Only 20.6 percent of the college-trained major leaguers had a working-class background, compared to 37.3 percent of the non-college men.

Besides regarding major leaguers as poor, ignorant men, the conventional wisdom also asserted that ballplayers came from rural regions and were recruited on a democratic basis. But in reality, professional ballplayers remained predominantly urban in origin in the early 1900s, although less so than in the past. Nearly three fifths (58.4 percent) were born in cities, compared to 35.4 percent of the national population in 1890. The ten largest cities comprised 11.7 percent of the white population in 1890, yet contributed 16.8 percent of the major leaguers, nearly 50 percent more than was warranted by their share of the population.

The domination by city boys reflected the strong urban baseball traditions. Baseball had originated and first became commercialized in cities. The presence of professional heroes provided important role models for city youths, who aspired to a big league career, and there was fierce competition for places on amateur teams sponsored by schools, businesses, ethnic groups, and religious organizations. The finest performers might receive some public recognition which could help them advance in their jobs or perhaps serve as a springboard into professional baseball.

The belief that everyone had an equal opportunity to become a major league ballplayer can be seriously questioned by examining the ethnic backgrounds of major leaguers. They were nearly all native-born Americans, Germans, or Irish. The Americans and Germans were solidly middle class whereas the Irish had been the lowest status whites in the nineteenth century. But by the turn of the century, the Irish were being replaced by the new immigrants from eastern and southern Europe, who were taking the least desirable jobs. Ambitious Irishmen who were deprived by lack of education, connections, or social position, might seek their fortunes in such areas as construction, crime, politics, religion, and boxing. They were also successful in baseball, one reporter estimating in the 1890s that Irish-Americans comprised one third of the major leaguers. Their prominence continued into the new century and was not restricted to the playing field, since in 1915 eleven of the sixteen managers were Irish. The sport was very popular among second- and third-generation Irish youths who played in school or on teams sponsored by their parish, tavern, or political clubs. The most proficient went into professional baseball.

The new immigrants, that is, the Italians, Jews, and Slavs, were rarely found on major league rosters in the early 1900s and were underrepresented in the sport for a generation. Between 1901 and 1906 there were five Bohemian, two Jewish, and no Italian rookies. There were no first-year men from these groups in 1910 and just one Czech and two Italians in 1920 out of 133 rookies. Thus baseball was not a notable means of upward mobility for some of the groups most in need of alternate routes to success.

Discrimination was not the main reason for their absence. The principal factor was that baseball did not fit in well with the new immigrant experience—unlike boxing, which was a useful skill for ghetto youths. Italians and Jews living in New York's Lower East Side or Chicago's West Side rarely became sufficiently skilled to compete with better equipped and better coached native-born Americans. There was little space for baseball diamonds in their crowded neighborhoods, they had little leisure time during daylight hours, and their parents frowned upon this strange American game played by men in short pants. Also, some able youths might have avoided this career because the rare second-generation new immigrant who made the majors was badly treated by old-timers, who resented his presence. Jewish ballplayers frequently changed their surnames to hide their ethnicity and avoid mistreatment. Veterans were afraid that these newcomers would take away their jobs, force down salaries, and diminish the prestige of their occupation.

Although baseball was theoretically open to all whites (including "Castilian" Cubans) and American Indians, the sport was closed to blacks after 1898. Beginning in 1872, about fifty blacks had participated in organized baseball, highlighted by Fleetwood Walker and his brother Welday, who played in the majors in 1884. But in the 1890s, club owners developed an unwritten policy to hire no more blacks. Much of the impetus for this move came from the white players, who felt the presence of blacks was a threat to their wages and status. It also reflected the pervasive racism of the period, since blacks were then being forced out of professional cycling and horse racing as well as more mundane occupations (catering, barbering, and cooking).

Skilled black athletes were restricted to all-black semiprofessional teams. These clubs were normally based in a large city but also toured the country scheduling games wherever they could, playing up to 200 contests a year. The ability of the best black players was acknowledged by sportswriters and by the major league players and managers, who competed against them on off days and after the regular season. Black players were encouraged by the success of light-skinned Cubans and Indians and hoped for their chance. However, no blacks were admitted into organized baseball until Jackie Robinson, in 1946, broke the color barrier when he signed with Montreal of the International League. The black experience in baseball was very different from that of the new immigrants. A sufficiently skilled second-generation white newcomer could sign a professional contract, although he might face prejudice from his teammates. The problem for the athletically inclined eastern or southern European was to obtain coaching and experience sufficient to reach a high level of competency. But blacks could never qualify, regardless of skill.

The careers of professional athletes were different from other careers since tenure was short. Few ballplayers played beyond their mid-thirties. The average major leaguer lasted about three years although, if we discount players who lasted just a few weeks, then the mean was closer to eight years. Facing retirement was a severe psychological crisis because of the uncertain future and the certainty of a loss in status and income. Examples of earlier players who ended up indigent worried even the most easy-going athlete as he grew older.

The conventional wisdom of the day was that ballplayers fared poorly after leaving the diamond. However, former major leaguers retired to jobs which were much better than their contemporaries realized (see Table 2). The principal job of nearly four fifths (78.8 percent) was non-manual; 3.4 percent became farmers; 13.4 percent became manual workers; and 4.4 percent were never employed because of illness or early death. Although their new positions did not pay as well as their jobs playing major league baseball, they were usually in "respectable" occupations. These results were much better than those of their cohorts from 1871 to 1882, who had a 35.6 percent drop into the manual class.

Nearly twice as many retirees worked as professionals compared to the male work force in 1910. This proportion reflected their high degree of education and was achieved even though it was difficult for them to sustain any professional standing while actively playing baseball. Indeed, there were instances when the retiree chose to drop his profession when he had a good opportunity to remain in baseball in a non-playing capacity. For example, David Danforth and Guy (Doc) White were both licensed dentists who had rarely practiced while active players, and they remained in baseball after retiring as competitors. However, there were cases of highly motivated men like David Jones and James (Doc) Casey who had studied pharmacy during the off seasons and later operated their own drugstores.

Retirees who held other high level white-collar jobs were primarily baseball executives or government officials, although there were some bankers, brokers, factory owners, and managers. At one time or another after retirement, 5 percent of the ex-players owned or operated a professional or semiprofessional club. Former players usually lacked the necessary capital, but might have been financed by friends or an old boss. Charles Comiskey of the White Sox helped Frank Isbell, a former employee, purchase a minor league team and in return expected first choice of any prospects that Isbell might develop. The other important leadership positions were usually in government. Retired nineteenth-century players often ended up working for their municipalities, mainly as firemen or policemen, but the later cohorts held more responsible roles, as commissioners, postmasters, or even mayors. An ex-major leaguer living in a small town might well have been

Table 2. Principal Occupation of Retired Major Leaguers Active 1900–1919

OCCUPATIONAL CATEGORY[a]	NUMBER	PERCENTAGE
High White-Collar		
Professionals	28	5.6
Managers, high officials, and		
major proprietors	91	18.2
Low White-Collar		
Clerks, sales, and kindred		
workers	48	9.6
Semiprofessionals	160	32.0
Petty proprietors, managers,		
and low officials	67	13.4
Total White-Collar	394	78.8
Farm		
Farmers—owners	17	3.4
—laborers	0	0.0
Total Farmers	17	3.4
Blue-Collar		
Skilled	18	3.6
Semiskilled and service	42	8.4
Unskilled	7	1.4
Total Blue-Collar	67	13.4
Other		
Inform or early death	22	4.4
Grand Total	500	100.0%

Source: Sample data of 593 men who played at least one year in Chicago or New York between 1900 and 1919.

[a] Categories from Stephan Thernstrom, *The Other Bostonians: Poverty and Progress in the American Metropolis, 1880–1970* (Cambridge, Mass., 1973), 290–292.

its most famous resident and he could use his fame for election to public office. In big cities the retirees might have relied on the political influence of their old boss to find a job for them.

Most ex-players were concentrated in the low status white-collar occupations, particularly in athletics. Retired ballplayers frequently maintained their middle-class status by securing a job in baseball where they could utilize their expertise to earn a living. The primary jobs of 29.2 percent were as coaches, managers, scouts, or umpires. Of the 593 men in the study sample

46.4 percent were involved in athletics at some time after retirement. This was a much higher percentage than the cohorts of 1871–1882; only about 11 percent of them held these jobs. The greatly increased opportunities in baseball resulted from its growing popularity and the enormous expansion of professional and amateur baseball throughout the United States. The job most sought was major league manager, although it was a tenuous position, rarely lasting more than a couple of years. But it was prestigious and well-paying, a fitting climax to an outstanding career. By 1910 the best managers were already earning salaries in five figures and were constantly in the limelight. Managers were recruited almost exclusively from former stars and their average playing tenure was fourteen years.

Outside of baseball, players had other opportunities to utilize their fame to secure a low white-collar job. Players hired as salesmen, real estate agents, or clerks were recruited by firms which hoped to take advantage of their famous names to lure potential customers. A job in sales, either in a firm or in his own business, suitably exploited an athlete's reputation because it placed him in a situation where he had a great deal of public contact.

Those athletes who became farmers were nearly always sons of farmers. But although one fifth of the major leaguers had farming fathers, only 3.4 percent made farming their life's work and another 4 percent worked on a farm some time after retirement. This small proportion is understandable since a retired athlete could not use his fame or athletic expertise to any advantage as a farmer.

Ballplayers who became manual workers suffered an enormous loss of income and prestige. The skilled retirees worked at crafts learned before becoming major leaguers, and some might have utilized their trade during the off season. These were secure, well-paying jobs, more remunerative than white-collar jobs as clerks, but they provided fewer chances for upward mobility. Service occupations had been popular amongst the men active in the early days of professional baseball (16.2 percent), but the proportion of ex-players working as policemen, firemen, or guards declined to 8.2 percent of the latter cohort, reflecting a better and wider choice of jobs for retirees. Still, government work at any level remained popular because of the adequate pay and benefits and the excellent security.

The new occupation of the retired player depended on such factors as his fame, length of service, social background, education, and even his personality. There was normally a close correlation between length of service and fame, but this was a crucial variable only when it came to seeking a baseball-related job. Blue-collar players had the shortest tenure, 7.8 years, compared to 8.2 for farmers, 8.6 for non-athletic white-collar men, and

10.1 for those who went into sports. The most important variables for non-athletic jobs were education and social background. Over 93 percent of the college-educated respondents to my questionnaire were white-collar, and virtually all the rest were farmers. But merely 67.5 percent of the noncollege men found white-collar jobs and one fourth ended up as manual workers. Social background was nearly as important in determining a player's future, even though he was in his thirties when he dropped out of the majors. Eighty-five percent of the fathers in non-manual labor, 77 percent of the farming fathers, and only 58 percent of the fathers in manual labor had sons in non-manual labor. Another way of looking at the relationship between father and son was that a farmer's son was four times as likely to become a farmer compared to the son of a father in manual or non-manual labor. A manual worker's son was three times as likely to become a blue-collar worker compared to the son of a father in non-manual labor and six times as likely as the son of a farmer. A typical player's future could be better predicted by his education and social class than by his batting average or won-loss record.

The conventional wisdom that professional baseball was an important alternate source of upward mobility for lower-class youths is inaccurate. The 368 major league jobs went mostly to well-educated, middle-class native American whites, Irishmen, and Germans who utilized the sport as a means of maintaining their social status and planned to use it as a ladder to future success. Although recruitment was generally meritocratic, it was not truly democratic since lower-class sons were underrepresented, having lacked the opportunities to develop the requisite skills. Blacks were completely excluded. Nevertheless, the myth of baseball's open recruitment policies was important for two reasons. It helped to certify in an increasingly compex society the continuing functionalism of traditional American values such as hard work and rugged individualism as well as traditional beliefs in democracy. The myth also promoted interest in baseball amongst recent immigrants who would ostensibly learn to become good Americans by participating in the rituals of the game.

MICHAEL S. KIMMEL

4. Baseball and the Reconstitution of American Masculinity, 1880–1920

Like the end of the twentieth century, the last decade of the nineteenth century saw Americans become fitness crazy, as they vigorously pursued all manner of activity that promoted physical health and well being. The list of cures pursued for ailments at the end of both centuries would be strikingly familiar. Physical health clubs, weight-lifting programs, cycling, running, bottled water, high-fiber diets, and consumption of large quantities of potions in the form of vitamins and herbs would all find their equivalents at the end of the nineteenth century. Then, as now, such concerns about individual health and fitness masked great uncertainties and fears about the future for a rapidly changing population. While current fads reflect the fears of the aging "baby boomer" generation that matured during the postindustrial, instant-gratification society, those of the previous century came of age at a time of great changes produced by the mechanization of American society.

Participation in sports around the turn of the twentieth century was seen as a patriotic duty calculated to reverse the slide into lethargy that came with lifestyle changes brought on by new technology. In a period heavily influenced by Social Darwinistic principles, many young men adhered to Theodore Roosevelt's notions that the "strenuous life" not only provided a means to rekindle a spirit of sexual and cultural dominance, but it was also necessary to achieve national greatness in a hostile world. Sports would create young men imbued with the attributes of physical, moral, and spiritual fitness. The strength of the nation was inextricably linked to the athletic

Fairmount College team, 1904. Though not dressed to take the field, a Miss Munn poses proudly with this turn-of-the-century team. Courtesy of the Special Collections Department, Wichita State University, Wichita KS.

vitality of its young men, disciplined with the attributes of physical, moral, and spiritual fitness.

Michael S. Kimmel examines the fitness craze of the late nineteenth century in the context of the perceived erosion of traditional middle-class masculinity. Not only forced to wrestle with an altered relationship with their work, men were also confronted by the closing of the American frontier as an outlet for their energies. Moreover, new waves of nontraditional immigrants as well as the emergence of an aggressive women's movement threatened male dominance in a whole array of social, cultural, political, and economic pursuits. The turn-of-the-century response to these forces that challenged their masculine dominance was manifested in many ways. Efforts to revitalize masculinity among the nation's manhood ranged from aggressive overseas imperialism to reconstituting the male vitality of earlier times by energetically embracing manly activities such as sports. Baseball proved to be an invaluable arena in which middle-class men could prove their manhood. The game provided the context of a new social and cultural order that allowed men to demonstrate their physical prowess, self-confidence, and social solidarity. In the process, they could fend off the social and cultural challenges from nonwhite immigrants, women, and the urban lower classes.

All boys love baseball. If they don't they're not real boys. – Zane Grey

Baseball is sport as American pastoral; more, perhaps, than any other sport, baseball evokes that nostalgic longing, those warm recollections of boyhood innocence, the balmy warmth of country air, the continuity of generations. More than this, baseball is a recollection of the America we have lost—languid and rural. The ballpark itself is a bucolic patch of green nestled in the burgeoning urban landscape. Baseball expresses the contradictions that lie at the heart of American culture.

And baseball is about both remaining a boy and becoming a man. Like other sports, baseball fuses work and play, transforming play into work and work into play, and thus smoothing the transition from boyhood to manhood. Play as work (the "professional" athlete who gets paid to play sports) generates adult responsibility and discipline; work as play (the incorporation of sport either literally, as in corporate softball leagues, or as metaphor as assembly lines compete with one another) allows one to enjoy the economic necessity of working. Some contemporary studies suggest that men who were successful as boyhood athletes become more successful in business; many cutting-edge corporations have introduced team sports among managers on the premise that such teamwork will increase productivity.

But unlike other sports, baseball inspires a literary eloquence that is unmatched, perhaps because it is so delicately poised between boyhood and manhood. No other sport has produced a Roger Angell or a Donald Hall, each of whom is preoccupied with the link between baseball and family memory. For Angell "going through baseball record books and picture books is like opening a family album stuffed with old letters, wedding invitations, tattered newspaper clippings, graduation programs, and curled up darkening snapshots," so that, for writer and fan, baseball players "seem like members of our family, or like trusted friends." And Hall underscores how baseball "connects American males with each other, not only through bleacher friendships and neighbor loyalties, not only through barroom fights, but, most importantly, through generations"; he continues: "Baseball is fathers and sons. Football is brothers beating each other up in the backyard, violent and superficial. Baseball is the generations, looping backward forever with a million apparitions of sticks and balls, cricket and rounders, and the game the Iroquois played in Connecticut before the English came. Baseball is fathers and sons playing catch, lazy and murderous, wild and controlled; the profound archaic song of birth, growth, age, and death. This diamond encloses what we are."

In this essay, I will examine one of the ways in which "this diamond encloses what we are," by looking at the historical links between baseball and masculinity in the United States. Focusing on the rise of baseball at the turn of the century, I will explore two themes, well developed by others, in order to make a third thematic argument. Looking back at the ways in which the rise of organized participatory sports was offered as a corrective to a perceived erosion of traditional masculinity in the late nineteenth century, and how the rise of mass-level spectator sports was part of the shift from a culture of production to a culture of consumption, I will argue that baseball was a key institutional vehicle by which masculinity was reconstituted and by which Americans accommodated themselves to shifting structural relations. Specifying the terms on which sports reconstituted American masculinity, I shall link participation and spectatorship, and explore how baseball provided an institutional nexus for a manhood that could be experienced as personally powerful while it simultaneously facilitated the emergence of a docile and disciplined labor force.

I. STRUCTURES AND FORCES

The early nineteenth century provided a fertile environment for an expansive American manhood. Geographic expansion combined with rapid industrial and urban growth to fuel a virile optimism about social possibilities. The Jacksonian assault against "effete" European bankers and the "primitive" Native American population grounded identity in a "securely achieved manhood." But by mid-century, "the walls of the male establishment began to crack" as social and economic changes eroded the foundations of traditional American masculinity. Westward expansion came to an abrupt end at the Pacific coast, and rapid industrialization radically altered men's relationship to their work. The independent artisan, the autonomous small farmer, the small shopkeeper, were everywhere disappearing. Before the Civil War, almost nine of every ten American men were farmers or self-employed businessmen; by 1870, that figure had dropped to two of three, and by 1910, less than one of three American men were as economically autonomous. Increased mechanization and routinization of labor accompanied rapid industrialization; individual workers were divorced from control over the labor process as well as dispossessed of ownership.

Simultaneously, social changes further eroded American men's identities. In the burgeoning cities, white Anglo-Saxon native-born men felt threatened by waves of immigrants. In 1870, for example, of the nearly one million people who lived in New York City, 4 of every 9 were foreign born. The rise of the women's movement in the late nineteenth century spelled the beginning of the end for men's monopoly over the ballot box, the college classroom, the professional school. The "New woman"—single, upwardly mobile, sexually active, professionally ambitious, and feminist— exacerbated men's insecurity and malaise.

The "crisis" of masculinity in the late nineteenth century emerged from these structural and social changes, as "the familiar routes to manhood were either washed out or roadblocked." This was not a generic crisis, experienced by all men in similar ways, but a crisis of middle-class white masculinity, a crisis in the dominant paradigm that was perceived as threatened by the simultaneous erosion of traditional structural foundations (economic autonomy, the frontier), new gains for women, and the infusion of nonwhite immigrants into industrial cities. It was a crisis of economic control, a struggle against larger units of capital that eroded workplace autonomy, and new workers (immigrants and women) who were seen as displacing traditional American men. And it was also a political crisis, pitting the traditional small town and rural white middle-class masculinity against new contenders for political incorporation. It was a crisis, in this sense, of gender hegemony, of whether or not the traditional white middle-class version of masculinity would continue to prevail over both women and nonwhite men. And therefore to understand how baseball articulated with these various dimensions of crisis in hegemonic masculinity, we will need to draw on analyses of the relations among various social classes, the relations between whites and nonwhites, and the relations between women and men.

Responses to the turn-of-the-century crisis of masculinity varied tremendously, especially given the simultaneity of the forces that seemed to be affecting middle-class white men. One reaction, the *antifeminist backlash*, sought to restore traditional gender arrangements in an effort to preserve a threatened masculinity. Antifeminists believed that if women would get out of the public sphere and go back to the private sphere, where, antifeminists argued, they belonged, the adverse impact of these social changes would be eliminated. A second reaction, the *profeminist reaction*, saw feminism as auguring important positive changes for men as well as for women. Thus profeminist men supported those reforms—coeducation, woman suffrage, women's entry into the labor force, birth control, higher education for women—that antifeminists opposed.

A third group believed that the problem lay not among women but among men, and specifically in the enervating effects of modern society on the nation's collective manhood. This *masculinist* response sought to revitalize masculinity, to return to men the vitality and strength which had been slowly draining from American men. Masculinism, both interpersonally and institutionally, articulated with other turn-of-the-century social currents, among them a rejection of the city as a den of corruption where healthy country men were transformed into effete dandies as hordes of unwashed immigrants threatened the racial purity of the nation. "Get your children into the country" one real estate advertisement for Wilmington, Delaware, urged potential buyers in 1905. "The cities murder children. The hot pavements, the dust, the noise, are fatal in many cases and harmful always. The history of successful men is nearly always the history of country boys." Frank Lloyd Wright's antiurban tirade in *The Future of Architecture* captures this sentiment, and links it to the perceived feminization of American culture: "A place fit for banking and prostitution and not much else . . . a crime of crimes . . . a vast prison . . . triumph of the herd instinct . . . outgrown and overgrown . . . the greatest mouth in the world . . . humanity preying upon humanity . . . carcass . . . parasite . . . fibrous tumor . . . pig-pile . . . incongruous mantrap of monstrous dimensions . . . Enormity devouring manhood, confusing personality by frustration of individuality." Antiurban sentiments were also fueled by a nativist racism that saw cities as the breeders of an immigrant threat.

Institutionally, the masculinist effort to stem the tide of feminization of American manhood included the development of the YMCA and the Boy Scouts, in which young boys could experience the remedial effects of the wilderness away from the feminizing clutches of mothers and teachers. If consumer society had "turned robust manly, self-reliant boyhood into a lot of flat-chested cigarette smokers with shaky nerves and doubtful vitality," as Chief Scout Ernest Thompson Seton had it, then the BSA could "counter the forces of feminization and maintain traditional manhood."

Masculinism included the Muscular Christianity movement, in which, through texts like Thomas Hughes' *The Manliness of Christ* (1880) and Carl Case's *The Masculine in Religion* (1906), the image of Jesus was transformed from a beatific, delicate, soft-spoken champion of the poor into a musclebound he-man whose message encouraged the strong to dominate the weak. Jesus was no "dough-faced lick-spittle proposition," proclaimed itinerant evangelist Billy Sunday, but "the greatest scrapper who ever lived." A former professional baseball player turned country preacher, Sunday drew enormous crowds to his fiery sermons where he preached against institutionalized Protestantism. "Lord save us from off-handed, flabby-cheeked, brittle-boned, weak-kneed, thin-skinned, pliable, plastic, spineless, effeminate, ossified three-karat Christianity." Masculinism also promoted a revived martial idealism, and found a new hero in Theodore Roosevelt, who believed that "the greatest danger that a long period of profound peace offers to a nation is that of [creating] effeminate tendencies in young men." Perhaps masculinity could be retrieved through imperial expansion, since, as General Homer Lea put it, "[as] manhood marks the height of physical vigor among mankind, so the militant successes of a nation mark the zenith of its physical greatness."

And masculinism also found institutional expression in the sports craze that swept the nation in the last decade of the century. The first tennis court was built in Boston in 1876, the first basketball court in 1891. The American Bowling Congress was founded in 1895 and the Amateur Athletic Union established in 1890. Sports offered a counter to the "prosy mediocrity of the latter-day industrial scheme of life," as Thorstein Veblen put it in *The Theory of the Leisure Class*, revitalizing American manhood while it replaced the frontier as "the outlet through which the pressure of urban populations was eased." Nowhere was this better expressed than in the rapid rise of baseball, both as a participatory sport and as a spectator sport. Baseball became one of the central mechanisms by which masculinity was reconstituted at the turn of the century, as well as one of the vehicles by which the various classes, races, and ethnicities that were thrown together into the urban melting pot accommodated themselves to industrial class society and developed the temperaments that facilitated the transition to a consumer culture.

II. PLAYING

The whole test of the worth of any sport should be the demand that sport makes upon those qualities of mind and body which in their sum we call manliness. – Theodore Roosevelt

In the late nineteenth century, America went "sports crazy." The nation had never been as preoccupied with physical health and exercise; Americans flocked to health spas, consumed quantities of potions and elixirs (like the 63 imported and 42 domestic bottled waters advertised by one firm in 1900), lifted weights, listened to health reformers extoll the tonic virtues of country air and bland high-fiber diets, raced through urban parks on bicycles, and tried their hands at tennis, golf, boxing, cricket and baseball. The search for individual physical perfection masked a deeper hopelessness about the possibility of social transformation, and also linked fears of cultural enervation and individual lethargy and failure of nerve.

Sports were heralded as character-building; health reformers promised athletic activity would not only make young men healthier, but instill moral virtues as well. Sports were a central element in the fight against feminization; sports made boys into men. In advice books, which counseled concerned parents about proper methods of child rearing, sports were invariably linked with the acquisition of appropriate gender-role behavior for males. Sports had been recommended as early as the 1840s and 1850s, when the "confusion and ambivalence within the baseball fraternity over the boundary between men and boys resembled the tensions between the culture of respectability and the culture of the street." Now they were *necessary*, according to D.A. Sargent, to "counteract the enervating tendency of the times and to improve the health, strength, and vigor of our youth" since they provided the best kind of "general exercise for the body, and develop courage, manliness, and self-control." Sports aided youth in "the struggle for manliness," wrote G. Walter Fiske in *Boy Life and Self-Government.* Sports were especially advised for boys because, as physical education professor Luther Halsey Gulick, Jr. put it, "athletics do not test womanliness as they test manliness."

Manhood required proof, and sports were a "place where manhood was earned," not as "part of any ceremonial rite of passage but through the visible demonstration of achievement." Such demonstration was particularly important because lurking beneath the fear of feminization was the fear of effeminacy and homosexuality, which had emerged in visible subcultures in urban centers. One English newspaper championed athletics for substituting the "feats of man for the 'freak of the fop,' hardiness for effeminacy, and dexterity for luxurious indolence."

Some were less sanguine about sports' curative value. Thorstein Veblen's blistering critique of the nascent consumer culture, *The Theory of the Leisure Class,* suggests that organized sports are an illusory panacea. For the individual man, athletics are no sign of virtue, since "the temperament which inclines men to [sports] is essentially a boyish temperament. The addiction to sports therefore in a peculiar degree marks an arrested development of the man's moral nature." And culturally, sports may be an evolutionary throwback, as they "afford an exercise for dexterity and for the emulative ferocity and astuteness characteristic of predatory life."

Most commentators saw sports as the arena for men to achieve physical manhood, but believed that organized sports would instill important moral values as well. Here, especially, the masculinist response to the crisis of masculinity resonated with the antiurban sentiments of those who feared modern industrial society. Sports could rescue American boys from the "haunts of dissipation" that seduced them in the cities—the taverns, gambling parlors, and brothels, according to the *Brooklyn Eagle*. Youth needs recreation, the *New York Herald* claims, and "if they can't get it healthily and morally, they will seek it unhealthily and immorally at night, in drink saloons or at the gambling tables, and from these dissipations to those of a lower depth, the gradation is easy."

And what was true of sports in general was particularly true of baseball. Theodore Roosevelt listed baseball in his list of "the true sports for a manly race" (along with running, rowing, football, boxing, wrestling, shooting, riding and mountain climbing). Just as horse racing had resulted in better horse breeding, Edward Marshall claimed in 1910, so baseball "resulted in improvement in man breeding." "No boy can grow to a perfectly normal manhood today without the benefits of at least a small amount of baseball experience and practice," wrote William McKeever in his popular advice manual, *Training the Boy*.

The values that baseball called into play were important to the man and central to the nation. The baseball player was "no thug trained to brutality like the prizefighter," noted baseball pioneer A. G. Spalding, nor was he a "half-developed little creature like a jockey" but an exemplar of distinctly "native" American virtues, which Spalding alliteratively enumerated in *America's National Game* (1911): "American Courage, Confidence, Combativeness; American Dash, Discipline, Determination; American Energy, Eagerness, Enthusiasm; American Pluck, Persistence, Performance; American Spirit, Sagacity, Success; American Vim, Vigor, Virility." Essayist Addington Bruce added: "Physical fitness, courage, honesty, patience, the spirit of initiative combined with due respect for lawful authority, soundness and quickness of judgment, self-confidence, self-control, cheeriness, fairmindedness, and appreciation of the importance of social solidarity, of 'team play'—these are traits requisite as never before for success in the life of an individual and of a nation." And Henry Chadwick tossed in "courage, nerve, pluck and endurance."

Such values were not only American, but Christian, replacing the desiccated values of a dissolute life with the healthy vitality of American manhood. Chadwick saw baseball as a "remedy for the many evils resulting from the immoral associations boys and young men of our cities are apt to become connected with" and therefore deserving "the endorsement of every clergyman in the country." McKeever added that "baseball may be conducted as a clean and uplifting game such as people of true moral refinement may patronize without doing any violence to conscience." Baseball was good for the body and the soul of men; it was imperative for the health and moral fiber of the body social. From pulpits and advice manuals, the virtues of baseball were sounded. Baseball "took manliness beyond a mere demonstration of physical prowess and linked it to virtues such as courage, fortitude, discipline . . . [and] concluded that if ball games called these virtues into play—as in fact they were critical to doing well at such sports— then ball playing was obviously one way of demonstrating manhood."

One central feature of the values that were instilled by playing baseball was that they appeared, on the surface, to stress autonomy and aggressive independence, but they simultaneously reinforced obedience, self-sacrifice, discipline, and a rigid hierarchy. This was also the case with the Organized Play movement, and other organizational efforts to counter cultural feminization. The Boy Scouts instilled a "quest for disciplined vitality," in which scouts are taught, in the words of founder Lord Baden-Powell, to "give up everything, their personal comforts and desires, in order to get their work done. They do not do all this for their own amusement, but because it is their duty to their king, fellow country-men, or *employers*" (emphasis added). The results of this and other efforts were noted with glee by Octavia Hill, the celebrated English social reformer in the 1880s: "There is no organization which I have found influence so powerfully for good the boys in such a neighborhood. The cadets learn the duty and dignity of obedience; they get a sense of corporate life and of civic duty; they learn to honour the power of endurance and effort; and they come into contact with manly and devoted officers. . . . These ideals are in marked contrast with the listless self-indulgence, the pert self-assertion, the selfishness and want of reverence which are so characteristic of the life in the low district."

For the boys learning to play baseball, these values were also underscored. The team always came first, and one always obeyed one's coaches and manager. What Veblen claimed about football is equally true about baseball:

> The culture . . . gives a product of exotic ferocity and cunning. It is a rehabilitation of the early barbarian temperament, together with a suppression of those details of temperament which, as seen from the standpoint of the social and economic exigencies, are the redeeming features of the savage character.
>
> The physical vigour acquired in the training for athletic games—

so far as the training may be said to have this effect—is of advantage both to the individual and to the collectivity, in that, other things being equal, *it conduces to economic serviceability* (emphasis added).

Sports reproduced those character traits required by industrial capitalism, and participation in sports by working-class youths was hailed as a mechanism of insuring obedience to authority and acceptance of hierarchy. Baseball's version of masculinity thus cut with a contradictory edge: If the masculinity expressed on the baseball field was exuberant, fiercely competitive, wildly aggressive, it was so only in a controlled and orderly arena, closely supervised by powerful adults. As such, the masculinity reconstituted on the baseball field also facilitated a docility and obedience to authority that would serve the maintenance of the emerging industrial capitalist order.

III. WATCHING

Just as on the field, so in the stands—baseball as a spectator sport was double edged, both facilitating accommodation to industrial capitalism as a leisure time diversion for the urban lower-middle and working classes, and, at the same time, being reshaped by them. Ballparks were located in the city and admission fees were low, so that "attendance at baseball games was more broadly based than at other spectator sports."

Baseball did not spring to such popularity overnight, as restorer of both individual virility and national vitality; its emergence as the "national pastime" was deliberately crafted. In fact, in the early half of the nineteenth century, cricket was hailed for its capacity to instill manly virtues in its players. "Whoever started these boys to practice the game deserves great credit—it is manly, healthy, invigorating exercise and ought to be attended more or less at all schools," waxed the *New York Herald*. In 1868, the *Brooklyn Eagle* informed potential spectators of a cricket match that they were about to see a "manly game." Baseball, in fact, was regarded as less than fully manly; one letter to the editor of a newspaper contended that: "You know very well that a man who makes a business of playing ball is not a man to be relied upon in a match where great interests are centered, or on which [a] large amount of money is pending."

By the late nineteenth century, this relationship between baseball and cricket had been reversed. The man who played cricket, Albert Spalding warned, thought that his match was a chance "to drink afternoon tea, flirt, gossip, smoke [and] take a whiskey and soda at the customary hour." How can we explain such a change? In part, the shift from cricket to baseball can be understood by looking at the changing class and regional composition of its players and its observers. Whereas earlier in the century baseball had been the domain of upper-middle-class men, by the end of the century it was played almost exclusively by lower-middle-class men. Similarly, the rise of mass spectator sports—the erection of the urban stadium, the professionalization of teams and leagues, the salaries of players—changed dramatically the class composition of the baseball fan. The values that were thought to be installed by *playing* baseball had made the imaginative leap to an ability to be instilled by *watching* baseball. And values of discipline, self-control, sacrifice for the team, and an acceptance of hierarchy were central to the accommodation of a rapidly developing working class to the new industrial order.

It was during this period of dramatic economic expansion in the late nineteenth century that baseball "conquered" America. In the first few decades following the Civil War, the baseball diamond was standardized, teams and leagues organized, rules refined, game schedules instituted, and grand tours undertaken by professional baseball teams. And though the earliest baseball teams, like the New York Knickerbockers, were made up of wealthy men, baseball was soon being played by small town lower-middle-class men and watched by their urban counterparts.

As Gunther Barth argues, the urban baseball park was one of the new important locations for social life in the burgeoning late nineteenth-century city, especially for white, middle- and working-class, native-born men. Like the vaudeville theater, the department store, and the urban park, the stadium provided a world of abundance and fantasy, of excitement and diversion, all carefully circumscribed by the logic of urban capitalism. Here the pain and alienation of urban industrial work life was soothed, and the routine dull grayness of the urban landscape was broken up by these manicured patches of green. The baseball park was a constructed "imitation of a pastoral setting" in the city, in which identification with one's professional team provided a "feeling of community" with anonymous neighbors; the ballpark was "a rural haven of shared sentiments" in the midst of the alienating city.

If masculinity had earlier been based on economic autonomy, geographic mobility, and success in a competitive hierarchy, baseball—among the other new social institutions of the turn of the century—allowed the reconstitution of those elements in a controlled and contained location. On the field, baseball promoted values essential to traditional masculinity: courage, initiative, self-control, competitive drive, physical fitness. In the stands, the geographic frontier of the mid-century was replaced by the outfield fences and by the mental frontiers between rival cities. (What we lose in reality, we recreate in fantasy, as a Freudian axiom might have it.)

Baseball was fantasy, and it was diversion. [According to Barth] "Men anxious to be distracted from their arduous daily routines provided a natural market for the product of the new industry." And baseball was viewed by boosters as a safety valve, allowing the release of potential aggression in a healthy, socially acceptable way; it was [Bruce stated] a "method of gaining momentary relief from the strain of an intolerable burden, and at the same time finding a harmless outlet for pent-up emotions" which otherwise "might discharge themselves in a dangerous way." For the fan, baseball was, Bruce noted, "catharsis."

To some supporters, the virtue of spectatorship was analogous to the virtues instilled by participation. Supporters of Sunday baseball extolled the healthy, invigorating and uplifting atmosphere of the ballpark. William Kirk, for example, called baseball "one of the greatest agents for clean living and temperate living." As he explained, "it is far better for the young boys and the old boys to be out in the light and the open air, watching a clean and thrilling struggle that is played where all may see, than to sit with legs crossed under some taproom table, dealing out grimy cards or grimier stories." In 1912, President William Howard Taft proclaimed himself a baseball fan, linking class, gender, and moral virtue: "Baseball takes people into the open air—it draws out millions of factory hands, of tradesmen and interior laborers of all kinds, who spend their afternoons whenever possible in a healthful, genuinely inspiring contest in the warm sunshine and fresh air, when many other sports, and in fact all natural tendencies conspire to keep them indoors engaged in various kinds of unwholesome and unhealthful pastime."

Like the frontier, the baseball park was also celebrated as "democratic." The experience of spectatorship, baseball's boosters claimed, was a great social leveler: "The spectator at a ball game is no longer a statesman, a lawyer, broker, doctor, merchant, or artisan, but just plain every-day man, with a heart full of fraternity and good will to all his fellow men—except perhaps the umpire. The oftener he sits in grand stand or 'bleachers,' the broader, kindlier, better man and citizen he must tend to become." "The genius of our institutions is democratic," Albert Spalding gushed, and "Baseball is a democratic game."

Supporters of Sunday baseball celebrated the "real democracy of spirit" that baseball embodied. "One thing in common absorbs us," wrote the Rev. Roland D. Sawyer in 1908, "we rub shoulder, high and low; we speak without waiting for an introduction; we forget everything clannish, all the petty conventionalities being laid aside." And novelist and former minor league ballplayer Zane Grey echoed these sentiments when he wrote: "Here is one place where caste is lost. Ragamuffins and velvet-breeched, white collared boys stand in that equality which augurs well for the future of the stars and stripes. Dainty clothes are no bar to the game if their owner is not afraid to soil them."

Such mythic egalitarianism, however, ignored the power relationships that made American democracy possible. For the experience of incorporation into community was based on exclusion: the exclusion of nonwhite men and the exclusion of women. The ballpark was a "haven in a heartless world" for white lower-middle-class men, and the community and solidarity they found there, however based on exclusion, facilitated their accommodation to their position in class society. Professional spectator sports maintained the "rigid gender division and chauvinist masculine identity," as well as the strict separation between whites and nonwhites that provided some of the main cultural supports of class domination. While providing the illusion of equality, and offering organized leisure time distraction, as well as by shaping working-class masculinity as constituted by its superiority over women, baseball helped white working-class men accommodate themselves to the emergent order. Embedded in a constellation of institutional and organizational solutions to the crisis of masculinity at the turn of the century, baseball was an expression of men's powerlessness—working-class accommodation to class hierarchy and workplace obedience—on the one hand, and simultaneously an expression of men's power—or at least the power of men over women and of some men (white, native-born) over other men, as well as the power of the working class to reshape the institutions in which they found themselves to better serve their needs. Thus it may have allowed men to experience their incorporation as alienated workers as a series of minor victories, so that their loss in the larger class war was far less painful.

IV. REPRODUCING

Baseball, as participatory sport and as spectator sport, served to reconstitute masculinity, whose social foundations had been steadily eroding, and in so doing, served to facilitate the reproduction of a society based upon gender, racial, and class hierarchies. For it was not just "masculinity" that was reconstituted through sports, but a particular kind of masculinity—white and middle class—that was elaborated. And part of the definition of that masculinity was hierarchy—the power of whites over nonwhites (including all ethnic immigrants to the cities), of the upper classes over the working classes, and of men over women. Baseball as a solution to the crisis of masculinity perpetuated hierarchy even as it seemed to challenge it.

By the end of the second decade of the century, some of the innocence of this illusory solution was lost. In 1919, this world was shaken during the World Series scandal that involved the infamous Chicago "Black Sox," who had apparently "fixed" the series. The scandal captivated American men. Commercialism had "come to dominate the sporting quality of sports"; heroes were venal and the pristine pastoral was exposed as corrupt, part of the emergent corporate order, and not the alternative to it that people had imagined. But by then it was too late: the corporate order had triumphed and would face little organized opposition from a mobilized and unified working class. The reconstituted masculinity that was encouraged by baseball had replaced traditional definitions of masculinity, and was fully accommodated to the new capitalist order. The geographic frontier where masculinity was demonstrated was replaced by the outfield fence; men's workplace autonomy and control was replaced, in part, by watching a solitary batter squaring off against an opposing pitcher. What had been lost in real experience could be reconstituted through fantasy. In collective terms, then, baseball was also designed, as A. Bartlett Giamatti quipped, to break our hearts, the hearts that yearned for collective solutions to class, race, and gender inequality.

The baseball diamond, as I have argued in this essay, was more than a verdant patch of pastoral nostalgia; it was a contested terrain. The contestants were invisible to both participant and spectator, and quite separate from the game being played or watched. It was a contest between class cultures in which the hegemony of middle-class culture was reinforced and the emerging industrial urban working class was tamed by consumerism and disciplined by the American values promoted in the game. It was a contest between races, in which the exclusion of nonwhites and non-European immigrants from participation was reflected in the bleachers, as racial discrimination further assuaged the white working class. And it was a contest between women and men, in which newly mobile women were excluded from equal participation (and most often from spectatorship); the gender hierarchy was maintained by assuming those traits that made for athletic excellence were also those traits that made for exemplary citizenship. The masculinity reconstituted on the ball field or in the bleachers was a masculinity that reinforced the unequal distribution of power based on class, race, and gender. In that sense, also, baseball was truly an American game. And if we continue, as I do, to love both playing and watching baseball, it is also a deeply ambivalent love, which, like the love of family or country, to which it is so intimately linked, binds us to a place of both comfort and cruelty.

JERRY MALLOY

5. Sol White and the Origin
of African American Baseball

Black Americans, like their white counterparts in northeastern cities, enthusiastically embraced baseball during the second half of the nineteenth century. Even before the Civil War black teams played, frequently against white clubs, in the Philadelphia and New York areas. Unfortunately, in the post-emancipation period black baseball players confronted an ever narrowing world of opportunity that reflected the experience of blacks in American society at large. Discrimination, bigotry, fear, and violence dogged black players and restricted their opportunities and progress in organized baseball. As early as 1867, the National Association of Base Ball Players, made up of supposedly "amateur" players, established a precedent by formally barring clubs that included black players. In the years that followed, other organized baseball leagues followed similar exclusionary policies, although many were informal and unwritten. The National League, for instance, adopted a "gentleman's agreement" that effectively excluded black players. Nevertheless, such practices were not uniform throughout the country, and evidence shows that more than fifty black players participated on integrated teams at various levels. Some, like Bud Fowler, Frank Grant, and George Stovey, displayed enough talent to play in the major leagues if given the opportunity. But by the late 1880s, the door had been slammed shut as a result of threatened player boycotts, including one by Cap Anson of the Chicago White Stockings, one of the most popular and influential players of his day. The social climate of racial discrimination gradually eliminated blacks from organized white baseball, and they completely disappeared by the turn of the century. However, blacks continued to play by organizing their own professional teams. As early as the 1880s most major urban centers and many smaller cities had one or more black teams. Many played in leagues mostly composed of white clubs. Other black teams barnstormed across the country playing against local amateurs or against each other or in exhibition games against white professional teams.

Sol White was a participant on many such teams. Highly skilled as a player and manager, he was also a keen observer whose baseball life spanned that of black baseball's difficult fledgling years. His book published in 1907, *Sol White's Official Guide: History of Colored Base Ball*, gives students of this period of baseball a unique insight into the world of black baseball during the last decades of the nineteenth century. The following essay is excerpted from Jerry Malloy's introduction to a recent reissue of White's history. Through an examination of Sol White's career, Malloy provides an enlightening context for the struggles of early black baseball to survive in an increasingly racist society.

SOL WHITE, BALLPLAYER

No colored ball player has had a wider experience in base ball than Sol, and no ball player has profited by experience greater than he has.
– H. Walter Schlichter

Sol White's considerable ability as a hard-hitting infielder during a period when ballplayers' careers (both black and white) tended to be peripatetic enabled him to move freely between the East and the Midwest to play for the best black baseball teams of his era. A review of his career as a ballplayer constitutes an overview of nineteenth-century black baseball.

THE MONEY PERIOD, 1885–1890

The figure of the African American in baseball has gone through various stages, from black players on white teams, to black teams in white leagues, to rivalry between independent black teams, to the formation of black leagues, to desegregation after World War II. The first African American player in baseball's sprawling minor leagues was John W. "Bud" Fowler, in Sol White's words, "the celebrated promoter of colored ball clubs, and the sage of base ball." Fowler, whose real name was John W. Jackson, was born in Fort Plain, New York, not far from Cooperstown in 1858. Twenty years later he pitched three games in Lynn, Massachusetts, then proceeded to become one of the finest second basemen in the country in ten scattered minor-league seasons.

In 1884, when Fowler was on the Stillwater, Minnesota, Northwestern League team, Moses Fleetwood "Fleet" Walker, a barehanded catcher, became the first African American in major-league baseball when his Toledo team joined the American Association, an early rival of the National League. Fleet Walker's younger brother, Weldy, also played a handful of games for Toledo, although they never played together in any game. They would be the last African Americans in the major leagues until Jackie Robinson in 1947 and the last black brothers until Henry and Tommie Aaron in 1962.

The stream of black players entering the various white minor leagues widened in the mid-1880s. In 1885, Fowler and Fleet Walker played in three minor leagues, and the following year saw Fowler, Walker, George Stovey, Frank Grant, and Jack Frye in four such leagues. The zenith of this early experiment in interracial play, which was not altogether harmonious, occurred in 1887, "a banner year for colored talent in the white leagues," according to White. Thirteen African Americans played that year on twelve white teams in five assorted eastern and midwestern minor leagues. Sol White and Weldy Walker were two of the four blacks in the Ohio State League that year, after having started the season as teammates on the Keystones, an early African American professional team from Pittsburgh.

But the most significant—and disquieting—events of 1887 occurred in the prestigious International League, just one level below the game's two major leagues, the National League and the American Association. Bud Fowler, Fleet Walker, George Stovey, Frank Grant, Robert Higgins, William Renfro, and Randolph Jackson played at one time or another for five International League teams that year. Fowler and Renfro were teammates in Binghamton, New York, while left-handed pitcher Stovey joined Walker in Newark, becoming organized baseball's first African American battery. Stovey, who won thirty-four games that year (an International League record that still stands), and Grant, Buffalo's hard-hitting, slick-fielding second basemen, were among the best players in a league rich in talent. In a caption accompanying a portrait of Grant that appeared in Sol White's *Guide*, White declared that Grant was "the greatest base ball player of his age."

Yet troubling racial episodes, fomented mostly by white players, occurred throughout the season. Most vexing were the symptoms of internal dissent on integrated teams, despite the obvious talent of the black players, ranging from intentional errors when a black teammate pitched to refusing to sit for team portraits including black players. *Sporting Life* (1 June 1887) asked, "How far will this mania for engaging colored players go? At the present rate of progress the International League may ere many moons change its name to 'Colored League.'" On 11 June, *Sporting News* noted that "a new trouble has just arisen in the affairs of certain of the baseball associations. It seems to have done more damage to the International [League] than to any other we know of. We refer to the importation of colored players into the ranks of that body." The *Toronto World* of 27 May 1887, under the headline "The Colored Ball Players Disgraceful," commented that a "number of colored players are now in the International League, and to put it mildly their presence is distasteful to the other players." White players, wrote the *World*, "dislike to play with these men," and this sentiment "may unexpectedly come to the front." They were right.

On 14 July, Cap Anson, major domo of Chicago's National League champions, demanded that Stovey be barred from pitching in an exhibition game at Newark. (Walker, Stovey's usual catcher, was not scheduled to play that day.) The same day, and probably not merely by coincidence, the directors of the International League announced that teams would not be allowed to sign African American players in the future. Sol White, as well as most writers after him, exaggerated Anson's role in the origin of the color line in nineteenth-century baseball. Robert Peterson was undoubtedly correct when he wrote, in *Only the Ball Was White*, "that [Anson] had the power and popularity to force Negroes out of organized baseball almost singlehandedly, as White suggests, is to credit him with more influence than he had, or for that matter, than he needed. For it seems clear that a majority of professional baseball players in 1887, both Northerners and Southerners, opposed integration in the game."

Although the league allowed Walker to play through 1889, as well as Grant and Higgins in 1888, the writing was on the wall for African Americans in the International League, a wall that was descending across the sport, imposing an apartheid in baseball.

When Fleet Walker's younger brother Weldy read an erroneous report in *Sporting Life* that blacks would be banned from the Ohio State League's successor, the Tri-State League, he wrote an open letter to the league president denouncing the ruling as "a disgrace to the present age [which] casts derision at the laws of Ohio—the voice of the people—that says all men are equal." Black players, he argued, should be as welcomed by team owners with the same warmth accorded to the black patron's money.

THE LIFER

Sol White, black baseball's first historian, was also one of its earliest "lifers."
Although White played briefly for a few white teams, his playing career was
predominantly within the world of African American baseball, which was
gradually driven underground until it became invisible to the mainstream
of white baseball. He was only nineteen years old when he was signed by
the Pittsburgh Keystones in the tumultuous season of 1887, and for the
next quarter century he traveled at the highest level of African American
baseball.

White was born in Bellaire, Ohio, directly across the Ohio River from
Wheeling, West Virginia, and not far from Steubenville, Ohio, in the
next county to the north, where Fleet and Weldy Walker grew up. As
a youngster, White was a fan of the Globes, one of Bellaire's three white
baseball teams, and the boyhood memory of his excitement at being pressed
into emergency service from the sidelines for his first game with them
was later embellished by the adult realization that the captain and second
baseman of the Marietta, Ohio, team that the Globes were playing was
none other than Byron Bancroft "Ban" Johnson, who would later found
the American League.

In 1887, White entered the ranks of professional baseball with the
Pittsburgh Keystones, charter members of the new, six-team League of
Colored Base Ball Players (often called the National Colored Baseball
League). The Cuban Giants, the country's first team of salaried black
ballplayers, had attained "great prominence," wrote White, since their
formation in 1885, which "led some people to think that colored base ball,
patterned after the National League, with a team in every big league city,
would draw the same number of people."

The new enterprise, a precursor to the Negro Leagues of the next century, was organized by Walter S. Brown, former Pittsburgh correspondent
to the Cleveland *Gazette*, an African American weekly newspaper. The
League of Colored Base Ball Players was born in a series of meetings in
Baltimore's Douglass Hall in the winter of 1886–87. At an early gathering,
J. W. "Bud" Fowler, the pioneering black player, represented a group of
potential investors from Cincinnati, where he worked as a barber in the
off-season, but they never joined the league. Also rejecting membership
were the Cuban Giants, and the absence of this famous African American
team from Trenton, New Jersey, was surely a deep disappointment to the
circuit's backers.

To the surprise of many, the fledgling league was granted admission
into baseball's official family when it was allowed to sign the National

Agreement, the pact that defined the polity of so-called organized baseball. In reporting this, on 13 April, *Sporting Life* remarked on its pointlessness. The National Agreement, it explained, benefited signatories because "it guarantees a club undisturbed possession of its players. There is not likely to be much of a scramble for colored players [due to] the high standard of play required and to the popular prejudice against any considerable mixture of the races."

Nonetheless, the league opened its season at Recreation Park in Pittsburgh on 6 May 1887. After "a grand street parade and a brass band concert," a crowd of 1,200 watched the Gorhams of New York City defeat the host Keystones, 11–8. Less than two weeks later, the Keystones lost, 6–2, to the visiting Lord Baltimores in the final contest of the league's thirteen-game existence. Insufficient financing proved fatal. Boston's Resolutes folded while the team was in Louisville, stranding its players. "At last accounts," wrote the *Sporting News* on 21 May, "most of the Colored Leaguers were working their way home doing little turns in barbershops and waiting on table in hotels."

A third of a century would pass before Rube Foster was able to forge a black league in 1920. Yet White points out that African American baseball benefited through this failed first attempt. "The short time of its existence served to bring out the fact that colored ball players of ability were numerous," he wrote. Furthermore, other than the Keystones and Gorhams, the league's teams were collections of local players in Boston, Philadelphia, Baltimore, and Louisville, who remained intact. "With reputations as clubs from the defunct Colored League, they proved to be very good drawing cards in different sections of the country." Several players, including Sol White, proceeded from the Colored League to play first for the higher-profile Gorhams and then the great Cuban Giants, among them Oscar Jackson, Andy Jackson, Robert Jackson (the latter two were brothers), William Malone, John Nelson, William Selden, Windsor Terrill, and John Vactor.

After the Colored League folded, White made his way back to Wheeling, West Virginia, where he played briefly with a local white club until being signed by the Wheeling team in white baseball's Ohio State League. He finished out the season playing fifty-two games at third base while hitting .370. In 1888 he returned to the Keystones, who played well in a four-team tournament in New York. Although the Cuban Giants won the contest, White recalled that "the surprise of the meet was the playing of the Keystones. Their only defeats were at the hands of the Cuban Giants; they won every game with the Gorhams and the Red Sox [of Norfolk, Va.]. The Keystones at this time were not professionals. They having one man

other than home talent." That "one man," of course, was Sol White, and
the larger fry of eastern black baseball quickly snatched from the Keystones
the greatest player they ever had.

Not only was White on his way to eventually joining the mighty Cuban
Giants, but for the next three seasons he played on African American
teams in white baseball's minor leagues. During these years, the attention
conferred on White in the local and national sporting press and the annual
baseball guides of the era suggests that he had considerable offensive ability.
Standing 5 feet, 9 inches, and weighing 170 pounds, he eventually played
all four infield positions, starting at third base and ending at first. White
played five seasons in white baseball, never hitting lower than .324. In a
composite of his 159 minor-league games, roughly equivalent to one long
season, he hit a robust .356 in 683 at bats. His 243 hits included forty-two
doubles, twelve triples, and seven home runs. He scored 174 runs and stole
fifty-four bases. Ordinarily not so humble, White was surprisingly reticent
in revealing his own considerable baseball talent, for clearly he was a player
of major-league caliber.

He spent all of 1889 with the Gorhams of New York City. Owned by Ambrose Davis, the first African American owner of a salaried African American
team, the Gorhams were perennial (and usually vanquished) early rivals of
the Cuban Giants for black baseball supremacy in the East. In the year
White played for the Gorhams, they represented Easton, Pennsylvania, in
the Middle States League, which White mistakenly called the "Pennsylvania
League." This association also included another African American team:
the Cuban Giants of Trenton, New Jersey. White's team fared poorly and
quit the league early, but the Cuban Giants challenged for the league title,
and apparently won it, in what White called a "bitterly contested" pennant
chase. The "Cubes" (57–16) barely edged out Harrisburg (61–20) in winning
percentage, .780 to .753. But a suspicious series of rulings on appealed games
during the postseason winter meetings resulted in the adjustment of the
totals to give Harrisburg a record of 64–19 (.771), just slightly ahead of the
Cuban Giants's 55–17 (.764).

THE COLORED MONARCHS OF YORK, 1890

Before the 1890 season, after four consecutive summers in Trenton, players
from the Cuban Giants fled the penury of John M. Bright's ownership en
masse to embrace the largess of J. Monroe Kreiter Jr. in York, Pennsylvania.
The Cleveland *Gazette* (5 April 1890) lamented that "the famous Cuban
Giants of '87, '88, and '89 will probably never again be seen in a team
together." But Kreiter assembled most of these renegade Cuban Giants

into a team he called the "Colored Monarchs of the Diamond" and gained for it admission into the Eastern Interstate League. While Bright stuffed his "Cuban Giants" uniforms with players of lesser talent, the *real* Cuban Giants were the team that White joined in 1890, the Monarchs of York.

Meanwhile, Harrisburg lured away Bright's slugging catcher, Clarence Williams, then secured Frank Grant (who had played the previous three seasons in Buffalo) after a legal battle with York, occasioned by Frank's having signed with both teams. In July, Harrisburg jumped to the Atlantic Association, and the Eastern Interstate League expired within days. White praised Harrisburg's directors for their insistence that Grant be included in the team's interleague transfer, which was good for both Grant and the team. But Clarence Williams was jettisoned to assuage the antipathy for black players expressed by the league's Baltimore, Jersey City, and Wilmington, Delaware, teams. "Williams has been released," reported the Cleveland *Gazette*, on 2 August 1890, "and the [Harrisburg] manager's only agreement was not to play or sign any other Afro-American player [besides Grant]."

THE BIG GORHAMS, 1891

In 1891, Bright rounded up his prodigal Cuban Giants and entered them in the new Connecticut State League. There they represented Ansonia, Connecticut, until the league folded in June, ending forever the Cuban Giants' presence in organized baseball. Perhaps it was an ominous sign to be representing a city that was namesake to Cap Anson, early black baseball's bête noire. *Sporting Life* reported on 20 June that the league had been "in a disorganized condition almost from the start." The Cuban Giants' decidedly noncollegial behavior contributed mightily to this unhappy state. On 20 May, the team traveled to Princeton, New Jersey, for an exhibition game rather than play a scheduled league game in Meriden, Connecticut. This was the team's second no-show of the young season and a bitter disappointment to the many Meriden fans eager to salute Grant, who had starred there five years earlier, just before signing with Buffalo. On 30 May, the Waterbury *American* decried the league's decision to include the supposed attraction of an African American team: "The Cuban Giants, representing Ansonia, as they conduct themselves at present, lend no strength to the league. They act as they see fit, paying not the slightest regard to schedule, the ordinary rules of the game or common decency. They were secured as a 'drawing card' and they have already begun to draw the wrong way. The Connecticut League has no use for them."

But by then, Bright's fealty to the struggling alliance had taken a back seat to more immediate concerns when, once again, his team began to lose ballplayers. After the Cuban Giants demolished Ambrose Davis's Gorhams, 18–10 and 17–2, in consecutive weeks in May, Davis responded with a tactic that would be repeated countless times in African American baseball's future: He simply gobbled up Bright's best players. But rather than wait for the end of the season, he embarked on the scheme immediately. George Stovey and Clarence Williams were the first to jump, joined later by White and Grant. On 13 June 1891, the Ansonia *Sentinel* wrote that "the Cuban Giants, or what remains of the original club, have gone to pieces and the Gorhams have absorbed the largest portion of the nine." Thus concluded the Cuban Giants' foray into organized baseball.

But J. M. Bright's misfortune was Ambrose Davis's finest hour. With the addition of Bright's Cuban Giants, Davis rechristened his revitalized team the Big Gorhams. Managed by former Cuban Giant skipper S. K. "Cos" Govern, the team's infield consisted of George Williams (first base), White (second base), Andy Jackson (third base), and Frank Grant (shortstop). Center fielder Oscar Jackson was flanked by one of the team's three pitchers, Stovey, William Selden, or William Malone, and one of its two catchers, Arthur Thomas or Clarence Williams. Every player on this team probably had skills equivalent to their major-league contemporaries.

White wrote that they lost only four games in more than a hundred, at one point winning thirty-nine straight—the Cleveland *Gazette* (29 August 1891) reported the string to be forty-one. Although *Sporting Life* (29 August 1891) wrote that their games "were mostly with weak amateur and semiprofessional teams," White ranked the Big Gorhams the greatest black baseball team of the nineteenth century, comparing it with the powerhouse Philadelphia Giants of 1905, a team White later coowned, managed, and played for. "A series of games between these two teams," he mused, "would have been worth going miles to see and would have rivaled the [1906] world's series which was played in Chicago."

Despite the team's success on the field, the 1891 season was a failure at the gate. Bright failed to present a Cuban Giants team in 1892 for the first time since 1885. The outlook was so bleak for African American baseball that year that not one professional black team made it to the field. From this point on, White's career as a player receded somewhat into the historical mist, though its outlines remain visible. In the barren year of 1892, he rejoined the scaled-down Pittsburgh Keystones and also played for a team at the Hotel Champlain in Bluff Point, New York, formed by headwaiter Frank P. Thompson, one of the cofounders of the Cuban Giants in 1885. In 1893 and 1894 he played for Bright's revived Cuban Giants, the only black professional team in the country in either season.

THE PAGE FENCE GIANTS, 1895

White began the 1895 season with the Fort Wayne, Indiana, Western Interstate League team, but he later joined an African American team from the unlikely rural community of Adrian, Michigan, some fifty miles southwest of Detroit. This team, the Page Fence Giants, was one of the earliest black teams in the Midwest. The notion of an African American team in bucolic lower Michigan was the brainchild of the ubiquitous Bud Fowler, who cooked up the scheme the prior year while playing in Findlay, Ohio. He quickly won over twenty-year-old Findlay native Grant Johnson, Fowler's only black teammate. Tall, lean, and muscular, he came to be known as "Home Run" Johnson for his prodigious power. By the turn of the century he was African American baseball's preeminent shortstop and would remain so until the blossoming of John Henry Lloyd. Johnson's essay, "Art and Science of Hitting," appeared in White's *Guide*.

Fowler originally wanted to base his African American team in Findlay and call them the "Findlay Colored Western Giants," but he failed to secure the requisite backing. Instead, he went to Adrian and entered a partnership with two white businessmen, L. W. Hoch and Rolla I. Taylor. They formed a black baseball team that would advertise for two companies, including the Monarch Bicycle Company, a Massachusetts firm cashing in on the national cycling craze. (At the turn of the century, during the peak of that sport's American popularity, Marshall W. "Major" Taylor, an African American from Indianapolis, was cycling's fastest man on earth.)

Fowler's other benefactor was the Page Woven Wire Fence Company of Adrian. Page Fence was not unfamiliar with inventive promotional techniques. As a permanent demonstration of the capacity of its product to contain livestock, the company maintained a park in town stocked with various animals corralled by its woven-wire fencing. This menagerie was transported by rail to nearby county and state fairs with Page Fence cages, thus displaying the strength and versatility of the company's line of goods. Consequently, Page Fence fencing and cages were purchased by zoos around the world.

The Page Fence Giants had no home field, playing continuously on the road as a full-time barnstorming team based in Adrian. However, they traveled in a manner that Rube Foster would emulate when he created the glamorous Chicago American Giants in the second decade of the twentieth century. The Page Fence Giants' home on the road was an opulent, sixty-foot-long private rail coach. It was fitted with sleeping berths and a galley and serviced by a porter and a cook, thereby obviating difficulties inherent in obtaining lodging and meals during a time when public accommodations were subject to Jim Crow practices. Their coach pulled onto a sidetrack wherever the team was booked, the players preceded their games with a boisterous parade through town astride gleaming Monarch bicycles, dressed in black uniforms with "Page Fence Giants" emblazoned in maroon letters—and topped off with firemen's caps provided by Monarch.

Augustus S. "Gus" Parsons, a hotel clerk and brother of one of Page Fence's directors, was the team's business manager, and he performed his duties well, booking the Page Fence Giants for 156 games in 112 towns of seven Midwest states. They won 118, lost 36, and tied 2, with 2 of their losses coming at the hands of the National League's Cincinnati Reds. Attendance varied from 800 to 7,100 for an average of 1,500 per game. In autumn the players traveled to Detroit for two games against an ad hoc team of players from five National League teams. They won both games, 18–3 and 15–0, with George Wilson, who joined the team for this series, allowing just three hits while striking out fourteen in the latter. Some Detroit fans were persuaded that the Page Fence Giants were "the best team in Michigan."

Bud Fowler's contacts enabled him to assemble what White called "a fine baseball team. They were hard to beat in '95 as their pitchers were among the best and their fielding excellent." The Giants signed some veterans of the Cuban Giants, such as White and Malone, and several exciting young players, like outfielder George Taylor and pitcher Joe Miller (both of whom were from Denver) and shortstop Grant Johnson. But Fowler's characteristic restlessness got the best of him, and he abandoned his creation on 15 July. He jumped to Adrian's entry in the Michigan State League for one game, then played thirty more with the Lansing team in the same league, hitting .331.

Adrian's white team, which won the league championship, was managed by Fowler's Page Fence partner Rolla Taylor and featured a black battery of Wilson and Vasco Graham. Wilson, a nineteen-year-old native of Palmyra, Michigan, pitched for the Page Fence Giants the following year and went on to a career in African American baseball, mostly in the West, so distinguished as to earn White's encomium as the black game's equivalent of the great Rube Waddell. For three weeks in 1895, Wilson and Graham were even teammates of Honus Wagner.

White left the team after one year. But Grant Johnson and George Taylor remained and the Page Fence Giants signed several talented players, such as outfielder George Wilson and Charlie Grant. The latter, unrelated to Frank Grant, was White's replacement at second base. In 1896 they soundly defeated a Cuban X-Giants team that included White in a series of fifteen games played in several towns in southern Michigan, winning ten of them. The Page Fence Giants prospered on the field but began to struggle at the gate. Since they were always traveling, press coverage in Adrian became sparse. They dissolved after the 1898 season, only to be reborn in 1899 as the Chicago Columbia Giants.

THE CUBAN X-GIANTS, 1896

In 1890 White had joined the stampede to York, Pennsylvania, which eviscerated the proud Cuban Giants of J. M. Bright. He did so again the following year, leading the exodus to the Big Gorhams. Now, in 1896, White was a key player in the final abandonment of Bright's parsimony when he and his teammates finally found an owner more to their liking, Edward B. "E.B." Lamar Jr. of Brooklyn. In summarizing Bright's role in nineteenth-century African American baseball, White called him "a lover of the game and a money-getting baseball man, . . . the leading spirit of his day in keeping the game before the public."

> "J.M.," as he was called by his players, was extremely selfish in his financial dealings and naturally shrewd. . . . [H]is players were always called upon to help him in an idea. When it came to getting money, "J.M." was full of ideas. He held up many games after his team reached a ground with a packed stand and demanded a boost in his stipulated guarantee. He generally got what he asked for. Bright spent his life in colored baseball, and he was not a millionaire when he died.

Unlike Bright, E. B. Lamar "spent his time and mind in making the game a lucrative calling for ball players." The result was one of American sport's most curiously named teams, not to mention a new eastern powerhouse in African American baseball. Lamar, whose brother Pete caught two games with the Chicago Cubs in 1902 and one with the Boston Red Stockings five years later, christened his team of ex–Cuban Giants the "Cuban X-Giants," creating no small confusion for both contemporary fans and future historians. For the next decade, the Cuban X-Giants would be among the best black teams in the East, while Bright's team carried on under the name of "Genuine" or "Original Cuban Giants." During the late 1890s, the two teams hurled various boastful claims and defiant challenges at each other during a rivalry in which the Cuban Giants were usually slightly inferior to their rival, much as the Gorhams had been to the Cuban Giants of the prior decade.

White closed out the century with the Cuban X-Giants. Following the 1899 season, the Xs played a series against the Chicago Columbia Giants. "Fourteen games were played in and around Chicago, the crowds on several occasions being enormous," White wrote. "The games were hotly contested all through the series but the superior hitting of the Cuban X-Giants won for them the title of Champions. They won nine of fourteen games played." The Columbia Giants were born that season of the remnants of the Page Fence Giants and managed by former Page Fence player John Patterson. To avenge the Columbia Giants' defeat, Patterson signed White for 1900.

THE CHICAGO COLUMBIA GIANTS, 1900

In a sense, this team was a throwback to African American baseball's earliest era in that it represented a black middle-class group in Chicago, the Columbia Social Club. For early black teams such as the Pythians and Excelsiors of Philadelphia, the Uniques and Monitors of Brooklyn, and the Mutuals of Washington DC, ballgames against similar clubs were little more than festive social romps, a sufficient excuse for the smashing buffet that inevitably followed. But by 1899, a new breed of upscale black professionals preferred simply to buy good players to nurture the honor and good name of the Columbia Social Club.

The Columbia Giants played at Wentworth Avenue and Thirty-ninth Street (now the intersection of the Dan Ryan Expressway and Pershing Road), just a few blocks south of the current incarnation of Comiskey Park, in the former grounds of the Chicago Cricket Club and future home of both Charles Comiskey's Chicago White Sox and Rube Foster's Chicago American Giants. Their players luxuriated in the extravagance of two sets of uniforms, whites for home games and grays for the road. Columbia Social Club members dispensed a generous amount of disposable income in outfitting its sporting representatives. Altogether, wrote White, "they were the finest and best equipped colored team that was ever in the business."

Chicago was the nation's powerhouse city in black baseball the year White played for the Columbia Giants. "While the Unions [another black team from Chicago] were thrashing the Cuban X-Giants, of New York, the Columbia Giants were walloping the Genuine Cuban Giants, of New York." In 1901, White returned East permanently, signing with the Cuban X-Giants.

White continued his career as a player until 1909, when he was forty-one years old. Indeed, in 1905 he teamed with Charlie Grant (second base), Grant Johnson (shortstop), and Bill Monroe (third base) in one of the finest infields of all time. This was the Philadelphia Giants club that White rated as the best team since the Big Gorhams of 1891. One need not cast aspersions on White's impartiality in rating two teams he played for so highly. He was, after all, a very good player. But his devotion to the Philadelphia Giants was accompanied by a special pride, for this brilliant team was assembled by White himself in his new role in African American baseball, that of team owner.

THE PHILADELPHIA GIANTS, 1902–1909

In 1902 Sol White entered a partnership with two white sportswriters from Philadelphia, H. Walter Schlichter and Harry Smith, to form the Philadelphia Giants. Schlichter, who later published *Sol White's Official Guide*, was the team's business agent, while White tended to matters on the field. For eight years, they operated one of the dominant eastern black teams in the bustling African American baseball industry.

The days were gone when one eastern team could dominate black baseball, as the Cuban Giants and the Cuban X-Giants had done so often from the late 1880s through the 1890s. Gone, too, were the dismal times of 1892 to 1894, when there was, at most, just one black professional team in the country. As the new century dawned, African American baseball blossomed with a profusion of new teams. By the time White wrote his *Guide* following the 1906 season, he could list nine such professional teams (plus two Cuban teams) within a hundred miles of that Queen Mother of African American baseball cities, Philadelphia. It is doubtful that many of these teams made much (if any) money, but the proliferation of teams suggests at least a thriving market for black baseball.

Both before and after, some African American teams were owned for reasons other than profits. The Page Fence Giants, as we have seen, were little more than a corporate advertising campaign, and the Chicago Columbia Giants existed primarily to adorn the prestige of a black social club. Similarly, John W. Connor formed the Brooklyn Royal Giants in 1906 to promote his Royal Cafe and Palm Garden, an advertiser in *Sol White's Official Guide*. In the future, Gus Greenlee would create the celebrated Pittsburgh Crawfords in the early 1930s as an embellishment of his Crawford Grill. Connor and Greenlee acquired African American teams to concoct a glamorous blend of sports, entertainment, and society—as if, say, a Toots Shor had aspired to own the New York Yankees in the 1950s.

MANAGERS' TROUBLES

In the first twenty years of the twentieth century, African American baseball was conducted within a context of frequent—indeed, bewildering—player movement among teams. As John Henry Lloyd, the "black Honus Wagner," later said, "Where the money was, that's where I was," and he certainly was not alone in this mercenary sentiment. Black baseball never developed anything similar to the white game's now discredited reserve clauses, which bound each player to a single team. African American ballplayers, unencumbered by such occupational slavery, became what we would now call unrestricted free agents after every season.

A few teams, even in the nineteenth century, were able to staff developmental teams. The Big Gorhams, for example, employed such a team, called—not surprisingly—the Little Gorhams. But black baseball never had a minor-league system. New players, often recruited while on tour in games against black or integrated amateur, semipro, town, college, or industrial league teams, had to be ready to jump directly into the highest level of performance to enter the ranks of big-time African American baseball. Star players, in the absence of a reserve clause, were ready, willing, and able to exploit a seller's market, a circumstance bemoaned by White in a section he called "Managers Troubles."

> In this day and time, when colored base ball teams are numerous and each striving for supremacy, the colored manager's path is not one of sunshine. With twelve or fourteen men under his command, twelve or fourteen different minds and dispositions to control and centre on the intricate points of play, with no National League of base ball clubs behind the rules and regulations, with the many complaints of players and threats of quitting ringing in his ears day after day, he passes many a sleepless night and will often ask for that "Patience he needs."

At the core of the first Philadelphia Giants team were shortstop Frank Grant, catcher Clarence Williams, third baseman Bill Monroe, and outfielder Andrew "Jap" Payne. The following year, 1903, they were defeated for the "colored championship" by a strong Cuban X-Giants team that included shortstop Grant Johnson, catcher Chappie Johnson, pitcher Danny McClellan, and rookie Preston "Pete" Hill, one of the finest outfielders in the pre–Negro Leagues era, a player with great speed and occasional power. But the dominating factor in the series was the pitching of a strapping young southpaw from Calvert, Texas, named Andrew "Rube" Foster. Foster threw a three-hitter in a 3–1 victory in the opener, the first of his four victories in the series, as the X-Giants beat White's team five games to two.

Following the established principle of "if you can't beat 'em, buy 'em," White reacted by hiring Foster, McClellan, Hill, and Chappie Johnson from the Cuban X-Giants in 1904 and replacing Frank Grant with Charlie "Tokohama" Grant, so nicknamed because John McGraw, while managing Baltimore's American League team in 1901, unsuccessfully conspired to foist him on white baseball as a Cherokee by that name. The 1904 Philadelphia Giants won all four games against the International League's Newark Bears, then run by Ed Barrow, future owner of the New York Yankees. They won the black baseball championship in Atlantic City, winning two of three games from the Cuban X-Giants, in a series in which "both players and spectators were worked to the highest pitch of excitement. Never in the annals of colored baseball," wrote White, "did two nines fight for supremacy as these teams fought." Once again, Foster was the key to victory. He struck out eighteen and allowed but three hits in the opener, then shut them down on just two hits in game three. He also led the Phils in hitting, with a .400 batting average.

What made the 1905 team the greatest of White's Philadelphia Giants was the addition of Home Run Johnson, the Cuban X-Giants' last remaining star. But Johnson left the Philadelphia Giants after just one year to manage Connor's new Brooklyn Royal Giants. Also in 1906, White lost catcher Chappie Johnson to the crosstown-rival Quaker Giants. White signed Nat Harris and Bill Francis for his infield and the Philadelphia Giants won 134 games while losing only 21. They clinched a four-way battle for supremacy in the East on Labor Day before a crowd of 10,000 fans in the Philadelphia Athletics' Columbia Park, "the largest crowd of spectators that ever attended a base ball game between colored teams," wrote White. This also was the first game between African American teams in a major-league ballpark. Flush with victory, Schlichter offered to take on the winners of the white "world's series" to "decide who can play base ball the best—the white or the black American," but the challenge went unanswered.

The beginning of the end came in 1907, when Foster jumped to the Leland Giants of Chicago and took Pete Hill and three other players with him. White responded by signing catcher Bruce Petway from the Brooklyn Royal Giants and, more important, John Henry Lloyd, the game's greatest shortstop. The following year, White took the Philadelphia Giants west to play the Chicago Leland Giants. White beat Foster's team four straight games in Detroit, and Foster refused to play the final three scheduled games in Chicago. The vengeful Foster did not allow White much time to gloat. In 1909, he signed both Lloyd and Petway from Philadelphia. Although White was able to discover yet another fine player, speedy Spotswood Poles (called "the black Ty Cobb"), after 1908 it was all over for the Philadelphia Giants.

In 1907, White had called Foster "one of the best colored pitchers the game has produced," so good, in fact, that he asked Rube to write a section in his *Guide* on "How to Pitch." But Foster would go on to play a much bigger role than that of a dominating lefthanded pitcher. The paterfamilias of the Negro Leagues, Foster had a career that would rival in variety and magnitude the achievement of white baseball's Al Spalding and Charles Comiskey combined, even serving as commissioner, unlike Spalding and Comiskey.

Just as White had destroyed the Cuban X-Giants by stealing John Henry Lloyd in 1905, so too Foster lured Lloyd from White in 1909, with a similar result. White's Philadelphia team was just one of the early victims of Rube Foster's ambition. Within a few years, he would nudge Frank Leland out of the picture in Chicago and found the Chicago American Giants, the most magisterial African American sporting organization of its time and a creation so closely identified with its creator that it was often called simply "Foster's Giants." In 1920 Foster founded the Negro National League, an alliance White could merely contemplate in 1907. Foster even fought white booking agent Nat Strong to a standstill, with Strong agreeing to undisturbed control of eastern black baseball in exchange for giving Foster a free hand in the Midwest. It was only Foster's mastery at booking that prevented Strong from controlling all of big-time African American baseball.

The year 1911 found White in Harlem, managing the Lincoln Giants, owned by white boxing promoter Jess McMahon and his brother Rod. White brought Spotswood Poles with him and signed several star players, including pitchers Smokey Joe Williams and Dick "Cannonball" Redding, catcher Luis Santop, and infielders John Henry Lloyd and Grant Johnson. But this team dissolved in July and Sol White headed back home to Bellaire, Ohio. There he lived removed from the world of baseball for eight long years, working in some unknown capacity.

When Rube Foster founded the Negro National League (NNL) in 1920, White served as secretary of the Columbus, Ohio, team. In 1924 he managed the Cleveland Browns of the NNL (alas, to a lastplace finish), and two years later he coached the Newark Stars of the Eastern Colored League, the eastern component in the 1920s of what we now call the Negro Leagues. But Sol White's impact on the game on the field was greatly diminished. He retained his enthusiasm for African American baseball and provided several helpful and informative newspaper articles for two black newspapers in New York, the *Age* and the *Amsterdam News*.

He lived in Harlem for the final third of his life, where he continued to follow the course of African American baseball and extol its history. In the 1930s he worked to secure Yankee Stadium as the home field for an African American team. He told the *Pittsburgh Courier* that he "like[d] to go to the library and read good books." He lived long enough to see the first African

American major leaguer in sixty-three years when Jackie Robinson joined the Brooklyn Dodgers in 1947. It is believed White died in New York City in 1955, at age eighty-seven, though his death record remains undiscovered and his place of burial unknown. Nor is it known if he ever married or had any children.

SOL WHITE, HISTORIAN

Nothing is known about White's childhood education in Bellaire. But, as the (black) Chicago *Broad Ax* wrote on 7 August 1909, he later had "the reputation of being the only professional Negro player who is a college graduate, having been educated at Wilberforce university, which is the oldest institution in America for the education of Afro-Americans." Wilberforce, named after England's foremost abolitionist, was founded in Xenia, Ohio, in 1856 by the African Methodist Episcopal Church.

Although it is doubtful that White graduated with a college degree, Wilberforce's records indicate that in the 1896–97 academic year he was a third-year student in the English preparatory department, though he may have begun his studies just the year before at the second-year level. He was also a private in the Corps of Cadets, the commandant of which was Lieutenant Charles Young, only the third African American to graduate from West Point. Young, who was in Wilberforce as an instructor of military science, eventually rose to the rank of lieutenant colonel after leading the all-black Tenth U.S. Cavalry Regiment with distinction during General John Pershing's pursuit of Pancho Villa into Mexico in 1916. Yet he faced discrimination in the military just as surely as White did in baseball. When the United States entered World War I, Army doctors declared Young unfit for active duty because of high blood pressure, which Young refuted by riding 500 miles on horseback from Wilberforce to Washington DC in sixteen days. Still, the Army held its ground and did not activate him until five days before the war ended.

One can only imagine how the gregarious White must have enthralled his fellow scholars with yarns from his summers spent playing baseball for the Page Fence Giants and the Cuban X-Giants. He received high grades in a curriculum that included reading, grammar, arithmetic, physiology, history, elocution, spelling, and U.S. history. Meanwhile, he developed the innate interest in history that ultimately made him the Livy of African American baseball.

The original edition of *Sol White's Official Base Ball Guide* was physically quite small, its 128 pages measuring only 5¾ by 3½ inches. Included were fifty-seven priceless photographs of various teams, players and executives, and even one of entertainer Bert Williams, who teamed with George Walker in one of the most popular song-and-dance comedy teams of the era. The (quite informal) Williams and Walker Base Ball Club antedated Bill "Bojangles" Robinson's later investment in the more formidable New York Black Yankees in the 1940s.

The book was underwritten with fourteen pages of advertisements, with three on each of two pages, two on each of two other pages, and ten full-page ads. Almost all of the advertising was purchased by Philadelphia business concerns, though Connor, owner of the Royal Giants, bought a page proclaiming his flagship enterprise, the Royal Cafe and Palm Garden of Brooklyn. Purveyors of alcohol and tobacco, who embraced the trade of the sporting set, predominate the roster of twenty advertisers, but the availability of Kimball's Anti-Rheumatic Ring, for those requiring "a general warming, quickening, strengthening and equalization of the circulation," was also announced. Two Philadelphia daily newspapers also advertised: the (white) *Item*, whose sports editor was Schlichter, and the (black) *Tribune*, half of whose page of space is allotted to a portrait of its city editor, G. Grant Williams.

The book was edited and published by Schlichter, White's Philadelphia Giants partner. In a caption accompanying a photograph of Schlichter, White identified him as the president of the "National Association of Colored Baseball Clubs of the United States and Cuba." This vaguely structured association, one of a handful of failed efforts to create a black baseball league prior to Rube Foster's success in 1920, lasted only one year. "Slick," as Schlichter was called, was lauded by White for "his ability as a press agent and booster." Sol White's *Guide* may have been produced, at least in part, as a promotional booklet for the Philadelphia Giants, then at the apogee of their existence. Schlichter also was in business with the influential New York booking agent Nat C. Strong, as revealed in an advertisement. Strong himself is identified in a photograph as the secretary of the aforementioned "National Association." In a 1936 letter to Sol White, Schlichter said that Strong was the only man he knew who made money on African American baseball. "And at that, I am better off than he is now," he remarked, sounding very much like an embittered former partner. "I am still living and have my health and Nat didn't take his wealth with him. There is no pocket in a shroud, you know."

Schlichter published *Sol White's Official Base Ball Guide* when White was at the apex of what the *Pittsburgh Courier* later called "the heyday of his glory of 1905, 06, and 07." Within the context of African American baseball, this was certainly true. But it was hardly a glorious time for all but a few of the country's black citizens. Rayford W. Logan's *Negro in American Life and Thought* (1954) was ominously subtitled, *The Nadir, 1877–1901*; a revised edition in 1965 was retitled *The Betrayal of the Negro: From Rutherford B. Hayes to Woodrow Wilson*. With Jim Crow ascendant, the history of African Americans of this sad era is a chronicle of despair.

A BARE-HANDED CATCHER'S HOME COLONY
The year after White's *Guide* appeared, Moses Fleetwood Walker, the bare-handed catcher who had entered the white man's preserve of major-league baseball in 1884, wrote a book having nothing to do with baseball. *Our Home Colony: A Treatise on the Past, Present and Future of the Negro Race in America*, published in Steubenville, Ohio, was a radical separatist tract that prescribed black emigration and a precursor to black-nationalist leader Marcus Garvey's "back-to-Africa" campaign. Walker's outlook was far more despondent than White's. The alarmingly commonplace practice of lynching illustrated to Walker that American racism "has reached such a degree of virulence that under its influence reasoning men perform like wild animals [with] the most horrible example of barbarism in a civilized country the world has ever seen." The so-called Negro problem, he averred, would more aptly be referred to as "the white man's Problem, for its solution . . . rests almost entirely with him."

Walker, who attended Oberlin College for three years and the University of Michigan for one, concluded that "the Negro race will be a menace and the source of discontent as long as it remains in large numbers in the United States. The time is growing very near," he warned, "when the whites of the United States must either settle this problem by deportation, or else be willing to accept a reign of terror such as the world has never seen in a civilized country." Since African Americans are "alien and always will be regarded as such in this country," the "only practical and permanent solution of the present and future race troubles in the United States is entire separation by Emigration of the Negro from America. Even forced Emigration would be better for all than the continued present relations of the races."

While Walker's views were extreme, there was no question that African Americans had been relentlessly and systematically deprived of opportunity and hope throughout American life and thought, despite the nation's self-designation as a paragon of equality and justice in the community of nations. In housing, education, and employment, in politics, government, and law, in literature, science, and philosophy, indeed, everywhere one turned, thoroughgoing racist policies and practices had stripped the African

American of justice and dignity, from matters trivial to vital, and proclaimed the United States to be "a white man's country."

As if the terrorist campaigns of the Ku Klux Klan did not sufficiently demonstrate the triumph of white supremacist rule in the South, where 90 percent of the country's black population still resided, politicians pandered to Negrophobia to garner lily-white voters, once black disfranchisement was complete in the former Confederate states. James K. Vardaman, campaigning for governor of Georgia in 1900, defended lynching as an antidote to rape, saying, "We would be justified in slaughtering every Ethiop on the earth to preserve unsullied the honor of one Caucasian home." Vardaman denounced the African American as a "lazy, lying, lustful animal which no conceivable amount of training can transform into a tolerable citizen."

In 1905, Georgia's Tom Watson voiced the callous attitude of many whites when he wrote, "What does Civilization owe to the negro? Nothing! Nothing!! Nothing!!!" When Benjamin R. "Pitchfork Ben" Tillman, the "one-eyed plowboy," was elected governor of South Carolina in 1890, he proclaimed that "the triumph of . . . white supremacy over mongrelism and anarchy is most complete." Later, as a U.S. senator, he ridiculed northerners for their hypocrisy (and probably made many squirm with guilt) after a three-day rampage of frenzied mob violence in Springfield, Illinois, home to Abraham Lincoln, in 1908 (a catalyst in the creation of the National Association for the Advancement of Colored People). So much for "the brotherhood of man," sneered the supercilious Tillman: "The brotherhood of man exists no longer because you shoot negroes [sic] in Illinois, when they come in competition with your labor, as we shoot them in South Carolina when they come in competition with us in the matter of elections. You do not love them any better than we do. You used to pretend that you did, but you no longer pretend it, except to get their votes."

Pseudoscientific theories misapplied Charles Darwin's principles of evolution, investing assertions of Caucasian superiority with a false patina of intellectual respectability. Thus, Charles Carroll wrote *The Negro A Beast* in 1900, and Robert W. Shufeldt's *The Negro, A Menace to American Civilization* was published in 1907, the same year that Sol White's *Guide* appeared. In 1906, Thomas Ryan Dixon wrote *The Clansman*, a best-selling novel set in South Carolina during Reconstruction that portrayed the African American in the most bestial terms. Nine years later, filmmaker D. W. Griffith used the novel as the basis of the first feature-length American movie, *The Birth of a Nation*, which was received with popularity and acclaim. Although it achieved technical and artistic virtuosity, the film's distortions and outright lies misinformed entire generations about the role of African Americans in the Reconstruction South. Woodrow Wilson, a friend of Dixon's from their college years, arranged for a private screening of the film at the White House and said it, "wrote history with lightning." In truth, though, art was merely the handmaiden of outrageous calumny.

THE STRANGE CAREER OF SOL WHITE

Yet race relations in the country had not always been so repressive, as the history of nineteenth-century baseball indicates. Sol White was a member of a tragic generation of African Americans, born within a few years of the Civil War. He and his contemporaries reached adulthood at a time, in the mid-1880s, when the brutal protocols of racial discrimination that soon would follow seemed by no means inevitable. It was, as C. Vann Woodward remarked in *The Strange Career of Jim Crow*, "a twilight zone that lies between living memory and written history," when "old and new rubbed shoulders—and so did black and white—in a manner that differed significantly from Jim Crow of the future or slavery of the past." "It was a time of experiment, testing, and uncertainty—quite different from the time of repression and rigid uniformity that was [to] come toward the end of the century. Alternatives were still open and real choices had to be made."

Sol White illustrated this development in baseball in a section titled "The Color Line." "In no other profession," he wrote, "has the color line been drawn more rigidly than in baseball." Yet White was able to recall a time, twenty years earlier, when the rules of racial engagement had been far less severe. The realm of public accommodations provides a clear example. The black player, he noted, "suffers great inconvenience, at times, while travelling," caused by the refusal of innkeepers to lodge African Americans. "The situation is far different today in this respect than it was years ago. At one time the colored teams were accommodated in some of the best hotels in the country, as the entertainment in [1887] of the Cuban Giants at the McClure House in Wheeling, W. Va., will show." Furthermore, "such proceedings on the part of hotel-keepers . . . will be difficult to remedy"— difficult, indeed.

In 1875 Congress legislated that "all persons within the jurisdiction of the United States shall be entitled to the full and equal enjoyment of the accommodations . . . of inns, public conveyances on land or water, theaters and other places of public amusement; subject only to the conditions and limitations established by law and applicable alike to citizens of every race or color." But in 1883, the U.S. Supreme Court ruled that such legislation was not sanctioned by the citizenship provisions of the Fourteenth Amendment to the Constitution. (When Congress passed the Civil Rights Act in 1964, virtually identical in purpose to the 1875 legislation, it avoided putting the Supreme Court in the inelegant position of reversing itself by basing it on the Constitution's interstate commerce clause rather than on the Fourteenth Amendment.)

As a result, people in such position as railroad conductors, ticket sellers, and hotel desk clerks gradually came to establish and enforce each community's racial boundaries. Through the Supreme Court's judicial sophistry, a law clearly intended to protect minority groups from racial discrimination was contorted into a ruling that threw open the door to Jim Crow codes. The Court's interpretations of the Fourteenth Amendment during the Gilded Age gratuitously shifted its benefits from black citizens to private corporations, thus abandoning African Americans to the tender mercies of implacable foes. In doing so, the Court may have helped white Americans heal the deep sectional wounds inflicted by the Civil War and Reconstruction, but white harmony was purchased, at a very steep price, with the coin of black repression.

The crippling effect of the ruling in the civil rights cases on the care and feeding of African American baseball teams was obvious. An example appeared in the 9 August 1890 issue of *Sporting Life* in an interesting account of Frank Grant's unpleasant experience, somewhat mollified by a rare (though modest) display of support from his white teammates, when the Harrisburg team of the Atlantic Association boarded at the Clayton House Hotel in Wilmington, Delaware:

> The . . . team was here a few days ago and all the members, including Grant, the Negro player, were quartered at the Clayton. Grant took his meals in the dining room with the rest of the guests, and was assigned a sleeping apartment in the guests' hall. The boarders protested against being obliged to eat in the same dining-room with a colored man, and threatened to leave the house unless the dusky-hued ball player was turned out. Mr. Pyle, however, allowed him to stay with his fellow players while they remained here. This morning the club returned and with them Grant. They applied at the hotel for board, and Proprietor Pyle informed them he would accommodate all but the colored man. The white players determined to stick by their sable-hued companion and all marched out of the hotel in high dudgeon over the refusal to accommodate Grant. Another hotel was sought, where the players were given rooms with the understanding that Grant must eat with the colored help or get his meals elsewhere. He accepted the latter alternative.

A few teams, as we have seen, such as the Page Fence Giants of the late 1890s and the Chicago American Giants of the early twentieth century, solved this vexing problem by traveling in a private railroad coach. But such opulence was rare. With the procurement of such mundane necessities as meals, lodging, and transportation becoming so complicated, the black baseball team owner's task became that much more challenging than that of his white counterpart.

THE PROPAGANDA OF SEGREGATION

Even worse than the inconvenience brought about by Jim Crow was the imposition on all African Americans, including those in baseball, of a dual personality. For the black American was always utterly aware that he was, simultaneously, both black *and* American—and the two components were not always in harmony. Indeed, in the mind of the white supremacist, the two were mutually exclusive, as expressed by Thomas Dixon in his 1902 novel *The Leopard's Spots*, when he wrote, "who thinks of a Negro when he says 'American'?" James Weldon Johnson in *The Autobiography of an Ex-Coloured Man* describes this dual personality as "the dwarfing, warping, distorting influence which operates upon each and every coloured man in the United States. He is forced to take his outlook on all things, not from the view-point of a citizen, or a man, or even a human being, but from the view-point of a *coloured* man."

W. E. B. DuBois put it more angrily in *The Souls of Black Folk*:

It is a peculiar sensation, this double-consciousness, this sense of always looking at one's self through the eyes of others, of measuring one's soul by the tape of a world that looks on in amused contempt and pity. One ever feels his twoness,—an American, a Negro; two souls, two thoughts, two unreconciled strivings; two warring ideals in one dark body, whose dogged strength alone keeps it from being torn asunder.

The history of the American Negro is the history of this strife,— this longing to attain self-conscious manhood, to merge his double self into a better and truer self. In this merging he wishes neither of the older selves to be lost. . . . He simply wishes to make it possible for a man to be both a Negro and an American, without being cursed and spit upon by his fellows, without having the doors of Opportunity closed roughly in his face.

In baseball, too, onerous, extraneous demands were placed on African American players for no other reason than their race, unknown baggage to white players. Even in the 1880s, before unrestrained *apartheid* came to prevail, the first rule of survival for the African American player was the clear comprehension that more was expected of him than just his ability. For the African American player, unlike his white compatriot, unprofessional talent was necessary but not sufficient, for he also was expected to contend with hostility and deprivation. All players had to become proficient with bats and balls, but only African Americans were expected to contend with brickbats and blackballs.

Sol White commiserated with the black ballplayer's plight, having known it himself. "In no other profession," he wrote, "has the color line been drawn more rigidly than in base ball." He was clear-eyed about the discouraging prospects of a career in African American baseball. "As it is," he lamented, "the field for the colored professional is limited to a very narrow scope in the base ball world. When he looks into the future he sees no place for him [in the white major leagues]. Consequently, he loses interest. He knows that, so far shall I go, and no further, and, as it is with the profession, so it is with his ability."

WAITING FOR ONE GOOD MAN

Yet despite the crippling layers of prejudice heaped on African Americans and their baseball, White remained hopeful that one day the barriers would tumble. In the meantime, he urged the black baseball community to prepare themselves to partake of the inevitable blessings of true athletic democracy: "Base ball is a legitimate profession. As much so as any other vocation, and should be fostered by owners and players alike. . . . It should be taken seriously by the colored player, as honest efforts with his great ability will open an avenue in the near future wherein he may walk hand-in-hand with the opposite race in the greatest of all American games—baseball."

He reported a rumor that an unnamed National League manager wished to break the color line by signing William Clarence Matthews, Harvard University's star shortstop from 1902 through 1905. White most likely was concealing the identity of John J. McGraw, blustery, innovative manager of the New York Giants, who is said to have employed two black stars, Rube Foster and Jose Mendez, known in his native Cuba as "El Diamante Negro" (the Black Diamond), at various times to coach his pitchers. White realized that the time was not yet ripe for mainstream white baseball to accept black players, but, for him, even such historical dead-ends as Matthews's truncated career bred optimism, for "when such actions come to notice there are grounds for hoping that some day the bar will drop and some good man will be chosen from out of the colored profession that will be a credit to all, and pave the way for others to follow." Matthews played in an informal league in Vermont, outside white baseball's organized structure, and even there faced resistance from his fellow players. He abandoned baseball, returned to Harvard, and became a lawyer. White would have to wait another forty years before his "good man," Jackie Robinson, would "pave the way for others to follow."

White's long-term optimism in the face of dire circumstances may have been bolstered by his knowledge, grounded in experience, that black talent had not always been eschewed by white baseball. He was aware, for example, that Stovey, Walker, and the Cuban Giants' Arthur Thomas all had attracted the interest of major-league teams in 1886 and 1887. White may have reasoned that race relations in baseball (and elsewhere) were not static but dynamic and a situation that had deteriorated in the past could improve in the future.

It also may be that White recognized the great truth of racial discrimination: white baseball, in banishing African Americans, was inflicting a wound on itself. Not only were white fans deprived of the joy of watching scores of the greatest baseball players over the many decades, indeed generations, of the Jim Crow era, but white owners were neglecting an ever-growing market of fervid black fans. American baseball would attain its fulfillment only when it cured itself of this disease.

NEITHER GIANTS NOR CUBANS

Despite the occasional minor errors in White's text, his account of the first twenty years of black professional baseball has withstood the scrutiny of subsequent historical research. Contemporary coverage, especially in the black press, pretty much confirms White's version of most events and testifies to his credibility and reliability as a historian.

One area, however, requires a somewhat closer examination, namely, his depiction of the birth of African American baseball's first team of salaried professionals, the Cuban Giants. This team is of special interest because it was the progenitor of what would evolve into the Negro Leagues, which was not only a source of pride and joy among black Americans in the twentieth century but also one of the most successful African American business enterprises during the bleak decades of racial exclusion.

Most accounts of the origins of this oddly named team of non-Cuban nongiants convey two vivid, colorful images, and in doing so, they recite, as if by rote, White's account. In his *Guide*, White introduced one element of the commonly told tale when he wrote that this team was formed in 1885 by Frank Thompson, headwaiter at the Argyle Hotel in the resort community of Babylon, New York, from among the African American staff. According to White, this fortuitous combination of menial hotel employees turned out to be quite auspicious for Thompson. Breaking free of its Long Island moorings, the neophyte team took to the road and signed several key players from the Orions, a strong black semipro team from Philadelphia. In 1886 they settled in Trenton, New Jersey, and called themselves the Cuban Giants.

The second prevailing image of the team's birth, as well as the usual explanation of its name, also derives from White, from an interview by Alvin F. Harlow for an article in the September 1938 issue of *Esquire* magazine:

> Most old-timers today are vague as to the origin of [the name Cuban Giants], but Sol White—who joined the club four years later, and may now be seen sauntering about Harlem on pleasant afternoons— says that the version which came to him is that when that first team began playing away from home, they passed as foreigners—Cubans, as they finally decided—hoping to conceal the fact that they were just American Negro hotel waiters, and talked a gibberish to each other on the field which, they hoped, sounded like Spanish.

How accurate is this picturesque tale, in "the version which came to him," of ballplaying waiters disguised as Cubans, jabbering in mock Spanish to avoid the disapprobation of racist white fans? Is it factual or fanciful, historical or apocryphal, or does it contain elements of both? Can it be that Sol White's story (or parts of it) of the birth of the first black professional baseball team has, as Samuel Johnson said of Shakespeare's histories, every virtue except that of being right?

A different account of the formation of the Cuban Giants appeared in the *New York Age* of 15 October 1887. The *Age*'s Boston correspondent, covering the Cuban Giants' appearance there, wrote that the team was born of a merger of three independent black semipro teams: the Keystone Athletics and the Orions, both of Philadelphia, and the Manhattans of Washington DC. The Keystone Athletics, according to the *Age*, were formed by Frank Thompson in May 1885 and hired as a baseball team by the Argyle that July. Thus, any duties the players performed in Babylon as waiters, bellhops, porters, and the like were incidental to their primary obligation, which was to play baseball for the hotel's guests. The merger with the other two squads, resulting in the creation of the Cuban Giants, took place a month later, in August.

For several reasons, this rendition of events is far more plausible than White's. First, it was written twenty years before White's book and only two years after the fact. Furthermore, the article probably was based on an interview with Thompson himself, who was employed by a Boston hotel at the time. The *Age's* version of the creation of the Cuban Giants also explains how S. K. Govern came to be the team's first field manager. Govern, a native of the Virgin Islands, had been managing the Manhattans of Washington DC as early as 1882, and some evidence suggests that he had taken that team to play in Cuba during the winter, even before the 1885 alliance that created the Cuban Giants. The Orions' contribution to the tripartite merger (George Williams, Abe Harrison, and Shep Trusty) was even more significant than that of Thompson's Athletics' (Ben Boyd, Ben Holmes, and George Parego), while the Manhattans pitched in with Arthur Thomas and Clarence Williams.

It is doubtful that the team ever attempted to babble in pseudo-Spanish, or if it did so the experiment must certainly have been quickly abandoned. For one thing, it is only remotely conceivable, at best, that nine baseball players could create spontaneous verbal chatter that sounded convincingly like Spanish. More important, not a single press report mentioned it. In fact, before White's statement in *Esquire*, there is no record of anyone, at any time, suggesting that this experiment in linguistic camouflage was ever employed by the team.

African American baseball teams used the name "Giants" with extraordinary frequency well into the twentieth century, in imitation of the National League's extremely successful and popular New York franchise. Referring to black players as "Cubans" was unlikely to deceive many nineteenth-century baseball fans, who were already accustomed to euphemistic references in the sporting press to black players as being "Cuban," "Spanish," or even "Arabian." Still, there may be a kernel of truth to the notion that bookings would be facilitated by implying that this team comprised Cubans rather than African Americans: so much so that nominal subterfuge may indeed explain the choice of the name "Cuban" Giants.

James Weldon Johnson, in his autobiography *Along This Way*, recalled confronting this curious breach in the wall of American racial discrimination during his youth. Johnson, who was raised in Jacksonville, Florida, learned to speak Spanish from a Cuban boyhood friend. On two different occasions while traveling by rail in the 1890s, he noticed that he was treated much better by railroad employees and fellow passengers after they heard him speak Spanish and surmised that he was not African American, but

Cuban. "In such situations," Johnson ruefully concluded, "any kind of Negro will do; provided he is not one who is an American citizen."

AVERTING OBLIVION

The flaws in the details of White's portrayal of the events that led to the birth of the Cuban Giants are attributable to his reliance on secondary accounts. Aside from this lapse, the modern reader can be assured that his work generally is corroborated by recent research. White's literary style, while workmanlike, is hardly redolent of Francis Parkman, or even Moses Fleetwood Walker. But he accomplished his purpose, which was "to follow the mutations of colored base ball, as accurately as possible . . . in the trust that it will meet the approbation of all who may peruse the contents of this book."

Apparently White had some intentions of bringing his story up to date annually, perhaps in the manner of the popular *Reach* and *Spalding Guides* of the era, which chronicled events in white baseball on a yearly basis. The National Baseball Hall of Fame Library, in Cooperstown, New York, has in its possession White's coverage of the 1907 season, written a year after the original book appeared.

Twenty years after *Sol White's Official Guide: History of Colored Base Ball* was published, White told Floyd J. Calvin of the *Pittsburgh Courier* that he had "a new book he would like to publish, a kind of second edition to his old one, bringing the game from 1907 down to date." The *Courier* passed along to its readers a request to hear from "anyone anywhere in sports circles . . . to help Sol print his record," but no one responded to his call. The same article also reported that "Sol's personal copy of his own book is the only one he knows about and it would be a historical tragedy if this should be lost."

Nine years later, H. Walter Schlichter, the volume's publisher, was down to two copies of the *Guide* himself, one of which he sent to White at his request. "The other one," he wrote, "I will not part with at any price." He suggested that White try to persuade one of his contacts in the African American press to run an article or series of articles on black baseball history. He informed White that he still had "all the cuts and pictures of the reproductions in the book," and he would gladly supply them to any editor willing to update the *Guide*. However, nothing ever came of this, either.

The historian's pulse quickens at such notions, quixotic as they may be, as that of Schlichter's artwork for Sol White's *Guide* being discovered some lucky day in a long-neglected chest in an attic in Philadelphia. But considering all the ways in which such artifacts as White's account of the birth of black professional baseball can be lost, forgotten, or destroyed over the course of time, one is thankful we still have his history to enable us to examine the past for clues as to what made us what we are. For Sol White's greatest triumph, in a lifetime of devotion to the game he loved so dearly, was the historian's quintessential bounty. To wit, he rescued merit from oblivion.

PART 2: THE GOLDEN ERA

DAVID Q. VOIGT

6. The Chicago Black Sox and the Myth of Baseball's Single Sin

The first year after the end of World War I was not a peaceful one for the nation or the baseball world. The war was over, but uncertainties existed about whether an enduring peace could be established. A threat loomed from the Bolsheviks, who had collaborated with the hated Germans, who repudiated capitalism, and who rejected God. Strikes, violence, race riots, and protests by unemployed veterans made it seem to many that the nation was coming apart at the seams. On the surface, at least, baseball appeared to be an island of tranquillity in the sea of political and social turmoil. As with the nation, however, professional baseball was still feeling the effects of the second decade of the twentieth century, which had been one of great disruption and challenges for the professional baseball establishment. The obvious crisis centered upon the war between the major leagues and the Federal League during 1914 and 1915, which produced a financial blood bath for both. No sooner had that war been won by the owners than the Great War in Europe led to America's involvement and the government's order to "work or fight." With their rosters seriously depleted, the 1918 season proved to be disastrous. Behind these obvious problems, however, lingered a host of other issues that threatened to tear apart the fabric of the game: low attendance, player unrest, escalating salaries, bitter dissension among the owners concerning rights to particular players, problems with the minor leagues, and a series of legal disputes fought out in the courts.

Nevertheless, baseball, like the nation at large, entered 1919 with considerable optimism, eager to return to normalcy. Returning war heroes included a good number of players eager to resume their profession. With the exception of two franchises, every club was playing in a steel and concrete stadium that had been built within the past ten years. But in the delicate mix of optimism and anxiety, and after exciting pennant races, the 1919 World Series gambling fix and Black Sox scandal blew up. The sordid story of the scandal's main developments has become well known, even becoming a subject of fiction, film, and folk tale. David Q. Voigt seeks to place the scandal in a broader context of the national pastime's most popular myths by widening the scope of culpability. In doing so, he reveals how the baseball establishment turned a negative event into a positive enhancement of the game's status and reputation through the myth that the corruption of 1919 constituted baseball's "single sin."

Forthcoming rites celebrating major league baseball's centennial season will draw heavily from gilded myths perpetuated by sportswriting troubadors. Despite the iconoclastic spirit of our age, the fairy-tale quality of our baseball legends persists. Perhaps the escapist world of the sports page with its colorful and stylized prose is the best environment for sheltering and nurturing myths—particularly two of the most persistent: the "immaculate conception myth" that professional baseball began in Cincinnati in 1869, and the "single sin myth" that only once has corruption tainted the game. That episode was the Chicago White Sox scandal of 1919.

A brief recap of the first of these myths is necessary for our understanding of the second, which is our chief concern. Apparently the immaculate conception theory is baseball's favorite way of explaining the appearance of its institutions. Despite abundant evidence showing that many players received money for their services before 1869, the official myth credits the Cincinnati Reds of that year with inventing the professional game by fielding the first paid team. When the Reds went undefeated for so long, this inspired the immaculate conception in 1871 of the first professional league, the National Association. This league lasted five years until its instability forced it to yield to another immaculate conception, the National League—a result of a coup promoted by Chicagoan William A. Hulbert and Albert Spalding. Then, after more than a quarter of a century of National League dominance, baseball legend reports the immaculate conception of the present dual major league system. After a brief war ending in 1903, the American League joined forces with the older National League to create a structural pattern for big league baseball that lasted until 1969 when the present four divisional pattern appeared.

So heavy a reliance on the immaculate conception myth to explain pragmatic evolutionary developments helps to explain why American baseball leaders came to feel a divinely guided sense of mission. Since the game was destined to be America's national game, its apologists believed that only flagrant dishonesty could thwart the divine plan.

The myth of baseball's single sin states that the game's promise was thwarted by the 1919 World Series scandal, which had been two years in the brewing. Back in 1914, desperate for a championship after eight years of drought, owner Charles Comiskey of the White Sox began purchasing star players. In 1915 he bought the hard-hitting outfielder Joe Jackson, and for an unprecedented $140,000 purchased second baseman Eddie Collins to go with the previously acquired trio of pitcher Ed Cicotte, catcher Ray Schalk, and infielder Buck Weaver. The key acquisition was Collins, who became field captain. Although an effective leader, Collins was unpopular with a cabal of players who resented his polish, his authority, and his high salary. Led by first baseman Chick Gandil, the clique included Cicotte, Weaver, Jackson, and pitcher Claude "Lefty" Williams. Together they made life miserable for Collins and for manager Clarence Rowland. At the same time, some of their off-field contacts with gamblers portended trouble for the White Sox. But in 1917 these troubles were masked by a world championship which the Sox scored over the National League Giants in the World Series. The following year America's total involvement in war drew attention away from baseball.

With peace restored, by 1919 baseball fortunes were rising sharply. War-weary fans returned in droves, thus restoring old profit patterns; and when Sunday baseball was legalized in New York, an era of greater profits loomed. Given exciting pennant races in 1919, which attracted droves of youthful fans, thousands cheered the Cincinnati Reds on to their first pennant in this century. And despite the bitter summer race riots in Chicago, even larger throngs backed manager William (Kid) Gleason's White Sox as they drove to a hard-fought victory over the challenging Cleveland Indians.

That fall the impending World Series clash of these rivals promised to eclipse all previous attendance records. Although the White Sox were favored, Cincinnati fans took heart when the Reds won the first two games, played in Cincinnati, by 9–1 and 4–2 margins. Moving to Chicago, manager Pat (Whiskey Face) Moran's Reds lost one to Chicago's little left-handed pitching star, Dick Kerr, 3–2, but the Reds rebounded to win the next two by shutout scores of 2–0 and 5–0. Now looking like sure winners and needing but one more win to clinch the nine-game World Series, the Reds trembled as Chicago battled back to win the next two by 5–4 and 4–1 scores. With the last two games scheduled for Chicago and with Claude "Lefty" Williams ready to pitch the first, Chicago fans waxed optimistic. But what followed was a cruel blow: Williams gave up four runs in the first inning, and Chicago went on to lose both the game and the 1919 World Series.

So runs the official account of the 1919 Series: if it had been allowed to rest, it might have ranked the Reds' victory somewhere behind the victory of the "Miracle Braves of 1914" in the annals of underdog victories. That it was not interred was due to persistent rumors telling of gamblers who had paid off some of the White Sox players for losing games. In 1920 the official *Spalding Guide* sniffed at these "rumors of collusion," but editor John B. Foster dismissed them as sour grapes. As Foster saw it, the experts simply had been wrong in failing to gauge the true strength of the Reds, whose superb teamwork was highlighted in the Series by Edd Roush's lusty hitting and by the pitching of Dutch Ruether, "Slim" Sallee, and Jim Ring. But the rumors would not be stilled. And baseball fans heard that Ray Schalk, the heroic White Sox catcher, had goaded Cicotte and Williams with obscenities matched in eloquence only by those of his manager. Indeed, fans of the Cincinnati Reds were talking about manager Moran's asking pitcher Hod Eller if gamblers had gotten to him. "Yep," Eller replied, and cheerfully admitted refusing a $5,000 bribe. Shocked by Eller's candor, Moran allowed him to pitch but watched him carefully as Eller won easily.

Had the rumors been confined to the playing field, the player code of "speak no evil" before outsiders would probably have preserved the official version of the lost 1919 Series games. But that fall the continuing rumors attracted the attention of Hugh Fullerton, a popular syndicated sportswriter. To a prying reporter like Fullerton, tracking rumors was the joy of life. His sleuthing helped to uncover the tangled tales of corruption that made the real story of the 1919 Series an American morality play. In lifting the lid on the Pandora's box, Fullerton was assisted by the great pitcher Christy Mathewson, who was doing feature stories on the Series for the *New York World.* No stranger to the seamy side of baseball, "Matty" was honestly worried about crookedness in the game. Hence, he became Fullerton's expert adviser and provided the reporter with diagrams of each questionable play in the Series games. With these diagrams and with his own findings, Fullerton wrote a series of sensational articles telling of a fix, the fixers, and their ill-gotten gains. Although widely read, the articles were generally discounted, one critic sneering that Fullerton was "always scoffing at the honesty of an institution, no matter how sacred."

Nevertheless, Fullerton's darts spurred four independent investigations as National League president John Heydler, American League president Johnson, Bill Veeck (Sr.) of the Cubs, and Comiskey each hired detectives to check out the rumors. Comiskey even offered $10,000 as a reward for bona fide proof of corruption.

At this point there was a chance the thing might blow over—a whirlwind lost amid gales of evil. After all, Americans of 1919 were daily reminded of bigger evils such as the Bolshevik threat and the threat of left-wing intellectuals, labor leaders, and sundry dissenters—all avidly pursued by patriotic witchhunters. Other stories told of looting in Boston in the wake of a police strike. And the year 1920 produced more lurid headlines about smuggling rings carrying booze for the revolt of American drinkers against national prohibition. In August there was also the exposé of stock swindler Charles Ponzi, a former convict who bilked $5 million from investors with a naive stock-jobbing scheme.

Notwithstanding all the stiff competition, news from the 1920 baseball campaign kept the rumor pot boiling. While Brooklyn coasted to an easy victory in the National League, the American League had a lively three-way race among Chicago, Cleveland, and New York. Before the season ended, fans read of Babe Ruth's home runs and the tragic death of the Cleveland shortstop Ray Chapman, who was killed by a wild pitch. Chapman's death made Cleveland the sentimental favorite of American League fans, and the team outlasted the White Sox by two games. The victory deserved celebration as a triumph of courage, but late-breaking news of more Chicago corruption sullied the Cleveland achievement.

Certainly a smart baseball man like Comiskey might have known that unpunished corruption breeds more corruption. For an agonizing period in 1919, he had considered not releasing the extra salary checks for World Series play to his suspected players, and he delayed mailing them their 1920 contracts.

In the end, to his lasting regret, he did both, thereby encouraging more dishonesty. Thus, late in the 1920 season new rumors told of some of his men receiving payoffs for losing key games, possibly enough to allow Cleveland to win. Game selling soon spread beyond Comiskey Park; and before the season ended infielder Lee Magee of the crosstown Cubs was fired for attempting to fix a game with the Phillies.

By September all these tales were generally known along with those of the 1919 Series. Drastic action was needed to save the majors from charges that gamblers were running the entire show. In mid-September, baseball faced a Cook County grand jury investigation into the 1919 scandal allegations.

Hard after this came James Isaminger's story in the *Philadelphia North American*, based on an interview with gambler Bill Maharg, who supplied details of the fix and the names of the fixers. As the story broke, the 1920 White Sox were only a game and a half out of first place, and at that point pitcher Ed Cicotte and infielder George "Buck" Weaver confessed to Comiskey. Angrily, Comiskey told both to go to the grand jury; and then he suspended the eight players whom all along he had known to be guilty. Comiskey thereby lost the services of the best players he ever had as well as the 1920 pennant. Beyond this he was unmasked as one who put personal profit ahead of integrity, for now he stood guilty of remaining silent in the face of suspected corruption. The consequences of his dilatory action were far reaching; by undermining the prestige of American League president Ban Johnson, Comiskey also undermined baseball's national commission system of rule. As a result, in 1921 the commission was replaced by a single commissioner, Judge Kenesaw Mountain Landis, whose theatrically stern rulings over a twenty-five-year period gave baseball a proper image of decorum—thereby reinstating the myth of the game's single sin.

The rest of the dismal story is well known, although its bizarre details yet defy understanding. Eight men from Comiskey's White Sox were branded as "Black Sox," including the great Joe Jackson, owner of a .356 lifetime batting average; pitchers Cicotte and Williams; infielders Weaver, Gandil (who retired from the game early in 1920), and Charles "Swede" Risberg; and outfielders Oscar "Happy" Felsch and utility man Fred McMullin.

Facing the grand jury, Cicotte tearfully told of getting $10,000, which he used to pay off a farm mortgage; Jackson testified that he got only $5,000 of a promised $20,000. Williams told the grand jury that gamblers had threatened to kill his wife unless he let down in the final game. All agreed that Gandil, who had received $35,000 in bribery, was the instigator and chief profiteer. According to later testimony, Cicotte admitted to making still more money by betting on the Reds to win the fixed games. Only Weaver said he got nothing, and he insisted that he had pulled out of the conspiracy but agreed to shut up about it.

Naturally the real winners were the gamblers. The grand jury managed to smoke out the "king of gamblers," Arnold Rothstein, who appeared as a friendly witness and named Abe Attell as the chief conspirator, himself disclaiming any part in the intrigue. Much later, after spending $10,000 of American League funds for a private investigation, Johnson in July 1921 accused Rothstein of a more active role. Although the charge was libelous, Rothstein refused to sue, perhaps acting on the advice of a colleague who once cautioned, "Never sue. They might prove it."

In June 1921, a conspiracy trial was held in Chicago before Judge Hugo Friend. It was only a farce, however, since the records of the grand jury and the confessions of Cicotte, Jackson, and Williams had mysteriously disappeared. Another bizarre development, it enabled the eight players to repudiate their confessions. Hopelessly crippled by lack of evidence, and confronted by a jury friendly to the players, the trial turned into a comic carnival. The trial ended on August 2, and the "not guilty" verdict brought cheers from the spectators, some of whom shouted, "Hooray for the Clean Sox." But if judged innocent under civil law, the eight were found guilty under baseball law. The final arbiter was commissioner Landis and as sole executioner he summarily barred all eight from baseball for life. For the rest of their lives the eight players wore the stigma of "Black Sox," and in spite of repeated appeals, Landis stubbornly refused to grant a single pardon.

To protest this artibrary judgment on any grounds is to run a twofold risk: that of undermining one of baseball's most sanctimonious myths and that of awakening the ghost of Landis. Yet the fact is that the players were denied their civil rights by the application of baseball law. Today such a ruling could never happen lest it evoke a heavy lawsuit; and even in 1921 its imposition was a legal error, resting on the moral consensus of baseball owners who were supported by the general public—all apparently unaware of the implications for civil liberties but overaware of their own pious definitions of sin and evil.

Those harried baseball Ishmaels lived furtive lives. Shunned by organized baseball, they were thwarted in any attempts to ply their trade. Some occasionally caught on with semiprofessional or outlaw leagues who played them under aliases, but exposure inevitably led to pressure which ousted them. Only Buck Weaver fought on with head high. He sued in the courts and won a partial payment on his 1920 contract. Six times he appealed to Landis for reinstatement, once armed with a petition bearing 14,000 signatures, but each time he was rebuffed. Jackson tried playing under assumed names until he could no longer bear the pain of exposure. In 1969 Cicotte died, after living for some years under an assumed name, yet later proud of a relative whom he coached and who made the majors under the Cicotte name. And in 1971 Gandil died; four months before he had vowed, "I'll go to my grave with a clear conscience." Yet he was dead ten weeks before word reached the *New York Times*. Of the unfortunate lot only Swede Risberg remains alive.

To understand why the eight men recklessly gambled their reputations on this ill-conceived intrigue is to probe the dark side of the human condition. They played on a clique-ridden team which pitted a sophisticated group, led by Collins, against their own earthy, boorish group, led by Gandil. Jealousy and verbal abuse marked the infighting as Gandil's faction attacked Collins' "dudish" manners and his $15,000 salary. Since none of the Gandil faction made over $6,000, this group continually groused about Comiskey's cheapness, and, indeed, his 1919 payroll was one of baseball's lowest.

The argument is spurious which says being underpaid gives license to cheat, and so is the argument that many wrongs make a right. But the Black Sox did have a point in using such defenses. The myth of baseball's single sin proclaims that the game has known but one case of proven dishonesty, yet the early years of the game were pockmarked with countless rumors of bribery and cheating similar to this episode. In 1877 a clique of Louisville players was expelled for selling games, and shortly thereafter an umpire was ousted for dishonesty. In the first modern World Series, played in 1903, catcher Lou Criger reportedly rejected a $12,000 bribe, and in the second Rube Waddell was offered $17,000 not to play. Coincidentally or not, he injured himself falling over a suitcase and did not appear. There were rumors of fixed games in the 1918 Series, and evidence of fixers centered about the victorious Reds of 1919. Outfielder Edd Roush later related that one suspected plotter got on base accidentally. To score would threaten the fix, so the player lagged on Roush's long hit that followed, but hot on his heels Roush goaded him to score, shouting, "Get running, you crooked son of a bitch."

Still other blotches spattered baseball's image. In 1908 some Phillies threw a gambler down the clubhouse stairs at the Polo Grounds after he offered them a bribe. With a torrid pennant race that ended in a tie, that same season found umpires Bill Klem and Charles Johnson reporting a bribe attempt in behalf of the Giants in their playoff game with the Cubs. And in 1916 the Giants were accused of lying down to help the Dodgers beat the Phillies—a charge Giant manager John McGraw thought to be true. Meanwhile persistent rumors of game selling centered about Hal Chase of the Giants. Inquiry into the Black Sox case dredged up evidence that Chase and Joe Gedeon of the Browns had made money betting on the Reds. By dragging their feet in the 1919 investigation, baseball men thus created a climate favoring more corruption in 1920. That year detectives found evidence linking two Giants and four Cubs with fix plots, and cast suspicion on some Yankees, Braves, Red Sox, and Indians players. No mere rumors these, for they led directly to the blacklisting of Magee and pitcher Claude Hendrix of the Cubs.

These are but documented incidents in a record of sporadic dishonesty extending through baseball history. A well-established, though clearly unethical, baseball practice of the time was the quaint custom whereby a contending ball club offered a suit of clothes to a noncontending pitcher for beating another contender; the custom sometimes had variations as in 1917 when the White Sox awarded suits to Detroit players for losing two doubleheaders. In 1921 Landis sternly ordered such practices stopped.

After two decades of holding their noses and indoctrinating newsmen with the myth of the incorruptible national game, baseball men at last made scapegoats of the most brazen cheaters. But they did not purge one of their own for withholding evidence that might have cleaned house in 1919 and possibly headed off the 1920 scandals. To save his own investment, Charles Comiskey had stood silent in the face of corruption. Knowing this, his colleagues isolated him after 1920. His last years were sick and lonely ones; his one consolation was that he kept his franchise.

In retrospect, the year 1920 was not a time for casting first stones. What Landis, the players, and fans seemingly sensed was that notions of sin were changing in a get-rich-quick, fast-buck America. Apparently the fans could overlook revealed corruption, for they kept coming, enabling the American League to top the 5 million attendance mark in 1920. Moreover, in spite of screaming scandal headlines about Black Sox, the 1920 Series drew well.

Had they kept cool under the fire of angry headlines and probing investigators, baseball leaders might have wielded power as of old. But they panicked, and a majority voted to bring in a famous outsider as commissioner to lend the game an honest image; the era of Judge Landis began in 1920 and lasted until 1944. By cleverly playing the role of "puritan in Babylon," Landis convinced most fans that baseball's "guilty season" was over. True, there were continuing scandals, but the Judge singled out enough scapegoats to keep baseball's reputation intact and the players cowed. As old Dan Cassidy, Cicotte's attorney in 1920, recently put it, "The players had no organization then. Now they do. This sort of thing couldn't happen today." Largely then, through Landis's efforts, the myth of baseball's single sin is alive today.

Judge Kenesaw Mountain Landis signs as baseball's first commissioner.

7. Here Comes the Judge!
The Origins of Baseball's Commissioner
System and American Legal Culture

Although baseball weathered the storms of the first two decades of the new century, the increased impotency of the National Commission as professional baseball's ruling body had been exposed. To be sure, the Black Sox scandal was the key event that finally pushed the owners into adopting an alternative. But the scandal was only the proverbial last straw. The infighting among the owners during the previous decade had threatened the existence of the National Agreement of 1903. Confronted with the dangerous impact of the scandal on the integrity of the game—and its profitability—the lords of baseball needed to pull together for their own well-being. They needed to restore public confidence in the game and their stewardship of it. Beyond the scandal's effects, however, loomed the impending Supreme Court case testing baseball's immunity from antitrust legislation. Although the Federal League challenge had been beaten back, that league's Baltimore franchise owners had sued organized baseball for monopolistic restraint of trade in violation of the Sherman Antitrust Act. A series of mixed verdicts had landed the case in the lap of the Supreme Court, where it met an uncertain fate.

Confronted with these twin crises, the baseball lords panicked. In November 1920 they offered a newly created position of commissioner of baseball to a man who had openly campaigned for it, Chicago federal judge Kenesaw Mountain Landis. A measure of the owners' desperation can be seen in the fact that they gave Landis the job on his own terms, conditions that they would eventually regret, but which in the short term served their purposes.

It was a stroke of genius. Landis had already built a reputation as a no-nonsense, trustbusting, some would say grandstanding, federal judge. He was viewed as an American patriot who hated the Germans during the war and the Bolsheviks afterward. Instantly recognizable by his gaunt, stern, white-haired appearance, the new "Czar of Baseball" exuded the confidence and virtuosity of one who would protect the integrity of the game as well as defend it against threatened court cases. By using his sweeping powers to investigate challenges to the "best interests of the game," Landis shrewdly dominated baseball for the next twenty years.

Norman L. Rosenberg places the events surrounding the rise of Landis and the development of the "Commissioner System" in the context of a broader changing legal culture that occurred during the first two decades of the century. With the support of the popular sports-writing establishment, a new internal legal system was adopted by baseball that went unchallenged for nearly half a century. At the same time, professional baseball won back the trust and allegiance of the sports public.

During the first two decades of the 20th century, legal architects designed a number of new juridicial structures. Small claims courts, workers' compensation tribunals, and juvenile courts, for instance, all date from the early years of this century. The successful implementation of these new legal forums, all of which departed in significant ways from traditional patterns and forms, required efforts to "sell" their virtues.

The magnates of professional baseball participated in this general process of legal reconstruction. In 1920 they created, and then lobbied on behalf of, a legal structure—the Commissioner System—that resolved problems that had bedeviled the national pastime since the late 1880s. Although historians of legal and popular culture can profitably view the origins of baseball's new legal order from several different perspectives, this essay will focus upon (1) the ways in which the Commissioner System departed from traditional legal ideals and models and upon (2) the ways in which the popular press, especially the sports-writing establishment, helped organized baseball legitimate its handiwork. In particular, the essay will examine how the "public" legal system's response to allegations that members of the Chicago White Sox had rigged the 1919 World Series helped smooth the way for the operation of baseball's own "private" legal order, one headed by a single, nearly absolute judicial patriarch.

I

The popular image of how American "law" should operate—an image that still dominates works of popular culture—merged the not-always-compatible strains of egalitarianism, individualism, and constitutionalism. This model of public justice contained at least four basic elements, all of which would be jettisoned in the legal structure adopted by organized baseball.

(1) Disputes were to be settled in governmentally operated courts of law, ones in which the official, supposedly neutral authority of the state clearly stood in the forefront of the entire process.

(2) Growing out of the late 18th- and 19th-century liberal principles, the traditional view of law centered upon legal conflicts between two theoretically equal individuals. As the image of "blind justice" suggested, the law was to ignore the social, economic, and political status of the litigants. Before the law, any party to any legal dispute stood on the same plane of equality with all others.

(3) In the courtroom setting, judges generally acted as passive, neutral arbiters. They allowed litigants, or their attorneys, to present evidence, frame arguments and summarize their positions. Over the course of the 19th century, common law judges did come to exert considerable power over the rules of procedure and evidence, but ultimate authority was still supposed to rest in the hands of jurors. Summoned from among the litigants' peers, the common law jury, after hearing both sides and receiving instructions from the judge, retired to render a final decision on its own.

(4) In those areas where judges did render decisions, such as on evidentiary matters or on cases appealed to higher tribunals, their individual authority was supposedly circumscribed by "the rule of Law." In theory, this meant that they deferred to the fact-finding authority of the original jurors, strictly followed prior legal precedents, and issued "reasoned" judicial opinions that rested upon the special insights of their "trained legal minds."

During the 19th century, exposés of the gulf between this idealized version of formal legal conflict and the realities of American jurisprudence became one of the staples of mass, popular journalism. As the historian Dan Schiller has argued, for example, crime reporting in the penny presses of the 1830s represented more than tawdry sensationalism. By focusing attention on how the legal system *really* operated in specific cases, the penny presses tried to show how political, class, and ethnic differences influenced legal outcomes. Championing the ideal of equality before the law, popular legal reporting rested upon the proposition that only a vigilant, informed citizenry could restore the idealized model of law. Even as they sold more and more papers with exposés of the failings of the legal system, popular journalists continued to hold up the traditional model as the ideal toward which the nation must strive.

Although 19th-century journalistic exposés and 20th-century scholarly critiques, in their own ways, deflated claims of the legal system's apologists, the notion of egalitarian-individualist justice retained considerable vitality, as both an ideal and a reality. Critical legal scholarship, for instance, has demonstrated that, contrary to legal mythology, doctrines underlying the 19th-century law of industrial accidents implicitly favored capital over labor. Yet, through the jury system, workers continued to recover damages for on-the-job injuries. Indeed, by the early 20th century, the volume of industrial lawsuits became so great that industrialists and their legal guardians ultimately designed workers' compensation courts, administrative tribunals that decided claims on the basis of "scientific" evidence and without jurors, in order to divert most industrial accident suits away from the traditional litigation process.

The pre-1920 law of baseball provides another example of the vitality of the traditional legal ideal and of the fact that the public legal system was not simply the tool of capitalist interests. From the 1880s to 1920, as the owners of baseball franchises created an elaborate business structure called "organized baseball," the question of the respective legal rights of ballplayers and owners, labor and capital, continually reappeared. Much of the controversy centered on the "reserve clause," the portion of the annual baseball contract that bound players to their teams for season-after-season. Owners justified the reserve clause as vital "for the good of the game." Since it prevented players from jumping from team to team and the wealthier owners from gobbling up the best talent, baseball's magnates lauded the reserve clause as necessary for both order and competitive balance. Ballplayers saw the situation quite differently. To them, the reserve clause perpetuated a type of wage slavery and provided owners a tool for holding down the game's salary structure. Led by John Montgomery Ward, a star pitcher and honors graduate of Columbia Law School, players unionized in the mid-1880s and then formed their own short-lived major league in 1890.

Club owners from the American Association and the National League, the two established "major leagues," successfully mobilized all manner of extra-legal pressures against the new Player's League; but they found, much to their dismay, that the nation's public legal system generally endorsed the player's interpretation of contract law. As John Montgomery Ward had predicted—his legal acumen was as sharp as his curve ball—court after court refused to prevent players from "jumping" to the new league. The legal argument was clear: any contract that bound one party, the player, to personal service for an indefinite series of years while it allowed the other, the owner, to cancel upon ten days' notice, simply lacked the kind of mutuality required of an equitable, enforceable contract. Unfortunately for the leaders of the Player's League, however, they could not live by legal victories alone.

In subsequent legal confrontations over the reserve clause, one of the pillars of organized baseball's system for disciplining its workers, club owners generally came out of the public courts as losers. In 1914, for example, when Hal Chase of the Chicago White Sox "jumped" to the new Federal League, the New York Supreme Court rejected any claim that the talented first-sacker's contract bound him to his old club. After a lengthy analysis of the standard baseball contract, the court condemned "the involuntary character of the servitude which is imposed upon the players by the strength of the combination controlling the labor of practically all of the players in the country." In fact, Judge Bissell compared baseball's labor system to the peonage arrangements forced upon Mexican immigrants in the Southwest. Baseball's established contractual arrangement was "contrary to the spirit of American institutions, and is contrary to the spirit of the Constitution of the United States." Free of old legal entanglements, Chase headed off to Buffalo, where he hit .347 and .291 before pressures from organized baseball and economic difficulties ultimately forced this third "major" league to fold after the 1915 season.

But baseball's establishment had not heard the last from either the Federal League or from Hal Chase. The dictum of the New York Court in the Chase lawsuit, language about "the strength of the combination controlling" the labor of ball players, implicitly raised the specter of a legal challenge, under the Sherman Anti-Trust Act of 1890, to the entire structure of organized baseball. The Federal League had filed such a lawsuit in January of 1915, but the baseball establishment found a legal protector in Federal District Judge Kenesaw Mountain Landis. Widely known for an impressive shock of white hair, a stern patriarchal visage, and an unorthodox approach to most legal issues, the judge was also a rabid baseball fan. He neatly "pocket vetoed" the Federal League's challenge until the league's final demise. As part of a peace settlement with the National and American Leagues, the

Federalist owners agreed to drop their joint lawsuit. In 1916, however, the holders of the old Federal League franchise in Baltimore, who were dissatisfied with the peace settlement of 1915, filed their own suit. This case, which challenged baseball's governing structure as violative of the Sherman Act, reached the Supreme Court of the District of Columbia in the spring of 1919. Fulfilling baseball owners' worst fears, the court did find baseball in violation of anti-trust laws, a decision that threw the game's legal arrangements into question.

Meanwhile, "Prince Hal" Chase had returned to the fold of respectable ball clubs, if not to the mold of a respectable ball player. Long considered too clever for the good of the game, Chase had been suspected, on more than a few occasions, of conniving to fix ball games for the benefit of gamblers. And in 1919 he ended up in the center of Major League baseball's biggest scandal: the alleged rigging of the World Series between the Chicago White Sox and the Cincinnati Reds. Rumors of a fix began to circulate during the series itself, but nothing concrete surfaced for nearly a year, until the tailend of the 1920 pennant race. Before allegations stopped flying, key members of the Sox (including stars "Shoeless Joe" Jackson and Eddie Cicotte), other baseball figures (including Hal Chase), and notorious gambling kingpins (especially Arnold Rothstein and the former featherweight boxing champion Abe Attel) had been fingered.

The official legal system quickly went to work. Always alert to career opportunities, several prominent politicians from Illinois had successfully pressed for a grand jury investigation into rigged games even before much was known about the 1919 series; then, in late September 1920, the pitcher Eddie Cicotte came before this Cook County grand jury. He became the first of several Sox players to "confess" a role in rigging series games, and newspaper headlines soon announced indictments against a number of prominent team members. After additional testimony, the grand jury returned final indictments against eight of the Sox, a group of alleged gamblers, and Hal Chase. Grand jurors coupled their rebuke of these alleged conspirators with a ringing defense of the game itself. "The jury is impressed with the fact that baseball is an index to our national genius and character. The American principle of genius and fair play must prevail, and it is all important that the game be clean, from the most humble player to the highest dignitary. . . . Baseball is more than a national game; it is an American institution, having its place prominently and significantly in the life of the people."

Despite such sentiments, baseball's magnates still faced a double-barreled legal challenge. The Baltimore anti-trust suit, by then winding its slow way through the appeals process, raised the possibility of the United States Supreme Court throwing out the basic legal agreements, including the reserve clause, by which baseball organized its own affairs. Like all oligopolistic business operations, baseball needed some type of regulatory structure that would tame the individual clubowners' self-interest—to raid, for example, the best players from rival teams—to suit the larger interests of the entire baseball business. If "public" legal institutions overturned baseball's private system of legal ordering, how could owners protect themselves from their own worst instincts? Or from a legally protected players' movement?

At this point, fears about baseball's status under the Sherman Act merged with the magnates' other major legal problem—the dark stain that was spreading out from the "Black Sox" scandal. Here again, the public law courts offered little help and additional difficulties. From the onset of their anti-trust problems, baseball's leadership had used claims that "the game" was an integral, and morally uplifting, part of American culture to bolster the dubious legal argument that the national pastime should not have to abide by the same rules as less pure aspects of American business. Revelations that baseball's premier attraction, the World Series, could be fixed hardly spoke well for the magnates' ability to police their own affairs. Moreover, as everyone associated with baseball recognized, a lengthy jury trial, during which all kinds of damaging testimony might emerge, would not likely help to clear the air.

Taken together, these two legal problems demanded a rapid solution to yet another legal difficulty: replacement of baseball's own self-styled "Supreme Court," the National Commission. Created in 1903, after the National and American Leagues ended several years of guerrilla warfare, the National Commission possessed theoretically broad authority—granted by the owners—to settle baseball's internal disputes. Composed of the presidents of the two leagues and August (Garry) Herrmann of the Cincinnati Reds, the Commission oversaw everything from umpire-player run-ins to charges of ball games being fixed. The Commission muddled through its early years, even helping the two leagues fend off the challenge from the Federalist circuit, but by 1920 it had fallen apart at the seams. Resentment at the power and arrogance of Ban Johnson, the American League prexy who was the real force on the three-member panel, helped to undermine this "Supreme Court's" authority. Shortly after the 1919 World Series, Garry Herrmann, long seen as a stooge for Johnson, resigned. Far from clearing the way for reorganization of the Commission, Herrmann's departure merely set off complex infighting, most of which involved pro- and anti-Johnson factions, over the future shape of baseball's legal order. Amidst persistent rumors of a rigged 1919 World Series and suspicious happenings during the 1920 pennant race, baseball staggered through the season with a crippled governing body.

Suddenly in the fall of 1920, baseball's magnates reached an accord. Little more than a week after the grand jury's indictments became public, the eight National League owners unanimously agreed to a new legal system; after more than a month of complicated negotiations, which included the threat of forming a new twelve-team league without the American League clubs loyal to Ban Johnson, baseball's moguls ratified a new legal structure that granted broad, quasi-dictatorial powers to a single High Commissioner, Federal District Judge Kenesaw Mountain Landis. Ever since he had helped baseball deflect the first Federal League lawsuit, Landis had been campaigning for such a job. Even so, he remained patient enough to wait for the sweeping authority he desired. Landis received, for example, power to investigate "either upon complaint or upon his own initiative, any act, transaction or practice charged, alleged or suspected to be detrimental to the best interests of the national game of baseball. . . ." In addition to such stated authority, Landis could also "take such other steps as he might deem necessary and proper in the interest and morale of the players and the honor of the game." Finally, Landis obtained a combination loyalty oath–gag order from baseball's magnates: "The owners pledge themselves to loyally support the commissioner in his important and difficult task, and we assure him that each of us will acquiesce in his decisions even when we believe them mistaken; and that we will not discredit the sport by criticism of him or one another."

As these clauses suggested, Landis came to the job of baseball Commissioner in an activist mood. And he soon underlined the fact that he had no intention of following the egalitarian-individualist line of jurisprudence. Formally assuming office in January of 1921, Landis quickly showed that he would not sit around as a passive legal arbiter and wait for disputes to find him. In March, he declared Gene Paulette, a first baseman for the Philadelphia Phillies, "permanently ineligible" because he had associated with suspected gamblers. Landis brushed aside Paulette's protest that he had neither discussed nor participated in any fixed games; the fact that he had admitted to knowing alleged gamblers, one of whom had been indicted by the "Black Sox" grand jury, satisfied Landis' guilt-by-association standards of justice.

Supporters of the new Commissioner System championed such decisions as examples of the superior, albeit harsher, legal order that had now supplanted the National Commission arrangement. Editorializing on Gene Paulette's suspension, for example, the *Sporting News* expressed pleasure at "the higher moral tone that has been pitched for baseball": "Time was when a Hal Chase might have been winked at, but that was in the dark ages; in the new era, there is no room for such gentry in baseball."

The *Sporting News* struck a theme common among baseball commentators: the game desperately needed more discipline and a tough legal character like Judge Landis. Indeed, Landis' pre-baseball reputation as a "hanging judge" now seemed one of his prime assets. In a column entitled "The Right Man," Robert Edgren of the Chicago *Tribune* exclaimed that no one could perform the "miracle" of cleaning up baseball "with less waste of time than a gent who has the habit of saying: 'Six months—next case!'" Similarly, other baseball writers suggested that Landis could help bring back the kind of tough, patriarchal discipline that too many players now lacked. Another *Tribune* columnist, I. E. Sanborn, denounced late hours and card-playing as off-the-field pastimes incompatible with a good performance at the ball park. During the 1920 "hot stove league" season, both the Chicago Cubs and White Sox announced their intentions of establishing a new moral tone among their charges: henceforth, craps and poker games were no longer approved activities for ball players from the Windy City. And at a banquet honoring Johnny Evers—the hard-boiled, no-nonsense manager of the Cubs—Judge Landis wagged his own, and non-too-subtle, finger over his "boys" on the field. "Never before in any activity in the United States has anything been scrutinized as will your activity this season," he warned. "If a man gets caught off first, if he muffs a ball, there will be winks of eyes in the stands and an 'I told you so' whispered around."

In April 1921, Landis showed that a patriarch's reach extended beyond the ball field when he suspended Benny Kauff, a New York Giants outfielder who became involved in an off-season scrape with public legal authority. Although nowhere near as talented (either on or off the field) as Hal Chase, Kauff still probably ran second for Prince Hal's title of baseball's leading problem child. Often suspected but never convicted of shady play, Kauff encountered the new Landis regime when he ran afoul of auto theft charges. The *Sporting News* quickly (and predictably) ratified Landis' legal judgment. It predicted that the ticket-buying and boxscore-reading public would agree with Landis that Benny Kauff's mere presence on a ball field would bring the sacred game into ill repute. Landis' action provided "refreshing evidence of the new moral consciousness in Organized Baseball." The facts that Kauff protested his innocence of the auto theft charges, that the Giants believed in him enough to invite him to spring training, and that traditional legal doctrines held him innocent until proven guilty carried no weight in Judge Landis' new court.

What the *Sporting News* left implicit—the fact that, for the purposes of the national pastime, ordinary legal rules were insufficient—a Chicago *Tribune* column by I. E. Sanborn made explicit. Writing in late 1920 on the still pending trial of the "Black Sox" defendants, Sanborn sketched his view of the legal hierarchy that the eight defendants would have to run before gaining readmission to the game. Even if they received vindication in the public court system, they would still confront three separate levels in baseball's own private justice system: the decision of their employer, Charles Comiskey of the White Sox; the verdict of the American League; and, finally, the decision of the High Commissioner, Judge Landis himself, who possessed "unlimited power to deal with all such cases involving the good name and future welfare" of baseball. "If any player succeeds in passing through that ordeal with a clean bill, it will be positive proof to the public that he is entitled to it, but there won't be a chance for a guilty man to get by."

Yet, Sanborn's assumption that "the public"—whom defenders of baseball's new legal structure constantly invoked—supported his view of the legal issues was unclear. A highly informal poll conducted by a Chicago *Tribune* sports columnist during December of 1920 found that many readers believed that "Black Sox" players should be returned to the game, under some type of probation arrangement, and given another chance. Moreover, most respondents, whatever their views about the players' culpability, also thought that baseball's magnates bore much of the responsibility for the "Black Sox" affair. Sympathy for the players, according to the *Tribune's* survey, ran much higher in Chicago than in rural areas, a fact that probably reflected the close identification between working-class urbanites and the "Black Sox" and one that definitely presaged the players' eventual acquittal.

Beset by delays and rumors of indefinite postponement, the "Black Sox" trial finally began in the summer of 1921. Since baseball's magnates obviously feared having their trade secrets—including Comiskey's scandalously tight-fisted salary schedule—exposed in a public trial, they did not simply allow "blind justice" to run its course. At the outset, for example, they helped the players, the very same ones whose salaries Comiskey continually tried to shave, obtain very expensive legal talent. And, at the other end of the legal process, the baseball elite seized upon the not guilty verdicts as proof positive that "baseball," including people who followed the national pastime, could not trust the public legal system but would have to rely upon the game's own superior legal apparatus.

In truth, the great baseball trial left something to be desired. Basically, legal officials found it difficult to discover any law that the "Black Sox," even assuming they had rigged the series, might have broken. In a similar situation, only six months before the Chicago trial, a judge of the Superior Court of Los Angeles had dismissed criminal charges against three Pacific Coast League players who had allegedly thrown games. Judge Frank Willis acknowledged that the charges, if true, indicated "reprehensible" moral conduct by the players; but, he continued, morality and legality did not always coincide: "There is nothing in the penal code of California providing for prosecution for the offense named in the indictment. The conspiracy [to throw games], if it existed and if it was carried out, constitutes a violation of a contract [between players and owners]. The remedy for that is in the civil courts. The contract broken provided that the men should play ball to the best of their ability."

Confronted by a similar legal problem, the prosecutors in the "Black Sox" case jerry-rigged an elaborate five-count indictment alleging conspiracy to defraud the public and Ray Schalk (one of the true "White" Sox), to injure the businesses of the American League and Charley Comiskey, and to carry on a confidence game. But conspiracy charges, as those involved with the political conspiracy trials of the 1960s rediscovered, have always been notoriously easy to allege and terribly difficult to prove. Moreover, trials for conspiracy have seldom displayed the strengths of the common law justice system. It was this way in Chicago in 1919 as in 1968.

In addition, the "Black Sox" trial seemed to mock the ideal of equality before the law. Arnold Rothstein, the reputed gambler-mastermind of the whole plot, used his considerable influence to escape even a grand jury indictment. Similarly, Hal Chase and Abe Attel, mobilizing their legal resources from the West and East Coasts respectively, slipped through the extradition process. While the ball players and an undistinguished crew of minor gambling figures suffered in the sweltering Middle Western courtroom, then, three of the central characters in the World Series caper watched from afar.

Finally, the conduct of the trial itself hardly inspired great confidence in the public justice system. State's Attorney George Gorman, for instance, had to admit that his office could no longer locate vital documents, including the four alleged confessions, gathered by the grand jury. Ban Johnson quickly charged that Rothstein had paid $10,000 to have the incriminating evidence spirited back to his New York City apartment. The defense, in turn, charged that Johnson himself was the hidden manipulator behind the scenes. They claimed that he had rigged the whole legal process, from grand jury indictments to courtroom trial, and had paid the players' accusers "to dig up the evidence" used against them.

After deliberating less than three hours and taking only one ballot, the jurors returned verdicts of "Not Guilty." The public legal process was over, and the defendants were cleared, at least in the eyes of the "law of the land." But Judge Landis had already been trying to establish the fact that baseball now followed an extra-terrestrial set of commandments. Within hours of the verdict, he issued this statement.

> Regardless of the verdict of juries, no player that throws a ball game; no player that undertakes or promises to throw a ball game; no player that sits in a conference with a bunch of crooked players and gamblers where the ways and means of throwing games are planned and discussed, and does not promptly tell his club about it, will ever play professional baseball.
>
> Of course I don't know that any of these men will apply for reinstatement, but if they do, the above are at least a few of the rules that will be enforced. Just keep in mind that, regardless of the verdict of juries, baseball is entirely competent to protect itself against crooks, both inside and outside the game.

Coverage of the trial in newspapers and magazines followed the Landis–baseball magnate line. First, the wire services and individual newspapers adopted the same story frame: the verdict had been returned in a circus-like atmosphere in which spectators, jurors, players, and even bailiffs joined in celebrating the result. All-the-while, the presiding judge, Hugo Friend, smiled down approvingly from the bench. A photo in the Chicago *Tribune* also followed this frame. It showed the acquitted players, friends, defense attorneys, and the other defendants—simply identified as "gamblers"—hugging one another in victory. The San Francisco *Chronicle* headlined the story this way.

CHICAGO "BLACK SOX" ACQUITTED

Diamond Stars are
Cheered Wildly When De-
cision is Read

Court Officials Take Part
in "Love Feast" After
End of Trial

And the New Orleans *Times-Picayune* carried this page-one headline.

Judge Friend Smiles, Hundreds Cheer, Bailiffs
  Join in Wild
Scenes of Disorder as Jurors Lift "Cleared"
  Players to Shoulders

Editorial opinion elaborated this dominant media frame. According to the *Literary Digest*'s survey of newspaper commentary, only a handful of papers accepted "the legal verdict at its face value." Expressing one of the central tenets of the egalitarian-individualist model of justice, for instance, the Buffalo *Times* announced that the verdict "ought to be an everlasting lesson to this country not to form opinion until it has heard the testimony." But the response of Leonard Sparrow, a sportswriter for the Baltimore *Sun*, was more typical. "The jury tells us that crookedness in sports is not a crime in Cook county, Illinois, in spite of guilt. The jury should now be placed on trial for libeling the moral atmosphere of the people of Cook county, Illinois."

There were, of course, reasons to criticize the shortcomings of the legal process in the "Black Sox" trial. But, in contrast to the calls for a return to a purified model of egalitarian-individualist justice, the type of media frame that had dominated crime reporting in the popular press of the 19th century, criticisms of the World Series trial ignored reformation of the public legal system and endorsed reliance upon the private system of baseball justice run by Judge Landis.

Invariably, newspaper writers framed the story in the same way: only the Landis model of private, patriarchal justice could adequately protect the larger interests of the national pastime. The jury's verdict would change no minds, according to a Chicago *Tribune* sportswriter. "A majority of fans believe the stories against the men. Apparently so does Judge Landis. Therefore it is his duty to rule as he does." Judge Landis had been charged with giving organized baseball "a character bath," editorialized the *Tribune*. "With the Black Sox back in the game, the bath would have looked worse than if it had been drawn from the Missouri River in flood time. . . ." A sports editor for the Boston *Globe* took heart that the "welfare of the game is not in the hands of juries," while his counterpart at the New York *Tribune* thought the ill-advised acquittals gave Landis the chance to show his "keen judgment and rigorous fearlessness." The New York *Evening World* neatly summarized the dominant frame.

> The supreme court of baseball is not governed by the same restrictions as a court of law. It is concerned primarily in protecting the game and not the technical rights of the players.

There are no two sides to the case. If the crooks who were acquitted try to show their faces in decent sporting circles they should be boycotted and blackballed.

II

Baseball's legal reformation solved the moguls' most pressing needs. The ascension of Landis—and the quick legitimation of his authority—settled quickly, if perhaps unjustly, the Black Sox affair. Although several of the tainted eight could make good cases for their innocence, Landis' lifetime suspensions remained in force. Similarly, baseball's new legal structure helped organized ball regain general public confidence. Throughout the early 1920s, Landis worked diligently and skillfully to assure the public that a firm patriarchal hand of justice ruled over the nation's pastime. Fans could go to the old parks and to the new stadiums without worrying about a rigged contest. And betters could place their wagers without fear that gamblers had more than the usual odds in their favor.

In addition to defusing the moguls' most immediate problems, the Commissioner System helped to resolve most of their long-term difficulties. The new legal order offered a private means of dispute settlement that proved much superior to the chaotic one established under the National Agreement of 1903. By setting up a single "czar," the Commissioner System eliminated the tripartite feuding that had undermined the old arrangement. The owners gave up some freedom to pursue their own individual advantage, but their common enterprise gained much needed stability and (at least until Landis' death in 1944) a means for settling disputes within the confines of their own legal baliwick.

With Landis presiding as a one-person court of both first instance and last resort, baseball could contend that there was no need for the public legal system to intervene in its perfectly ordered affairs. For many years, baseball's defenders had claimed that the game offered a private, orderly refuge from the tangled problems of public life, a semi-pastoral haven that was better than the surrounding society. Now, they could draw a corollary: baseball also possessed a private legal order far superior to the one that existed in the public realm.

In its comments upon Judge Landis' new court, the *Sporting News*, baseball's self-styled "bible," reiterated the frame of the general press. The *Sporting News'* post-acquittal editorial, highlighted by black borders, announced that "JURY VERDICT PUTS BASEBALL ON ITS OWN." In subsequent weeks and months, stories in the *Sporting News* showed how baseball's system of swift and informal justice not only punished the guilty but quickly cleared the innocent. Only weeks after the "Black Sox" affair, for example, Landis absolved Emil Meusal of allegations of "indifferent play" for the Phillies and gave the club's deposed skipper, "Wild Bill" Donovan, a clean bill of health. On the other hand, in September of 1921 Landis declared Benny Kauff's acquittal on car theft charges "one of the worst miscarriages of justice that ever came under my observation" and refused to lift his earlier suspension.

Baseball, then, settled its immediate and longer-range legal problems by creating a means of private ordering that differed significantly from the egalitarian-individualist system of public justice. And with the media steadily criticizing the public courts for bobbling the ball in the "Black Sox" episode and extolling Judge Landis, baseball's ruling elites found it relatively easy to legitimate their new order. Although this "higher" legal order subordinated the "technical" rights of players—including their freedom to contract, to bargain collectively, and even to seek justice in the public courts—its defenders praised Landis' legal game as being every bit as fair and square as the game on the field. It protected, they claimed, the needs of the sport and the general interests of the fans.

Baseball's new legal system highlighted the major ways in which the broader American legal culture was changing. Most obviously, the Commisioner System represented an increasingly important trend: the proliferation of more effective private systems for settling disputes and dispensing justice. The business of law was fast becoming one for private as well as for public courts, and baseball's new legal arrangement both reflected and helped to legitimize this important legal development.

The Commissioner System departed from the traditional legal model in several other important ways. As we have already seen, Landis seized an activist judicial role, and he decided disputes without reference to a clearly stated body of rules. His statement barring the "Black Sox" typified his approach: the legal standards he suggested for any possible reinstatement hearing comprised "only a few of the rules that will be enforced," a clear message that the High Commissioner possessed the authority to develop others if he thought the integrity of the game demanded them. And despite the fact that his legal authority extended only to organized baseball, Landis continually sought to enlarge his sway over amateur, semi-professional, and outlaw baseball, especially when it came to players who had been banned by the Commissioner or disciplined by their employers. This meant, among other things, that players holding out for higher wages found it difficult to pick up salaries playing for teams outside of organized ball. Thus, baseball's new order rejected the ideal of a passive judge operating according to known

formal rules in favor of a highly activist, much more flexible system of
legal ordering.

Finally, the new order differed from the traditional public model by
avowedly treating the legal rights of the people brought before the Commissioner as flowing from their special status in society. The Commissioner
System, in this respect, resembled the new legal model then being adopted
for juvenile court systems. Just as individuals brought before juvenile judges
had many of their legal rights determined by their status as minors, so did
the young men coming to Judge Landis' chambers find their rights, at least
as they pertained to organized (and perhaps even unorganized baseball)
resting upon their status as athletes. And Landis treated players not as
adults, able to make intelligent decisions on their own, but as PINS, persons
in need of supervision and fatherly guidance.

This PINS-style of "diamond justice" fitted the kind of baseball played
and the type of player associated with the post-"Black Sox" era. In the days
of scientific, "inside" baseball, the dominant style of play from the 1890s to
about 1920, the player to emulate had been Tyrus Raymond ("Ty") Cobb.
Cobb exemplified the kind of shrewd, always calculating individualist who
could have weaved his way through traditional contract-law disputes as
skillfully and ruthlessly as he roared around the basepaths. In contrast,
the post-1920 style of play downgraded the intense "inside" game—whose
practitioners included Hal Chase as well as Ty Cobb—in favor of a more
naturalistic, less calculating approach. The home run and the big inning
replaced the sacrifice bunt and the stolen base.

Here, of course, the preeminent figure was not Cobb (though he continued to play throughout the twenties) but George Herman ("Babe") Ruth.
Raised in a Baltimore orphanage, brought into baseball by a fatherly priest,
Ruth was portrayed by the media as an overgrown kid, one who always
needed others to handle his affairs. A 1921 confrontation between Ruth
and Commissioner Landis, over the Babe's right to defy Landis' authority
and sign up for a post–World Series exhibition tour, raised a clear choice:
Ruth's right to make an honest living by contracting to play baseball versus
Landis' power to bring order and patriarchal discipline to the game. In
the end, "Father" Landis prevailed over his "big spoiled boy," and the
Commissioner even made baseball's greatest attraction sit out the first
eight weeks of the 1922 season as punishment for his defiance. Once again,
the dominant media frame supported Landis; the larger "public interest"
demanded invocation of his immense powers.

Most important, the public court system put its stamp of approval on
baseball's own legal arrangements. Confirming an appellate court ruling

overturning the finding that baseball's structure violated the Sherman Act, the Supreme Court of the United States held in 1922 that the national pastime was not subject to anti-trust actions. Although the opinion by Justice Oliver Wendell Holmes, Jr., a firm supporter of corporatist as against egalitarian-individualist jurisprudence, said nothing directly about Landis' authority, the Commissioner System itself soon received judicial endorsement from Judge Walter Lindley of the Federal District Court for the Northern District of Illinois. By establishing a kind of code of fair conduct and creating a central czar, baseball's legal order seemed intended "to foster keen, clean competition in the sport of baseball, to preserve discipline, and a high standard of morale," and to structure baseball's affairs in a rational, orderly way. And though conceding that Landis possessed "all the attributes of a benevolent but absolute despot and all the disciplinary powers of the proverbial pater familias," Lindley flatly rejected claims that such a delegation of legal authority was "contrary to public policy."

In contrast to the earlier legal structures by which organized baseball was governed, the Commissioner System succeeded in winning support from both the sports public and the official legal system. Baseball's post-1920 structures seemed to fit nicely into the emerging American legal order, one that exhibited both a growing solicitude for informal, private alternatives to officially dispensed justice and a declining attachment to individualistic, contractual models of legal ordering. Indeed, Judge Lindley seemed to view baseball's arrangement as a model of rational and efficient legal reconstruction. The legal ghosts raised by John Montgomery Ward and the Players' League—reflections of the social-legal turmoil of the late 19th and early 20th centuries—would remain buried until the upheavals of the 1960s unearthed old legal goblins from baseball's past.

Babe Ruth and Ty Cobb, photographed on 25 May 1920 at the Polo Grounds in New York City. ID U1146INP © Bettmann/CORBIS.

8. The Changing Style of Play: Cobb vs. Ruth

In light of the considerable debate during the last decade of the twentieth century concerning the great increase in home runs and runs scored, it should not be too difficult to project oneself back to an earlier era when a similar dramatic increase in offense occurred. During the 1920s, the nature of the game changed to such an extent that it never was returned to its earlier style. In fact, much of the change occurred during a three-year period, 1919 through 1921, when aggregate batting averages increased from .263 to .291, runs per game jumped from 7.75 to 9.71, and home runs per ten games leaped from 3.9 to 7.6. Perhaps even more indicative of the changed nature of the game was the increase in seasonal home runs, from 384 to 1915 to 1,565 in 1930. To be sure, a variety of factors help to explain the increased offense: a livelier ball, the outlawing of trick pitches, such as the spitball, and, after the beaning death of Cleveland's Ray Chapman, the frequent substitution of new white balls into the game. While these changes undoubtedly would have increased offensive production to some degree, the impact of Babe Ruth was the dominant factor. Not only did he revolutionize the way the game was played, offensively and defensively, but he may well have pulled the game back from the abyss created by the problems of the previous decade, capped off by the Black Sox scandal of 1919.

In retrospect, the Babe was a man of his times—indeed, the symbol of an age. The ongoing transition of American society from a rural-agricultural world to one that was largely urban-industrial generated considerable tension in its psychological, cultural, and social values. Ruth came along at a time when his irrepressible nature, combined with the new medium of the newsreel, undoubtedly stimulated the public's fascination with his actions on and off the field. His face became and remains one of the most enduring and instantly recognizable of the twentieth century. Far beyond his prowess with the bat, the Babe was a self-made man from the wrong side of the tracks who had defied the odds to become an American hero. This was the stuff for the making of legend—the common, unsophisticated individual who had achieved fame and glory in an increasingly complicated, impersonal world. The Babe was the embodiment of the American dream.

Leverett T. Smith Jr. assesses Ruth's impact on the game and society by focusing on the contrast between Ruth's free swinging, slugging style of play and that which dominated the first two decades of the century, the controlled, scientific, "inside game" best typified by the play and passion of Ty Cobb. In juxtaposing the most conspicuous symbols of the two eras, Smith studies the contemporary popular sporting press to gauge how such changes were appreciated. At the same time, he attempts to underline the shift in values that occurred between the earlier, grimly unimaginative era to the spirited, free-swinging American society of the 1920s.

It is safe to say that no single baseball player, before or since, made such an impact on the game of baseball as Babe Ruth did during the years 1919, 1920, and 1921. During these three years offensive play in baseball was radically altered, with some effect on defensive styles as well, and Babe Ruth was a major force, though by no means the only one, in accomplishing this change. Our interest here will be to see how the public press understood the change that occurred, and to underline the shift in values that accompanied it. This may be easiest accomplished by focusing on the representatives of the two styles of play: Ty Cobb, regarded by Ring Lardner in 1915 as the greatest of offensive players, and, of course, Ruth himself.

We can turn to the sporting journals, *The Sporting News* and *Baseball Magazine*, for some initial impressions as to what the significant differences in style are. Ernest Lanigan offers the following opinion in *The Sporting News*:

> It is saying nothing new to say that all the world loves a hitter and that Ruth has a legion of admirers. So has Cobb. It doesn't seem to

me that the Babe has taken any constituents away from the Peach and I don't think he is likely to for some time to come.

Tyrus Raymond may not be as speedy as he once was, undoubtedly isn't, but there is one thing in which he hasn't slipped, and that is in his brain play. He can still outthink any past-timer in the profession and the dear public prefers brain to brawn.

Here the contrast is simply drawn: brains vs. brawn. *Baseball* Magazine was more analytic about the situation, and more interested in viewing it as a part of the evolution of baseball. Consequently, they focused on the change that was occurring. In the July issue of 1921, F. C. Lane considered the phenomenon of "The Home Run Epidemic" as follows:

> Baseball, year by year, had grown more scientific, more a thing of accepted rules, of set routine. This slow evolution of the sport displayed itself in batting, in the form of the bunt, the place hit and various other manifestations of skill. . . . Ty Cobb, perhaps, had as much to do with this batting evolution as any one man. Ty taught the world the supreme value of place hitting. . . . Under his magnetic leadership, batters tried for safe hits rather than long hits. . . . And because Ty was supreme among batsmen, no one even dared to question the merit of the system he employed.
>
> We do not intend to question it even now. To our mind, Ty is the greatest batter who ever lived. He was the supreme exponent of scientific hitting and science has a surpassing value in baseball just as in everything else. But every so often some superman appears who follows no set rule, who flouts accepted theories, who throws science itself to the winds and hews out a rough path for himself by the sheer weight of his own unequalled talents. Such a man is Babe Ruth in the batting world and his influence on the whole system of batting employed in the Major Leagues is clear as crystal.

The metaphor of evolution controls *Baseball* Magazine's understanding of the situation. Cobb represents the ordinary course of baseball evolution: Ruth represents those cataclysmic events that occasionally occur in the course of geological time. "Science" takes its place beside brains on the one hand: Ruth's activity is pictured as anti-scientific, he "throws science itself to the winds and hews out a rough path for himself by the sheer weight of his own unequalled talents." It is natural talent rather than scientifically acquired skill that enables him to accomplish what he has.

The following quotation from a 1908 edition of *Baseball* Magazine will serve to give us a sense of how baseball, Cobb's game, was regarded previous to 1920:

> Baseball is not merely an interesting and scientific game. It is the game which calls into play the dominant traits of Americans in its demand for agility, quick thinking, and a tremendous exertion and excitement. It is peculiarly popular and fascinating to us because it means a contest, a personal hand-to-hand encounter. Baseball has all the elements of the personal battle which makes every red-blooded American itch to see a glove contest.

Baseball here is scientific and it is a context, with "quick thinking" as a necessity. Ty Cobb's autobiography provides a passage that seconds and deepens this view of what baseball is.

> When I played ball, I didn't play for fun. To me it wasn't parchesi played under parchesi rules. Baseball is a red-blooded sport for red-blooded men. It's no pink tea, and mollycoddles had better stay out. It's a contest and everything that implies, a struggle for supremacy, a survival of the fittest. Every man in the game, from the minors on up, is not only fighting against the other side, but he's trying to hold his own job against those on his own bench who'd love to take it away.

Baseball for Cobb is a mirror of the commercial world, a competitive jungle in which each has an equal chance to survive. This is the system which results in the best coming to the top.

We are concerned immediately with the scientific aspect of the old game, and the most necessary quality to have in order to be successful at it was thought to be "brains." As the Chicago White Sox approached the 1919 World Series, one thing that was celebrated about them was their braininess. Charles Comiskey was quoted, just before the series started, as saying: "I have merely spoken of the physical aspects of baseball, the trade ability of the men to perform. I have always believed that brains count as much as base hits—sometimes even more. I think I have a fast-thinking team, and the Lord knows I don't like a slow thinker. If we can't outthink and out-play Cincinati we will lose, and I'll have no kick coming if it happens. But it won't."

Tris Speaker was of the same opinion. He saw the White Sox as a "brainy lot of players who will make few, if any, mistakes." The brainiest player of them all was apparently Eddie Cicotte. A poem by Grantland Rice appeared in *The Sporting News* in September of 1919, in celebration of Cicotte, in which he was praised for "A noodle that was packed with brains." Later commentators considered Cicotte's case with some confusion. Billy Evans, commenting on Cicotte's banning for taking a bribe, considered some of the things he had contributed to baseball. "In the passing of Eddie Cicotte, baseball loses one of the craftiest pitchers that ever stepped on the rubber. Not only was Cicotte a master workman, who carefully studied his batters, but to him goes the credit or discredit of originating a lot of the new fangled deliveries that, for a time, had baseball agog."

F. C. Lane, in an article on the men who had turned crooked, was also rather taken aback that Cicotte had sold out. He had always considered Cicotte an honest and intelligent man. Cicotte had, according to Lane, "a keen business mind." Others began to wonder about the crafty workmen with keen business minds who had taken bribes to lose games. George Phair's "Breakfast Food" column in the Chicago *Herald & Examiner* began to contain sayings like "clever ball playing is much desired in a world's series, but it has been demonstrated that a ball player can be too clever." Clearly, other qualities might be more important than braininess in baseball.

What was the offensive style of these brainy ball players? How did they approach the task of making runs? The various techniques they used are for the most part described in articles which bemoan the disappearance of various lost arts; bunting, base stealing, and so forth. We can get an idea of how the game was played from these articles. In his 1961 autobiography, Ty Cobb described the old game as the "game of hit-and-run, the steal and double steal, the bunt in all its wonderful varieties, the squeeze, the ball hit to the opposite field and the ball punched through openings in the defense for a single." These are all techniques of offense as "an act of skill rather than simple power," which, according to Cobb, contained "fine, scientific nuances."

These "fine, scientific nuances," according to many writers, were becoming fewer and fewer. James Isaminger reported the following in *The Sporting News* in June of 1921:

> In the slam-bang style of ball played at Shibe park during the series with the Western teams only in the games with Cleveland has any real baseball cropped out. The champions of the world won a game from the Macks Wednesday through a display of inside stuff that reminded one of baseball of previous years. In this game Tris Speaker opened the eleventh inning with a single and stole second. A land sacrifice put him on third and then a sacrifice fly let him tab the winning run home. With whole series being played here without a sacrifice hit, two such hits in a row startled the fans. . . .

Baseball used to be a contest of wit, skill and courage, but this
season it had degenerated into a mere tug of brute force.

"Force" has replaced "real baseball" according to Isaminger, and real baseball
involves skills of more subtlety and value than simple brute force. *Baseball*
Magazine ran an article in July of 1920, with the peculiar title "Gladstone J.
Graney, a Player Who Bats With His Brains" in which it made this statement
about batting. "The fan's idea of batting is primitive. In his mind batting
consists of hitting the ball. . . . There are other ways of showing batting
ability besides the crude and obvious one of leaning on the ball. And he
comes to the conclusion, in time, that these finer, more subtle methods
are even more effective than lambasting the horsehide to the far corners of
the lot." John B. Sheridan is a great deal more specific in describing what
goes into this more scientific offensive play when he describes Ty Cobb and
what he likes about him as an offensive player.

Like most lovers of baseball I like to see long hitting, but I got
more than enough of it in 1920 and 1921. Much as I like to see hitting
I find, upon examination, that I love base running better than I love
slugging. I know this: Cobb's work on base always intrigued me more
than not only his actual hitting but more than his really wonderful
work at the bat, more than the amazing manner in which he worked
pitchers and out-guessed them, outgeneralled them, made them do
what he wanted them to do, or did what they tried to keep him from
doing. It always has been a delight to watch Cobb hit, more of a
delight to watch him work the pitchers, but greatest delight of all to
watch him run bases.

These were the things at which the scientific batter was accomplished,
but there now seemed no reason for them. They were taken up, one by one,
by *Baseball* Magazine, and analyzed to see why they were dying out. A May
1921 article described "the Bunt as 'Scientific' Batting." The article began
by quoting Rogers Hornsby to the effect that "a good batter is a slugger,
for slugging is natural batting." The article went on to point out that while
Hornsby's statement might be perfectly true, there were not many batters
around who had the batting skills to afford to be natural. For them, brains
were more important than brawn. "Bunting is skill and practice and self
control all in one and where did you ever find a slugger with self-control?"
The article concludes that "Bunting is the last word in batting skill because
it marks the furthest departure from slugging, which is natural batting.
Bunting is scientific batting because it is science which takes us from the

beaten path of the merely natural." Two articles in *The Sporting News* announced that the bunt was now out of fashion as an offensive weapon. The first, published somewhat before the *Baseball* Magazine article, told of the lack of good bunters active in the major leagues, then spoke of the excellent bunters of the past. "The bat became an instrument rather than a bludgeon in the hands of such men as Keeler and Browne, an instrument of which they, more than others, realized the possibilities. I don't suppose any other two batters harassed a pitcher more than did Thomas and Huggins. You couldn't play in on these men because they'd shift and hit them past you." Ty Cobb is the chief of the modern players mentioned, but with the comment that "he is such a hard, versatile batter that we do not think of him particularly as a bunter." The second article in *The Sporting News* simply announced that "the sacrifice bunt" is "no longer . . . considered an important part of the training of a ball club." It is no longer, the writer concludes, considered an effective play.

Baseball Magazine next considered the fate of the stolen base in the new era. In two articles, "Is Base Stealing Dead?" in the June 1921 issue, and "The Sensational Decline of the Stolen Base" in the May 1922 issue, F. C. Lane argued that "As Major League baseball develops, base stealing declines. Increased efficiency in pitching and fielding automatically crowds out the stolen base." In spite of this evolutionary trend, Lane felt that base stealing "should be encouraged so far as possible for it offers greater scope for individual initiative and varied attack than batting." The gradual extinction of the stolen base was, to Lane, a product of the gradual evolution of baseball. The play is to be "sacrificed on the altar of mechanical perfection." "In this painstaking effort, to make of baseball an exact science, the managers, however, have overlooked one very important point. . . . Beyond and above all rules and regulations must be placed human daring and ingenuity." John B. Sheridan suggested another reason for the decline of the stolen base in his column.

> Yet it seems to be a pity that play at many of the fine points of the game, notably at base running, must be permitted, for the present at least, to decay while the slugger is making his brief strut upon the stage. With slugging at its apogee base running, naturally, declines. There cannot be any sort of sense in breaking a leg to steal a base when the giant at the bat is liable to make a four-base hit and chase the runner home ahead of him.

Sheridan here suggests that it is the fad for slugging that has caused the decline in the stolen base. He also suggests that the slugging style is a fad, and that it will not last long, which, as we will see momentarily, is an opinion shared by many.

F. C. Lane joins John B. Sheridan in both these opinions in a 1922 essay, "What's Wrong With the Three Base Hit?" This offensive weapon is also not as much used as in the past. Lane calls the three base hit "about the nicest hit of all, a line drive of terrific force, well placed between the outfielders, combined with nice judgment and speed of foot in base running." He is quite clear as to why this kind of hit is no longer in use.

> When Babe Ruth ceases to be the dominant influence in modern day batting and the bubble of home run popularity is exploded, then the three bagger along with other suppressed baseball features will come into its own. And the return of the triple to its normal position will probably mark a saner, less feverish, better balanced contest than has been possible under the brilliant but irrational domination of the home run.

For all these men who espoused "scientific baseball," the popularity of the home run seemed an "irrational domination." Before Ruth, apparently, no one thought of actually swinging the bat with the purpose of hitting the ball out of the park. The only home run of the 1919 World Series was shrugged off by the pitcher whose pitch was hit as "an accident that is likely to happen to any pitcher." Babe Ruth is thought of as "a freak, an unknown quantity." Thomas Rice, in speaking in defense of other aspects of baseball than the home run, said in *The Sporting News* that "there is a thrill in the home run, but there is an equal, and more protracted, thrill in the steady fielding behind a good pitcher that is saving him hits. A home run is a spectacular incident." W. A. Phelon summarizes the view of the situation held by these men in the following manner: "The Home Run has been set up and established as the idol of baseball. The brilliant, snappy game of old; the intricate methods of defense; the fast subtleties of the attack; the stories of magnificent pitching—all these have been subordinated to the God of Slug." Thus we find that Ring Lardner's estimate of the condition of professional baseball concurs with that of other experts in the field.

The man these men all idolized for his ability on the field was Ty Cobb. A great deal of verse was composed to celebrate his offensive capabilities, one of the better stanzas of which came from the pen of one Howard T. Walden, II (with apologies to Kipling).

He is Cobb! Cobb! Cobb!
When they want a run he's always on the job;

Either hits or sacrifices,
When the game is at its crisis
There's one man you can count on—Tyrus Cobb!

Cobb is a money ball player, and he treats his profession seriously. One sports writer lectured major league players by holding Cobb up as an example to them: "Ty Cobb is a living example of the value of brains and courage in baseball, but more than half the big league players fail to realize why he is so great a star. It is because he outgames and outthinks the average player. With Cobb, baseball is a serious business in which he has earned a large salary for many years and he considers it worthy of his attention." The chief value of brains is in the learning of new things, day after day, and this is what Ty Cobb was popularly believed to be able to do. Grantland Rice describes him early in his career.

. . . Ty Cobb . . . the greatest offensive player of the game. . . . Cobb saw that he was only a fair base-runner, so he went forth alone, to slide and practice by himself, hours at a time. He kept plugging at this art until he knew that he could handle himself around the bases.

Shortly afterward he began to find that he was weak against left-handers. . . . At morning practice he got all the left-handers he could find to pitch to him. And if there were none available from the team he would pick up corner lotters or camp followers, and set them to work, blazing away at his weakness.

The man who compiled the highest batting average of all time was admired by his contemporaries not for his talent but for the hard work he put in acquiring the various skills of scientific play.

Cobb himself had this advice to give to others who wanted to follow in his footsteps: "Scheme, scheme and keep scheming." This seems definitive. Cobb is the representative of the kind of crafty braininess that Lardner liked to see in ball players. Cobb himself seemed to worry about the lack of this characteristic in other players. He was quoted as saying in 1919,

Although the game has grown faster and more scientific in my mind, there has not been the individual improvement you might look for. The boys of today play scientific baseball because it has been taught them, not because they dope it out themselves. They don't study the game like young doctors or young lawyers or engineers study their professions. After a game these kids are through with baseball until the next day. They don't take their chosen profession seriously enough. My success was due entirely to self-application and study.

There is no role for a community to play here; the statement seems totally individualistic.

Part of the reason for the change from this point of view lies in the public figure of Babe Ruth. The public response to Ruth was overwhelming. Paul Gallico insists that it was unique. "In times past," he reflects, "we had been interested in and excited by prize fighters and baseball players, but we had never been so individually involved or joined in such a mass out pouring of affection as we did for Ruth." It is hard now to imagine what it must have been like to watch Ruth perform. Gallico says that "the home runs amassed by Babe Ruth, and in particular his great record of 60 in 154 games, was the sheerest pioneering and exploration into the uncharted wildernesses of sport. There was something almost of the supernatural and the miraculous connected with him too." Ruth in 1920 hit 54 home runs which record, as the *Times* noted in awed tones, was "a greater number than any entire team in either major league compiled." Then in 1921, Ruth broke his own record again, hitting 59 home runs. Feats of this sort prompted players to make remarks like the following by Chet Thomas, a Cleveland catcher: "I am not so certain now that Ruth is human. At least he does things you couldn't expect a mere batter with two arms and legs to do. I can't explain him. Nobody can explain him. He just exists." Clearly Ruth's impact on the game was awesome.

His home run hitting was thought to inaugurate a new style of play, but opinions on the importance and permanence of this style of play varied immensely, beginning with the attitude that he was a freak, held by many exponents of scientific baseball. John McGraw exemplifies this point of view in his explanation of how he had his pitchers pitch to him during the World Series. The central fact to remember was that "Ruth . . . is a ball player of the freak type that is likely to bust up a game at any moment." Sam Hall of the Chicago *Herald & Examiner*, in an article on Ruth during the 1920 season, spoke of Ruth's desire to raise his batting average in the following terms: "Yes, the Babe longs for a big batting average now more than he wished home runs. Not that he won't sock them if he gets a chance. But he's going to quit swinging with all his might at every pull, cease hitting with two and three balls and no strikes on him and bat like a regular hitter and not a freak—for a high average, and the good of the team." This essentially friendly paragraph contains many assumptions that are not friendly to Ruth's style of hitting.

Slugging as a batting style was generally looked down upon and those hitters who were merely sluggers were ordinarily depreciated. John B. Sheridan's remarks on Frank "Home Run" Baker show how a slugger was looked down upon. In speaking of the New York Yankee team in general, he dismissed Baker with the following words: "What has Frank Baker ever been? A slugger. That's all. Never could field or run bases. Could hit." There was also considerable resentment of the fact that sluggers always got all the glory, though they weren't always the best players. The following verse by George Phair, called "Science," speaks of the same sort of man as Sheridan's version of Frank Baker:

His feet were like a pair of scows,
    But he could hit.
There was a void behind his brows,
    But he could hit.
He fielded like a four-wheel hack—
He never seemed to get the knack—
And yet he always got the jack,
    For he could hit.

Like Baker, this player can do nothing but slug. He can't run, he can't think, he can't field. In short, he can't play scientific ball.

Some people felt that Babe Ruth fell into this mold. Jack Doyle, Pacific Coast scout for the Chicago Cubs, voiced their attitude clearly in a statement for *The Sporting News* in which he criticized "bum ball players like Babe Ruth." He maintained that "baseball is an athletic science that requires nine men working in harmony to produce teams of championship caliber" and that Ruth disturbed that harmony. He went on to assess Ruth's talents.

Ruth is a third-rate outfielder. As a base runner, he is in a class by himself. I'm not complimenting him, either.

As a batter, Ruth is an accident. He never plays inside baseball at the plate. He goes up trying to take a swing on every strike, a style that would cause any other player to be benched. He either knocks home runs or strikes out. Any man who strikes out as many times as Ruth did last year can never be classed as a great hitter. . . .

These are the classic criticisms of an old style baseball man. One of the ways Ruth was defended was to argue that he had, really, all the talents of the old ball players in addition to his special talent for hitting home runs. William B. Hanna's reply to Jack Doyle was structured in this way. He argued that Doyle was all wrong in his assessment of Ruth's talent, that Ruth "is a good base runner and a smart and bold one. Match him against such wide-awake citizens as Cobb and Speaker, and he holds his own."

The Independent, in a feature article on Ruth, denied the "freak" theory to the extent that they attributed to him the same background of study and preparation for his calling as was usual in reviewing the case of Ty Cobb. In speaking of his home runs, the article reads, "he does not do this by any accident or by reason alone of some special gift of nature. He does it very largely by art, the result of long and careful study and practice."

The revolution in baseball styles Ruth brought on led to the domination of sheer strength and speed over brain power on the baseball diamond. Baseball had become largely a "simple, primal game"—as John B. Sheridan called it—"hit it a mile and run until you are put out." F. C. Lane sums up the shape of the revolution in an interview with Ruth: "It may be a triumph of brawn over brain. It may even suggest the dominance of mere brute strength over intelligence. It may show a preference for the cave men over the finished artist. . . . Rest assured it's a fact. Babe Ruth is the uncrowned king of the diamond, the master figure of the baseball season, the big noise in the biggest game on earth." To most writers, it might be true that Ruth could be a brainy ball player, but it wasn't relevant to the situation at hand.

Lane and *Baseball* Magazine could never make up their minds as to precisely how Babe Ruth fit into their scheme of the evolution of baseball style. The title of Lane's July 1921 article, "The Home Run Epidemic," suggests that they might see it, as many saw the baseball scandals, as a momentary illness of which baseball could eventually be cured. The substance of this article, though, suggests something else. In it Lane calls Babe Ruth a "superman."

> Now and then a superman arises in the domain of politics or finance or science and plays havoc with kingdoms or fortunes or established theories. Such a superman in a narrow, but none the less obvious field, is Babe Ruth. The big bat wielder might not make much impression in the fine arts or classical literature. . . . Nevertheless, in his own particular field, Babe is a true superman.

The article goes on to present Ty Cobb as the prototype of hitting style followed by most players before Ruth came on the scene and then concludes that "the home run was a victim on the altar of improved methods and general development just as we saw last month that the stolen base was a victim. Batting flourished as never before. But the home run became more and more of a rarity." Lane refers then to the statistics of the last two years, which shows a 156% increase in the number of home runs hit. He declines to accept two possible causes for this: a restriction on the use of certain popular pitching deliveries such as the spit ball, and the introduction of a "livelier" ball into the game. The rise of home runs is due rather to a change in batting styles. Ruth, according to Lane, "has taken the place-hit [Cobb's specialty] from its pedestal as the batter's universal model and has set up in its place the home run."

> . . . can there by any doubt that Babe Ruth was the man who showed the world the value of the circuit clout? . . .
>
> A leader in any field speedily obtains a following. . . . We do not mean to contend that the chop hitter who chokes up on his bat and punches out an occasional feeble single is hitting any more home runs than he ever did. But we do say and the records bear us out, that almost every batter who has it in him to wallop the ball, is swinging from the handle of the bat with every ounce of strength that nature placed in his wrists and shoulders.
>
> . . . Babe has not only smashed all records, he has smashed the long-accepted system of things in the batting world and on the ruins of that system he has erected another system or rather lack of system whose dominant quality is brute force. . . .
>
> Does Babe's advent into baseball herald a new era of development? We cannot say. For a time, at least, the old order of things is in complete eclipse. . . . We are in for a true carnival of true home run hitting which evidently has not yet reached its peak.

Here, certainly, Lane is prevented from understanding Ruth's batting style as a new model for players only by his understanding that baseball is to evolve in scientific ways. He cannot understand Ruth's style as a scientific improvement on that of Cobb. Consequently, when he speaks of Ruth's system, he qualifies this, saying, "or rather lack of system whose dominant quality is brute force." Later Lane pulled back even from the position he had taken in this article. A year later he spoke of the "home run epidemic" again, and this time he was a little truer to the implications of the word "epidemic": "Just how long the epidemic of home runs will endure is not clear. That it is a permanent trend in baseball is hardly probable. More than likely it is a transient demonstration of brute force à la Babe Ruth, which will pass with the passing of the great hitter who invoked it."

There are some indications that others saw Ruth's hitting as the basis of a new offensive style. *The Sporting News* suggested

> That many batsmen are following Ruth's system is an open fact, and it will be only a short time when big league teams will encourage

one or more in the line-up who possess the ability, which means giant
strength and a keen eye, to try for homers every time. . . . There
is no reason why George Ruth should have a monopoly of divine
right to absorb all the glory and home runs derived from this style
of hitting. If club owners and managers come to the conclusion that
this mode of attack is effective and really a valuable asset in winning
games, then there will be a general training in that direction and in
a few seasons the woods will be full of more or less Babe Ruth style
of swatters.

Of course the crucial point here is the question of whether this style, if
pursued, would contribute more to winning games than the style presently
followed. In 1919 and 1920, this was a real question. In 1919, when Ruth had
begun to hit home runs, the Boston Red Sox, on which team he played,
had changed from a championship team to a second division team and, in
fact, the owner of the Red Sox announced that he had traded Ruth to the
Yankees because he was a disruptive force on the team. In 1920, despite the
fact that Ruth hit 54 home runs and drew monstrous crowds everywhere
the Yankees played, the team still finished third in the pennant race. Since
the Yankees won pennants in 1921, 1922, and 1923, the argument might be
said to have completed its first phase by then.

Numerous short statements that spotted the Chicago newspapers tended
to indicate that Ruth's home runs were magnificent, but that other than
that they seemed quite meaningless. George Phair, for instance, printed
the statement that "Babe Ruth's forty-seventh home run was a noble
achievement, but it didn't mean anything." Presumably he meant that
it had no effect on the outcome of the game, and therefore had no
significance. In the same column appears a poem on the relation of home
runs to winning.

> A home run hit may cause a grin
>   Upon the rooter's face,
> But four-base wallops do not win
>   A pennant race.

The problem of the relation of slugging to winning was discussed by Christy
Mathewson in his New York *Times* column. Mathewson wrote

> There seems to be a great demand these days for star sluggers. There
> is no doubt of their value to a team, and the man who can rap out
> a home run frequently furnishes the fans with the most spectacular
> play in the game.

But from the point of view of winning contests, my experience has taught me to prefer an aggregation of good base runners to a batting order of hard hitters. I believe the former can do more to help a pitcher win games. . . .

When a man is pitching for a team of base runners he knows that every time a player with a reputation for stealing bases gets on the bags, with half a chance, he is pretty sure to score a run. Then, too, when a club has a name for possessing base runners it helps to get the opposing pitcher's goat. He has to devote a lot of his energy to watching the men on the circuit and has less to devote to his pitching.

On the other hand, a hard hitter who is slow on the bases is only a hindrance.

This puts the case against the slugger well. A little more than a year later, Hugh Fullerton spoke of a heated argument among ball players and managers "concerning the value of long distance hitting and its effect upon baseball teams and baseball leagues." Fullerton feels that whether or not one argues for or against slugging depends entirely on whether or not one is on the same team with a slugger or not. He points out that the fans love slugging but suggests that "there may be a sharp reaction of sentiment when the fans discover that long distance hitting is not winning baseball, but even that is doubtful." He concludes that "the real baseball is the middle ground, the judicious mixture of real baseball and slugging, with the manager deciding when and how the batters shall hit." This essay suggests that things are beginning to change. Fullerton has moved the "reality" of baseball more toward the position of the slugger, even though his language ("the judicious mixture of real baseball and slugging" is a phrase that still refuses to admit slugging to the realm of "real" baseball) is inadequate for this task. Slugging is becoming a legitimate tactic, even in the minds of the defenders of the old style.

We should speak finally of some of the personal qualities of Babe Ruth as a public person. They too suggest a shift in values from a commercially oriented individualistic community to one hierarchically structured. Where Cobb had a rural, Protestant background, Ruth was a Catholic from Baltimore. Though in his public image, Ruth was first presented in the same way Cobb had been, soon it was found that his personality was vastly different and a new way of presenting him had to be found. One thing Cobb and Ruth had in common and that Ruth was proud of all through his life was the fact that he had risen to the top of his profession from lowly origins. He made this point very early in his autobiography.

Too many youngsters today believe that the age of opportunity has passed. They think it ended about the time people stopped reading Horatio Alger.

There are more opportunities today than when I was a boy. And all these opportunities are open to every type of American. The greatest thing about this country is the wonderful fact that it doesn't matter which side of the tracks you were born on, or whether you're homeless or homely or friendless. The chance is still there. I know.

Ruth's is the story of the American boy, but, we shall see, even though his story fits the American success story mold in this respect, that, like the story of his successor as Yankee, Joe DiMaggio, his image reveals a different set of values than those usually found in the American success story in all other respects.

Early articles worried rather ineffectually about Ruth as a capitalist. *Current Opinion* remarked that "in winter he manages his cigar factory in Boston and is possessed of shrewd business sense as well as a sense of humor." The article fails to give any examples of his "shrewd business sense" other than the existence of the cigar factory and goes on to describe his sense of humor. Much the same thing happens in an article in *The Independent*:

> His outlook on life is kindly but shrewd. He has various sources of income in addition to his salary and he is not spending all he makes. When baseball finishes with him Ruth will have money. Being a likeable young man he will also have friends who are willing to do real services for him. He will probably have his choice of a dozen good business offers.
>
> And he may turn them all down and decide to go it alone in some field of big business. If he does, his admirers will expect him to make good. They say he has business sense.

Again, his business sense is not documented. It seems only a pious hope in the minds of his interviewers.

Instead of a burgeoning capitalist, Ruth was pictured in various images that relate the natural, the instinctual, and the childlike. He was pictured as a natural force, as a man who plays the game for love, not money, as a kind of foolish or simple person, and finally as a child. "Brute force" is a familiar term with which to describe Ruth by now, but it seemingly applies to his character as well as his physical strength. The following quotation appeared in the New York *Times* on the occasion of Ruth's fiftieth home run of the 1920 season:

Baseball has never before developed a figure of such tremendously picturesque proportions as this home-run king of the Yankees. With no weapon but a primitive club, he has manipulated it in a manner which would make the famed clubbers of the Stone Age look like experts in battledore and shuttlecock. Ruth has hit almost as many home runs as Heinz has pickles. In fact, he is a greater pickler than the world has before known.

Here Ruth stands for the primitive, the brutish and the natural. His bat is a club, not an instrument. Furthermore, as we learn from the following quotation, his knowledge of baseball is instinctive rather than learned. The occasion is speculation on whether Ruth will be asked to manage the Yankees: "Unquestionably Cobb is a great player and in his day better than either Speaker or Sisler, but as an attraction, Ruth has him beaten. And the Babe knows baseball. Knows it and plays it instinctively. He may make errors—they all do—but you'll rarely, if ever, hear of him pulling a bad play." That a player of this sort should be the largest gate attraction in the game was something new. The greatest players before had always had great talent, of course, but always they had worked and worked to improve and perfect their talent. This Ruth was not doing.

One of the things that saves Ruth from himself is, according to writers, his love for baseball. Hugh Fullerton writes of this quality in him in an article in *American* Magazine.

> In the past two years the baseball public of New York has fallen into the same habit. The fans flocked by millions to see the Yankees play ball, apparently caring little whether the team won or lost, so long as Babe Ruth made a home run.
>
> Yet "Bambino" himself is exactly the opposite. With him the game *is* the thing. He loves baseball; loves just to play it. I remember one day in Boston, when he was with the Red Sox, fighting for a game which meant perhaps the winning or the losing of a championship. He started in the game as an outfielder, stepped into the breach as a pitcher, and finally won the game with a smashing hit.
>
> It was almost dark when some of us emerged from the park and started downtown. Two blocks away, a bunch of kids was assembled in a vacant lot, playing ball. And there was Babe, hitting the ball, just for the fun of it; just because he loved it; not to win something, or to keep from losing something, but just for the sake of doing it. . . .

Here we find that Ruth is interested in playing baseball, not merely working at it. This is what his "love" of the game seems to mean. It is hard to imagine

Ty Cobb in a sandlot game, with his "scheme, scheme and keep scheming" motto for human action. Ruth himself explained his behavior with reference to a love of baseball. On the occasion of being suspended for five days for arguing with an umpire, Ruth made this statement to the press:

> I do not regret being out of the game because of the money it costs me. I really don't need the money, but I do love to play baseball. For that reason it hurts when I can't get into the game.
>
> Another thing that hurts is the criticisms. Some persons are saying that I welcome the suspensions because it gives me an alibi for not equalling my home run record of last year. That is ridiculous, as I realize that that is impossible. Others claim that I have a "swelled head." My friends know different. I want to be in there every minute because I love to play baseball.

Here Ruth uses his love of the game to remove himself from the suspicion of having commercial motives for his actions. These kinds of images center eventually on the image of Ruth as a child. In defense of Ruth, when he was being criticized by Harry Frazee just after Frazee had traded him to the Yankees, *The Sporting News* attacked Frazee and told its readers that Ruth was "pretty well spoiled, but a good boy at heart." Again, W. J. Macbeth in the New York *Tribune* defends Ruth against detractors by describing him as a child at play.

> Ruth is nothing if not a big grown up kid. Nobody in camp is working harder than he. He runs out every hit as if sprinting for a base knock in the real show and already runs them out past second base. Afield in fly chasing Ruth has shown a judgment and speed that matched the best efforts of Sammy Vick. Samuel was one of the speediest of Huggins' 1919 aggregation.
>
> Babe is working to improve his speed and range as instance a sample of his day's work. After his hitting practice he indulged in about an hour's "shagging" of fungoes while the infielders practiced fielding. Then Ruth came in to third base for a half hour more. He finished up the day with a few clownish antics for the benefit of the grand stand managers.

Without the first and last sentences, this could be a paragraph about Ty Cobb. But the two sentences give the activity an entirely different context. Billy Evans has the final word on Ruth as a child. This particular passage concerns the size of his head and the effect that being a celebrity has had on him.

What kind of a fellow is Babe Ruth? That is a question I have been asked hundreds of times since Babe hogged the sporting spotlight. Ruth's remarkable ability to hit home runs has made him the most discussed individual in the history of the game. Thousands of fans wonder what kind of a fellow he really is, when not engaged in busting them over the fence.

No doubt a great many people have the impression that Ruth feels his greatness. Nothing could be further from the truth. Ruth is a big, likeable kid. He has been well named, Babe. Ruth has never grown up and probably never will. Success on the ball field has in no way changed him. Everybody likes him. You just can't help it.

Ruth the child is the perfect representative citizen of Judge Landis' kingdom. With this picture of Ruth the change of the community of professional baseball from a community identified with a democratic capitalistic world to a community which sees itself as authoritarian and above commercial concerns is complete. Far from being a capitalist engaged in competition, Ruth is a child exercising his talents out of love for the game. Professional baseball has become a big, happy family.

To summarize, as a result of the scandal, which uncovered deep areas of corruption in the democracy that could not be handled by a democratic government, baseball chose the option of calling in a dictator to purify itself. Coincidentally, a style of play which emphasized the virtues of a paternalistic, hierarchical society arose. Thus by 1922, professional baseball was able to view the American community at large from a position of superior purity, a position it would hold until the 1960s, when the public discovered that professional football made a better representation of the alternatives to the confusions of a democratic society.

JASON PENDLETON

9. Jim Crow Strikes Out: Interracial Baseball in Wichita, Kansas, 1920–1935

During the past couple of decades, historians of baseball have focused increasing attention on the integration of major league baseball and on the black professional leagues beginning in the 1920s. Even the barnstorming teams dating back to the 1880s have drawn a fair bit of attention. Such studies inevitably focus on the urban areas of the North and East, where the concentration of the black population was heaviest. Neglected in the story of the black experience in baseball, however, has been its amateur and semiprofessional presence at the local community level, where innumerable town teams played. Indeed, it is at the local and regional levels that one can most fully understand the far-reaching social, cultural, and economic aspects of racial segregation. Yet the more one studies the specific nature of the local relationship between race and baseball, the more the conventional wisdom and stereotypes break down.

The story of the local black baseball experience is difficult to tell due to the peripatetic nature of local teams, the inconsistent local press coverage of games, and the incomplete statistics and financial records left behind. Oral testimonies, while valuable for providing context, are often too inaccurate and embellished to be relied upon to complete the record and provide understanding of the dynamics of black baseball during the period of local Jim Crow laws. Beyond baseball, such local studies reveal much about the social consciousness, cultural expression, and economic status of the larger local black community. They also disclose how the entire local community interacted, formally and informally, with blacks within the bounds of racial segregation. The incongruities of baseball and social relations between blacks and whites at the local level provide an interesting and instructive backdrop to the breakdown of national segregationist barriers following World War II, for the playing of local interracial and integrated baseball in the interwar years provided a vehicle for expanding racial tolerance that undoubtedly was mirrored in other areas of social activity.

Jason Pendleton traces the emergence of interracial baseball in Wichita, Kansas, during the interwar period. In doing so, he analyzes the particular local conditions that permitted such incongruous behavior as a game between a Ku Klux Klan team and a local black club. The game was played in 1925, when local Jim Crow laws were ascendant and the Klan had reached the peak of its white supremacy influence. The fact that it was played without incident reveals a good deal about attitudes unique to segregated Midwestern society.

As Satchel Paige stood behind the pitcher's mound facing the outfield, his mind likely raced with excitement and a sense of accomplishment. With two outs in the ninth inning, the African American hurler and his Bismarck (North Dakota) teammates were on the brink of the first-ever national semi-pro baseball championship. The eleven thousand black and white fans on hand in Wichita, Kansas, to see the Bismarcks battle the Duncan (Oklahoma) Cementers for the ten-thousand-dollar first-place prize, however, were witnesses to something more significant than a championship game. The huge crowd that filled Lawrence Stadium on a humid August night in 1935 saw a Bismarck team represented by both black and white players. It is unclear whether the fans recognized the importance of a racially integrated team competing in an era of racial segregation. Satchel Paige, however, barred from playing major league baseball because his skin was black, understood the significance of playing on an integrated team in 1935. Stepping back onto the mound, Paige faced the Cementers' top power hitter, who had collected hits in his three previous at bats. Utilizing his famous windup, Paige unleashed three consecutive fast balls that struck out the Cementers' big first baseman and clinched the national title for the Bismarcks. That Paige had struck out fourteen batters in the championship game was of secondary concern to him; rather, the importance of the moment inspired him. Commenting later in his life about his experience with the Bismarcks, he remarked: "I'd cracked another little clink in Jim Crow."

The championship for the Bismarcks was the culmination of a tournament that brought thirty-two teams to Wichita, Kansas, from twenty-five different states, including California and New York. The historical significance of the tournament, however, has less to do with the Bismarcks being crowned the first national semi-pro champions than with the presence of racial diversity among the participants. "Four different races will be found in the list of 32 clubs," reported the *Wichita Beacon*. The Memphis Red Sox, San Angelo Sheepherders, Denver Stars, Texas Centennials, and Monroe Monarchs were teams comprising all black players. In addition to all black teams, the Nipponese Stars were Japanese and the Stanolind Indians were Native Americans. However, the most racially diverse team was the Bismarcks, considered one of the best teams in the country with its victories over both the American League All Stars and the Kansas City Monarchs the previous year. The Bismarcks presented a team of five white and six black players.

Twelve years before Jackie Robinson broke the color barrier of major league baseball, the integrated Bismarcks, as well as the other black teams, played without incident before tens of thousands of fans in Wichita, Kansas. The participation of black players without incident in the 1935 Wichita tournament was no accident. The previous fifteen years had exposed Wichitans regularly to African Americans and whites playing interracial baseball. This history had largely prepared them to accept teams like the Bismarcks in 1935. The question, however, remains as to why white Wichitans, as well as many other Americans at the local community level, accepted integration in baseball but refused to allow African Americans such as Satchel Paige to stay in their hotels or eat in their restaurants.

During the first decades of the twentieth century racial segregation had spread to nearly all social aspects on local and national levels. The 1896 U.S. Supreme Court decision in *Plessy v Ferguson*, which established the doctrine of "separate but equal" as a constitutional principle, ushered in a wave of segregation statutes known as "Jim Crow" laws, which increasingly excluded African Americans from interacting with whites. Subsequently, racial animosity and resulting tension further separated black and white social interaction. The "Red Summer" of 1919 was the worst period of interracial violence in the history of the United States. In the last six months of the year approximately twenty-five race riots occurred throughout the country.

Racial violence was not absent on the Great Plains. In September a riot broke out in Omaha, Nebraska, when Willie Brown, a black man, was accused of attacking a white girl. A mob of whites destroyed the county courthouse, captured Brown and dragged him through the streets. Reportedly shot a thousand times and mutilated beyond recognition, Brown's body ultimately was hanged from a downtown trolley pole. The trend of violence continued into the 1920s. In Tulsa, Oklahoma, twenty-seven people were killed and three thousand African Americans were left homeless due to a riot that caused $1.5 million in property damage to the black community. Kansas did not escape the prevailing attitude of racial hatred. In December 1920 Independence, Kansas, was the scene of what the *Wichita Beacon* referred to as a "race riot" when violence erupted between black and white citizens after a black man reportedly shot a white grocer. According to the *Negro Star*, a group of white men organized a posse to arrest "colored men who spoke out in defense of the man accused of killing the grocer." Fearful of the mob, African American men also united. The two groups reportedly squared off in a two-hour melee that resulted in the deaths of a white schoolboy and a black man. As with the riots throughout the country, the Independence riot provides evidence of the deep division between black and white citizens in Kansas.

By the 1920s racial segregation was firmly entrenched in Kansas. African Americans consistently were denied access to public accommodations that whites enjoyed. Black Kansans hoping to enjoy a cafe-cooked meal routinely were denied access to restaurants that catered to whites and most often used the back door to place take-out orders. Movie theaters throughout the state also were segregated. Although African Americans generally were granted access, they were forced to sit in sections exclusively for black patrons. Along with the humiliating *de facto* segregation prevalent in theaters and restaurants, black Kansans faced similar forms of discrimination in housing and employment opportunities, as well as *de jure* segregation in some public elementary schools.

In the urban environment of Wichita, Jim Crow attitudes made it increasingly difficult for the growing black population. In terms of employment African Americans had few opportunities for well-paying jobs. According to historian Craig Miner, "more than twenty percent of the black population pursued menial occupations and lived far below the level of decency and comfort." Consequently, many black Wichitans lived in "squattertowns" on the edges of the city. Those African Americans who had adequate employment still faced housing discrimination that led to a concentration of black residents and consequently a black community separate from that of white citizens. In 1924 an interracial conference examined the status of African Americans in Wichita and questioned "whether school

segregation resulted in equal education and whether black institutions . . .
were getting enough aid and attention from the city." As a result of its
study, which also questioned "whether blacks were treated fairly in hiring
in the city police and fire departments as well as in private industry," the
interracial conference concluded that Wichita did "have a negro problem."
Thus, discrimination in Kansas largely mirrored the prevailing trend of
racial separation that existed throughout the country.

Racial segregation and the resultant constraints on African American access
to white-dominated social institutions led black Americans to create parallel
social institutions. As a reaction to black exclusion from professional major
league baseball, Andrew "Rube" Foster, a former star pitcher for the Cuban
Giants at the turn of the century, organized the Negro National League
(NNL) for professional black baseball. Foster wanted an organized black
professional league that provided stability and structure similar to the
white majors. Foster understood that the league would be dependent
on the support of black fans and thus targeted cities with large black
populations. In the inaugural season of 1920 the league had representatives
in Chicago, Cincinnati, Dayton, Detroit, Kansas City, and St. Louis.
Foster's motivation for separation was based on Booker T. Washington's
ideas of advancement through self-help. "In all things purely social,"
Washington declared in 1895 in his famous Atlanta exposition address, we
can be separate as the fingers, yet one as the hand in all things essential
to mutual progress." Organizing a successful league comprising black
players and black owners would serve two purposes. First, the league would
provide black men the opportunity to participate in professional baseball.
Second, and most important, Foster and the other black owners believed
that if they could prove professional black baseball was economically
successful and had a quality standard of play comparable to that of whites,
eventually segregation would be broken. Thus Foster's ultimate goal was
more integration than separation.

The Negro National League became black America's counterpart to
the white major leagues. Under Foster's direction the NNL turned a profit
immediately. In 1923 the league drew more than 400,000 fans and grossed
approximately $200,000 in attendance. The Chicago American Giants,
owned by Foster, grossed approximately $85,000 a game in 1924. Foster's
success in creating a separate professional league for black players motivated
other African Americans throughout the country to organize leagues. The
Eastern Colored League formed in 1923, joining the NNL that same year.
The Southern Negro League (SNL) also emerged in the 1920s. Comprising

the top southern independent teams, these organizations drew from a talented pool of players in the large black population areas of the South. Satchel Paige was just one of many athletes who played in the SNL. In addition, the Texas Negro League blossomed in the 1920s, serving as a minor league way station for future Kansas City Monarch's pitcher Hilton Smith.

Along with being segregated from playing with white professional teams, African American baseball players in the Midwest also were geographically isolated from the all-black leagues in the North and South. Possessing the same desire to play baseball as did their counterparts elsewhere in the country, black players from Kansas, Oklahoma, Nebraska, and Missouri organized the Western League of Professional Baseball Teams (Colored Western League). The nine-team league, representing Oklahoma City, Tulsa, Omaha, St. Joseph, Coffeyville, Topeka, Independence, Kansas City (Kansas), and Wichita, began play on June 4, 1922. In the first league game in front of "a large number of enthusiastic fans of both races," the Wichita Monrovians beat the Tulsa Oilers eight to one. The Monrovians, named for the capital of the African nation of Liberia, were a strong organization apparently operated solely by black Wichitans. Prior to the organization of the Colored Western League, the Monrovians had been in Wichita the previous two years under the name Black Wonders. In 1922 the Monrovians secured their own ballpark in Wichita at Twelfth and Mosley. The field allowed the Monrovians to schedule league games on their field and host games with black teams throughout the Midwest.

The Monrovians played outstanding baseball their first season, winning the Colored Western League. No exact record for the entire season has survived, but the *Negro Star* reported at the end of July that after sixty games the Monrovians were fifty-two and eight. In addition to enjoying success in league play, this team, as was customary for black teams throughout the country, played games outside its league schedule. The Monrovians scheduled such games against the Arthur Gosset Post American Legion team and the Hutchinson Aces Up team—both black—because they provided additional opportunity for income. In these nonleague affairs, teams might play for a percentage of the gate receipts or put up a monetary forfeit with the winner taking all. The majority of the time each team received something, win or lose.

The Monrovian Corporation, which had a state charter with capital stock valued at ten thousand dollars, appears to have become one of the leading social forces of Wichita's small black community. The Monrovian baseball park provided black Wichitans a place to socialize and be comfortable among other blacks without feeling the stinging pain of racism. Whites who attended the games were more likely to be less openly prejudiced toward black Wichitans than the mass of the city's population. The games became social events with black families and couples attending; women sometimes received free admission when accompanied by ticket-buying escorts. In addition to providing a friendly atmosphere of entertainment, the Monrovian organization participated in the Kansas Black Elks convention and also utilized its popularity to help raise money for the Phillis Wheatley children's home in the black community. The active role that the Monrovian organization assumed in assisting Wichita's black community was part of the same self-help motivation that led the Monrovians to join the Colored Western League.

Unfortunately, the Colored Western League collapsed following its inaugural season. No articles appeared in the Wichita papers indicating the details of the demise; likely it resulted from managerial squabbles that occurred during the first season. The collapse of the league, however, did not doom the Monrovian organization. Although the black league provided a stable organized schedule for the Monrovians, its survival was not dependent on the league. Following the collapse, the Monrovians returned to playing Wichita teams and barnstorming throughout the state, playing both black and white teams.

Amid the racial turbulence of the early 1920s interracial baseball was prevalent at the same time that social interaction between African Americans and whites was virtually nonexistent. Although inconsistent with the pervasive segregation throughout the country, including Kansas, the Monrovians' custom of playing white teams was not uncommon in Wichita. The Monrovians' doubleheader victory over the all-white Campbell Merit Bread Company team in August 1922 (which, according to the *Wichita Beacon*, was played before "one of the largest crowds to ever attend a game at Monrovia Park [and] which consisted of both white and colored fans") suggests that baseball at the local level did not follow the norms of segregation. The paradox of local toleration of interracial baseball is evidenced by the following advertisement in the *Wichita Beacon*: "The Southwest Cracker company would like to establish their claim to the city championship by meeting the best baseball club in the city. The Gold Medal Boys have an open date at the league park . . . and will play any club in the city . . . [f]or a purse or for the gate receipts. This pertains to all comers, white or black." No black team reportedly filled the open date; nonetheless, that this white team openly stated its desire to play black teams represents the tolerance some Wichitans had toward interracial baseball.

Despite white Wichitans' apparent attitude of toleration for interracial baseball, interracial participation did not extend into organized city league play. Among five leagues comprising thirty-eight teams in the city in 1924, not one team was black. In 1925 the trend continued with no black team represented in any of the eight leagues, collectively comprising forty-nine teams. In fact, between 1920 and 1935 no black team played organized city league baseball among white teams in Wichita. Considering the precedent that teams such as the Monrovians had established playing against white teams such as the Kirke Tire Company, the absence of black teams among Wichita city leagues seems unusual. Yet the Monrovians' absence, at least, is explainable: the team did not play because it was a professional team. Participation in nonprofessional city leagues would have prevented the players from touring throughout Kansas and surrounding states, and stops in small towns were essential because they provided the bulk of the players' salaries. The absence from city leagues of other black teams such as the Gray Sox and the ABCs, who won the 1920 Wichita "Colored Championship," raises questions about the inconsistency between league and nonleague practices.

Although Wichitans frequently engaged in interracial ball games, it remains unclear why all-black teams were absent during city league play. Although no official written policy forbade black teams from participating in Wichita's city league, their absence raises questions. Were black teams excluded because whites felt threatened by the possibility of crowning a black city league champion? White teams could easily justify losing individual games to black teams as simply bad luck or an "off" day. However, crowning a black team as city champions, which was determined over several months with an established schedule, would have forced white teams to acknowledge that the black team was better. That possibility could have potentially threatened the idea of white racial superiority. Crowning a black city champion also would have left white Wichitans vulnerable to verbal assaults from white Kansans about the teams' inferior showing. Despite hypothetical rationales, the absence of black teams does not necessarily mean they were excluded by white teams. It is plausible that black teams did not play simply because they did not want to. Considering nonleague practices, however, it seems unlikely that black teams collectively had no desire to compete for the city championship. Regardless of the possible explanations, the absence of black teams demonstrates that limitations remained in interracial baseball participation in Wichita.

Outside the city leagues, interracial games continued. The Monrovians maintained their practice of playing the best teams in the city, including a

1924 contest against the Wichita Advertisers, the leading team in the city's Industrial League. The newspapers did not publish the contest results, not an uncommon occurrence when games involved black teams. Cudahy Rex, an all-black team sponsored by the Cudahy packing company, played three games against white teams in 1926, all of which were announced in the *Wichita Beacon*. Despite the newspaper's announcement, only the white team's victory over the Rex team appeared in print. Why the newspaper did not report the other games is uncertain, but it is possible the results were omitted because the Rex team was victorious. Although the *Wichita Eagle* and the *Wichita Beacon* journalists did not appear prejudiced in their articles, they may have expressed their attitudes about African Americans by omitting stories in which the all-black teams proved victorious. Not all black victories over white teams were excluded from the paper, but their defeats of top white teams, which could have undermined the idea of white racial superiority, frequently lacked follow-up stories with game results.

The Ku Klux Klan is one of the leading symbols of American white racial superiority. Originally designed to destroy Republican political power in the Reconstruction-era South, the Klan reemerged in the 1910s with an expansion of its hatred to include, in one historian's words, "Jews, Catholics, bootleggers, adulters [*sic*], atheists, and others who offended against the Klan's vision of a racially morally pure America." In 1921 the new Klan's national leader, William Simmons, sent a representative to Wichita. The representative claimed that the Klan was present in at least ten Kansas cities and stated that the Wichita membership included "native-born, white, gentile, American citizens who believe in the tenets of the Christian religion and owe no allegiance to any nation other than the United States, either civil, political, or ecclesiastical." Such a message was popular in Kansas. In early 1922 the *Wichita Eagle* reported that membership in the Wichita Klan totaled five thousand. By 1924 the Klan was present in almost every town in the state and its statewide membership approached one hundred thousand. The Kansas Klan of the 1920s was an ultra-patriotic organization concerned less about white supremacy than perpetuating anti-Catholicism. Although the Kansas Klan's antipathy focused primarily on Catholics, the organization by no means ignored African Americans.

Among the tenets of the Wichita Klan, as printed in the *Wichita Eagle* in November 1922, was the repression of African Americans in the city. The local Klavern "support[ed] Jim Crow laws; the abolition of secret societies among Negroes; . . . [and] no employment of Negroes under any circumstances." In 1923 the Montgomery County Klan also used violence to intimidate African Americans. According to historian Paul Franklin Harper, white attackers shot Sam Stevens (a black man) in the leg on his way home because some white citizens did not want Stevens's children "to attend the same school with their white children." The malicious violence directed at Stevens and others prompted *Emporia Gazette* editor William Allen White to charge that the "Klan [was] directing terror at honest law abiding citizens, Negroes, Jews, Catholics," and indicates that the Kansas Klan intimidated African Americans in its attempts to create a "racially morally pure" state.

Although the Wichita Klan expressed anti-Negro sentiments among its tenets, apparently black and white participation on the baseball field was not a problem. In fact, the Wichita Klan Number 6 baseball team played a game against the all-black Wichita Monrovians in 1925. The failure of baseball—and the Klan—in Wichita to follow the general trends of a segregated society was exemplified by this game. In the article announcing the game, the anomalous—and unpredictable—quality of Klansmen playing against African Americans is visible:

> Strangle holds, razors, horsewhips, and other violent implements of argument will be barred at the baseball game at Island Park . . . when the baseball club of Wichita Klan Number 6, goes up against the Wichita Monrovians, Wichita's crack colored team.
>
> The colored boys are asking all their supporters to be on hand to watch [the] contest . . . due to the wide difference of the two organizations. . . . The novelty of the game will attract a large crowd of fans altho [*sic*] both teams say that all the fans will see is baseball.

As the teams predicted, the game was played without any hint of violence before a large interracial crowd, even though the Monrovians prevailed ten to eight. The almost inexplicable presence of an all-black team playing against the historical archenemy of African Americans suggests that Wichitans were developing an attitude of toleration toward African Americans in the area of baseball that was inconsistent with the pervasive racist segregation that dominated American society. Although it is unlikely many whites in Wichita were completely race tolerant, their participation and attendance at the game indicates the degree to which white Wichitans accepted limited black and white interaction on the baseball field.

As the end of the decade drew near, Wichitans witnessed increasing numbers of interracial baseball games. As the Monrovians began to fade from the sports pages, other black teams emerged to fill the void. Cudahy Rex proved capable of succeeding the Monrovians as the best black team in Wichita.

The team frequently battled its white rivals, the Cudahy Puritans, splitting two games in 1927. The continuation of interracial baseball between the two Cudahy teams, although important, illustrates the limitations in baseball's ability to challenge segregation. Separate teams from the same company shows the breadth of division in the 1920s. The Puritans played in the city league and participated in numerous nonleague games, while the Rex team did not play city league ball; rather, it scheduled games against small-town and individual city league teams. Despite the tolerance of interracial baseball in the late 1920s, white Wichitans' views on racial integration probably would not allow Cudahy to have one integrated team. The company's willingness to sponsor a separate team exclusively for black employees, however, suggests an acceptance of baseball as a limited sphere of toleration.

Although black teams such as the Monrovians and Cudahy Rex were important in exposing Wichitans to interracial baseball, the Kansas City Monarchs of the Negro National League expanded the practice and introduced thousands more Wichitans to talented black baseball players. In 1926 the Monarchs drew three thousand fans to their game in Wichita. In 1927 the Monarchs' return prompted the local promoter to sell advance tickets for the two-day event. Featuring Joe "Bullet" Rogan, who was considered one of the greatest pitchers in baseball during the 1920s, and T. J. Young and Newt Joseph, both former members of the Monrovians, the Monarchs drew a collective six thousand fans in their two victories over the white Wichita Advertisers team.

The appeal of the Monarchs crossed racial lines in Wichita and elsewhere. As the leading stars of the Negro National League, black players were heroes to the black communities they visited. The presence of local black Wichitans on the Monarchs team who were exalted as stars likely created great excitement among the Wichita black community. African American fans no doubt enjoyed the Monarchs' regular victories over their white counterparts. Their reported record of 577 wins and three losses against semi-pro teams (black and white) provided a source of pride for many. African Americans, moreover, likely recognized the irony of segregation as the Monarchs, prohibited from playing in the white major leagues or even from dining with whites, methodically beat white teams before thousands of spectators in mixed crowds. The Monarchs' appeal was broad and included a large number of whites who flocked annually to the ballpark to witness the great talents of the professional black players.

In 1928 the Wichita fans were again exposed to the talents of professional black baseball when the Cuban Stars of the NNL came to town. Along with playing in the NNL, the Stars also played winter baseball in Cuba, winning the championship of the Cuban winter league in 1928. The Stars' appearance in Wichita demonstrated the prevailing attitudes about race. Although most Americans regarded race in simple terms of black and white, Cuban players, like many African Americans, were not uniform in the color of their skin. The players' skin hues ranged from dark brown to what was considered nearly white. Yet, despite their Cuban ethnicity, white Wichitans recognized the players by the racial conceptions they understood, white and black. Of the fourteen Cubans who played in Wichita in 1928, thirteen were termed black and one was termed white. The thirteen dark-skinned players participated in the NNL, while the lone light-skinned player received a contract in the Boston Red Sox organization. Although the players were Cuban, in America they could not escape the prevailing divisions of the color line. Consequently, the players' shared history and the cultural connections they maintained as Cubans were overshadowed by an American concept of race that classified people by skin color.

It is uncertain whether Wichita's black community accepted this prevailing racial view or placed more emphasis on the Cubans' ethnicity. But considering their shared experiences with oppression and segregation, black Wichitans likely viewed the Cubans as black. Such distinctions notwithstanding, the Stars were a talented team. In a doubleheader against an all-star team of Wichita's best white players, the Cuban team pummeled the locals fifteen to two and twenty-three to five.

By the end of the 1920s Wichita was a regular stop on the Monarchs' midwestern tours. Unlike the Cuban Stars, who humiliated opponents, the Monarchs appear to have kept the contests fairly close. Recognizing the financial importance of the tours, the Monarchs used public relation schemes to drum up fan interest and make the games appear competitive. In 1929 the Monarchs issued an ultimatum to Henry's Clothiers, their scheduled opponent in Wichita. If the Henry's team did not defeat the Wallenstein-Raffman all-girls' team in July, the Monarchs threatened to cancel their game in August. Henry's four to zero victory over the girls' team ensured that its game with the Monarchs would be played. The Monarchs' ultimatum was probably a calculated move to generate interest for the game and help boost attendance. Different rules were adopted in the game to make it appear more competitive. Similar to match play in golf, the winner of each inning, rather than the final tally of runs, determined the score in the game. For example, if the Monarchs scored ten runs in the first and Henry's scored only one run, the Monarchs would win the first inning one to nothing. Whichever team won the previous inning would bat first in the next inning. The different rules were used to avoid lopsided victories and help keep the game competitive, with the maximum points a team could score being five. Unfortunately, newspapers did not report the game winner. The different format illustrates that the Monarchs understood the importance of the illusion of competitiveness for fan interest.

In the 1930s interracial baseball was increasingly common in Wichita. In 1930 the Monarchs made their seasonal trek to the city, bringing with them night baseball. At a reported cost of fifty thousand dollars, the Monarchs traveled with generators and temporary lights that could be assembled quickly. The lure of the Monarchs and the intrigue of night baseball drew more than three thousand fans. In the same season, local African American teams such as the Wolverines, Grays, Blue Devils, and Black Sox all played on Wichita's baseball fields. New teams of all hues sprang up yearly, including the Aztecs, an all-Mexican team. The Aztecs played white and black teams in Wichita and also traveled to surrounding cities to battle other Mexican teams. Baseball served as a vehicle to expose people of different backgrounds to each other. Wichitans who attended baseball games regularly witnessed people of diverse racial and ethnic backgrounds competing on the diamonds. The ballpark engendered an arena for social interaction that existed nowhere else in the city's segregated corridors.

By 1932 a dozen years of interracial social interaction had paved the way for the appearance of minority teams in official city baseball contests. The first nonwhite group to play city league baseball, however, was not black. Despite more than a decade of local competition between black and white teams, two all–Mexican American teams, with only a two-year playing history in Wichita, became the first minority group in city league play. The Mexican Midgets played in the Wichita junior league, and the Aztecs played in the adult city league. Why Mexican Americans were the first minorities to play in the city league is unclear—possibly because their skin color was not dark enough to be considered black. Not being black, and consequently not completely subjected to racial segregation, Mexican Americans likely were the beneficiaries of the established tradition of black and white baseball in the city. Although white Wichitans were not yet ready to compete with black players in the city league, the atmosphere of tolerance relative to baseball had broadened to allow Mexican Americans to participate. The limited racial toleration that surrounded baseball in Wichita was slowly expanding.

Unable to break the color line of city league play in 1932, African Americans appeared that year for the first time in the Kansas state semi-pro championship tournament. The Colored Devils from Wichita, with the aid of players recruited from Oklahoma, won their initial game of the state tournament against the Reformatory Boys, a team of delinquents. Despite losing their next two games and being eliminated from the tournament, the Devils and the black community of Wichita and Kansas logged a victory by their very participation. Since the Devils previously had been denied the opportunity to play organized baseball with whites, their participation was the first change regarding the status of African Americans and baseball in the city.

In 1933 Wichita newspapers openly discussed allowing an all-black team to play in the city league. T. J. Young, former Monrovian and Monarch catcher, attempted to organize an all-black team for city league play, but his efforts proved unsuccessful. With the presence of several all-black teams in Wichita, Young undoubtedly found enough talented black men to play in the league. The absence of Young's team was more likely a result of white resistance than lack of black support. Despite the failure of his effort, Young achieved an important, albeit limited, victory when he was allowed to play for the Mulvane team of the Oil Belt League. Participation of a single black player in the city league was not insignificant. Young had cracked the color line, an indication that toleration of African Americans in baseball was continually expanding.

In the state tournament held in Wichita in 1933, black baseball in Kansas achieved its first official organized success. Although only two teams out of forty were black, their abilities proved unmistakable. The Ninth Cavalry team of Fort Riley and the Beavers of Arkansas City both had established themselves as top teams in the Midwest. The Ninth Cavalry was considered second only to the Monarchs, and the Beavers had proved their abilities by defeating four Class A white minor league teams in 1933. Although the Ninth Cavalry team did not live up to its billing and was ousted early in the double elimination tournament, the Beavers performed well. The team easily won its initial contest behind forty-two-year-old Army Cooper, former pitcher for the Monarchs, against the Dickey Oilers of McPherson twelve to two in front of three thousand fans. The victory set up a game between the Beavers' "most hated rivals," the Arkansas City Dubbs, whom the Beavers had beaten four of six times during the 1933 season. The trend continued as the Beavers defeated the Dubbs by a single run in extra innings before forty-five hundred fans. Wichita Water dealt a punishing blow to the Beavers' drive for the championship with a seven to three defeat. Despite the setback, the Beavers were determined to win the championship. The team's right fielder and coach, Hurley McNair, a veteran of the NNL, expressed its attitude: "Listen[,] you just tell the boy's [sic] there's going to be plenty of smoke behind our next game. And we're going to rap that fence so hard out there that the game will have to be called in the second inning on account of no fence. By losing to the Wichita Water team our confidence and desire to win the tournament has increased one hundred percent." Despite the Beavers' determination the team was eliminated in the semi-finals by the Shell Dubbs eleven to ten. The Beavers' fourth-place finish served notice that black teams would have to be taken seriously in the future.

The state tournament of 1934 featured several strong black teams. Joining the returning Ark City Beavers were the Kansas City Colts, Wichita Wolverines, Topeka Darkies, Colored Stars, and Wichita Elks. The extreme competitiveness of the tournament and the compulsion to produce a winner led some cities to hire professional teams to play for them during the tournament. The Topeka Darkies actually were the Cuban All Stars, now hired by white merchants from Topeka to represent their city. Apparently no teams objected to Topeka's actions since most were guilty of hiring minor league professionals to play with their teams. The Wichita black community hired a Texas team to represent it in the tournament. Despite an opening round loss to the Topeka team, the Wichita Elks battled back to finish third and collect $887.74. The Topeka contingent also fared well, finishing fourth and collecting $591.83, while the Kansas City Colts finished fifth and took home $295.93. Three all-black teams were represented among the top five places. The tournament's two-week duration exposed thousands of fans to interracial baseball. Following the tournament, fans also witnessed an integrated all-star game with three black players, including Army Cooper, who was unanimously selected to be the starting pitcher in the charity game against the all-white state champion Arkansas City Dubbs.

The continual evolution of racial tolerance on the baseball field was present in the 1935 state tournament. This gathering in Wichita witnessed the return of the Kansas City Colts and Topeka Darkies (again, actually the Cuban All Stars). The Elks club of Wichita once more secured a professional team from Texas (Dallas Steers) to represent the black community of Wichita. African Americans in Fort Scott did the same, hiring the San Angelo Sheepherders to represent their community. Unlike the previous year, only the black contingent representing Fort Scott fared well in the tournament. Its third-place finish was important because it helped expose black baseball to the forty-one thousand fans who attended the tournament, and it qualified the team for the National Semi-pro Baseball Tournament.

The dominating performance of the Bismarcks in the National Semi-pro Baseball Tournament symbolizes the progress Wichitans had made regarding racial tolerance on the baseball field. The integrated Bismarcks represented the culmination of the previous fifteen years of interracial participation on the baseball fields of Wichita. From the Monrovians of the early 1920s to the integration of black teams into the state tournaments in the early 1930s, the citizens of Wichita generally accepted African Americans in baseball in an era when black people gained access to few other realms of white society. The failure of baseball to follow the established norms of racial segregation in Wichita focuses the attention on the prevailing ideas about race in America.

The complexities of racial segregation in Wichita derive their inconsistencies from the incongruent racial concepts inherent in American life. America's legacy of slavery, which once separated slaves and masters on the premise that black Africans were inferior because of their skin color, engendered a pervasive ideological construct of race based largely upon color. Historian C. Vann Woodward contends that "the long experience of slavery in America left its mark on the posterity of both slave and master and influenced relations between them more than a century after the end of the old regime." America's history of treating African Americans as inferiors because they were not white offered a foundation for the emergence of Jim Crow attitudes that dominated all parts of America. In her examination of social relations in the American West, historian Patricia Limerick contends "race . . . was the key factor in dividing the people of Western America." Similarly, historian Robert Hine in *The American West* states that "sources of prejudice were not sectional or urban, western or rural. They lay deep in the National experience." Wichita's maintenance of racial segregation reflects how deeply embedded was this ideology in which white residents viewed African Americans as a separate and inferior race.

Yet, despite Wichita's general conformity to the prevailing national racist ideology, regional factors peculiar to the Midwest contributed to an attitude of limited racial tolerance in baseball. According to historian Barbara Fields, "ideology is a vocabulary for interpreting social experience. . . . [and thus] ideology must convey different meanings to people having different social experiences." The social experience of whites in Wichita, confronted with only a small number of black citizens, was certainly a different social experience than in the cities of the South and East, or even to those in parts of the Midwest more affected by the Great Migration. In Chicago in 1930 one hundred thousand African Americans were spreading into white neighborhoods, while black Wichitans totaled just 5,623 and represented only 3.7 percent of a 111,110 population. African Americans were considered a threat to whites in Chicago, but the small segregated black community in Wichita largely was not. Thus the social experiences of Wichita whites, faced with only a small number of blacks, allowed whites to view black and white interaction somewhat differently than did whites in the East and South. There white citizens in cities such as Baltimore and New York were confronted daily with black populations ranging from 140,000 to 220,000 respectively. Thus the disparity in population contributed to varying regional social experiences and spawned different local attitudes about race.

In the 1920s and 1930s the Midwest was the scene of thousands of interracial baseball games. Lacking regional major league teams, people in small towns openly accepted black teams on their baseball fields. Why did midwesterners, seemingly as racist as their eastern counterparts, initially accept interracial games and finally integrated teams? An examination of Kansas, Colorado, and North Dakota, where integrated baseball first occurred, shows the common denominator to be that African Americans represented only a fragment of the total population. In Kansas in 1930 African Americans totaled 66,344 and represented 3.5 percent of the population. In Colorado, where Denver hosted the region's first tournament with an integrated team, African Americans totaled 11,828 and represented 1 percent of the population. In North Dakota, where integrated baseball flourished with an entire league of integrated teams, the black population totaled only 377 and represented one-tenth of 1 percent of the state's local population. In these sparsely populated areas, interracial and integrated baseball not only existed but flourished because the presence of black and white players on the baseball field together would not threaten the segregated relationship outside the lines. In Bismarck, North Dakota, Satchel Paige, whose team owner paid him four hundred dollars a month and gave him a car, slept in an abandoned freight car with his wife in the lone black section of the town because he could not find available lodging elsewhere. Despite the inconsistency of baseball relative to social relations, black citizens in the Midwest, lacking in numbers and isolated because of their skin color, were powerless to successfully change the notions that gave credence to Jim Crow.

Although racial segregation was still prevalent in the 1930s, baseball in the Midwest provided an arena for social interaction that previously was nonexistent for black and white citizens. Interracial baseball in the Midwest served as the vehicle for bringing whites and African Americans together as equals on a consistent basis. The experience helped modify and expand the racial tolerance of Midwesterners relative to baseball. When Jackie Robinson broke the color barrier of major league baseball in 1947, many Kansans had already grown accustomed to witnessing integrated baseball and were surprised with the attention surrounding the event. Historian Larry G. Bowman fondly recalled the six years he lived in McPherson, Kansas, during the mid-1940s when his father took him to see Wichita tournaments that boasted numerous integrated teams. Bowman stated, "I would sit with a group of men with . . . my father and I never recalled hearing a derogatory remark made about the black players." When Robinson broke into the majors, Bowman vividly remembered wondering what the excitement spreading across the country was all about. According to Bowman, his experience viewing interracial and integrated baseball in Wichita helped shape his view as a young adolescent that interracial interaction in baseball and other areas was normal.

Consequently, the numerous fans who attended games in Wichita and other parts of the Midwest where interracial and integrated baseball was played developed attitudes that were inconsistent with prevailing racist segregation. Admitting African Americans on the playing fields made it easier to break down other segregationist barriers in the ensuing decades. The acceptance of African Americans in baseball—first by Midwesterners, later by people in the East, and last of all by the South—opened some of the first doors of the civil rights struggles of the 1950s and 1960s. Players such as Satchel Paige, who have been correctly acknowledged both for their athletic talent and their impact on race relations, should not completely overshadow the heroic efforts of men such as T. J. Young and other members of the Monrovians who bucked the restrictions of Jim Crow segregation in the 1920s and 1930s to play interracial baseball on the dusty fields of Kansas.

WILLIAM M. SIMONS

10. The Athlete as Jewish Standard Bearer: Media Images of Hank Greenberg

The history of baseball necessarily involves the study of broader issues of diversity and ethnicity in America. During the 1930s the ethnic makeup of the major leagues began to change. Long dominated by the English, Irish, Germans, and other northwest Europeans, the rosters began to reflect the changing ethnic, religious, and geographic origins of the country's population. Italian names like DiMaggio and Lazzeri, eastern European names such as Simmons (actually Szymanski) and Picinich, or Hispanic names like Lopez and Luque appeared on the rosters of big league clubs. Baseball was viewed as a microcosm of the great American "melting pot." Increasingly larger numbers of recent immigrants from southern and eastern Europe had replaced earlier groups on the bottom rungs of the urban social ladder in the nation's major cities. Despite claims to the contrary, players from such backgrounds frequently found themselves the targets of verbal abuse from fans and bench jockeys from opposing teams, to say nothing of crude hazing from fellow teammates. But in baseball, with the notable exception of blacks, if one could display the requisite professional skills of pitching, hitting, and fielding, rapid promotion was possible. Why and how organized baseball became adept at absorbing such ethnic groups after decades of exclusivity has been the subject of considerable debate, but one suspects that the pursuit of profits among the owners weighed in heavily. Not only would an ethnic player's skills make a team more competitive on the ball field, but such a star would also have the potential advantage of attracting fellow ethnic city dwellers to the ball park.

Like many other ethnic groups, Jewish Americans occupy a particular niche in the history of baseball. Prior to the 1930s few Jews had made it to the big leagues, and those who did so encountered open hostility and anti-Semitism. To avoid such harassment, some had even changed their names. Considerable contemporary speculation existed about why so few made the grade. Some observers claimed that Jews were simply not inclined to team sports, preferring boxing instead, while others emphasized Jewish preference for more cerebral pursuits. Nevertheless, if Jews had trouble making it into the melting pot, Walter Harrison argues that baseball was one of the features of America's life that Jews quickly assimilated and fused with Judaism to form a new "secular faith." More than fifty Jewish players had ascended the ladder of professional baseball by the end of the 1930s. The most notable of these, a Manhattan-born son of Romanian emigrants, Hank Greenberg, would prove to be the most important Jewish baseball star until the emergence of Sandy Koufax in the 1960s.

William M. Simons examines Greenberg's role as an ethnic standard bearer, especially among second-generation Jews, who saw in him a symbol of their own prospects for assimilating and succeeding in mainstream America. Press commentators played a key role in the creation of the public image of Greenberg as an individual and, by extension, the Jewish community as a whole.

Throughout the first half of the twentieth century baseball reigned as the undisputed "national game." At times it evoked a depth of concern that suggested a secular religion as the following paean by a sporting enthusiast suggests: "[baseball had] all the attributes of American origin [and] character. . . . [it was] the exponent of American Courage, Confidence, Combativeness; American Dash, Discipline, Determination; American Energy, Eagerness, Enthusiasm. . . ." Also, during World War II *The Sporting News*, which unabashedly referred to itself as the "Bible," pontificated that " . . . Japan never was converted to baseball. . . . No nation . . . could have committed the vicious, infamous deed of . . . December 7, 1941, if the spirit of the game ever had penetrated their yellow hides." As a microcosm of the American mind, baseball thus provides one means of evaluating attitudes toward important social phenomena, including ethnicity.

This article analyzes media depictions of baseball's premier Jewish standard bearer, Hank Greenberg, during the 1930s. After surveying the general status of ethnicity in press coverage of 1930s baseball, recurrent images of Greenberg are identified. Then, the focus shifts to the journalistic controversy surrounding Greenberg's decision to play baseball on the Jewish New Year in 1934. Finally, the assimilative connotations of Greenberg's image for fellow ethnics receives attention. Detailed examination of 1930s' print media, including the Anglo-Jewish press, sporting publications, national magazines, contemporary books, and general circulation newspapers, from all cities with major league baseball teams, provides the empirical base for the content analysis that follows.

The 1930s furnish particularly fertile ground for probing perceptions of ethnicity in the "national pastime." Although Anglo-Saxon Protestants from small towns constituted baseball's largest contingent, the major leagues possessed a significant ethnic dimension. During the 1930s, however, baseball's ethnic composition changed substantially, and this highly visible transformation attracted extensive contemporary comment. While "the English, Irish and the German," noted a Depression-era sportswriter, " . . . were well grounded in the fundamentals and spirit of the game before the other lads from the continent," the German and Irish presence waned somewhat by the 1930s. Another 1934 article noted that "in recent years there had been a grand invasion of other nationalities," prominently featuring players with southern and eastern European antecedents.

Jews, sons of immigrants who fled eastern European *shtetls* between the assassination of Tsar Alexander II and the outbreak of World War I, contributed, albeit in a limited form, to the ethnic recasting of baseball during the 1930s. As with their counterparts from other ethnic groups, Jewish major leaguers confronted the universal dilemma of the second generation, resolving the conflict between the "old world" values of their immigrant parents and those of the larger society, embodied in the "national pastime." Beyond the shared "marginal man" phenomena, however, Jewish major leaguers of the 1930s faced additional anxieties often not encountered by gentile athletes. American anti-Semitism, fueled by the social and economic abrasions of the Depression, peaked during the 1930s. Thus, given the ambiance of the 1930s, the second generation's struggle to resolve the tension between ethnic and host society expectations assumed a special dimension for Jewish athletes.

Depression-era commentators frequently asserted that "one race . . . that was always weakly represented" in baseball "was the ancient Jewish stock." Although they depicted the presence of Jews in baseball as on the rise, Depression-era journalists devoted considerable print to the reasons for the supposed paucity of Jewish major leaguers. *The Sporting News'* Fred Lieb, one of the most influential sportswriters of his time, claimed that " . . . Jewish boys are smaller than kids who spring from other races. The

Jewish boy was pushed aside on the playground diamond by the bigger youth with an Irish, German or Scandinavian name. Also, . . . the Jews did not possess the background of sport. . . ." In a 1934 article, which appeared in both the New York *Evening Post* and *The Jewish Advocate*, Phil Weintraub, a Jewish outfielder on the New York Giants, blamed Jewish parents for opposing the athletic ambitions of their sons: "Jewish mothers don't want their sons to be ballplayers. They dream of them becoming professional men, successful in business. But first of all they want them to become educated." Several articles also claimed that boxing reflected the Jewish temperament more fully than did the "national pastime": "For centuries, the Jew in his individual business had to fight against heavy odds for his success. It sharpened his wit and made him quick with his hands. Therefore, he became an individualist in sport, a skillful boxer and ring strategist, but he did not have the background to stand out in a sport which is so essentially a team game as baseball."

Although a number of coreligionists preceded Hank Greenberg, baseball's original "Hammerin' Hank," in the big leagues, scribes hailed him as the first "really great Jewish player." Greenberg became "that long-sought Hebrew star." Except for Sandy Koufax, the pitching sensation of the 1960s, no rivals challenge this Hall of Famer's status as baseball's premier Jewish player. Born in 1911, the New York City native's major league tenure spanned the years 1933 to 1947 with four and one-half years lost to military service during World War II. Aside from his final season with the Pittsburgh Pirates, he spent his entire major league career with the Detroit Tigers.

Greenberg, a first baseman–outfielder, ranks with the most powerful sluggers who ever played the game. Four times Greenberg led the American League in home runs, and no right-handed batter has ever surpassed his 1938 total of 58. Although a plethora of evidence exists to support Greenberg's position as the game's greatest Jewish player, a middle-aged man, writing during the 1970s, summed it up best: "Imagine a boy of today, growing old in 2018. When he looks back at the seventies, which sports hero will he remember? If there is one whose specific individual feats he can recall as clearly as I recall so many of Hank's, he will have something special to think about. . . ."

1930s' sportswriters frequently noted Greenberg's ethnic identity even in accounts of mundane incidents. Numerous ethnic sobriquets attached to Greenberg, including "Hebrew star," "the Tigers' great Jewish first baseman," "the Jewish slugger," and even "a conscientious orthodox Jew." At times the press demonstrated imagination in its allusions to Greenberg's ethnicity as with *The Sporting News'* explanation that he "does everything in orthodox fashion." Too, a New York *Evening Journal* article repeatedly referred to Greenberg as "Henry David," "David's" connotation being more obvious than "Benjamin," Greenberg's actual middle name. The press of the 1930s also did not neglect the antecedents of other Jewish players. Journalists described outfielder Morrie Arnovich of the Philadelphia Phillies, for example, as a "Jewish athlete," "the chunky Hebrew lad," and "the little Hebrew."

In identifying the ethnicity of Jewish players and designating that background as a race, reporters were not treating Jewish big leaguers differently than their gentile counterparts. A myriad of evidence, including such press excerpts as "An Italian Baseball Guide," "the fiery Frenchman," "the even-tempered Bohemian," "McCarthy . . . the Buffalo Irishman," "Urbanski . . . hard-working, likable Polish recruit," and "Lou Novikoff . . . the mad Russian," illustrates the pervasiveness of ethnicity in baseball literature of the Depression. Sportswriters repeatedly portrayed baseball as the "great American melting pot," which facilitated the assimilation of its heterogeneous participants. *The Sporting News* preached that "baseball . . . [provides] the world an example of how nations may be brought together through the universal brotherhood of sport." The New York *Evening Journal* depicted the Detroit Tigers as a veritable League of Nations: "Greenberg is a Jew and his boss, Cochrane, is a Catholic, and there are other Catholics and Protestants and nonbelievers on the Club. Yet it functions like a well oiled machine. . . . The players have been fused into a unit. . . . They are willing to make any sacrifice for the sake of the club."

The press portrayed players with ethnic antecedents as symbols of the assimilation process at work. Although scribes thus viewed these players as transitional figures, leading their co-ethnic to the figurative melting pot, writers enthusiastically approved of publicizing ethnic standard bearers to attract fans and increase game profits. *The Sporting News*, for example, endorsed the Cincinnati Reds' exploitation of Alex Kampouris, "the only Greek in the big show," as a useful device for luring other Greeks to the game: ". . . for the last three seasons, a delegation of swarthy citizens would march to the home plate. . . . The swarthy citizens always are Greeks. And when the Greeks come bearing gifts where the Reds are playing, it is Alex Kampouris, dashing second baseman of Cincinnati's team, who gets them."

Even without the ethnic dimension, sheer size rendered the six foot four inch Greenberg conspicuous in an era when the average player stood approximately five feet eleven. Sportswriters incessantly attached the adjectives "big," "giant," "huge," and "tall" to Greenberg's name. More significantly, however, a constellation of related media images orbited around

Greenberg's Jewishness. By means of phrases such as "late of Bronx" and "slugging first baseman from the Bronx," scribes highlighted Greenberg's association with New York City, "the hub of the Hebrew population of the United States." The *Saturday Evening Post* portrayed Greenberg as more attached to urban life with its "theater, nightclubs and bright lights" than "most ballplayers." With repeated assertions that "Hank was born with a silver spoon in his mouth," the press exaggerated the economic situation of Greenberg's parents, thus paralleling prevailing, and erroneous, stereotypes about Jewish wealth. Although Hank's father, a Rumanian immigrant, did own a cloth-shrinking plant, the Greenbergs were not wealthy.

Greenberg, according to 1930s' writers, also differed from most gentile contemporaries owing to the aspirations of his parents. Journalists emphasized that his parents "wanted him to go to college, then into business." Moreover, sportswriters depicted Greenberg as the quintessence of traditional Jewish respect for learning, which America transformed into a passion for secular knowledge. Commentators lingered over his cerebral qualities. Some of the descriptions of Greenberg's intellect conjure up a Talmudic scholar more readily than an athlete: "put more thought . . . into his work than any other player"; "has demonstrated . . . intelligence and imagination"; "the most energetic . . . researcher"; and "he studies the best methods and practices as earnestly as a young physician." In addition to intellect, the press suggested that Greenberg shared another trait commonly associated with his coreligionists, an oversensitivity to criticism. Numerous journalists declared Greenberg "inordinately sensitive to public opinion." Yet not one 1930s' article ever acknowledged the anti-Semitic taunts fans and opponents showered on Greenberg.

In distinguishing Greenberg from his gentile peers, most of whom were natural athletes, sportswriters repeatedly depicted the Detroit slugger as a self-made ballplayer. Numerous articles portrayed the young Tiger as "clumsy," "naturally slow," "awkward," and "[possessing] little natural ability." With near unanimity, however, pundits cast Greenberg as a Jewish Horatio Alger hero, who "overcame . . . [his] glaring weakness" by "hard work and determination." A *Saturday Evening Post* article, entitled "Hank Made Greenberg," contended, "Greenberg is purely a self-made star. . . . His enormous capacity for work staggers everyone. . . . He has spent so much time in Tiger Stadium that the groundskeeper once suspected he had set up light housekeeping there to save rent." The Detroit *Evening News* glowingly reported that "Greenberg is a good first baseman because he works at the job. . . . He works at it 24 hours a day. . . ." Although the press gave significant attention to several financial controversies involving

Greenberg, most scribes believed that Greenberg, through hard work and tenacity, merited his success." "No one will begrudge Greenberg honors," declared the Detroit *News*, because "he has earned them." Many writers repeated the refrain that "no ballplayer probably worked harder to prepare himself for success" than Greenberg. In the 1930s' press the Jewish Greenberg appeared as a symbol of the rewards that hard work could bring to even the awkward son of an immigrant in baseball's melting pot.

Media portrayals of Greenberg as a Jewish standard bearer burgeoned during September 1934 owing to controversy over whether the Detroit slugger should play on the Jewish High Holidays. Although rookie Greenberg's decision not to play on the 1933 High Holidays attracted little attention, the improved play of the twenty-three-year-old Greenberg and of his team during the 1934 season created new pressures. Not since 1909 had the Tigers won the American League pennant, and the Bengals' 1934 surge, which culminated in a first place finish, created a "frenzied public." The Dearborn *Independent* claimed that one overzealous fan succumbed to a coronary while listening to a radio broadcast of a Tiger game. And the *New York Times* reported, "The old Tiger town has gone baseball crazy." Apart from loyalty to the Tigers, social bonds between Detroiters, residents of a "tough town," hard hit by the Depression, were "frail."

Historian Ralph Jones asserts that "Detroit's . . . susceptibility to economic, ethnic, racial, and territorial outbreaks is impressive and persistent." Also, Greenberg's High Holiday dilemma hardly occurred during a golden age in Detroit's ethnic dynamic. Greenberg's Detroit has a propensity for lifting bigots, such as Henry Ford and Father Charles Coughlin, to the status of folk hero. Neither the city of Detroit, which had a Jewish population of only 5 per cent, nor Greenberg's Tiger teammates, over 80 per cent of whom hailed from parochial areas of the South and Southwest, entered September of 1934 with much understanding of the reasons for observing the Jewish High Holidays. According to the press, however, Tiger players and fans clearly understood the importance of Greenberg to their feverish dreams of a pennant.

Publications varied markedly in the extent of coverage they granted Greenberg's High Holiday conflict. Most journalistic depictions of the episode, however, shared a core of common assumptions. Some minor differences in nuance did occur. Nevertheless, a widespread consensus of interpretation dominated press portrayals of Greenberg's behavior during the 1934 High Holidays.

When Greenberg casually mentioned he might not play in the 10 September home game against the Boston Red Sox since the contest fell on Rosh Hashanah, the Jewish New Year, the media promptly recited Greenberg's secular responsibilities. Although the Tigers led the second place New York Yankees by four games on the eve of the Jewish New Year, the press still referred to a "neck-and-neck pennant race." Scribes also noted the Tigers suffered from flagging momentum. The Philadelphia *Evening Bulletin* stated, "the Tigers look pretty sad at this moment." Alone of "the Tiger mainstays," Greenberg continued to hit well despite the general team slump. Thus, the Tigers needed Greenberg's presence more than ever during this crucial phase of the season.

Given the tight pennant race, journalists stressed Greenberg's obligation to the city of Detroit. People wrote letters to Detroit newspapers pointing out that "whereas Rosh Hashanah came every year, Detroit had not won a pennant since 1909." In addition, sportswriters emphasized Greenberg's special "duties toward his teammates. . . ." The New York *Evening Journal* stated that Greenberg's Rosh Hashanah absence from the line-up would have constituted a massive "loss to his companions." Moreover, every member of the Tiger infield had thus far played "every inning of every game," a record that Greenberg's observance of the Jewish New Year would snap. Finally, and least important of the secular responsibilities cited by the press, Greenberg needed, on the eve of Rosh Hashanah, "only 11 more [doubles] to equal the American League record of 67. . . ."

During September 1934 the media also gave prominent attention to Greenberg's religious responsibilities although journalists ultimately found them less imperative than his secular obligations. The Anglo-Jewish press and several general circulation journals described the nature of the Jewish New Year as Rosh Hashanah approached. The Detroit *Evening Times,* for example, stated: "Essentially, Rosh Hashanah is not a joyful but a thoughtful day. Unlike the celebrations of the New Year among other nations the New year of the Jew is devoted to supplications and to the searching of one's self." Some newspapers, including the Detroit *Free Press,* noted that Orthodox Jews, such as Greenberg, "did not work . . . [or] play" on Rosh Hashanah. Nevertheless, references to the Jewish temple or synagogue as a "church" in a number of papers, suggests a muted understanding of the High Holidays by the media. Furthermore, whereas the press related Greenberg's secular re-sponsibilities to loyalty to community and teammates, it tended to depict re-ligious obligations as largely a matter of individual conscience or preference.

Several newspapers reported and analyzed the formal statement of Dr. Leo M. Franklin, chief rabbi of Detroit, concerning Greenberg's prob-lem. Rabbi Franklin's comments, issued just prior to the Rosh Hashanah game, appeared in a number of journals:

In the Jewish faith there is no power granted to the rabbi to give dispensation to anyone for doing anything which reads contrary to his own conscientious convictions—indeed we insist upon the doctrine of personal responsibility.

In such a case as this, Mr. Greenberg, who is a conscientious Jew, must decide for himself whether he ought to play or not.

From the standpoint of Orthodox Judaism the fact that ballplaying is his means of livelihood would argue against his participation in the Monday game. On the other hand, it might be argued quite consistently, that his taking part in the game would mean something not only to himself but to his fellow players and, in fact at this time, to the community of Detroit.

But in the last analysis, no rabbi is authorized to give or to withhold permission for him to do so.

Despite the ambiguous tenor of Dr. Franklin's remarks, writers, while conceding the impossibility of a dispensation, eagerly noted that the rabbi's comments constituted no fiat against Greenberg's participation in the Rosh Hashanah game. *The Sporting News*, for example, interpreted Rabbi Franklin's proclamation to mean "that the question lay strictly between Greenberg and his conscience and that the Church had no right to . . . criticize him if he played." Thus the terse headline of a Detroit *Evening Times* story on Dr. Franklin's statement read "Greenberg Decision Own."

Some journals also reported and examined another Detroit rabbi's position on Greenberg's conflict, that of Joseph Thumim. Rabbi Thumim's declaration, which was even more Delphic than that of Dr. Franklin, implied that "Greenberg . . . can play ball today" subject to "three stipulations": " . . . no tickets could be bought by the Orthodox on the day of the match; that there should be no smoking; and that the refreshments distributed should be kosher." Oblivious to the three restrictions Rabbi Thumim cited, a Detroit *News* article, entitled, "Talmud Clears Greenberg for Holiday Play," proclaimed, "Henry Greenberg need have no pangs of conscience because he plays baseball during the Jewish holidays. . . ." The Detroit *Jewish Chronicle*, the only Anglo-Jewish newspaper published in Michigan, agreed with the *News'* interpretation of Rabbi Thumim's statement. No paper consulted gave detailed attention to strong rabbinical pleas that Greenberg not play on Rosh Hashanah although *The Sporting News* reported that Greenberg received "telegrams from rabbis and Jewish advisers from all over the country. Some told [him] . . . of the mistake [he] . . . would make if [he] . . . did not observe the day properly."

While the media assessed Greenberg's secular responsibilities for their impact on other people, which it largely eschewed in its examination of his religious responsibilities, the press portrayed the intense pressures converging on Greenberg as emanating largely from two competing value systems rather than from the articulated demands of specific individuals or groups or the press itself. Thus, journalists, to a significant degree, abstracted the struggle between the divergent forces contending for Greenberg's conscience. Nevertheless, some scribes noted pressure from specific individuals and groups. Not surprisingly Anglo–Jewish newspapers levied the strongest claims that Greenberg was hectored to play. The Detroit *Jewish Chronicle* and the *Jewish Daily Bulletin* asserted that ". . . a flood of telephone calls came to him (Greenberg) from Manager Mickey Cochrane, from Frank and Charles Navin, the owners of the ball team, from teammates and leading citizens. 'This is a civic duty,' they told him. 'If Detroit is to win the pennant you must play.'" Conversely, the Boston *Post* reported, "A larger number of Detroit Jews tried to keep Henry Greenberg out of today's game in observance of Rosh Hashanah." More characteristically, however, *The Sporting News* and the Detroit *Free Press* quoted Greenberg's comment that Tiger manager "Mickey Cochrane told me it was a personal matter that I must handle myself." By juxtaposition, the New York *World Telegram* linked the decisions of Mickey Cochrane, the symbol of secular authority, and Rabbi Franklin, the symbol of religious authority, to "let Greenberg decide the question for himself."

Most journalists emphasized that the real conflict occurred internally within Greenberg's conscience. Moreover, media images of Greenberg's problem assumed titanic proportions as the Detroit slugger "waged a terrific battle with himself" over "conflicting duties to his religion and to his team." The press generally treated Greenberg's ordeal and consequent suffering with utter seriousness and dignity. In the pages of the Detroit *Free Press* the beleaguered Greenberg almost assumed the dimensions of a tragic hero:

> . . . He is an orthodox Jew and practices his religion faithfully. . . .
> Hank started his day by attending services in the congregation Shaarey Zedek. . . . But he was worried about the ball game. Should he play? or should he take the day off and risk depriving the Tigers of a chance in the World Series? Hank did not know. . . .
> . . . All Sunday he had debated that question with himself. Like Jacob of old, he spent the night wrestling with the angels. He sat up late wondering, wondering. And when he went to bed he tossed uneasily as he tried to make up his mind.

Greenberg had reached no decision as to playing when he arrived at the ball park yesterday.

Several writers stressed that Greenberg remained "conscience stricken" even after making a reluctant decision to play. Indeed, Greenberg half expected some sort of divine retribution: " 'I'll probably get my brains knocked out by a fly ball,' " Greenberg, according to the Detroit *Free Press*, "said gloomily as he left the dugout. 'But I'm going to play.' "

Both the Anglo-Jewish and the general circulation press approved of Greenberg's decision to play for "the welfare of the Tigers and the interests of the community," as he "subordinated his own inclinations for the good of the whole." A Detroit *News* headline read, "Playing for Community . . . Tiger First Baseman Serves His Fellows on Jewish Holy Day. . . ." The Detroit *Jewish Chronicle* and the Jewish *Daily Bulletin* both recorded sportswriter Ty Tyson's tribute to Greenberg's "sacrifice." The media stressed the positive consequences of Greenberg's decision.

The Tigers triumphed 2 to 1 over the Boston Red Sox in the crucial Rosh Hashanah game, extending their American League lead to four and one-half games. Moreover, emphasized the press, Greenberg "almost single-handed[ly] won . . . the ball game with two home runs." The Detroit *Free Press* exclaimed, ". . . Greenberg . . . had enjoyed the best day of his career. . . . Ruth at his best never hit a baseball to more effect or never won a ball game more dramatically." Given the heroic victory of Greenberg's Tigers, some sportswriters interpreted the triumph as heavenly approval of his Rosh Hashanah activities. According to *The Sporting News*, for example, Greenberg concluded, "Some divine influence must have caught hold of me that day." Moreover not only did God bless Greenberg's nontraditional observance of Rosh Hashanah, but the Tiger manager did as well: "What he did at the plate led Mickey Cochrane the next day to elevate him to the clean-up position. . . ."

According to the press, Greenberg read Rabbi Franklin's statement for the first time after the Rosh Hashanah game, "which caused him to brighten visibly," since he construed it to mean that "I didn't do the wrong thing after all." Also, several newspapers noted Greenberg still had time to go "back to the synagogue" after the game. Moreover, the Detroit *Jewish Chronicle*, emulating locker-room jargon, enthused that Greenberg was "acclaimed by boys in the synagogue." Indeed, no less an authority than Tiger third baseman Marv Owen advised Greenberg that all he had on his "conscience" was "a couple of home runs." Apparently once Greenberg had recognized the primacy of community needs over ethnic considerations, the painful crisis yielded to glorious success.

The postgame trivialization of Rosh Hashanah markedly differed from the tone of respect accorded this solemn holiday in pregame commentary. The Detroit *Free Press* saluted Greenberg's hitting with the refrain, "A Happy New Year for Everybody." A woman reporter for the Detroit *News* coquettishly wished "every day were Rosh Hashanah, [so] our [baseball] worries would be over" as Detroit fans, "grinning broadly," yelled "Happy New Year." "Iffy the Dopester," august commentator for the Detroit *Free Press*, magnanimously declared, "I'm here to testify to the world as a baseball expert that the two hits he (Greenberg) made in the ball game were strictly kosher." Stuart Bell of the Cleveland *Press* demonstrated a dubious sensitivity: "Only one fellow blew the shofar yesterday so you could hear it. He was Hank Greenberg. He blew the shofar twice, and the ears of the Boston Red Sox are still ringing. Blast No. 1 from his shofar was a homer. . . . Blast No. 2 from Hank's shofar was a home run . . . will you please take me home shofar?" Amid the postgame euphoria the press depicted the solemn Rosh Hashanah as a near twin of the larger society's raucous first of January.

Although Greenberg still faced a conflict over whether to play on Yom Kippur, this episode generated much less media attention than his New Year's ordeal as the Tigers had the pennant "in the bag" by Yom Kippur. Nevertheless, a number of articles claimed that Greenberg's observance of Yom Kippur entailed some sacrifice from his fans and teammates. Several newspapers, for example, noted that Greenberg's absence would terminate the Detroit infield's streak of starting the same four regulars at 143 consecutive games. Although in recent questioning, Greenberg, second-baseman Charles Gehringer, and sportswriter Fred Lieb all characterized the consecutive game mark as a "trick record," the media termed it "one of the most amazing streaks in history" when Greenberg missed the Yom Kippur contest. Nevertheless, despite the infield record and the defeat of the Tigers by the Yankees on the Day of Atonement, the press generally felt Greenberg, after having contributed to the pennant's inevitability by his Rosh Hashanah heroics, merited Yom Kippur off. Overall, however, the press commented on the Yom Kippur incident, just as it had during the Rosh Hashanah controversy, with the assumption that responsibilities to the secular community transcended those to the ethnic group. By its application of baseball criteria, the press implied that if the Tigers still had to fight for the pennant and if Greenberg's past performance had fallen within the mediocre range, he could not justify missing the Day of Atonement game. Even the tribute to Greenberg by the syndicated folk poet Edgar Guest defended the former's Yom Kippur observance by reference to secular achievements:

In July the Irish wondered where he's ever learned
  to play . . .
But upon the Jewish New Year when Hank Greenberg
  came to bat
And made two home runs off Pitcher Rhodes—
  They cheered like mad for that.

Scribes acknowledged that Greenberg might serve as a symbol "that hard work, determination and perseverance can take a man to the top" to all "the youth of America," but the press emphasized Greenberg's position as an ethnic standard bearer. Many nonsectarian journals noted the honors, awards, and adulation Greenberg received from his coreligionists. A few days before Rosh Hashanah 1934, for example, the Detroit *Free Press* described how nine-year-old Sammy Kaufman attempted to carry the 215-pound first baseman's heavy traveling bag for him. The Detroit *Jewish Chronicle* reported that when he attended synagogue services during the 1934 High Holidays, a "youngster pleaded to be permitted to sit in Greenberg's seat," which the paper likened to a " 'Chassi' and 'Rebbe' fad." Moreover, the Anglo-Jewish press heralded Greenberg's 1934 selection by "Jewish admirers," in a poll conducted by the Jewish Telegraph Agency, as the "Greatest Jewish Baseball Player of All Time."

Both the Anglo-Jewish and general circulation press perceived a lesson for Greenberg's coreligionists in the slugger's September 1934 behavior, the appropriateness of an ethnic standard bearer, and by implication his followers, giving priority to the demands of the secular community over those of the ethnic group. Pundits claimed even "the most orthodox Jews" "respected" Greenberg for subordinating his religious preferences "for the good of the whole" on Rosh Hashanah. According to the media, "the public judges people by the idols they produce," and the Jews ought then to take pride in Greenberg, "a credit to . . . Jewry." "The Jewish people are to be congratulated," editorialized the Detroit *Jewish Chronicle*, "that Greenberg is such a splendid type of their people. He is in a position to do untold good in breaking down the mean and vicious prejudices against an ancient and honorable people." For the most part, the press portrayed Jewish standard bearer Greenberg as a symbol of assimilation, leading the way toward the melting pot. Greenberg's baseball heroics, suggested most

1930s' commentators, facilitated the Americanization of his fellow Jews. *Baseball Magazine*, for example, cast Greenberg as a latter-day Moses:

> . . . He had led his ancestral race into a new promised land, the field of major league baseball, a field where they have been comparative strangers.
>
> Since America is the melting pot of all nations, it is quite fitting and appropriate that baseball should be represented by players of all racial strands and stocks.

By taking pride in a coreligionist's accomplishments in the "national pastime," Jews hastened their collective entry into the main currents of American life. The Anglo-Jewish press, sensitive to "What do the Gentiles say?," acknowledged that their standard bearer was the "only . . . Jewish lad [who] mattered to" the larger community on Rosh Hashanah 1934 and praised Greenberg for fulfilling his secular responsibilities, thus combating anti-Semitism by winning "the admiration and affection of the [gentile] fans."

From the vantage point of Greenberg commentators then, individual standard bearers rather than Jewish values constituted the appropriate contribution of Jews to America. A few highly atypical articles, however, depicted Greenberg as an instrument through which Jewish principles enriched American society. The Detroit *Free Press*, for example, related his honest refusal to settle for a two-base hit on a triple, which would have facilitated his assault on the American League record for doubles, to his ethnicity: "Hank Greenberg, being Jewish, has an innate sense of values." Nevertheless, typical 1930s analysis depicted notable individuals, not Jewish principles, as the Jewish contribution to the "national pastime." During the 1930s both Anglo-Jewish and general circulation publications invariably depicted ethnicity in a fashion similar to that utilized by many Depression-era historians of immigration. In *We Who Built America* (1939), for example, the influential scholar Carl Wittke, by listing a plethora of specific immigrants and their progeny who contributed to American advancement in various ways, suggested that individuals with "old world" antecedents, not ethnic groups as a whole, "built America." Wittke believed pride in ethnic heroes instilled a sense of potential and security in the foreign-born and their children, thus fostering Americanization. Hence, eponymic standard bearers, not the immigrant groups that nurtured them, constituted the appropriate ethnic contribution to America.

Anglo-Jewish journals, similar to the general circulation press, almost invariably adopted a Wittke-type approach to Greenberg and other Jewish athletes. English-language Jewish papers noted scores and scores of Jewish athletes, often either of limited ability or in esoteric sports, without usually demonstrating anything distinctively Jewish about the individuals cited or their achievements, save, as Wittke had in *We Who Built America*, "old world" antecedents. The Chicago *Jewish Chronicle*, for example, did not usually probe for a Hebraic legacy in the character, training, or ring style of those it designated as "Jewish boxers." The Detroit *Jewish Chronicle* exulted, without identifying the Jewish mores typified by the numerous individuals listed, "We as Jews can be proud of the fact that we have a champion in almost every field of sport. It almost appeared at times as though Wittke freelanced for the *Jewish Advocate*:

> In the long and arduous climb of Jewish athletes to fame and success the year 5694 [1934] will rate as a landmark, for during the past twelve months more Jews reached the top rung of athletic achievement than in any other similar period within memory. . . . If the sensational playing of a number of Jews in the minor leagues means anything the National and American League will have a dozen Jewish players next year. . . . The American Association also swarms with Jewish talent: Milt Galatzer of Toledo . . . Andy Cohen of Minneapolis, Si Rosenthal of St. Paul. . . .
>
> No year in the last decade has passed without the inclusion of at least one Jew on the mythical All-American eleven. This past season developed two Jewish All-Americans, Aaron Rosenberg of Southern California and Paul Geisler of Centenary. . . . Other outstanding Jewish gridiron heroes of the past season were Chick and Leo Kaufman of Princeton. . . .

The *Jewish Advocate* concluded with a copious list of Jewish boxers, basketball players, tennis stars, golfers, auto racers, bicyclists, horse trainers, swimmers, wrestlers, fencers, rugby enthusiasts, track and field participants, softball standouts, and ping pong athletes. Greenberg, however, "the outstanding Jewish figure" in "the national pastime," reigned as the premier standard bearer.

Both the Anglo-Jewish and general circulation press applauded Greenberg for demonstrating to his coreligionists the American way. The Detroit *Free Press*, for example, approvingly reported Greenberg's participation in Detroit's 1934 "Community Fund Drive." Contemporaneously, several newspapers lauded Greenberg for declining a tribute the Jews of Detroit planned for him:

While the Tigers were on the road the biggest and wealthiest members of Detroit Jewish life made arrangements for a big testimonial banquet to the Hebrew star. . . . They arranged for a sumptuous feast . . . and . . . were going to buy him a valuable present. Hank had no inkling of the affair until his return to Detroit. . . . "Nothing doing," replied Hank after offering his heartfelt thanks for the honor. . . . Members of the committee, at first aghast and deeply disappointed, finally saw the point. Now they are prouder of the first baseman than ever before.

The Detroit *Jewish Chronicle*, fearful that the proposed Greenberg tribute would have alienated Detroit's gentiles, vigorously applauded Greenberg's decision: ". . . Hank vetoed the idea. He displayed good sense in doing so and his arguments were sound. There are K. C. members on the Tiger team, are there not he asked. How come that Catholics do not offer to sponsor testimonials in their honor? It is simple, he concluded, that the triumph of the Tigers is not the concern of any one group or of several groups. It is a community affair." According to the Detroit *Jewish Chronicle*, "outstanding Jewish leaders" fully endorsed Greenberg's decision to place community over ethnic considerations. The *Jewish Chronicle* deemed the vetoed Greenberg dinner particularly offensive because it would have taken place "in advance of the event planned in honor of the Tigers by the Detroit Board of Commerce at the end of this month." As with the contemporaneous High Holiday controversy, the press felt Greenberg deserved to participate in ethnically based events, such as being guest of honor at a B'nai B'rith dinner some time after he cancelled the earlier testimonial, provided it did not detract from community interests, such as the Detroit Board of Commerce's salute to the Tigers or an important baseball game.

Essentially, the media depicted the Jewish standard bearer as a transitional phenomenon. Since parochial attachments continued to exist, Americanizers paradoxically employed those ethnic attachments for assimilationist ends. Although Jews, not far removed from the world of the *shtetl*, still deviated somewhat from the mainstream, Greenberg's success in the "national pastime," a microcosm of United States society, would inspire coreligionists to follow his "All-American" example. Thus, ethnic groups and the standard bearers they spawned, implied the press, would become an anachronism. Ironically the press emphasized Greenberg's position as an ethnic standard bearer to illustrate assimilation in baseball's melting pot.

The assimilationist implications of Greenberg's press image coincided with aspirations harbored by many Jewish Americans during the Depression era. As progeny of immigrant parents, many Jews of this period belonged to the second generation. The second generation, ambivalent about its religious heritage, eager to acquire middle-class respectability, and anxious about the opinion of the gentile community, found Greenberg an appropriate standard bearer. Unlike the often flamboyant, braggadocious, poorly educated, financially imprudent Jewish boxers, who flaunted their ethnicity with the Star of David emblazoned on their trunks, engaged in nocturnal adventures with *shiksas*, and carried the ambience of ghetto pugnacity with them, "modest," "retiring," "clean-living" Hank Greenberg, as portrayed by the press, was an Americanized *mensch*. The Greenberg of the media, who eschewed calling attention to his private religious beliefs, offered fellow Jews an example of an upwardly mobile lifestyle that attracted relatively little animosity from gentile neighbors. The New York *Evening Post* in 1934, for example, linked Greenberg's personal success with the movement of Jews from the Lower East Side ghetto: "The last time Detroit got into the October set of games there were not nearly as many Greenbergs in the Bronx as there are now." Newspaper photographs of the articulate Greenberg, who had attended New York University for a year, often displayed a neat, immaculate gentleman, dressed in tie and jacket with a newspaper in hand and resembling a young professional or businessman more than he did a baseball player.

Both the Anglo-Jewish and general circulation press perceived Greenberg as the most exemplary of the Jewish athletes and commented critically on world welterweight boxing champion Barney Ross' decision not to fight on Rosh Hashanah 1934. When rain cancelled his match with "Irish Jimmy McLarnin," Ross refused to have it rescheduled on Rosh Hashanah. Instead, the pugilistic champion suspended training and attended synagogue services on the Jewish New Year. Rather than emphasizing Ross' piety, however, several newspapers related Ross' Rosh Hashanah observance to financial calculations. According to the Chicago *Tribune*, "the promoters know that New York's Orthodox Jews also would decline to attend." Too, the Boston *Post* cynically asserted, ". . . the ordinary two-day postponement would have resulted in a financial flop. . . ." The Anglo-Jewish press also did not note Ross' High Holiday observance sans caveat. The Jewish *Daily Bulletin*, for example, while conceding the pugilist's sincerity, argued that Ross' example of refusing to participate in an athletic contest on Rosh Hashanah did not, and ought not to have, unduly impressed Hank Greenberg:

The controversy hinged on whether Hank Greenberg was "Right" in playing ball on Rosh Hashanah. It was pointed out that Barney Ross refused to fight on this holiday and that Greenberg could have done likewise. . . . [But] neither Ross nor McLarnin could have put up a decent show if the fight . . . would have been held, after being postponed three nights, on Monday. . . . The fighters would not have been able to give the same top-notch performance after such a lay-off . . . the fighters needed plenty of time to whip themselves back into the pink after a three day lay-off.

Thus, implied the Anglo-Jewish press, Ross' observance of the Jewish New Year furthered his boxing interests, while Greenberg's violation of normative Rosh Hashanah practices constituted "a civic duty."

Throughout the 1930s the press continued to emphasize Greenberg's ethnic identity. After 1934, however, the press never again depicted Greenberg as engaged in a soul-searching choice between his personal religious beliefs and community interests. Precedent and circumstance served as a prophylactic against the intense pressures that peaked in September 1934. In 1935, for example, as a 1979 Greenberg letter notes, "I did not play on Yom Kippur in the World Series of 1935 against Chicago, as I was injured at the time, no decision was necessary." More importantly, from the viewpoint of media image, the premier Jewish standard bearer had already made the irrevocable choice between community and ethnic interests in 1934.

Although 1930s newspapers printed numerous articles about antisemitism, neither the Anglo-Jewish or general circulation press acknowledged its existence in baseball. Interviews reveal that Greenberg served as the target of many antisemitic taunts, but contemporary writers refrained from any mention of the phenomenon. During the 1934 World Series, for example, the St. Louis Cardinals, a raucous ensemble embodying the small town provincialism cherished by Henry Ford, continually referred to Greenberg as "Moses" and reviled him with antisemitic epithets. While the press noted Henry Ford's fondness for Dizzy Dean's "Gashouse Gang," sportswriters attributed the tenseness Greenberg displayed to the pressures of playing in his first World Series and indicated the taunts the latter received from the Cardinals related to some errors on the playing field. Perhaps sportswriters felt impelled to protect the pristine image of the "national pastime," an idealized reflection of American society at large. Moreover, acknowledging antisemitism would have brought into question the efficacy of baseball's melting pot.

Media references to Greenberg as a Jewish standard bearer declined during World War II. Greenberg, the only baseball superstar ensnared by the pre-Pearl Harbor draft, received his Army discharge on 5 December 1941, but reenlisted immediately after Pearl Harbor. Dissimilar to many baseball players, who served as athletic directors, Greenberg, noted the press, volunteered for combat, serving "in the China-Burma-India Theater with the Twentieth Bomber command, the first B-29 unit to go overseas." Comments germane to Greenberg's ethnicity became infrequent. The media now portrayed the big slugger, not as a Jewish standard bearer, but rather as the embodiment of "the national pastime," and thus "the American way of life." A *Sporting News* cartoon, for example, depicted Greenberg trading a bat for a rifle. Ethnic depictions of Greenberg did not resurge or again become common after the war. When Greenberg returned to baseball, the media viewed him as a heroic symbol of veterans seeking to regain their civilian skills. The "Jewish first-baseman" of the 1930s had become "Captain Henry," a designation repeatedly used by scribes during Greenberg's post-World War II career.

The decline of press references to a Jewish standard bearer paralleled the general decline of media attention to ethnicity. The chronological distance from the era of mass immigration, the appearance of the third generation, the consensus created by World War II and sustained by the Cold War, and the growing mass culture, soon to be buttressed by the "new suburbs," interstate highways, franchises, and television, reduced the need for ethnic standard bearers. After Branch Rickey signed the incomparable Jackie Robinson to a contract in the Brooklyn Dodger system during late 1945, race filled the vacuum left by ethnicity. As the *Sporting News* realized, the age of the racial standard bearer had arrived: ". . . Jackie . . . will be haunted by the expectations of his race. To 15,000,000 Negroes he will symbolize not only their prowess in baseball, but their ability to rise to an opportunity. Unlike white players, he can never afford an offday or an offnight. His private life will be watched, too, because white America will judge the Negro race by everything he does. And Lord help him with his fellow Negroes if he should fail them." A journalist might have written similarly about Greenberg a decade before.

The press no longer sought a Jewish standard bearer because assimilation and time had largely dissipated the constituency for one. Greenberg and other second generation Jews had significantly ameliorated the secular community—ethnic group dichotomy by the end of World War II. As Hank's father David recognized, the second generation resolved their conflict in ways that often deviated from the traditions of their immigrant fathers: "I take keen pride in my son, in his work, in his accomplishments. . . . I have seen him in every game he played in the Yankee Stadium. I did not see him in the World Series this year because of the Jewish holidays. I believe in religion—in every man's religion for himself." The third generation, scions of the "marginal men," needed no Jewish standard bearer to symbolically resolve their conflicts, facilitate their Americanization, or attract them to ball parks. When Greenberg's son Steve, captain of the Yale baseball team, agonized over whether to take the field during the Spring 1970 campus strike, humanistic concerns about war and justice, devoid of overt Jewish imperatives, formed the criteria for decision-making. The differences between Hank Greenberg's 1934 conflict and that of his son thirty-six years later largely define the distance between the second and third generations. During the 1930s Hank Greenberg served as potent media symbol for second generation Jews, who applauded the success of a coreligionist in the "national pastime" because it provided reassurance of their own ability to resolve the strain of assimilationist-ethnic polarities and to succeed within the American mainstream. In 1979 a Jewish writer recalled Greenberg's meaning for the second generation:

> I found the heroes of my time: Hank Greenberg and Bess Myerson. I can think of no public personages in all the succeeding years whom I've followed with such feeling. . . . Hank and Bess were winners, like DiMaggio and Grable—only smarter. They were as American as apple pie and the Fourth of July—and as Jewish as *Knishes* and Yom Kippur. They belonged to a race of victors, not victims. They transcended the categories which trapped other Jewish luminaries of that era . . . for the first time, Jews had successfully crossed over from ethnic favorites to national heroes. . . . They had arrived.

Part 3: The National Game

Jackie Robinson is tagged out by Yankee third baseman Bill Johnson in a 1947 preseason game at Ebbets Field. Robinson broke the barrier in baseball that season by being the first African American to play in the major leagues. ID BE044161 © Bettmann/CORBIS.

11. A Spectacular Season: Jackie Robinson Breaks Through

By the beginning of the 1940s, it had become abundantly clear that numerous black ballplayers were gifted enough to play in the major leagues. During the interwar years the black professional leagues had flourished in the form of the Negro National and American Leagues. They drew big crowds as paying tenants in major league stadiums, with their own world series and all star games, and with a widespread season of exhibition games. Consequently, the names of many black players, like Satchel Paige, Josh Gibson, and Buck Leonard became highly recognizable in white athletic circles. Moreover, the winds of change had begun to blow during the depression-ridden years of the 1930s. In many communities around the country the Jim Crow laws began to be repealed. As additional blacks migrated to the cities of the North, their sense of identity, potential political influence, and economic clout grew, and they increasingly forced city fathers, newspaper publishers, and community activists to reconsider the status of race relations. Undoubtedly the nation's sports fans had been caught up in the exploits of boxer Joe Louis and the astounding feat of track star Jesse Owens in the Berlin Olympics of 1936. Such prowess may have thrown Nazi racism back in Der Führer's face, but it also exposed America's own racial hypocrisy to those who wished to look.

Even so, it took World War II to bring serious attention to America's race relations and to provide impetus for breaking the informal ban on black participation in major league baseball. When many blacks fought and died for their country, in mostly segregated units, and when many of them flocked to cities to help fill the labor shortage in the war production plants, living in mostly segregated housing, the incongruities between their contribution to the nation's well-being and their social restrictions were laid bare. Nevertheless, for the duration of the war professional baseball, under the bigoted and autocratic control of Judge Kenesaw Mountain Landis, made no headway at integrating the game. Despite the obvious skilled-player shortage caused by players going into military service, all attempts to tap the pool of qualified black players were stifled by Landis, even as he continued to claim publicly that no regulations barred their participation. When a one-armed outfielder and a fifteen-year-old pitcher made it to the big leagues but no black player was hired, the hypocrisy was starkly revealed. With the death of Landis in 1944 and the end of the war a year later, the door cracked open to a new era in the game and the nation. Nevertheless, it took the remarkable partnership of two of baseball's courageous figures, one white and one black, both thick skinned, to cross the threshold and finally break the game's long-standing discriminatory practice.

For the fiftieth anniversary of Jackie Robinson's breakthrough, Jules Tygiel reviewed the conditions of the times, the characters of Branch Rickey and Jackie Robinson, and the difficulties they confronted. While their motivation may still be debated, it is undeniable that their success had an impact that far transcended the baseball world.

Extraordinary lives often reveal ordinary truths. Jackie Robinson was born in 1919 and died in 1972. He crammed into his too few fifty-three years a legacy of accomplishment, acclaim, controversy, and influence matched by few Americans. Even before his historic baseball breakthrough, he was an athlete of legendary proportions. He won fame and adulation as the first African-American to play in the major leagues in the twentieth century, launching an athletic revolution that transformed American sports. He garnered baseball's highest honors: Rookie of the Year, Most Valuable Player, and election to the Hall of Fame the first year he was eligible. Even more significant, Robinson became a symbol of racial integration and a prominent leader in the civil rights struggle of the 1950s and 1960s. His half-century among us illuminates not only the contours of an exceptional life but also the broader African-American experience of those years.

Jackie Robinson, the grandson of a slave and the son of sharecroppers, was born in Georgia in the heart of the segregated South. When Jackie was an infant, his father, Jerry Robinson, abandoned the family. His mother, Mallie, seeking a better life for Jackie and his four older siblings, joined the post–World War I Great Migration of African-Americans out of the South. Most blacks traveled to the Eastern metropolises or to Midwestern manufacturing centers like Chicago and Detroit. On the advice of a brother, Mallie Robinson headed West to California.

African-Americans were relatively rare in California in the 1920s. Although Mexican-born blacks had figured prominently in the settlement of the region, by the early twentieth century blacks accounted for only around one percent of the state's population. They confronted a pattern of discrimination common to the American West. Few hotels, restaurants, or recreational facilities accepted blacks, and restrictive covenants and other less formal practices barred them from living in most neighborhoods. Job discrimination impeded economic advancement. African-Americans met hostility at almost every turn from strangers, neighbors, and police.

Thus Jackie Robinson grew up in an environment similar to that of other children of the Great Migration. Raised in a family without a father and sustained by their mother's income from domestic work, the Robinson children lived in poverty but were held together by their mother's indomitable spirit and strong Methodist morality. As a teenager in Pasadena, Jackie ran with local street gangs and had inevitable confrontations with the easily provoked local police, resulting in at least one arrest.

However, if Southern California offered a harsh existence, it also held opportunities unavailable in most other places. The absence of tenements and the predominance of single-family houses allowed Mallie Robinson to buy a home for her family. The lack of restrictions on black participation in athletics opened to her sons an avenue of success. First Jackie's brother Mack starred in track and field at Pasadena Junior College and the 1936 Olympic games, where he won a silver medal; then Jackie himself won renown in four sports at Pasadena Junior College and at the University of California at Los Angeles.

Robinson's years at UCLA introduced him to high-level interracial competition. He was not the first African-American athlete at UCLA; he was preceded by the All-American Kenny Washington—another extraordinary athlete, who starred in football, baseball, and basketball—and the future movie actor Woody Strode. Robinson's childhood friend Ray Bartlett was a fourth black starter on the 1939 UCLA football team. While most black athletes of the era played for Negro colleges, in the Negro Leagues, or on clown teams like the Harlem Globetrotters, Robinson achieved his initial stardom on integrated playing fields.

In his senior year at UCLA Robinson met his future wife, Rachel Isum. She was three years younger than Robinson and came from a more secure black middle-class background. She was a third-generation Californian, a rare status among African-Americans, and she had earned an academic scholarship to UCLA and maintained a straight-A average. Her calm, warm, thoughtful manner complemented Robinson's fiery impetuousness. They formed an enduring bond of mutual love and support that girded them for the challenging years ahead.

Robinson and Isum found their courtship interrupted by World War II. Robinson's Army career typified the African-American military experience. Drafted in April 1942 and assigned to Fort Riley, Kansas, he ran an endless gauntlet of racial discrimination. He was barred from Officer Candidate School, blocked from playing on the camp baseball team, and restricted to segregated facilities. But he used both his aggressiveness and celebrity to demand better treatment. He rose to the rank of lieutenant and waged a campaign to improve conditions for black soldiers at Fort Riley. After his transfer to Fort Hood, in Texas, he refused to move to the back of a military bus and defied the officers who tried to discipline him, precipitating a court-martial that might have led to dishonorable discharge. A military tribunal acquitted him of all charges, but the episode left its mark and intensified his commitment to racial justice.

Upon his release from the Army, Robinson faced a predicament familiar to African-Americans. Although at the peak of his athletic talent and good enough to star in any major American team sport, he, like his brother Mack and Kenny Washington before him, had few professional options. Neither organized baseball nor the National Football League nor most major basketball teams accepted black players. Robinson's best alternative was to cast his lot with baseball's Negro Leagues, and in the spring of 1945 he signed with the Kansas City Monarchs.

There can be little doubt that at their best the Negro Leagues played first-class baseball, featuring some of the game's greatest stars. In 1945 the Monarchs' roster included two standout pitchers, Satchel Paige and Hilton Smith. On opposing teams were the future baseball Hall-of-Famers Buck Leonard, Josh Gibson, Roy Campanella, and Martin Dihigo. For Robinson, however, the Negro Leagues proved a distasteful experience. Accustomed to the highly structured training of major college sports and hostile to any compromise with segregation, Robinson considered the Negro Leagues a step down rather than a leg up. The long, hot bus rides through the South, the degrading treatment at gas stations and other white-owned facilities, and the players' informal approach to most nonleague contests frustrated him. An intensely private individual who neither smoked nor drank nor enjoyed what Paige called the "social ramble," Robinson never really fit in among the Monarchs. Although he performed well with Kansas City and gained invaluable training and exposure to top-flight baseball competition, Robinson, unlike most of his teammates and rivals, always disparaged his stint in the Negro Leagues.

Unbeknownst to Robinson, his performances with the Monarchs had attracted intense scrutiny. The Brooklyn Dodgers' president, Branch Rickey, secretly decided to bring blacks into the major leagues. With the pretext of forming a new black squad, the Brown Dodgers, he had assigned his top scouts to evaluate Negro League talent. From the start Robinson had been high on Rickey's list of prospects. In April 1945 the Pittsburgh *Courier* sportswriter Wendell Smith arranged a tryout with the Boston Red Sox for Robinson and two other Negro League stars. The Red Sox, who agreed to the audition in the face of local political pressure, never considered signing Robinson. Shortly thereafter Rickey quizzed Smith about potential players for the Brown Dodgers. Smith, who might have suspected Rickey's true intentions, recommended Robinson.

Branch Rickey offered various reasons for his historic decision to desegregate baseball. Sometimes he spoke of his need to make peace with the memory of a black college player he had coached in 1904 who had wept when barred from staying with his teammates at a Midwestern hotel. At other times he expressed moral and religious concerns. Just as frequently he denied any noble intentions and invoked his desire to field the best possible team. "The Negroes will make us winners for years to come," he accurately predicted. He also surely recognized that by attracting fans from New York City's growing African-American population and by fielding winning teams he would boost Dodger attendance. In the end it was probably a combination of these factors—and a desire to make a mark in history beyond the boundaries of baseball—that motivated Rickey.

What is often forgotten in light of the success of the Rickey-Robinson alliance is the extraordinary risk Rickey assumed in signing Robinson. Although Rickey correctly guessed that integration would bring profits, most major-league owners believed that luring more blacks to the ballpark would, in the words of the New York Yankees head Larry MacPhail, "result in lessening the value of several major league franchises."

Furthermore, although a seasoned athlete, Robinson had had minimal baseball experience. Other than his one season with the Monarchs, he had not played serious competitive baseball since leaving UCLA five years earlier. Few considered him the best player in the Negro Leagues. Even more ominous, Rickey, who had traveled to California and done research on Robinson's background, was well aware of the athlete's tempestuous nature and capacity for controversy. "Jackie had a genius for getting into extracurricular scrapes," remembered one Los Angeles sportswriter. Robinson's problems in the Army, also known to Rickey, reinforced this image. Rickey discounted many of these reports, noting that most of Robinson's difficulties arose from asserting his rights or responding to discrimination. If Robinson had been white, Rickey said, his aggressiveness both on and off the field would have been "praised to the skies." This behavior in an African-American, however, was "offensive to some white people." Rickey believed that Robinson's racial pride and combativeness, if consciously curbed, would not offend whites but rather rally them to his cause.

Other elements of Robinson's history and personality appealed to Rickey. Robinson boasted a college education and had been an Army officer. He was intelligent, articulate, and comfortable in the limelight. Unlike most Negro League players, he had had extensive experience in high-level interracial competition. In addition, he had the athletic skills Rickey admired in a ballplayer: speed (the only crucial skill that Rickey believed could not be taught), daring, and a fierce competitive drive.

Before signing him, however, Rickey elicited a promise from Robinson. Regardless of the savage insults he might face from opposing players and people in the stands, when off the field he was not to respond. He was to curb his naturally combative instincts and turn the other cheek. Robinson, who understood and welcomed the challenge confronting him, readily agreed.

In February 1946 Robinson married Rachel Isum in a Los Angeles church. Shortly thereafter they departed for spring training in Florida. The South that the young couple entered in 1946 was a land of rigid segregation, lynchings, and racial oppression; the dismantling of Jim Crow seemed a distant dream. Two years later President Harry S. Truman would order the desegregation of the armed forces. Eight years would pass before the U.S. Supreme Court issued its landmark *Brown v. Board of Education* decision. Seventeen-year-old Martin Luther King, Jr., was attending classes at Morehouse College. Robinson thus became what one writer has called "a one man civil rights movement."

From the moment of their arrival in Florida the Robinsons encountered Jim Crow. In Sanford threats of violence forced the couple out of town. In Jacksonville and De Land public officials refused to let Robinson play. On one occasion a local sheriff marched onto the field and demanded his ouster in mid-game. Yet Robinson, assigned to the Montreal Royals, of the International League—the Dodgers' top farm club—participated freely in games at the Dodgers' base in Daytona Beach, and both black and white fans greeted his appearances enthusiastically. Local business leaders in many Florida communities, aware of the profits and publicity generated by baseball training camps, courted the integrated Dodgers for future seasons. Although Rickey did not bring Robinson and the Dodgers back to Florida in 1947, the team had established an important precedent. Within three years cities throughout Florida and the rest of the South would clamor to host the Jackie Robinson Dodgers.

Throughout the 1946 season Robinson, in the words of the New York *Amsterdam News* columnist Joe Bostic, "ascended the heights of excellence to prove the rightness of the experiment. And prove it in the only correct crucible for such an experiment—the crucible of white-hot competition." During the Royals' opening game, in Jersey City, New Jersey, Robinson unveiled his ability to convert challenges into transcendent moments. The Montreal second baseman garnered four hits, including a three-run home run; scored four times; stole two bases; and twice scored from third by inducing the opposing pitcher to balk.

This extraordinary debut proved a prologue to an equally remarkable season. Despite a rash of brushback pitches, spiking attempts, vile harassment by opposing players, and threats of race riots in the league's southernmost city, Baltimore, Robinson led the International League in batting (.349) and runs scored (113). He finished second in stolen bases and had the highest fielding percentage of any second baseman. Anchored by his inspirational play, Montreal won the league pennant by nineteen-and-a-half games. The team returned to the South to defeat the Louisville Colonels in the Little World Series, securing the championship of the minor leagues.

Although Robinson's spectacular season at Montreal dispelled doubts about his right to play in the major leagues, Branch Rickey kept him on the Royals' roster throughout spring training in 1947. Rickey embarked on several stratagems that he hoped would ease Robinson's way onto the Dodgers. He avoided the pitfalls of Florida segregation by dispatching the Dodgers and the Royals to Cuba and Panama, and he transformed Robinson into a first baseman, the Brooklyn club's greatest need. Rickey believed that a demonstration of Robinson's undeniable skills would generate a groundswell of support for his promotion among the Dodgers' players.

Robinson responded with a .429 spring batting tear, but rather than demand his ascension, several Dodgers, led by the Southerners Dixie Walker, Kirby Higbe, and Bobby Bragan, circulated a petition to keep him off the team. Other key players, however, notably the Kentucky-born shortstop Pee Wee Reese, refused to sign the protest, and Rickey and the manager Leo Durocher quickly quashed the rebellion. On April 10, five days before the start of the season and with no groundswell yet in evidence, Rickey simply elevated Robinson to the parent club as the Dodgers' first baseman.

Around the National League Robinson's arrival produced undercurrents of dismay. The Philadephia Phillies, under the leadership of the manager Ben Chapman, subjected him to a stream of racist abuse. Opposing pitchers regularly targeted him with brushback and bean-ball pitches, hitting him seven times—a league record—in the first half of the season. Hotels in Philadelphia and St. Louis barred him; one in Cincinnati compelled him to take his meals in his room, fearing his presence would offend other guests.

Against this backdrop of pressure and challenge, Robinson carved out not just an extraordinary rookie season but a monument to courage and equal opportunity. After an early slump, he removed any remaining justifications for the exclusion of blacks from baseball. He batted above .300 for most of the season, led the league in stolen bases, and trailed just one other player in runs scored. He paced the Dodgers in home runs and led them to the pennant. *Sporting News*, which had consistently opposed the inclusion of blacks in organized baseball, named him Rookie of the Year.

Yet Robinson's rookie-year statistics and honors, impressive as they are, fail to capture his achievement. By introducing the more aggressive and flamboyant base-running and batting styles of the Negro Leagues, he transformed major league baseball. In the process he changed the nation's outlook as well.

Robinson began the 1947 season as a curiosity; he emerged as a national phenomenon. Wherever the Dodgers played, fans turned out in record numbers to witness the spectacle of integration. While he doubtless benefited from the more liberal racial attitudes that had emerged during the Depression and World War II, Robinson helped forge a new consciousness that would accelerate the civil rights movement of the 1950s. African-Americans saw him as their standard bearer, leading the onslaught against segregation. Whites discovered in him an individual who won their admiration not only as an athlete but as a man, compelling them to reassess their views both of African-Americans and of American race relations.

Although few people realized it at the time, Robinson had launched a revolution in American athletics. Only two other major league teams signed African-American players in 1947, and the pace of integration seemed agonizingly slow. Yet within a decade blacks from the United States and Caribbean countries had appeared on all but one team and emerged as the stars of the game. This pattern proved even more pronounced in other team sports. By the late 1960s African-Americans predominated in the National Football League and National Basketball Association. The black influx into college football and basketball forced Southern universities to abandon policies barring competition against integrated squads and ultimately to recruit African-Americans themselves. Sports became the primary symbol of social mobility in the black community, eventually prompting concern about an overemphasis on athletics among young African-Americans.

In the wake of his triumphant rookie season, Robinson transcended baseball and sports to become an American icon. Numerous articles showing Jackie and Rachel Robinson living in integrated neighborhoods and their children attending predominantly white schools portrayed the family as the vanguard of the new racial enlightenment. As the nation's foremost representative of interracial improvement, Robinson found himself embroiled in 1949 in a Cold War confrontation with the singer and actor Paul Robeson, whose pessimistic assessment of American race relations had led him to a flirtation with Soviet communism.

Robinson's dynamic playing for the Dodgers reinforced his charismatic appeal. In 1949 he led the National League in batting, won the Most Valuable Player award, and began a string of six consecutive All-Star Game appearances. With the addition of the catcher Roy Campanella, the pitcher Don Newcombe, and other former Negro League stars, the Dodgers continued to showcase the benefits of integration. Equally important was the fact that Robinson, the African-American firebrand, was clearly the leader and dominant personality on the National League's most accomplished and celebrated squad.

Yet amid these growing achievements, Robinson's "genius for getting into extracurricular scrapes" reasserted itself. In 1945 he had promised Branch Rickey that he would ignore insults and assaults. By 1949 both men agreed that this chapter had ended; Robinson no longer needed to restrain his instinctive responses to opposing players or anyone else.

Thereafter Robinson seemed forever surrounded by controversy. He complained that some umpires had it in for him and warred with the Giants' manager, Leo Durocher. He objected to the Yankees' failure to sign black players, protested the continuing discrimination faced by black athletes during spring training, and demanded that blacks be considered as candidates for managers. His unrepentant outspokenness and civil rights militancy attracted criticism and acclaim both inside and outside baseball.

In January 1957, after ten tempestuous seasons, Robinson retired. It is fitting testimony to his baseball prowess that his career record alone, without any consideration of his pioneering social role, merited his first-ballot election to the Hall of Fame five years later. His lifetime batting average was .311, and his .410 on-base percentage puts him among the top twenty-five players of all time. In addition, the Dodgers won pennants during six of Robinson's ten years with the club and finished second three times. Moreover, he accomplished all that he did after discrimination had robbed him of at least five years of prime productivity, for he was already twenty-eight years old when he joined the Dodgers.

Unlike most athletes, Robinson did not retreat from the public eye after his retirement. He accepted a job as vice president of Chock Full O'Nuts, a chain of New York City fast-food restaurants that employed many African-Americans. He chaired the NAACP Freedom Fund Drive and became one of the organization's primary spokespersons and fundraisers. He immersed himself in the civil rights movement as an ardent supporter of Martin Luther King, Jr., raised funds for the Student Non-Violent Coordinating Committee (SNCC), and marched in many of the major demonstrations of the 1960s.

Yet he also became engulfed in the shifting racial and generational tides of that decade. Always defiantly independent, he forged his own distinctive path in politics and protest. In 1960 he endorsed Richard Nixon for President over John F. Kennedy, the favorite of most civil rights activists. Although the majority of African-Americans supported the Democrats, Robinson allied himself with New York's governor, Nelson Rockefeller, and became the nation's most prominent black Republican. As white and black radicals increasingly attacked the American economic and political system, Robinson reaffirmed his faith in "black capitalism" as the vehicle for African-American progress, establishing the Freedom National Bank and investing in other black-owned enterprises.

In 1960 young SNCC activists successfully approached Robinson for assistance, seeing him as a kindred spirit. By the late 1960s, however, he had publicly feuded with Malcolm X and other Black Power advocates and split with King over the latter's opposition to the Vietnam War. Indeed Robinson, who came to be regarded by many militants as a pillar of the mainstream establishment, was even called an Uncle Tom. Ironically, these attacks coincided with his resignation from the NAACP because, he said, it was dominated by a "clique of the Old Guard," and had failed to incorporate "younger, more progressive voices."

Accustomed to contention, Robinson confidently navigated these controversies. Personal tragedy, however, took a far greater toll. Twenty-one-year-old Jackie Robinson, Jr., wounded in action in Vietnam, had returned addicted to heroin and turned to a life of crime. On June 4, 1968, police arrested him for possession of drugs and a firearm. Where Jackie Sr. had been a herald of the "new Negro" of the civil rights movement, his son became a harbinger of the devastation that awaited many African-American males in the 1980s and 1990s.

After a stay at Daytop Village, a drug-rehabilitation center, Jackie Jr. emerged cured of his addiction and devoted to helping others afflicted by drugs. Fate allowed him little time to savor his triumph. In the early morning hours of June 17, 1971, the sports car he was driving veered out of control and crashed on the Merritt Parkway, near the Robinson home in Connecticut. Jackie Robinson, Jr., was dead at twenty-four.

His son's ordeal and death transformed Robinson. The tragedy had been played out, as had so much for the family, in public view. "I guess I had more of an effect on other people's kids than I had on my own," he remarked, after Jackie Jr.'s arrest, as unsparing in self-criticism as in his attacks on others.

Around this time Robinson's physical condition declined precipitously. Plagued for several years with diabetes, he found his eyesight fading. He suffered a heart attack, and poor circulation made walking difficult. He was told that one of his legs would have to be amputated. After King's assassination, in 1968, and the election of Richard Nixon, with whom he had long since parted company, the troubles of Jackie Jr. led Robinson— like many other African-Americans—to re-evaluate his faith in America's ability to overcome its history of racism.

This reassessment culminated in the publication, in 1972, of Robinson's remarkable final testament, his bluntly titled autobiography, *I Never Had It Made*. Characteristically frank and outspoken, he expressed pride in his accomplishments but acknowledged his errors: his castigation of Robeson, his endorsement of Nixon, his split with King over Vietnam, and other episodes. He wrote honestly and movingly about Jackie Jr. Having for a quarter of a century symbolized the possibility of integration in America, he now sounded a profoundly pessimistic note. "There was a time I believed deeply in America. I have become bitterly disillusioned," he wrote. "Personally, I have been very fortunate [but] I cannot say I have it made while our country . . . speeds along a course toward more and more racism."

Yet the image of Robinson in his final years as broken and dispirited belies the reality of his indomitable personality. The publication of Roger Kahn's book about the Brooklyn Dodgers, *The Boys of Summer*, in 1971, awakened a new generation to the power and the glory of the Robinson saga. Those who saw and spoke to Robinson in 1972 describe him as ebullient despite his personal grief and physical difficulties. In a final telephone conversation Kahn found him "as enthusiastic as a twenty-year-old" while discussing his latest business venture. When, during the 1972 World Series, major league baseball celebrated the twenty-fifth anniversary of Robinson's debut, he joked with his former teammates about his impending amputation, needling Pee Wee Reese by saying that he would return to best him on the golf course. Then, before a national television audience, Robinson offered America one final, enduring memory. After accepting the accolades of the dignitaries, he challenged organized baseball to fulfill his legacy by hiring black managers.

Nine days later, on October 24, 1972, Robinson died of a heart attack. He was only fifty-three years old. To deliver the eulogy Rachel Robinson, who had shared her husband's triumphs and heartbreaks, chose not someone from Robinson's baseball past nor one of his long-standing allies from earlier civil rights struggles but the thirty-one-year-old Rev. Jesse Jackson, an African-American leader who embodied the hopes of the future rather than the disappointments of the past.

Jackson, like Rachel Robinson, understood Robinson's final testament. Robinson, preached Jackson, had "created ripples of possibility," "turned stumbling block into stepping stone," and bequeathed the "gift of new expectations."

In his autobiography Robinson vented his disappointment with the state of race relations in the 1970s, but he also reaffirmed the message that has made him an enduring figure: that individuals of courage and commitment can confront bigotry and create change. He tempered his disillusionment with an uplifting epitaph: "A life is not important except in the impact it has on other lives." By that measure, a quarter-century after his death and half a century after his historic feat, the import of Jackie Robinson's life continues to resound.

DEBRA SHATTUCK

12. Playing a Man's Game: Women and Baseball in the United States, 1866–1954

As with black players, aspiring women baseball players faced limited opportunities to develop their interest and display their skills. As with blacks, too, the study of women in baseball necessarily involves the examination of a wide range of issues within the broader evolving social and cultural fabric of the nation and prevailing social roles affecting women. During the nineteenth century, prevailing "correct" codes of behavior for women were severely restrictive, enjoining them to pursue a life of moral domesticity and delicate submissiveness. Victorian ideals of a woman's place left little opportunity for vigorous athletic activity. Young girls undoubtedly participated in games and contests, but upon reaching adolescence they were relegated to the grandstands as spectators of male athletes. Not only did social codes prevent women from vigorous athletic competition, so too did prevailing dress codes. Encased in corsets that inhibited their physical movements and encumbered by petticoats and long dresses designed to enhance their image of femininity, it is little wonder that serious athletic activity was impossible. Ironically, however, their presence at sporting events was desired to provide a semblance of respectability to the unruly world of men's sports.

Some of these limitations eased following the Civil War. Respectable women's colleges with dull curricula began to provide a greater variety of recreational activities. Although far from the prying eyes of male spectators, baseball became the first team sport adopted by respectable women. On the other hand, barnstorming teams of women such as baseball's "Bloomer Girls" offended sedate sensibilities by openly flaunting their talents for financial gain before gawking spectators. Prevailing wisdom dictated that women's sports should be played only for one's individual health, but not too vigorously, for physicians feared the effects of such activity on women's child-bearing ability. Such notions that women's sports should be neither strenuous nor spectator oriented dominated well into the twentieth century. But as an improved standard of living and more leisure time resulted from new technology, sporting activity increasingly became an element of women's desire for emancipation. Just as women gradually broke into previously all-male occupational bastions, they also began to force changes on the sporting scene. The pace of such changes was clearly accelerated by the two world wars of the twentieth century.

In her survey of the fitful advances in baseball made by women players, Debra Shattuck examines some fundamental questions about those who played the game for nearly a century before the sports and sexual revolution of the 1970s. She identifies the kind of women who played the game: what class of society were they from and what motivated them? In doing so, she sheds new light on some of the neglected women pioneers of the game.

Baseball has long been considered a man's sport. Books and articles on baseball history abound, but few give serious consideration to women's involvement with the national pastime. Articles that do mention women generally focus on their role as spectators or on the social derision they faced for daring to play a man's game. But women were playing baseball as early as 1866 and their defiance of social mores dictating separate roles for men and women raises some interesting questions to challenge baseball and social historians: What kind of women played baseball? Were they women's rights activists trying to make a social statement? Were they playing simply for the money such a novelty might net? Were they from the upper or lower classes, white collar or working class, married or single? Did their participation alter certain cultural attitudes toward female athletes?

This brief overview of the history of female baseball players cannot possibly permit in-depth analysis of the motivations and aspirations of female players, but a few generalizations will be offered. The women in this study came from all classes of society and walks of life. Some were married, some were single and most were white. But while all of them shared the distinction of challenging social mores by playing a "man's game," there is little indication that the female players in this study, from the pioneers at Vassar to the professionals of the All-American Girls Professional Baseball League, were specifically trying to change social mores. In fact most of the women went out of their way to demonstrate that they could still conform to social definitions of femininity even while playing baseball.

It appears that female baseball players were motivated by the same reasons that women took up activities like cycling, basketball and tennis before those were socially accepted pursuits for women—they simply enjoyed the game and found ways to play it. There is little evidence female baseball players saw themselves as anything particularly phenomenal. Sophia Foster Richardson and Minnie Stephens attributed the origins of baseball at Vassar and Smith colleges to the desire of students for some "vigorous exercise." When female players from Philadelphia were asked in 1883 why they played baseball, they remarked that it was "partly for the fun of it and to see the country." These are hardly the statements of women out to change the status quo.

Whatever their motivations, it is still significant that women were playing baseball at all in the nineteenth and early twentieth centuries when social custom dictated that a woman's place was in the home and that her greatest aspiration should be to bear and raise children. This article will introduce these women whose involvement with the national pastime may not have always been readily accepted but who, because of their actions, have enriched baseball's colorful history.

Women who wanted to participate in sports or games in early nineteenth-century America faced a host of social and cultural obstacles. Throughout this period, women were told that their ideal strengths were "moral and emotional and nonphysical." Physicians warned women that failure to severely curtail physical activity after puberty, and especially during menstruation, would result in severe consequences including disease, miscarriage and possible sterility.

Women who chose to participate in physical sport despite the warnings of well-meaning physicians often faced social ostracism. One article, published in 1834 in *New York Sporting Magazine*, summed up the attitude of many men toward women involved in sporting activities: "[W]e have a peculiar antipathy to ladies in gigs; . . . we nauseate all skating in the feminine gender; and . . . we have an extraordinary aversion to ladies riding to hounds." The article concluded with a threat which many self-respecting nineteenth-century women must have found hard to ignore: "We would not marry a downright, thoroughgoing, hurdle jumping, racing pace, fox hunting lady, if she had the planet, Jupiter, for her portion."

Despite the threat of spinsterhood or debilitating physical maladies, scores of women participated in physical exercises in the first half of the nineteenth century ranging from horseback riding to dancing to ice-skating. Croquet was an especially popular sport for women in the mid–nineteenth century. In 1866 *Harper's Weekly* called croquet the "greatest outdoor game for women yet invented."

If croquet was the greatest outdoor game for women, baseball was the greatest outdoor game for men—at least as far as Charles Peverelly, author of *The Book of American Pastimes*, was concerned. "The game of Base Ball," he asserted, "has now become beyond question the leading feature of the out-door sports of the United States." Also "beyond question" was the fact that baseball was not a game for women. "There is no nobler or manlier game than baseball . . . ," *Harper's Weekly* proclaimed. *Cassell's Complete Book of Sports and Pastimes* went so far as to say that baseball, "when played up to the highest mark," was not even suited for boys, due to the "fatigue involved, and the injuries frequently sustained."

Surprisingly, in this era of cumbersome hoop skirts, tightly laced corsets and high button shoes, there were women who were determined to play baseball. The archives of the nation's earliest women's colleges have preserved the history of what may well have been the country's first female baseball players.

In June 1866, *The Vassariana*, Vassar College's student newspaper, reported the existence of the Laurel and Abenakis Base Ball Clubs. Thirty years later, in a speech to the Association of Collegiate Alumnae, Vassar alumna Sophia Foster Richardson (class of 1879) provided valuable insight into the game of baseball as played at Vassar in the 1870s. Richardson related that when she was a freshman at Vassar, "seven or eight baseball clubs suddenly came into being." She added: "The public, so far as it knew of our playing, was shocked, but in our retired grounds, and protected from observation even in these grounds by sheltering trees, we continued to play in spite of a censorious public."

Pressure from the "censorious public," and "disapproving mothers" prevailed and baseball did not flourish for long at Vassar although, according to Richardson, "those of us who had learned the value of vigorous play succeeded in keeping alive enough interest in the game to support two clubs until our senior year."

Vassar was not the only college where women had learned the value of vigorous play. An interesting account of baseball's first appearance at Smith College is provided by Minnie Stephens (class of 1883) in a letter to her former schoolmates: "Way back in Seventy Nine [1879], I was more or less active and full of fun.—It seemed to me that we ought to have some lively games in the way of wholesome exercise so I got a few friends together and we organized a base ball club." The Smith girls formed another team soon after and, in Stephens' words, they "had a wonderful match game, never equalled in the history of athletics for 'intelligent gentlewomen.'" The restrictive clothing styles of the day must have made the game especially challenging but, as Stephens related, fashion had its good points too: "One vicious batter drove a ball directly into the belt line of her opponent and had it not been for the rigid steel corset clasp worn in those days, she would have been knocked out completely."

Baseball players at Smith College fared little better than their contemporaries at Vassar. "We were told . . . that the game was to violent," Stephens recalled, "and also there was great danger in breaking windows in the Hubbard House, so we were politely ordered to give it all up." She added that a tennis club was soon begun but "the fire of the base ball club still smouldered and we did want a safe place to play."

As it turned out, the women at Smith College had to wait until 1891 before the college president approved baseball as an official club sport. The "safe place to play" was assured in 1899 when Stephens' husband, Frank Gates Allen, donated an athletic field to the college on behalf of his wife and daughter.

While female college students had the advantage of trespassing on the male sphere of baseball in the relative seclusion of all-girl campuses, other women challenged social dictates off-campus. An illustration from an unidentified source in the files of the National Baseball Hall of Fame Library shows women playing baseball in front of a large crowd of well-dressed male spectators. The caption reads: "The Last [Latest?] Illustration of Womens' Rights.—A Femele [sic] Base-Ball Club at Peterboro, N.Y." The drawing is dated Saturday, July 3, 1869. The caption also mentions an article about the game, but until the source of the illustration can be determined, little else can be learned about the team.

It is impossible to tell whether the Peterboro women played baseball by official rules but, consistent with the times, none was wearing baseball gloves. Also, while the caption attributes the game to an "illustration of women's rights," there is no way to substantiate that. The women wore bloomer style pants which many "proper" ladies shunned, but all the players were wearing typical high button shoes and many wore earrings—a feminine touch to what might otherwise have been construed a rather masculine style uniform. It is very possible the reference to "women's rights" was made by a disgruntled male observer and was not an accurate reflection of the players' motives. If the women at Smith and Vassar are any indication, women played baseball because they enjoyed it; they weren't necessarily trying to use baseball to challenge cultural definitions of male and female spheres.

While women on campus and off played baseball for enjoyment, it didn't take long for a few enterprising men to see the financial possibilities of promoting women's baseball as a spectator sport. Consequently, sometime in 1875, three men organized two women's baseball clubs in Illinois for the sole purpose of making money. The "Blondes" and "Brunettes" played their first game on September 11, 1875, in Springfield, Illinois. One newspaper called it the "first game of baseball ever played in public for gate money between feminine ball-tossers," a claim which may or may not be true. The women used modified rules and equipment. Baselines were only 50 feet instead of the regulation 90 feet, and a lighter ball and smaller bats were employed. There is no indication whether the pitching was overhand or underhand. A box score of the game makes it evident that the women were not experienced ball players. Though the final score in the 2 hour and 45 minute game was 42 to 33 in favor of the Blondes, only three of their runs were earned. The Brunettes managed only one earned run. Errors abounded: the Blondes reached first base 13 times on blunders; the Brunettes nine times.

Poor ball playing probably did not concern the clubs' organizers much since financial success did not depend on their clubs' win-loss record. As one newswriter put it: "The troupe contains some pretty fair players, but as a general thing the attraction is the novelty of seeing eighteen girls prettily attired in gymnastic dress playing in a game of baseball."

Apart from their names, listed in newspaper accounts of their games, nothing else is known about the women who made up the "Blondes" and "Brunettes." It is significant, however, that one article refers to them as "a selected troupe of girls of reputable character." Projecting a clean-cut image of their players was critical to the clubs' owners. The novelty of the game was women acting like women playing a man's game, not women acting like men playing a man's game. Spectators would have been especially critical of the latter and gate receipts would have dwindled.

Fortunately for women, after 1880 social mores did grant women far more freedom to pursue vigorous physical exercises like cycling, field hockey, golf and track. As historian Lois Banner states, "The ancient belief that a woman was controlled by her reproductive organs was on the way out." Author Henry Hall reflected the view of an increasing majority when he wrote in 1887: "Exercise . . . adds materially to woman's charms and greatly to her effectiveness and the ease and safety with which she performs the great functions of her life." This view still emphasized women's traditional roles as housewife and mother, but acknowledged that exercise could actually benefit women in those endeavors.

Society's more lenient attitude toward female exercise did not extend to women who wanted to play baseball, however. "The female has no place in base ball, except to the degradation of the game," proclaimed an editorial in the *St. Louis Globe-Democrat* in 1885. Five years later, a disgusted gentleman lamented: "Probably the most disgraceful feature in base ball is the female base ball crowd now travelling over the country giving a burlesque of the sport." And indeed, it did seem there was a "crowd" of women who had decided that, socially approved or not, they were going to play baseball.

The campuses of women's colleges continued to offer a relatively safe haven where girls could pursue their love of baseball. The women at Mount Holyoke organized their first formal team in 1891 although photographs in the school archives indicate students played baseball there in the mid-1880s. At Wellesley College, beginning in 1897, women could play baseball on club teams, and in 1911 the physical education department began offering formal instruction in the sport. The records of the Radcliffe College Athletic Association first mention baseball in 1915 and the student handbook issued in 1920 for the Women's College at Brown University noted: "Last year was the very first year that baseball at the Women's College was a definite sport."

Unless specifically stated in contemporary sources, it is difficult to determine which form of baseball rules were used on college campuses. There were many from which to choose. In addition to regulation men's baseball or softball (the first women's softball teams appeared in the mid-1890s), schools could adopt any number of variations of indoor baseball rules available. Indoor baseball had been invented in the late 1880s by a group of men determined to play baseball despite inclement weather. The game was soon modified for all sorts of conditions and players. In 1920, in *Basketball and Indoor Baseball for Women*, Helen Frost and Charles Digby Wardlaw described indoor baseball games using 12" balls with 35' baselines, 14" balls with 27' baselines and 16" balls with 18' baselines.

Since there were no official standardized rules for women's baseball until the Sub-Committee on Baseball of the National Committee on Women's Athletics of the American Physical Education Association adopted rules devised by physical educator Gladys E. Palmer in 1926, schools played one or more modified versions of baseball. (Even the official rules, once approved, allowed for four different-sized diamonds, four different-sized balls and either overhand or underhand pitching depending on the size of the diamond or the ball. The Sub-Committee specifically rejected the official men's 90-foot diamond on the grounds that it was not suited to the "abilities and needs of the average girl.")

There were a few women's colleges which played baseball by official men's rules. Frost and Wardlaw observed in 1920: "Certain women's colleges have been playing baseball for years, and some under outdoor rules with a regulation ball, gloves, masks, etc." One of these schools was Barnard. When baseball was officially added to the list of approved sports at Barnard in 1910, an article in the *Cincinnati Enquirer* noted: "The Barnard girls will play on a diamond of regulation size, with bags, mitts, bats and other accouterments from a regulation sporting goods house. They will play genuine baseball, with all its complications and regulations."

Despite more lenient attitudes toward women playing sports, women playing baseball on college campuses couldn't entirely escape criticism. A scathing commentary in *The Reach Official American League Guide for 1911* viewed the addition of baseball as an official sport for women's colleges as "One more indictment against the modern unsexing system of female education and training." The anonymous writers continued: "We hold, and we know, that base ball is not a game for any woman, not even the most masculine of that sex." They concluded bluntly: "So far as such essentially masculine games as base ball and foot ball are concerned women's only relation thereto should be as spectator."

While female college athletes continued playing baseball despite occasional criticism, a growing number of women outside of the colleges took up the sport. Some played on organized teams; others, like a group of women in Gilmore, Pennsylvania, played, what might be termed today, "pick-up" games. An article in the *New York Clipper* on October 2, 1886, reported that a "novel" game of baseball had been played the week before in Gilmore between two women's teams, the "Marrieds" and the "Singles." A woman umpired the game, which was witnessed by a large crowd, and terminated at the end of seven innings in a victory for the married women by a score of 27 to 17. The women all wore long dresses and gave a good exhibition."

A few women had the opportunity to play baseball on organized teams. In August 1883 the "Young Ladies Baseball Club" was founded in Philadelphia. Like the women's team at Springfield in the 1870s, the Young Ladies Baseball Club was organized by men eager to capitalize on the financial potential of women's baseball. The owners billed their club's games as entertainment spectacles, not serious competition and, like the Springfield managers, stressed the femininity and moral respectability of their players.

A newspaper account of one of the club's first games relayed the management's claim that players were "selected with tender solicitude from 200 applicants, variety actresses and ballet girls being positively barred." The article further stated: "Only three of the lot had ever been on the stage, and they were in the strictly legitimate business. . . . Most of the others were graduates of Sunday-schools and normal colleges. . . ."

While the players' social pedigrees may have been impeccable (according to their managers) their playing abilities were questionable to say the least. When the Young Ladies Baseball Club played its first game on August 18, 1883, at Pastime Park in Philadelphia, 500 spectators laughed themselves silly as the girls attempted to play baseball on a regulation diamond. As one writer observed: "A ball thrown from pitcher to second base almost invariably fell short, and was stopped on the roll. The throw from first to third base was an utter impossibility."

When the Club played again at the Manhattan Athletic Club on September 23, 1883, the players were still woefully lacking in playing skills. While one writer did concede that "four of the girls had become expert—for girls," the remainder of his lengthy article described the comical antics of their teammates. The score was 16 to 3 after only one inning and by the fifth inning the players were exhausted. Many "doggedly refused to run from one base to another, until it became morally certain that the other side was hopelessly tangled up with the ball."

Evidently "novelty" as opposed to quality continued to be enough to draw fans to contests between female baseball teams. The Young Ladies Baseball Club endured under various managers for at least two years and possibly longer. Newspaper articles attest to their appearance in cities like Chicago and New Orleans. In the winter of 1884, a group of the players made an extensive trip throughout the south. During this trip the women were pitted against men's teams instead of against each other. Despite the new tactic of using competition between male and female teams to draw fans to the games, the managers continued to promote games the same way. Advertisements stressed novelty and entertainment as selling points. In New Orleans, the players "paraded the streets in full uniform, and created an impression that base ball, played by shapely, activs [active] girls, must be attractive."

By the late nineteenth and early twentieth century, scores of "Bloomer Girls" baseball teams were traversing the country demonstrating their baseball prowess—or lack thereof. As one writer noted, Bloomer Girls was "a name without copyright" adopted by a variety of barnstorming baseball teams "trying to scratch a buck out of the sandlots of early 20th century America." There were Bloomer Girls teams organized in Texas, Chicago, New York, Kansas City, Boston and anywhere enough interest could be generated. Bloomer Girls was actually a bit of a misnomer since it did not refer to teams composed entirely of women. Many of the teams contained one or more "toppers," baby-faced boys or men dressed in women's wigs. Despite the abundance of Bloomer Girls teams, they did not play each other and no formal league was established. Instead, they journeyed from town to town challenging men's amateur and semi-professional teams.

Unlike the women's teams of the past little, if any, emphasis was put on promoting the femininity of Bloomer Girls players. In fact, at least one manager stressed just the opposite. This gentleman, mentor of the Tennessee Bloomer Girls, claimed his girls "were equally talented at playing baseball and chewing tobacco."

It is hard to say why managers would no longer wish to promote the femininity of their players. One reason may be that since Bloomer Girls teams often contained a number of male players, managers realized the futility of trying to claim respectability for women who blatantly disregarded social mores against women playing on the same teams as men.

If managers could not promote the fine morals of their female players, at least they could promote their playing skills. One female player who received a great deal of praise in newspapers for her playing ability was pitcher Maude Nelson (sometimes spelled Neilson), who began her career with the Chicago Bloomer Girls as early as April 1899 and was still playing six years later with a group called the Chicago Stars. Her excellent pitching was frequently cited as the main attraction at her team's games. Nelson's teammate, "Miss" Day (first name unknown), also received acclaim. One sportswriter contended: "She is without doubt the greatest lady ball player in the business, and deserves all the nice things that have been said by the press throughout the country about her."

Despite the occasional praise of a kind-hearted sportswriter, life for a Bloomer Girl was difficult. Teams played grueling schedules (the Boston Bloomer girls once played 28 games in 26 days without a loss) and there were no luxury airliners or air conditioned tour buses to take them from place to place.

The Bloomer Girls teams were not the only option available to baseball-playing females. There were numerous women's teams and co-ed teams throughout the country. On August 31, 1903, an article in the *Boston Herald* announced an upcoming game at Forest Hills between the "Hickey and Clover clubs," both composed of five women and four men. The article noted that the Hickey team had already played a number of similarly organized teams with great success due in large part to the excellent play of pitcher, Elizabeth Conry, and catcher, Mary Howe. One year later in Flat Rock, Indiana, a group of women organized two baseball clubs, one consisting of only married players, the other only single players. The *Cincinnati Enquirer* commented that a game played between the two teams "would make the bloomer girls sick with envy."

It is difficult to determine the social class of most female ball players. While the majority of female players in colleges were from the middle and upper classes, the majority of "Bloomer Girls" were probably from the lower classes. It is unlikely that upper class women made up the contingent of tobacco chewing players about which the Tennessee Bloomer Girls coach boasted. Another questionable group of "ladies" was the New York Bloomer Girls team which, according to one account, "ended a tour of North Carolina [in 1913] by wrecking a hotel in Raleigh." When a police officer arrived on the scene, they pelted him with "shoes, bats, masks and baseball weapons."

There is evidence that upper class women did play baseball outside of a college setting, however. For example, two of the women who played in Flat Rock, Indiana, were wives of prominent members of that community. In addition, in April 1908, Roy Somerville penned an article called "Feminine Baseball De Luxe" for *The Baseball Magazine*. Somerville introduced the "charming daughters of Mr. Howard Wood, multi-millionaire iron manufacturer," who had organized two baseball teams of "society buds." Somerville contrasted these players with the "collection of 'pie-faced' females, in spotted uniforms who travel through the bush countries as 'professional ball-players.'"

Somerville attributed "society's invasion of the plebeian baseball field" to the girls' love of outdoor sports, but added: "Secure in their social position, they could afford to show the natural American love for the game of baseball." His statement indicates that women baseball players were not highly respected. The Wood sisters could "afford" to play because their social position was secure. Few would dare speak ill of them. Such was not the case for lower-class female baseball players who were frequently denounced by the public as whores and freaks.

Considering public disapproval for women baseball players and the social taboo regarding women competing "against men in the more rugged masculine sports," it is surprising to find evidence of a number of women who played on otherwise all-male teams. One of the most successful of these women was Ohioan Alta Weiss.

Born in Ragersville, Ohio, on February 9, 1890, Weiss was the daughter of a prominent physician, Dr. George Weiss. Perhaps because he had three daughters and no sons, Weiss enthusiastically nurtured the athletic talent Alta demonstrated from an early age. When she was 14 she played baseball with a local boys' team. According to a history of Ragersville, her father, acting in his capacity as president of the Ragersville Board of Education, even established a two-year high school "so Alta could play with a high school team." He later had a private gymnasium built near his home so Alta could keep her pitching arm in shape during the winter months.

Alta's rise to fame as a baseball player began in the summer of 1907 when her family made a trip to Vermilion, a popular resort town about 20 miles west of Cleveland on the shores of Lake Erie. During the visit Vermilion's mayor, purportedly "elected five straight terms on nothing less than a 'baseball' ticket," spotted Weiss playing catch with some local youth and convinced the manager of the semi-professional Vermilion Independents to give her a try. Fortunately for Weiss, the team had just lost one of its best pitchers and needed help in that area.

More than 1,200 fans showed up for Weiss's pitching debut on September 2, 1907, in Vermilion. She pitched five innings giving up only four hits and one run. By the time Weiss made her second appearance on September 8th, she was already being heralded as the "Girl Wonder" in the press. The *Vermilion News* reported that so many fans were expected for Weiss's next game that "an effort is being made to have either the LS & MS or the Nickel Plate run a special train from Cleveland so as to give the Cleveland people a chance to see this girl wonder."

Weiss attracted more than 13,000 fans to the eight games she pitched for the Independents in 1907. The following year her father bought a half-interest in a men's semi-professional team in Cleveland which became known as the Weiss All-Stars. Weiss played in more than 30 games for the All-Stars in 1908 as the team travelled throughout Ohio and surrounding states. She generally pitched five innings and then played first base for the remainder of the game.

Weiss was very popular with Cleveland sportswriters. They even began a half-serious campaign to get her signed with Cleveland's professional team, the Naps. A headline in the *Cleveland Press* on March 22, 1908, questioned: "If the Nap Pitchers Can't Win Regularly, Why Not Alta Weiss to Help?" Larry Lajoie, the Naps' manager, was not about to sign a female player although, after seeing her pitch a game with the Independents, he had conceded: "I was surprised to find that she could pitch so well."

After the 1908 season Weiss dropped out of the limelight to enroll in college. She attended the University of Wooster and later studied at the Starling Ohio Medical College where she became the only female graduate in the Class of 1914. She served in the medical profession for more than three decades.

After entering college, Weiss did not completely give up baseball. In 1910 a newspaper reported that she had signed to pitch with an all-male team in Ragersville and would "twirl in all the big games." An article in the *Vermilion News* dated October 5, 1922, noted that Weiss "again appeared in action and is still a marvel among women baseball players."

Weiss's enduring popularity among northern Ohio baseball fans went beyond her feminine gender. She was not just a female ball player, she was a good female ball player. One sportswriter commented that though there were many "would-be women ball players" in the country, "Miss Weiss can easily lay claim to being the only one who can handle the ball from the pitchers box in such style that some of the best semi-pros are made to fan the atmosphere." His remarks are typical of the numerous accolades Weiss received from the press.

Thanks to the abundant source material available on Weiss it is possible to address her motives for playing baseball. The newspaper articles about her playing days make it clear that she loved the game and was thrilled to have the opportunity to play it. She was not a women's rights activist. Her reluctance to wear bloomers is one indication of this. A few years after becoming a baseball sensation Weiss told a newswriter how she had finally been forced to give up skirts in favor of bloomers: "I found that you can't play ball in skirts. I tried. I wore a skirt over my bloomers—and nearly broke my neck. Finally I was forced to discard it, and now I always wear bloomers—but made so wide that the fullness gives a skirtlike effect." Weiss also had ample opportunity in the press to speak out on behalf of women's rights but never did so. At one point she even stated: "No, I don't believe that there ever will be any distinguished women base ball players. Women haven't the nerve. . . . They may get up some wishy-washy girls' nines, but they'll never have any real players." (Weiss was obviously a better ball player than a seer, however, as the later section of this article on the outstanding athletes of the All-American Girls Professional Baseball League will attest.)

Though Weiss was far and away the most well-known female baseball player in northern Ohio at the time, she was not the only one. When she returned to Cleveland in 1908 to begin her second season she was already facing competition from other female pitchers. Her scrapbook contains numerous clippings about her female rivals like 14-year-old Carita Masteller, Irma Gribble, Anna Singleton, Verds Bailagh, "Miss" O'Brien and sisters, Irene and Ruth Basford.

None of these girls received near the acclaim Weiss enjoyed. Part of Weiss's success was, no doubt, related to her social standing. Her father was a respected physician and community leader. He had the financial means to build her a gymnasium for winter workouts and to assure her a place on the Weiss All-Stars by purchasing a half-interest in the team. These financial advantages were not available to Elizabeth Murphy, who, from about 1915 to 1935, was known as the "Queen of Baseball" throughout New England and eastern Canada.

Born Mary Elizabeth Murphy in Warren, Rhode Island, on April 13, 1894, "Lizzie," as she liked to be called, was the daughter of a mill hand. At the age of 12 she joined her father in one of Warren's woolen mills. But, according to Murphy, she spent much of her time in front of the looms "dreaming of the outdoors and baseball." She recalled that even when she was too small to play: "I used to beg the boys to let me carry the bats."

It was not long before Murphy impressed her playmates with her baseball savvy. By the time she was 15 she had earned a spot on a number of men's amateur teams in Warren. Not long after, she was being paid to play. The 1913–1914 edition of the *Bristol, Warren & Barrington Rhode Island Directory* listed the occupation of "Mary E. Murphy," boarder at a home on Arlington Avenue, as "ball player." Few women could make such a claim in 1913.

Murphy was indeed a ball player—and a good one at that. Like Alta Weiss, she did not depend on her gender alone to draw fans; she was an expert player. She played first base and, as one of her managers put it: "She swells the attendance, but most important, she produces the goods." After earning $5 per week plus a share of the gate receipts playing for local Warren teams, Murphy signed with the semi-professional Providence Independents in 1918. A few years later she signed with Ed Carr's All-Stars of Boston and spent a number of seasons touring with them through New England and Canada.

Murphy played baseball until 1935 when she returned to Warren and settled down. She married in 1937 but her husband died a few years later. Unlike Weiss, Murphy had not been as frugal with her earnings and was forced to work in the woolen mills and on oyster boats to support herself. During this period her love for baseball diminished considerably. Toward the end of her life she rarely reminisced about her baseball glory days and once remarked, "It's hard to explain why I liked baseball so much. And the more I think about it the less I understand the reason." Murphy died on July 27, 1964.

It is difficult to ascertain exactly how much money female ball players like Weiss and Murphy were paid. One article in Weiss's scrapbook stated that she was to receive $100 for her debut at Cleveland's League Park. It is highly unlikely she earned anything close to that sum for every game. Another article did note, however, that during at least one game in which

Weiss appeared, the fans threw money on the field whenever she stuck out a batter or reached first base.

A look at Murphy's earnings indicates that female players were sometimes exploited by managers. After her initial appearance on a semi-professional team in Warren, Murphy failed to receive a penny of the $85 gate receipts. She subsequently refused to play until the manager guaranteed her $5 per game and an equal share of the gate. When she played for Carr's All-Stars she earned somewhat more though the exact figure is unknown. Another ploy Murphy used to bolster her small salary was to sell autographed pictures of herself in the stands between innings. At one game in Dorchester, Massachusetts, she reaped almost $50 in this manner.

While Elizabeth Murphy was impressing New Englanders with her baseball expertise, 14-year-old Margaret Gisolo was helping her Blanford, Indiana, American Legion men's baseball team win county, district, sectional and state championships in 1928. In seven tournament games, Gisolo had nine hits in 21 at-bats for a .429 batting average. She scored 10 put-outs and 28 assists in the field with no errors charged against her. A protest filed by opposing teams against her participation in the games went all the way to the American Legion's National Americanism Commission, who referred it to Major League Baseball Commissioner Kenesaw Mountain (Judge) Landis. Landis determined that American Legion rules did not specifically ban the participation of women and the protest was disallowed.

Little did Landis know, but just three years after he approved Gisolo's participation in the American Legion tournament he would have to address a similar situation in minor league baseball when the "Barnum of Baseball," Chattanooga Lookouts manager Joe Engel, signed 17-year-old Jackie Mitchell to a contract with his Class AA team. Engel knew that the novelty of seeing the first female ever signed to a professional contract in organized baseball would draw fans to his ball park, but he also knew that Mitchell was a superb pitcher. She had been taught to pitch by major leaguer Dazzy Vance and had once struck out nine men in a row in an amateur game. Engel wasted no time putting Mitchell's abilities to a true test—he immediately scheduled her to pitch against the visiting New York Yankees in an exhibition game on April 2, 1931.

That date has forever gone down in baseball history as the day that a woman struck out Babe Ruth and Lou Gehrig back-to-back. Speculation continues as to whether Ruth and Gehrig were merely putting on a show or really trying to hit Mitchell's pitches. Mitchell contended that it was not a setup, and that the only instructions given to the Yankee hitters was to try not to hit the ball straight through the pitcher's box. A number of Yankee players later commented they were not aware of any special agreement to take it easy on Mitchell. Other witnesses pointed out that Mitchell was a left-handed pitcher pitching to two left-handed batters, and that she had an excellent sinker pitch—sufficient advantage for many pitchers to accomplish the same feat.

Unfortunately, Mitchell never had an opportunity to repeat her performance as a professional ball player. A few days after her debut, Landis informed Engel that he had disallowed Mitchell's contract on the grounds that life in baseball was too strenuous for a woman. Mitchell spent the next six years barnstorming the country with a number of men's teams and then settled down to live out a quiet life in Chattanooga.

While Murphy and Gisolo and Mitchell dazzled fans with their baseball savvy, the social debate over the propriety of strenuous athletic competition for women continued. Despite the political gains made by women's rights activists during the early 1920s, and the symbolic defiance of thousands of young "flappers" challenging the mores of Victorian culture, many physical educators were determined to keep men's and women's athletics in two separate spheres. In *Athletics in Education*, published in 1930, physical educators Jesse Feiring Williams and William Leonard Hughes wrote: "The error in athletics for women is not in allowing them to play games but in permitting them to imitate both the activities of men and the manner of conducting men's competitions."

One key organization of physical educators which worked to keep women from merely copying men's athletic endeavors was the Women's Division of the National Amateur Athletic Federation (WD/NAAF). In 1926 the WD/NAAF resolved to "promote the study of existing rules of all sports to the end of adapting them, wherever indicated, to the special needs of girls and women." Throughout the 1930s and into the 1940s, the WD/NAAF represented a bastion against women's involvement in serious competition. By the 1930s, the Women's Division had succeeded in eliminating gate receipts for women's competitions at almost all schools and colleges.

While the WD/NAAF could exert considerable influence over collegiate sporting activities for women, it had little influence over the female athletes, both amateur and professional, who competed outside the collegiate arena in national and international competitions. In addition, as more women entered the nation's work force, especially during World War II, the WD/NAAF found itself unable to counter a trend toward female participation on industrial league teams coached by men and under men's rules.

In 1942, 32 amateur women's softball teams from the Midwest banded together and created the International Girls' Major League (IGML), and by

1943 there were 40,000 women's semi-professional teams scattered across the country. One contemporary noted that "every city of any consequence" had a women's softball league made up of teams sponsored by various businesses and industries. Another observed: "It has been no secret to sports fans in the Midwest that girls' softball in Chicago has been outdrawing the major-league baseball clubs."

Major league baseball struggled throughout the war and many minor league teams were forced to shut down completely due to lack of players. In 1943, to conserve fuel and money, 16 major league clubs broke a long-standing tradition and agreed to conduct spring training in or near their home cities. This measure, coupled with a shortened season, was still not enough to guarantee baseball could survive the war. Although President Roosevelt believed "it would be best for the country to keep baseball going," he emphasized to Baseball Commissioner Landis that "individual players who are of active military or naval age should go, without question, into the services." Roosevelt refused to exempt players from the draft, pointing out that baseball would retain its popularity even if older or less skilled players were used.

Faced with the bleak possibility that major league baseball might have to suspend operations, Chicago Cubs owner Philip K. Wrigley decided to capitalize on the popularity of women's softball to provide entertainment for war-weary industrial workers. In 1943 he created the All-American Girls Professional Softball League with the intent that the teams would play their games in the major league baseball stadiums for the duration of the war. As it turned out, few league games were played in major league stadiums and, within a year, the league modified its rules and became the first women's professional baseball league.

Wrigley was not content to merely create another IGML. He knew that female softball players were often referred to as "Amazons" in the press and that many tried to mimic the mannerisms of male big league players. Wrigley was adamant that his girls would be ladies first and ball players second. According to one writer, Wrigley's challenge was to convert "somewhat uncouth Amazonian spectacle into something nearer to the Wellesley, Vassar, Smith, and Stephens standard of competition." The challenge was one Wrigley had every intention of meeting. As had been the case with promoters of women's baseball in the past, Wrigley was determined that his league would gain "respectability" in the eyes of the general public.

The official contract of the All-American Girls Professional Baseball League (AAGPBL), as it came to be called, stated that the league's purpose was to oversee baseball in such a manner that it would "secure approval of the American public." One of the most visible manifestations of Wrigley's emphasis on the femininity of league players was the dress code. On the field the players wore skirts; off the field, they were admonished to "always appear in feminine attire when not actively engaged in practice of playing ball." In 1951 this general guidance was clarified: "Masculine hair styling, shoes, coats, shirts, socks, T-shirts, are barred at all times." Players were forbidden to appear in public wearing slacks or shorts. Proof that the league placed high priority on proper dress is that while players were fined $10 for being ejected from a game for arguing, they could be fined $50 for appearing in public with an unkempt appearance.

Wrigley was not content with having his players just look like ladies; he wanted them to act like ladies too. For awhile he even insisted that every member of his league attend charm school. To ensure that league rules were upheld and to convince wary mothers that their daughters were involved in a respectable enterprise, Wrigley stipulated that every league team have its own chaperone. The chaperones were combination policewomen, nurses, business managers, surrogate mothers and best friends for the more than 500 girls and women who played in the AAGPBL during its 12-year existence.

The AAGPBL made its debut in 1943 when four teams, the Rockford [Illinois] Peaches, the South Bend [Indiana] Blue Sox, the Racine [Wisconsin] Belles and the Kenosha [Wisconsin] Comets, squared off during the league's 108-game schedule. Attendance that year was 176,000 which, according to one source, meant the league was "drawing a higher percentage of the population [in league cities] than major-league baseball ever did in its greatest attendance years." (AAGPBL teams were located in communities with populations ranging from 50,000 to 150,000.) In 1944 the Milwaukee Chicks and Minneapolis Millerettes joined the league (neither team lasted more than one season) and attendance soared to 259,000 for a 152-game schedule.

Wrigley's idea to provide wartime entertainment to the American public was a resounding success and the AAGPBL continued to flourish after the war. Attendance figures climbed year after year, reaching a peak in 1948 when the league's 10 teams drew almost 1,000,000 fans. League cities fell in love with their teams and their players. Sportswriters in these communities devoted as much attention to AAGPBL teams as was given to major league teams in other cities. At least one city, Racine, introduced live, play-by-play coverage of its team's games on the radio.

The success of the AAGPBL goes beyond its emphasis on the femininity of its players. While a few prospective players were turned away for being "too uncouth, too hard-boiled or too masculine," league scouts signed some of the premier female athletes in the country. Every player in the AAGPBL was a top-notch athlete. Many were veterans of championship school, community or industry softball teams and some, like Wilma Briggs, Glenna Sue Kidd, Mary Lou Studnicka and Sarah Jane Ferguson, had even played on boys' or men's baseball teams.

It is impossible in this article to give an adequate recounting of the tremendous skills of the AAGPBL players. Just as men's baseball had its Babe Ruths and Ty Cobbs, women's baseball had its standouts as well; women like Jean Faut, who pitched her way to three pitching championships, hurling two perfect games in the process, and Joanne Weaver, who won three consecutive batting titles from 1952–1954, amassing a .429 average in 1954.

Contemporary articles about the league are filled with comments about the superb playing abilities of the players. Sophie Kurys was dubbed "Tina Cobb" by one sportswriter for her ability to steal bases like the great Ty Cobb. (Kurys averaged over 100 stolen bases per season and swiped a phenomenal 201 bases in 1946. She was thrown out only twice in 203 attempts that year.)

The baseball expertise of AAGPBL players can be attributed, in part, to the men who taught them the finer points of the game. Many of the AAGPBL managers were experienced professional ball players; some, like Bill Wambsganss (the only player to achieve an unassisted triple play in a World Series), Max Carey, Jimmy Foxx, and Dave Bancroft, were legends.

Despite enjoying great support from fans and the press for many years, the AAGPBL eventually folded in 1954. League historians and former players have offered a number of explanations for the league's demise, ranging from the resurgence of men's major league baseball after the war, to a change in the AAGPBL management system which saw the individual team owners taking over the league and drastically cutting publicity and recruiting budgets. The most significant factor in the league's final collapse was probably the advent of television. League teams had always been sponsored on a non-profit basis by local communities (any profits made were used in the communities for special projects and charity work), but once television arrived on the American scene, it became harder for communities to maintain fan interest and keep their teams out of debt. Many men's minor league teams failed during this same period as television began broadcasting major league games to a wider audience.

Some effort was made to sustain interest in women's professional baseball after 1954. When the league folded Bill Allington, a team manager, took a selected group of players on a cross-country barnstorming tour. The women played 90 games in 107 days against a host of men's teams. The venture enjoyed some success and was repeated in 1956 when the players travelled throughout the North and West playing 65 games in 88 days. By 1957, however, women's professional baseball was breathing its last gasps. Jean (Geissinger) Harding and Fran Janssen related the tribulations of the travelling team: "endless hours on the road, cheap motels, living out of a suitcase; eating, sleeping and laundry done when time allowed." The glory days of women's baseball, when one million fans turned out to watch league games and when players earned good salaries and slept in fine hotels, were over.

Had the All-American Girls Professional Baseball League continued to flourish until today, this article would merely have been a chronological survey of the transformation of baseball from a male-dominated sport, to a non-gender-specific sport as occurred with games like tennis, golf and basketball. But the AAGPBL did not endure—and baseball continues to be dominated unofficially and officially by men.

Baseball has been able to maintain its status as a "man's" sport despite the number of women who have been serious baseball players. While no specific quantitative figures can be offered concerning the number of women who played baseball during the period studied, enough examples have been given to demonstrate that more women played baseball than previous literature on baseball has admitted.

One possible reason baseball is still regarded as a man's sport is that it has been identified as such far longer than sports like basketball and tennis. These sports were introduced in the United States in the late nineteenth century at a time when women were gradually being allowed more freedom to participate in athletic activities. But baseball had been dominated by men for decades prior to that and, as such, it was easier for them to maintain dominance over the game.

For years social disapproval of women competing against men was sufficient to keep most women from playing baseball, but when these social restrictions weakened, and women like Alta Weiss, Lizzie Murphy and Jackie Mitchell began competing against men, baseball's upper hierarchy resorted to written legislation to ban women from men's major and minor league professional baseball teams. This legislation was officially passed on June 21, 1952, after the Class B minor league Harrisburg Senators attempted to sign Eleanor Engle to a contract as a publicity stunt. Minor League President George Trautman and Baseball Commissioner Ford Frick moved quickly to block the attempt and succeeded in barring all women, capable or not, from organized baseball. It is impossible to predict how long the ban against women in professional baseball will stand in the face of determined efforts by women to change it.

In 1974, in the wake of a series of lawsuits, the courts ordered little league baseball to admit female players. In 1984 a women's baseball team attempted to join the Class A Florida State League—unsuccessfully for the time being. In June 1987 the first issue of *Base Woman: Darlene Mehrer's Newsletter of Women in Baseball* was published. One of Mehrer's goals is to unify efforts to challenge male domination of baseball. She abhors softball, the baseball surrogate for women, and lumps its invention in with such infamous events as the Chicago Fire, the St. Valentine's Day Massacre and the Black Sox scandal (all originated in Chicago). Mehrer's attitude is shared by many women determined to extend equal rights to the baseball diamond.

As more and more young girls play baseball on little league teams, and as more women's teams attempt to gain access to minor league circuits, baseball may well become, as basketball, tennis and golf before it, a game for either sex. It may take legal battles to break organized baseball's ban against women, but it seems quite possible that an exceptionally talented female baseball player (most likely a pitcher) will someday get the chance to prove her abilities on a men's major league team and open the door for baseball to become an accepted sport for women.

BRUCE KUKLICK

13. The Demise of the Philadelphia Athletics

By the end of the twentieth century, franchise instability and transitory ownership became a prominent feature of professional baseball. Increasingly, teams became part of larger business empires, which made it difficult for even the most dedicated fan to keep abreast of who owned them. The decision of Peter O'Malley to sell the Los Angeles Dodgers in 1998 marked the end of family-owned and -operated teams that had typified many of the most storied franchises earlier in the century. But a harbinger of this process was already apparent in the 1950s, when one of baseball's icons, Connie Mack, was forced to give up the reins of his team, the Philadelphia Athletics.

Since 1903 the same sixteen teams had played in ten cities, mostly in the northeastern quadrant of the nation. Rebounding from the effects of the Great Depression and World War II, baseball enjoyed an unparalleled popularity and prosperity in the euphoric postwar period. With pent-up savings in hand, fans flocked to the ballparks and were treated to some of baseball's greatest heroes, returning from the service. Moreover, several close pennant races, two of which required one-game playoffs, and many games played under lights stimulated the interest. Unthinkable in earlier years, in 1948 the Cleveland Indians drew 78,382 fans to their spacious park for a night game pitched by a black man, Satchel Paige.

Such prosperity did not last long, however. By the early 1950s the major leagues were in trouble again. Basic demographic shifts resulted in decaying inner cities and exploding suburbs. The automobile and improved arterial roads made it easier to head out of town than to drive back into the old neighborhood to watch a game. Even if one decided to attend a game, the problems of finding parking and encountering street rowdies in order to purchase uncomfortable seats in a dilapidated stadium proved a daunting experience that one did not often repeat. A great many other leisure pursuits became available to attract the recreational dollar, and, of course, television threatened the ballpark just as it did the movie theater. Declining attendance especially affected cities that hosted two teams. As a relatively small city, St. Louis had chronic problems supporting its two teams, and the Cardinals under Branch Rickey's guidance had built a dynasty second only to the Yankees. The Browns were doomed. In Philadelphia it had been the Athletics who had traditionally dominated the allegiance of the city's fans rather than the lowly Phillies. Indeed, Connie Mack had produced more American League championships by mid-century than any team except the Yankees. Moreover, he had proven adept at surviving in tough times. While modern-day owners such as Charlie Finley or Wayne Huizenga have been excoriated for emasculating championship teams, it is often forgotten that Mack did it not only once but twice. During the Federal League challenge, he sold or traded his high-priced players, including his famed $100,000 infield. During the Depression he unloaded key parts of a team that had beaten the Yankees' "Murderers' Row" for three straight years.

Bruce Kuklick examines the forces, personal as well as structural, that combined to topple one of the game's legendary franchises. In doing so, he provides insight into the growing irrelevance of fan allegiance and the growing complexity of operating a major league franchise.

The 1950s began an era of change for baseball tradition as franchises shifted for the first time in over a century and expanded to the south and west. Many patriarchal sports businesses crumbled. A simple pattern emerged as the weaker team in the two-team cities moved elsewhere. The Browns left St. Louis, the Braves left Boston, the Giants and Dodgers left New York. This essay analyzes the forces at work in the departure from Philadelphia of the American League Athletics in 1954. The A's were in many respects a much less beloved franchise than, for example, the New York teams, but they were also exceptional in some ways. Their longtime manager and owner, Connie Mack, was the most famous figure in professional sports. Although by the 1950s he had not produced a winner for two decades, he had earlier been responsible for two of the great baseball dynasties, his teams of 1910–1914 and 1927–1932.

From 1901, financial direction of the A's had rested in the hands of baseball manufacturer Benjamin Shibe. He owned 50 percent of the stock, the franchise and, in 1909, put up the cash to build Shibe Park, the first concrete-and-steel stadium, to house the club. In 1913, Mack became a co-owner, but Shibe and members of his family continued to run "the front office," while Mack was premier on the field. When Shibe died in 1922, the Shibe interest in the A's passed into the hands of his four children but primarily to his two sons, Tom and Jack. They continued to run the business while Mack managed the team. Tom Shibe performed ceremonial duties during his father's later years and was president from 1922 until his death in 1936. His younger brother Jack, always in charge of the money, briefly became president, but Mack took over at the beginning of 1937, shortly before Jack's death. Mack bought Jack's share of the Athletics from his widow and, with this block of stock, controlled the A's and Shibe Park for the first time, although the Shibes still had considerable holdings in the franchise.

Mack set about dividing his shares among his heirs. He first married in 1887, and his wife had three children before her death in 1892. Mack had long thought that the two sons from this marriage, Roy and Earle, would carry on the business. Earle had played with the A's for a short while and managed in the minor leagues before assisting his dad, sitting next to his father on the Shibe Park bench. Connie assumed he would serve as manager, while Roy, like the Shibes in the earlier period, would run the front office where he had been for some time.

Connie, however, had married again in 1910, eighteen years after the death of his first wife. He had five children by his second spouse, including a son, Connie, Jr., some twenty years younger than his stepbrothers. Because the father had laid his plans when Connie, Jr. was a child, Connie, Sr. did not know how his youngest son would fit into the business. In the 1930s, however, the young man began to devote himself to the club's concessions, then becoming an essential part of the franchise. Connie, Sr. envisioned the three male heirs ruling the franchise in concert.

To this end he split his majority holdings. He kept a block of shares for himself, and apportioned the rest among his wife and his three male children, giving nothing to his four surviving daughters. Perhaps having in mind the Shibe stock, which Ben Shibe's daughters partly owned, Mack did not want the affairs of the club "muddled." He would not include a group of women in ownership. The club, Mack said, would go to his sons so that "the name of Mack," "the House of Mack," would go on.

His wife had other ideas. Mack's plan would empower Roy and Earle, the surviving children of the first marriage. The second Mrs. Mack proposed that her husband distribute stock in equal shares to her, to each of her five children (four of whom were female), to Roy, to Earle, and to the children of Mack's deceased daughter from his first marriage. Controlling interest in the club would go not to the men but to the family of the second marriage (and, indeed, to the ladies).

So adamant was Katherine Mack that the couple finally separated, her husband leaving the house when they could not agree. Mack, well over eighty, had his humiliating estrangement become public knowledge in the winter and spring of 1946 and 1947. The couple were reconciled after several months, although Connie did not compromise on the stock allocation. The feud, however, was just the sort of family quarrel Mack wanted to avoid.

Undistinguished men, Roy and Earle lived in the shadow of their father. Roy was a mediocre executive, given to talking too much. Earle was better known as his father's field lieutenant, but seemed without motivation of his own. The older brothers fought between themselves "like cats and dogs," one observer said, but a generational bond and a lengthy baseball association that antedated Mack's second family united them. Their stepmother's plan crystalized an alliance between the two. Connie, Jr. and his mother needed allies and turned to the Shibe heirs, who among themselves owned some 40 percent of the Athletics' stock. Now failing, Connie, Sr. was unwilling or unable to settle disputes between the first family and the second family *cum* "Shibe faction."

The prosperity of the postwar period initially masked the problems of the franchise. Baseball attendance soared. Before World War Two, 10 million patrons for all of major league baseball signaled a banner year. In 1946, however, attendance climbed to 18.5 million, and topped 20 million in 1948 and 1949. The Philadelphia franchises profited. In 1946, over 600,000 saw the A's, in 1947 and 1948 over 900,000, and in 1949 over 800,000.

The crowds compared to those in the great twenties era of Athletics prosperity. Connie, Jr. in particular seems to have wanted to move the franchise more surely in the direction of the most successful major league clubs and wished for new managerial and promotional skills for the A's. His brothers, however, were determined to let the fortunes of the franchise rest on the enormous prestige of their father.

From the 1930s, the public doted on Mack, "the Grand Old Man of Baseball" or "Mr. Baseball." His birthdays at Shibe Park occasioned yearly celebrations sponsored by local sports commentators. Writers and players spoke of him—and to him—as "Mr. Mack." Writing in the *Atlantic Monthly* in 1940, John R. Tunis described Mack as "an institution," "the first citizen of Philadelphia." During the war, American G.I.s trapped disguised German soldiers passing through their lines by asking if they'd heard that "Connie Mack pitched a shutout against Brooklyn." What American wouldn't know this was nonsense? In rare disputes on the field, umpires would respectfully come over to the dugout for discussion with the old manager. Later, in the early TV age, when Mack might view a game from his office, A's officials would bluff umps by saying that the elderly owner had seen a play on television and disagreed with the ruling. Mack was, said one analyst, "one of the most popular figures sports has ever known . . . unique in the game's annals."

But this public approbation could not hide from insiders, and in time from the fans, the deterioration of Mack's mind. In 1946, he traded future Hall of Fame third baseman George Kell to the Detroit Tigers. Wish Egan, who made the deal, stated that "I was a little ashamed of myself for taking advantage of the old man." On the field players would ignore incorrect signals, or the coaches would overrule obvious mistakes. "My goodness, yes," Mack would say in acknowledgment. Things got worse. His memory failed, and by the late forties he would call out the names of stars of bygone days—Baker! Foxx!—to pinch-hit.

Sportswriters commented euphemistically on these "mental lapses," and Mack refused to quit. "If I did," he said, "I'd die in two weeks." In a widely read and sympathetic article in *Life* magazine in 1948, Bob Considine wrote that both players and coaches noted their manager's errors of judgment. The same year, Mack exploded in public and fired pitcher Nelson Potter in front of the dugout as he came off the mound. He now occasionally broke into stormy emotions, reduced to tears. The manager was "off the beam." Historian David Voigt described him as "an anachronism." Mack's downward slide and the disagreements within his family, wrote a commentator, began to accustom fans "to sudden, sometimes calamitous moves." All sorts of people now knew of his senility.

At the same time Mack constructed a curiously interesting postwar team, assembling draftees, waiver players, and promising youngsters. In 1945 and 1946 they finished last. Yet in 1947, 1948, and even 1949, these bargain-counter discoveries, though they wound up only fifth, fourth, and fifth, respectively, were in the thick of the American League race for much of the season, collapsing in August and September as their lack of reserve strength became critical. To some extent their modest prowess accounted for the high attendance. Nonetheless, Mack overestimated their talents as well as his ability to make up for their deficiencies by clever strategy.

The year 1950 was Mack's fiftieth as A's manager. He was 87, but baseball in April is a siren, and the spring of the sport is a season of eternal youth. Should Mack retire? He would not. His team had shown some mettle, and, as one writer put it, "The will o' the wisp that danced ahead each spring" captivated the old man. Mack would manage, and he predicted a pennant for his "Ath-l-etics." Roy and Earle agreed, and overrode the doubts of their younger brother. The *Elephant Trail,* the A's newsletter, expected the club's attendance to pass the million mark for the first time. The magazine also urged fans to send in ideas to boost the gate to that figure, but asserted that patrons would come out because the A's would be contending for the pennant and because Mack would be receiving nationwide honors throughout the season. Honoring Mack's golden anniversary as manager, a motorcade from City Hall to the park began the festivities on opening day.

Things went downhill from there. The year proved disastrous as the A's tumbled deep into the second division and stayed there. Bill Veeck was asked if a rumored purchase of the A's involved him, "They haven't got a ball club," he said. "All you get is the ball park." In June, the family's internal squabbling, intensified by bad baseball, became more serious and more public. The youngest son and the Shibes failed in their attempt to force Mack's retirement, but they did succeed in removing the nondescript Earle as assistant manager. Voting his faction's stock against his father for the first time, Connie, Jr. made his brother take a job with the franchise's farm system.

The crisis came later in the 1950 season when the A's were in last place. The youngest son agreed to a plan that would permit Roy and Earle to buy out the other shareholders. If they could not come up with the money, Connie, Jr. had the right to buy them out. In either event, the senior Mack would remain as titular head.

Both sides competed to raise money. Local businessmen wanted to buy stock in the team. The newspapers reported that Phillies' owner Bob Carpenter refused a half-interest in Shibe Park and its concessions. Connie, Jr. talked to James Clark, president of the Philadelphia Eagles football team, and the press said that wealthy builder John McShain wanted a piece of the franchise.

Roy and Earle triumphed. They needed approximately $1.75 million to buy the 60 percent of the stock of the other side. To finance the transaction, the brothers took a portentous step: they mortgaged Shibe Park, the franchise's single real asset.

Appraisers valued the park at $436,000 and the land at $250,000. But the stadium made money, including a $40,000 rental from the Eagles and 10 cents per head from the Phillies' gates, which in 1950 would generate more than $100,000. Concessions were also important. "Following a careful analysis of the value of Shibe Park and its earnings record," Connecticut General Life Insurance Company issued Roy and Earle a $1.75 million loan over ten years. In addition to the mortgage on the park, the A's turned over to Connecticut General the rent they got from the Phillies. A representative of the insurance company joined the A's board. To raise more cash, Roy and Earle leased the concessions, no longer run by Connie Jr., to Jacobs Brothers, a pioneer food service organization.

These steps changed the club's business. Concessions made big profits and had expanded beyond Shibe Park; a separate Athletics corporation sold wares at the ballpark, at the stadium of Temple University, and at other places. Now the A's got a pared-down amount from concessions at the same time they gave to Connecticut General some of their other income. Thus, in mortgaging Shibe Park, Roy and Earle took on an interest burden— of $250,000 a year—at a time when their cash flow was declining. Much hung on the elder brothers' ability to draw people to Shibe Park. The A's had based their 1950 budget on 800,000 admissions, from which they estimated earnings of $800,000. But when Roy and Earle took over in August, the A's were thirty-five games out of first, "locked in a death battle," the *Bulletin* wrote, "with the St. Louis Browns for last place." The A's won, finishing eighth and drawing 310,000 fans, 500,000 off their budgeted number, 700,000 off the million patrons they had wished for.

To add insult to injury, Bob Carpenter's Phillies won the first Philadelphia pennant in twenty years, drawing over 1,200,000. Part of the A's problem, though not the Phillies', was that baseball attendance began to slacken in 1950 after the postwar rush and did not stop declining until the latter part of the decade. The consequences for the A's were dire. At the end of the season, the Athletics were deeply in debt and mortgaged to the hilt.

The most knowledgeable commentator on the family's fortunes wrote that Roy and Earle forced Connie's retirement in October of 1950. As the abysmal year unfolded, patrons proclaimed with Connie Mack, Jr. that the senior Mack should go. In the seventeen years prior to 1950, the A's had finished in the first division only once. "He should know the parade has passed him by," said one. "Why doesn't he step down and give a younger man a chance?" Philadelphians voted with their feet. Roy and Earle totaled the books and recognized that their younger brother had been right. Their father must retire: "the fans would never be content with any other move."

Sportswriters who had snickered in private about Mack's failings now flooded newspapers and magazines with platitudes about the octogenarian manager. Only the communist *Daily Worker* criticized Mack, a fact that highlighted the vapidity of sports journalism.

The franchise was sick, but the elder Mack brothers tried to restore its health. Connie remained the nominal president, and Roy and Earle did everything they could to capitalize on his name. In 1951, they opened the Elephant Room under the park's first base stands. The Macks wanted to attract "baseball men," and filled it with memorabilia from the A's great days. To replace Mack as manager, the older sons appointed the popular Philadelphia figure Jimmie Dykes, a stalwart of the dynasty of the twenties and early thirties. Arthur Ehlers, a savvy baseball executive, took over as general manager. In 1951, marginally better results occurred as the A's came in sixth, but then in 1952 they finished a surprising fourth and drew over 600,000. As Roy Mack later commented, however, the middling prosperity of the team did not depend on management. Robert Clayton Shantz made the A's solvent.

"Little Bobby" Shantz was a left-handed pitcher, 5'6", 140 pounds. Born in Pottstown, Pennsylvania, he played semipro ball after the war in the Frankford section of Philadelphia. In the late 1940s, he recalled, for the price of "maybe a few car tokens to Shibe Park and home," he signed with the A's. In 1949 and 1950 he compiled mediocre statistics, and labored under Connie Mack's suspicion that he was too small to win. In 1951, however, Shantz displayed real ability and compiled an 18–10 record under Dykes' management. The next year he won twenty-four games and lost only seven; the American League named him its Most Valuable Player.

Shantz was a likable and modest young man whose "diminutive stature," as the sportswriters put it, gained him the affection of fans everywhere, but particularly those in Philadelphia. Ray Kelly of the Philadelphia *Bulletin* wrote:

Atop the Shibe Park pitching tee
the village hero stands . . .
the shrimp has muscles in his arms
as tough as rubber bands.

The Year the Yankees Lost the Pennant, later made into the hit musical "Damn Yankees," was an early 1950s novel about middle-aged Joe Boyd, who signs a baseball pact with the devil. Set in the then future of 1958, the novel has Boyd win the pennant for the Washington Senators. In one scene at Shibe Park, Washington faces Shantz in "the late afternoon of a great career." In the ninth inning, Boyd homers over the right field wall to ruin "the diminutive portsider's" no-hitter and win the game for the Senators. But Shantz is such an icon that Boyd spends a miserable, sleepless night turning over what he has done.

Shantz' crowds in Philadelphia in 1952 averaged almost 18,000. When he didn't pitch, the A's drew less than 8,000. His sixteen Shibe Park appearances accounted for almost 44 percent of the Athletics' home gate. In the 1952 All-Star game at Shibe Park, Shantz pitched the fifth inning against the National League and struck out the side: Whitey Lockman, Jackie Robinson, and Stan Musial. The "hometown crowd," said Shantz, cheered as if he had won a World Series game. Then, the inning over, the umps called the game because of rain. The rain-out left the city's fans believing that Shantz would have gone on to duplicate or overshadow Carl Hubbell's 1934 All-Star feat of striking out five batters in a row. Later in 1952, on August 5, Shantz won his twentieth victory before a packed Shibe Park audience. The *Inquirer* editorialized that the triumph brought to "countless Philadelphians" "the comfortable assurance that no matter what else was happening, the world was a pretty good place to live in. Something about Shantz moved thousands to have some minor part in the occasion." The editorial concluded that "there'll not be another such time in Philadelphia for many days."

The *Inquirer* was right. Shantz won four more games, and then, in late September, a pitched ball fractured his wrist. He never again had a winning record in the city. In 1953 the A's dropped to seventh place and drew 362,000; in 1954 they were last with 305,000. If only Shantz had stayed healthy, said Roy Mack later, the club would have remained in the black. After a few years of precarious profits, Roy and Earle Mack were broke once more.

The problem, again, was not just the team but more family squabbling that hurt the franchise in public. Allied so long as they competed with Connie, Jr. and the Shibes, the elder brothers now feuded openly. When Earle and his wife separated, he moved into the small suite that the franchise provided for him off the A's clubhouse in the stadium. Still in charge of the front office, Roy turned the water off so that his brother could not bathe or use the toilet. They sniped at one another from two different Shibe Park offices, to and from which reporters scurried in their quest for stories.

As early as the fall of 1951, after they took over, the brothers denied tales they would sell the team. In truth, however, only Roy wanted to stay. In the middle of the poor 1953 season, he countered rumors of a sale by saying "we have been here for fifty-two years and will be here for fifty-two more"; the club was "part of Philadelphia . . . as much a part of the community as Fairmount Park." But Earle wanted to get out. The brothers never had a united front, and conflicting stories attributed to their father worsened the situation. By the fall of 1953, lack of money and internal strife troubled the Macks; pressure also came from the American League. The A's tiny attendance affected the receipts visiting clubs got from trips to Philadelphia, and other owners demanded change. The powerful voice of the Yankees pushed for the transfer of the A's to Kansas City, where New York had a farm club.

At the start of the 1954 season, knowledgeable sportsmen talked about the A's debts and their failure to meet their Shibe Park mortgage. Then, in the middle of June, the Macks advised Philadelphia Mayor Joseph Clark that they would have to sell or shift the franchise unless the A's attendance leaped dramatically. Roy and Earle hoped that they could turn public feeling to the A's advantage, but the mayor was an insubstantial friend.

Clark was not really interested in baseball, and professional sports in the city held a low priority for him. He did form a "Save the A's" committee. But it had 100 members and fifteen subcommittees. In his July announcement, the mayor also said that he personally rooted for the Phillies and that he was "no socialist"—government would not subsidize sports. Clark vaguely thought that his committee might come up with some long-term solutions to the A's woes. But publicists immediately attempted to encourage more people to turn out to the park. The Macks needed 550,000 patrons to earn the money to meet their obligations and stay in the city. The committee tried to boost attendance for the remaining games.

As "Save the A's" mobilized its forces, the newspapers asked Philadelphians to express their views. The torrential response surprised the papers and yielded arresting insights into the fans' minds.

Appropriately enough, a few letter writers recalled better days. "As a small boy," said one, "we saw the opening of Shibe Park, and we remember the fans, like swarming bees clinging to the outside of summer trolleys." "I learned to love baseball and the A's as a boy following Connie Mack's great team of 1929–32," said another, "I don't want the A's to move from Philadelphia." "Save the team," wrote still another, "that so often brought a thrill of pride in being a Philadelphian"; "it would be like losing something very dear. . . ." The most poignant mail noted how significant baseball was "for the kids." "My son is an A's fan," wrote one father now too ill to go to the park. "I took him to his first game when he was five years old to see Babe Ruth. The future of all things are in children."

More often, however, letters displayed the rage and frustration that loyal rooters felt about the Athletics. For the first time the public alluded to the park and the neighborhood. The *Inquirer* reported that parking stirred "bitter complaints." Driving to the stadium "exhausted" patrons. One said, "Get out of that undesirable neighborhood and get a bigger home, where parking will be no problem." Fans wanted "spacious acreage"; motorists did not want to endure "intimidation" or "gangster mob damage" to their cars. Inside the stadium, they demanded "modernistic improvements," escalators, better lighting, roomier seats, more restrooms, and drinking fountains. Finally, fans complained about the concessions, angry about the "ridiculous" price of hotdogs and soda.

To the extent that the stadium and its community were the main issue, Mayor Clark did not help. The city at this time was collecting land and generating construction capital for projects that would revitalize Philadelphia's industrial base and central business district; and other towns interested in the Athletics—Kansas City, Minneapolis, and San Francisco— proposed bond issues to finance new playing fields. But Clark did not think that such bond issues should assist sports facilities. Although he came to accept the principle, he evinced little enthusiasm.

In any event, the stadium was not the main issue. As the A's public relations director asked: if parking kept people away from the A's, why didn't they desert the Phillies (who were drawing twice the fans)? Letters emphasized that the real problem was the Macks and the teams they fielded. "Get rid of the Macks," said the letters. Connie Mack had "surrendered to the years" and a new generation could not "rest on memories" or listen to "sentimental drivel about . . . past glories." The Mack dynasty had "overstayed its welcome by about twenty years." For the preceding two decades, the Macks had run "a bush league circus." One man wrote that he was "tired of watching a franchise made up of second-string ball players . . ."; another said the Macks had done little "to earn the fans' support," consistently fielding second-division teams and selling off good players. Under Bob Carpenter, said one writer, "the Phillies' star" had risen and Philadelphians need not accept the Macks' "take it or lump it" attitude. To the Macks' repeated statement that fans "will not support a winning team," wrote one exasperated rooter, let them compare "the cellar years to the pennant years." "The Macks," concluded one perceptive citizen, "are on the same path as all venerable one-man family businesses." "Family expansion" proves ruinous. A disgruntled father who had faithfully gone to see the A's through thick and thin and had made fans of his children was more blunt: "Roy and Earle Mack ain't worth a shit."

These sentiments affected the "Save the A's" campaign. In early July, the club needed a turnout of 13,000 per game, as opposed to the approximately 6,000 it was then drawing. But as each home date passed with much ballyhoo in the papers, the average draw required for the remaining games climbed as a mere three, four, or five thousand patrons turned out. By the end of July "Save the A's" neared collapse. The committee reported apathy to the franchise in the business community. The Mack family had "a public relations problem to solve," and "a struggle in the family for power" accentuated the problem. The Macks rejected the committee's advice that well-to-do sportsmen be permitted to buy into the franchise and that the team search for playing talent.

Although the Macks did not help in their particular case, the willingness of American cities to aid the baseball clubs they already had was minimal. Urban areas without franchises easily stirred up the civic pride and public funding necessary to entice teams. This combination was equally necessary to rescue existing enfeebled clubs, but it was not forthcoming. Early on in the debate over the A's, the *Bulletin's* Hugh Brown analyzed the club's "deep-rooted" miseries. The stadium needed "a complete refurbishing" inside, and outside "swifter and more direct transit" and "extensive parking." In examining the Athletics' specific problems, Brown said that "no city, no matter how large and charitable, can be whipped or cajoled into supporting a team that has finished in the cellar eight times in the last thirteen years."

In early August, Chicago businessman Arnold Johnson, who was connected to the Yankee farm team in Kansas City, offered to buy the A's for about $3.375 million and move them to Kansas City. As completed in early November, the deal paid the three Macks, Connie, Sr., Earle, and Roy, about $1.5 million. In addition, Johnson assumed the team's debt, estimated between $400,000 and $800,000, mainly to the Jacobs Brothers concessionaires who had taken over park sales and lent the Macks money. Finally, Johnson liquidated the stadium mortgage, standing at about $1.2 million. The A's had paid off $500,000 of the mortgage, but at the cost of indebting themselves to the vendors.

The transfer of the franchise honored the ability of baseball capitalists to profit from the American commitment to the sport. One cannot help but remark on the contrast between the attractive power of the game for millions of ordinary people and the avarice and imperfection of those who controlled it. What is striking is not that the institutions of baseball were part of an acquisitive society, but that in the affection of fans the game transcended American culture. Roy and Earle Mack took over a weak franchise in 1950 for $2,000 a share. In four years they had run it into the ground, dismissed advice that might have helped them, and demanded that someone else save them. Assisted by a spiritless Mayor Clark, however, their incompetence was self-serving. When they sold out to Johnson, they did so at an effective price of $2,250 a share.

Arnold Johnson's even greater gain demonstrated adeptness at joining civic pride to his real estate manipulation of the Philadelphia and Kansas City ballparks, the latter of which was Johnson's major asset. He purchased the Philadelphia A's with little or no outlay of cash. Stock in the new club paid off Roy Mack. Connie Mack's money came from Johnson's sale of the minor league Kansas City park, to Kansas City. (The city rebuilt the facility to major league standards and leased it back to Johnson.) The new franchise's profits gradually liquidated what the A's owed to Jacobs Brothers.

Bob Carpenter of the Phillies put up the cash in the transaction. After a series of negotiations he bought Shibe Park for $1.7 million. The money satisfied the mortgage on the ballpark and paid off Earle Mack. Carpenter recalled that Johnson was a slick speculator getting by on the skin of his teeth. He picked up the Athletics' franchise on the strength of Kansas City's willingness to underwrite a major league baseball team.

In the summer of 1954, before Johnson made his purchase, Carpenter said he did not want "to buy the park under any circumstances." He let it be known that the stadium was a dubious real estate investment and elaborately looked for land for a new field in West Philadelphia that would have 6,000 parking spaces. No one, said Carpenter, could renovate the present stadium: it would cost $1 million to modernize, and enlarging the seating was impossible. At one point, when it looked as if the A's sale would not go through, he said that purchasing a stadium had not interested him but that he "wouldn't have had any alternative."

The Phillies were leasing the field until 1957, which gave them a short breathing period, and apparently Johnson suggested a new lease. It called for 20 cents a head rental, double the old rate, plus payment of maintenance expenses that the A's had previously carried. Staying in the park without buying would be very expensive. In addition, the value of Carpenter's franchise would leap if the Athletics left. If Johnson would not take the Athletics unless Carpenter bought Shibe Park, was it worth sabotaging the move? He did not covet a ballpark but had few options. Indeed, the price of the property was just what Connecticut General figured four years before, appraising the site as valuable and income-producing. Later, as part of the franchise shift, Carpenter bought the property from the Philadelphia American League franchise.

Johnson's initial offer to the Macks energized Philadelphia business and sports leaders. Harry Sylk, head of the Sun Ray Drugs, pointed out that "What we stand to lose is not only the A's but the whole American League." Prominent realtor Albert M. Greenfield added that the "loss of the team would be a blow to Philadelphia's prestige."

In August and September of 1954, before the transaction with Johnson was concluded, various local businessmen tried to purchase the Athletics. They focused on Roy Mack, a weak man who yet seemed determined to keep the team in Philadelphia, as opposed to Earle, who saw no alternative to leaving. No Philadelphia plans had panned out, however, when the American League owners approved the sale of the franchise to Kansas City in mid-October. But Roy Mack wasn't sure. The day before the deal was final, the Macks sold the A's to a local syndicate. Two weeks later, amid a flurry of rumors, charges, and countercharges by various members of the Mack family—including Connie Mack and his wife—the American League met again in New York and vetoed the move to keep the A's in Philadelphia. Led again by the Yankees and conscious of their profits, the owners turned down a plea from Connie Mack himself, whom a chauffeur had taken up from Philadelphia. "The Grand Old Man" was a useful symbol for the sports entrepreneurs, but not a person to listen to in his dotage. Sentiment did not govern the League; the Kansas City move stood.

Ten days later, a remnant of the rejected syndicate raced Johnson to the senior Macks' Germantown apartment to buy Connie's share of the club. Apparently this group wanted to obtain his stock and force the American League to keep the Athletics in Philadelphia. Whether such a move would have worked is doubtful, but it did not as Mack refused four proffered checks from the locals in favor of a single check and some talk from Johnson. "There must be some less excruciating way to spend money," said one of the rejected principals, "than trying to buy the A's." In the end, all the Macks broke down and wept.

New York Times columnist Art Daley wrote that Connie Mack "gave Philadelphia fans a pride in the Athletics. Without him there is nothing left but a dwindling force of habit." The new Athletics spent thirteen years in Kansas City before they picked up again for Oakland, California. Although they drew large crowds and profited their owners, the A's in the midwest performed worse than they had in their last twenty years in Philadelphia. The Kansas City A's were nicknamed the "Yankee Farm Club," as Johnson scandalously traded with his patrons in New York. The transfer assisted the dominance of the Yankees through the 1950s but also upped the league's income.

The removal finally sealed the triumph of New York over Philadelphia during that part of the century when they were the two preeminent American cities. In defeating John McGraw's Giants in the second decade of the century and in battling (sometimes successfully) the Yankees of Ruth and Gehrig, the A's established Philadelphia's credentials as an urban competitor of New York. But by the time the Yankees swept the Phillies in the World Series of 1950, Philadelphia was less significant. The transformation of the A's into a midwestern affiliate of New York ended an era of great rivalry between the two towns. New York writers had good reason for their comfortable, smug feeling that the transfer was an unmixed blessing.

Back in Philadelphia in early 1955, two trucks carried off memorabilia to Kansas City from the Elephant Room at the stadium. Johnson planned to display them for a couple of years. For the time being, Connie Mack was driven to and from his old tower office with the benign consent of Bob Carpenter. But Mack was going downhill rapidly and died just over a year later.

Another, less noticed, death more fully embodied the minor tragedy of the Philadelphia Athletics in the 1950s. "Yits" Crompton lived in the neighborhood of the ballpark and came to the stadium as an A's batboy when he was fourteen. Later he was a fixture as clubhouse custodian. He followed the new A's to Kansas City in 1955 but returned to his old community a year later, disconsolate and unemployed. On August 23, 1956, he hung himself in his home around the corner from Shibe Park. He left a note: "I can't get baseball out of my life."

Some time afterwards, two years before his own death, Roy Mack reminisced: "People always say to me 'I wish the A's were still at 21st and Lehigh.'" Years later many old-time fans agreed when they tried to puzzle out how Philadelphia lost the franchise of the $100,000 infield and of Al Simmons, Jimmie Foxx, Lefty Grove, and Mickey Cochrane and got stuck with the Phillies, perhaps the worst franchise in baseball.

14. More Legacy of Conquest: Long-Term Ramifications of the Major League Baseball Shift to the West

One of the dominant features of baseball outside the lines during the last half of the twentieth century was the fact that the game became a pawn in a competition between widely disparate elements. Sports entrepreneurs, politicians, developers, urban planners, super-agents, and media empires, among others, have sought to use the game for their own purposes. For their part, of course, the clubs have often been willing accomplices. Perhaps the best indicator of this complicity was the expansion of the major leagues beginning in 1961; it came on the heels of the franchise shifts that had begun during the previous decade. One could argue that such expansion, which saw the major league teams nearly double in thirty years, provided one of the great business and entertainment success stories of the period. Baseball became truly a national game for the first time in its history as the leagues were courted by communities from coast to coast.

Using the proposition that "If you build a stadium, we will come," or "If you do not, we will leave," the owners and would-be owners launched an unparalleled raid on the public coffers of America's major metropolitan areas, including many of the newly arrived communities created by the dynamic demographic changes that had occurred in postwar America. All too often franchise moves were made as a result of perceived political challenges from Washington threatening baseball's exemption from antitrust laws, or they were expedient responses to financial offers of lucrative tax subsidies and broadcast revenues that were too good for baseball's self-centered moguls to refuse. A classic case of doing the right thing for all the wrong

Dodger Stadium, Los Angeles, CA. Courtesy of Los Angeles Dodgers, Inc. Photo by John Cordes. © 1993 Los Angeles Dodgers.

reasons, franchise hopping and expansion were made with little long-term planning or consideration of their impact. The result was a period of increased tension off the field between the various affected parties in an environment fundamentally different from earlier times. Yet, ironically enough, such difficulties were played out against a backdrop of unparalleled prosperity for the game. Unimaginable player salaries, record-breaking attendance figures, a wave of new stadium construction, and spiraling franchise valuations seem to attest to the game's basic health. Critics have derided the use of public funds that subsidize a few millionaires at the expense of civic projects that could benefit many people. But they have been most often swept aside by waves of public enthusiasm for seeing a community labeled a major league city.

Using the approaches of the "new western historians," Ron Briley examines the issue of franchise expansion, especially the westward expansion of the 1960s. By examining the motivation for such movement, as well as its consequences, he identifies complexities and implications that challenge the popular perception about expansion. Clearly, baseball is not immune to the law of unintended consequences.

In an April 2, 1995, article for the *New York Times Magazine*, veteran sportswriter Robert Lipsyte bemoaned the loss of traditional American values in baseball. Lipsyte argued that the ideas championed in the sport— "honoring boundaries, playing by the rules, working together for a common goal, submitting to authority"—were the characteristics that had allowed Americans to conquer the Western frontier. Obviously irritated by the 1994–1995 major league baseball players' strike, Lipsyte concluded that the changes in baseball, such as the shifting of franchises and free agency, "have made it impossible to count on a player, a team, an entire league still being around for next year's comeback. The connection between player and fan has been irrevocably destabilized, for love and loyalty demand a future. Along the way, those manly virtues of self-discipline, responsibility, altruism, and dedication seem to have been deleted from the athletic contract with America."

It is worthy of note that in his jeremiad, Lipsyte uses the imagery of the American frontier. Like Frederick Jackson Turner in his frontier thesis, Lipsyte perceives the Western experience as the embodiment of the traditional American values of progress and improvement. Many American scholars would certainly agree with Lipsyte's perspective. In *The American West in the Twentieth Century,* Gerald D. Nash maintains that for much of the century, the American West "has been ahead of the rest of the nation by about one generation." In support of his conclusion, Nash points to the emergence of a consumer-oriented economy hospitable to social dissent, the application of science and technology to modify the environment, the growth of service industries, a political cooperation between government and private business, and cultural experimentation. Seeking to tap the economic and cultural possibilities described by Nash, major league baseball executives turned to the West, establishing franchises in Los Angeles and San Francisco in 1958, followed by expansion and realignment to include Houston, Anaheim, San Diego, Seattle, Oakland, Dallas, Denver, and, in 1998, Phoenix.

While this expansion has resulted in tremendous profits, especially for the Los Angeles Dodgers and Colorado Rockies, and has brought major league baseball to millions who were long denied this opportunity by the Eastern establishment of the sport, the blessings of the Westward movement in baseball have proven to be mixed. The origins of the lack of community- and civic-mindedness among professional athletes, of which Lipsyte complains, may be found in the franchise relocations set off by the Dodgers' move from Brooklyn to Los Angeles.

A younger generation of Western historians might well have warned the lords of baseball that the Western experience is one of complexity rather than unimpeded progress. In her pioneering work *The Legacy of Conquest: The Unbroken Past of the American West,* Patricia Nelson Limerick emphasizes the American West as an epic of conquest with consequences for the conqueror and the conquered. Thus, from the perspective of the New Western History, the American West is a place where sexism, racism, exploitation of the environment, and capitalistic cycles of prosperity and recession characterize the region. Limerick asserts, "A belief in progress has been a driving force in the modern world; as a depository of enormous hopes for progress, the American West may well be the best place in which to observe the complex and contradictory outcome of that faith." Her conclusions on the broader implications of Western history may also be applicable when considering the long-term ramifications of the major league baseball shift to the West.

Seeking an El Dorado in the West, baseball ownership found lucrative financial veins to exploit. However, this expansion brought with it troubling questions that have yet to be resolved: the impact of franchise shifts on minor league operations such as the Pacific Coast League, civic loyalties to abandoned cities such as Brooklyn and Washington DC, the economic future of small markets such as Seattle, and a general loss of place, community, and time as the major league baseball map stretches across four time zones, reflecting the mobile nature of American society, which in the search for new opportunities is always in danger of losing its identity.

During the 1957 season, the Western outpost of major league baseball was Kansas City, demonstrating the Eastern domination of baseball. Indeed, stability reigned between 1903 and 1953, until the owners approved the shift of the Boston Braves to Milwaukee, followed by the move of the St. Louis Browns to Baltimore in 1954, and the realignment of the Philadelphia Athletics to Kansas City in 1955. However, the great quest for new markets and opportunities in the West was set off by the departure of the Brooklyn Dodgers and New York Giants for the greener pastures of Los Angeles and San Francisco. These franchise shifts and major league expansion were the products of demographic changes in American society as well as political pressures.

In 1951, New York Congressman Emmanuel Celler's subcommittee on monopoly investigated allegations of antitrust violations against baseball, which traditionally enjoyed antitrust exemption dating back to a 1922 Supreme Court ruling written by Oliver Wendell Holmes. Congressman Celler questioned numerous aspects of organized baseball, including the reserve clause, the "mere pittance" of a $5,000 minimum annual salary for major league players, and the failure to expand in the past 50 years despite the considerable geographical shifts in American population. However, the final report of the subcommittee paid homage to baseball as America's national pastime and extolled the democratic values of the game. And, of major significance to baseball executives, no legislative remedies for the plight of organized baseball were suggested, allowing the court's antitrust exemption to stand. However, Congressman Celler strongly urged organized baseball to take the opportunity given by the subcommittee to get its house in order. In response to critics of the sport, Baseball Commissioner Ford Frick asserted, "Baseball must resurvey itself and make territorial changes to keep pace with the economic and population shifts in this country in the last fifty years." Accordingly, the path was paved for the first franchise transfer in over 50 years, the move of the Boston Braves to the untapped Midwestern market of Milwaukee.

In 1957, with rumors circulating in the nation's press that the Dodgers and Giants might be moving West, Commissioner Frick was once again confronting the investigative powers of Congress, where bills were being introduced calling for baseball to be stripped of its antitrust exemption. Seeking to antagonize neither representatives who sought the expansion of major league baseball nor those who feared the loss of valuable franchises, Frick played the role of the careful bureaucrat, pointing out that in meetings between minor and major league executives expansion as well as reclassification of many minor league cities was under consideration. However, a wary Frick told Congress that tampering with baseball's legal status might endanger this orderly process of change. Predicting chaos if Congress interfered with baseball, Frick argued that without clear territorial rules established by organized baseball, "Clubs presumably could relocate at will and without notice or compensation to other clubs and leagues. Under these conditions, I question whether responsible persons would be willing to invest in unprotected clubs in either major league or national association cities. I am also apprehensive that, under those conditions, baseball would not be sufficiently well organized to finance and operate the players' pension plan." Frick's obfuscation and threats to renege on negotiated agreements with the players, along with the testimony of other executives and players, convinced Congress to forestall legislative action once again. But it was clear that the sport would have to expand to head off further legislative inquiry.

Demographics also reinforced Congressional demands for realignment. In the affluent post–World War II society, the West experienced unprecedented growth rates. In the 30-year period between 1945 and 1975, the population of Houston climbed from 385,000 to 1,400,000; Phoenix from 65,000 to 755,000; and San Jose from 68,000 to 446,000. And in the 1990s Texas has now surpassed New York in population, trailing only California, whose gross domestic production would make it one of the ten leading economic powers in the world. In *Power Shift: The Rise of the Southern Rim and Its Challenge to the Eastern Establishment,* Kirkpatrick Sale identified six pillars to the economic emergence of the West: agribusiness, defense spending, technology, oil, real estate, and leisure, of which sports such as baseball constituted a vital component.

Confronted with aging ballparks and urban population shifts, which reduced suburban attendance, the Giants and Dodgers decided to gamble on the growing economic prosperity of the West. As David Voigt has noted, their Westward movement "rocked the foundations of the major leagues." Efforts by Branch Rickey and William Shea to launch a third major league, the Continental League, in 1959, resulted in a compromise whereby the threat of a rival league was crushed by absorbing the more promising proposed Continental sites into the existing major league structure. Thus, in 1961, the American League added the Los Angeles Angels and Washington Senators (the original Senators had departed for Minnesota after the 1960 season), while in 1962 National League expansion brought the New York Mets and Houston Colts into the major league fold.

While certainly welcomed in the virgin territories of the West, in his history of baseball Ben Rader has demonstrated that Westward expansion was the type of mixed blessing that Patricia Limerick attributed to the Western experience. Rader observed, "By the 1950s and 1960s, baseball could no longer ignore the shifting character of leisure in American cities, the rapid growth of new metropolises, or the new technological marvel of television. In response, the big leagues moved to exploit the new population centers, embarked on a new stadium-building boom, and sought to control the dangers and capitalize on the opportunities presented by television." But an orgy of expansionism, from 16 teams playing a 154-game schedule in 1950 to 26 teams in 24 cities playing a 162-game schedule in 1990, failed to solve the problems of major league baseball. A 70 percent increase in the number of regular season games enhanced gross attendance, but per game attendance has continued "to lag proportionately to the population areas served by big league clubs," and the game has never recovered the popularity that it lost in the 1950s.

The chief architect of baseball's paradigm shift was the owner of the Brooklyn Dodgers, Walter O'Malley, who has been described as a heartless, greedy despot for abandoning Brooklyn. The devil perception of O'Malley is well developed in Peter Golenbock's *Bums,* in which the author dismisses O'Malley's complaints of declining attendance as a "red herring," pointing out that the Dodgers were the most profitable team in baseball. However, Neil J. Sullivan, in his study of the Dodger franchise relocation, paints a very different portrait of the Dodger owner. According to Sullivan, O'Malley was forced to abandon a deteriorating Ebbets Field, that he would have been willing to stay in Brooklyn if the New York City government had been more accommodating in acquiring title to land for the construction of a new stadium. Municipal and county government in Los Angeles was forthcoming, assisting O'Malley in the acquisition of Chavez Ravine where the owner built Dodger Stadium. Sullivan perceives O'Malley not as a greedy exploiter but as an opportunistic businessman who was willing to take a chance on the unproven Los Angeles market, despite court challenges and a voter initiative questioning the Chavez Ravine agreement between Los Angeles and Dodger ownership. While tears were shed in Brooklyn over what Doris Kearns Goodwin described as an "invidious act of betrayal," citizens of Southern California thronged to the vacuous Los Angeles Coliseum, exceeding two million fans in the Dodgers' pennant-winning season of 1959. In the spirit of civic boosterism, the *Los Angeles Times* celebrated the Dodger World Series triumph by editorializing,

> Their triumph is that they have created one of those centers of attachment that the Metropolitan area of Los Angeles needed so desperately. The team has made the people for a couple of hundred miles around aware that they have a common interest. A major league baseball club does not a city make, but in our agglomeration of Southern California communities any joint enterprise which excites a wide interest serves as a sort of civic glue.

The Los Angeles love affair with the Dodgers continued to grow after the opening of Dodger Stadium in 1962, with season attendance figures of over three million fans annually the norm by the mid-1980s. However, the Dodgers were not able to create a sense of community that would prevent Los Angeles from exploding in racial tension during the 1960s and 1990s.

While the Dodger exodus from Brooklyn and their love affair with Los Angeles has attracted the attention of numerous academics and journalists, the history of the Giants' move from New York to San Francisco has received far less scrutiny, perhaps because the Giants had never developed the geographical attachment to a New York City borough such as Brooklyn.

In addition, Giants' owner Horace Stoneham was often perceived as having
been duped by the crafty Walter O'Malley into abandoning New York. In
reality, Stoneham had considerable incentive in his own right for seeking
gold in California. The Polo Grounds were deteriorating, attendance had
slumped to only slightly over 600,000, and the citizens of San Francisco
pledged the construction of a new ballpark for the Giants.

Even though the Giants opened the 1958 season in the minor league
Seals Stadium, which seated fewer than 23,000 spectators, Stoneham was
able to double his home attendance. The Giants also enjoyed instant
gratification on the playing field, finishing third in 1958 and remaining in
contention for the 1959 National League pennant until the last week of the
season. Fortunately, they did not win and have to play in October, as Seals
Stadium had already been booked for a convention of the American Medical
Association. With the opening of Candlestick Park in 1960, attendance
soared to 1.8 million, a new club record. However, Candlestick Park proved
to be a somewhat cold, windy, and inhospitable site from which to witness
a baseball game, and attendance soon declined. Club owners did little to
relieve the plight of the Giants when in 1968 they allowed Charles Finley
to move the Kansas City Athletics across the bay to Oakland. Fluctuating
attendance figures and the failure of Bay Area voters to approve public
construction of a replacement stadium for Candlestick have led to repeated
discussions of another franchise shift for the Giants (in 1992, National
League owners blocked a transfer to St. Petersburg, Florida).

Why did the Giants fail to find El Dorado in the West as had the Dodgers?
The ambiguous legacy of the Western conquest was again apparent. Perhaps
the instant success of the Giants spoiled Bay Area fans, who had a rich
legacy of successful minor league baseball with the San Francisco Seals and
superstars such as Joe DiMaggio. While the imperialistic perpetrators of
baseball's "manifest destiny" seemed somewhat impervious to this tradition,
the players were not. Thus, Giant outfielder Hank Saur lamented that
San Francisco fans never embraced Willie Mays the way New York City
loved the centerfielder. Saur complained, "They never treated him like the
superstar that he was. Supposedly, they were still partial to San Francisco-
native Joe DiMaggio as baseball's great centerfielder." A sensitive Mays
was only too aware of the situation and blamed Manager Bill Rigney for
establishing unrealistic expectations in an effort to stir up fan interest.
A disgruntled Mays also encountered racism in finding housing in San
Francisco, which he had not encountered in New York. San Francisco
crowds adopted the Latino Orlando Cepeda, who never played in New
York, as their favorite.

Perhaps the Giants could never quite replace the indigenous Seals, DiMaggio, and Pacific Coast League, or compete successfully with the many other cultural options available in San Francisco. In his survey of minor league baseball, Neil Sullivan argues that if the Pacific Coast League had been allowed to evolve into major league status, "with its character, traditions, and rivalries intact, it would have made a special contribution to major league baseball. Instead, the majors engulfed the West Coast by transferring three of its historic franchises and creating three new ones. Baseball in the West is a hodgepodge of clubs from the eminent Dodgers to the marginal Mariners with little to suggest the deep traditions of the game in that part of the country."

Indeed, the search for gold in the West by the Dodgers and Giants, along with Congressional pressures and the threat of antitrust legislation, set off a new wave of expansionism akin to the European imperialist scramble for African colonies following the Berlin Conference in the late 19th century. In 1961, the American League moved into Southern California with the Los Angeles Angels under the ownership of cowboy actor and singer Gene Autry, a most appropriate symbol for Western baseball. In 1962, playing in Dodger Stadium, the Angels challenged the dominant New York Yankees for the pennant, before fading in the final weeks and settling for a most respectable third-place finish in the standings. The success of the Angels caught the attention of the Hollywood crowd, and the young Angels players developed a considerable reputation for the party scene. However, in 1963 the Angels came back seriously to the game, and most of the Hollywood crowd deserted them for the more consistently successful Dodgers. In 1965, the Los Angeles Angels became the California Angels, and in 1966 moved to their current home in Anaheim. Although Autry opened his saddlebags and spent lavishly in the free-agent market, the team never captured the hearts of Southern California like the Dodgers, nor an American League pennant, although coming close in 1982 and 1986. The Angels have struggled to establish a tradition and identity of their own in Anaheim, where they were initially overshadowed by Walt Disney's version of the California dream, and now have been incorporated into the Disney empire.

Another Western city that has struggled to find its major league baseball identity is Houston, which, as another proposed site for a team in the defunct Continental Leagues, was awarded a National League franchise in 1962. Appealing to the frontier image still associated with Texas and its largest city, the initial logo for the Houston team was the Colt .45's, often shortened to Colts—a fitting image for the city, according to historians of Houston. Francisco A. Rosales and Barry J. Kaplan maintain that

19th-century values (and symbols) have retained a stronghold in Houston, remarking, "Individualism, opportunity, capitalism, limited government, virtual dogma in American government before the 1929 crash, have remained sacred in Houston."

Overwhelmed by the publicity generated by their hapless expansion cohorts, the New York Mets and the irrepressible Casey Stengel, the Colts played in the virtual obscurity of a temporary structure, Colt Stadium, with a seating capacity of 32,000 and located on the same lot as the projected domed stadium. Relief pitcher Hal Woodeschick described the problems of playing in hot and muggy Houston, observing, "It was so hot in Houston . . . we started playing our home games at night. The problem was that the mosquitoes were worse at night . . . . The ballplayers would have to be sprayed before every game. If we didn't have the stuff on our bodies, they would eat us up in the bullpen."

In addition to combating mosquitoes, Houston players were expected to wear Western suits on the road. On a road swing from Cincinnati to Chicago, ten players refused to wear the suits, complaining that the outfits had caused negative comments and contributed to a "circus-like" atmosphere. In Chicago, airline passengers reportedly asked Colts players such questions as "Where is the rodeo?" and "Where's your horse?" But Manager Harry Craft made it clear that wearing the cultural symbols was not a negotiable issue. He reminded the players that they had voted for the Western suits before the season, and they would wear them. The early 1960s represented a time period in which management dominated, and player options were limited through strict enforcement of the reserve clause. Conformity and compliance were still the watchwords of ballplayers, and player representative catcher Hal Smith announced that the Colts would adhere to the wishes of management.

However, in 1965 Houston management attempted to shed the frontier image with the opening of the Harris County Domed Stadium, now called the Astrodome. The Colt .45's logo was abandoned in favor of the rainbow-colored Astros, a futuristic look for a city that was playing a key role in the nation's space program. Despite changes in symbolic imagery, baseball attendance in Houston has been inconsistent, and the team has yet to win a National League pennant.

Still seeking gold in the West and the growing California market, American League owners approved the transfer of the Kansas City A's to Oakland for the 1968 season. Following the 1955 move of the A's from Philadelphia to Kansas City, the team's attendance and play on the field had improved; but in 1967 the team finished last for the third time in four years, and fan interest lagged. However, with their bright kelly green uniforms, mustaches, and long hair, the youthful Oakland A's seemed to embody the values of the counterculture that found a home in the Bay Area during the late 1960s and early 1970s. In reality, these contemporary fashions were encouraged by A's owner Charles Finley, a businessman whose journey from the steel mills in Birmingham, Alabama, and Peoria, Illinois, to multi-million-dollar Chicago insurance executive personified the Horatio Alger saga of rags to riches and 19th-century production values. Finley, seeking to boost sagging ticket sales, paid Oakland players $300 each to adorn themselves with facial hair. The A's owner sought to co-opt the fashion of the counterculture, but he did not count on having to deal with the questioning of authority inherent in the movement.

Thus, led by such outstanding players as Joe Rudi, Vida Blue, Catfish Hunter, Reggie Jackson, Rollie Fingers, and Sal Bando, the A's won world championships in 1972 (when the A's defeated the well-disciplined and well-groomed Big Red Machine from Cincinnati), 1973, and 1974, before Finley, in response to increasing player demands, disassembled his dynasty. Despite tremendous success on the playing field, Oakland's attendance lagged behind performance, and many in major league baseball still question whether the Bay Area is able to support two major league franchises.

Following the Oakland franchise transfer, baseball expansion in 1969 placed new Western franchises in San Diego and Seattle. The National League San Diego Padres wanted to tap the lucrative Southern California market, which had proven to be so for the Dodgers and to a lesser extent for the Angels. Baseball was not an instant success in San Diego, however, with only one winning season during the first 15 years. Home attendance for the inaugural 1969 campaign barely topped half a million. By 1974, team owner Arnholt Smith was prepared to sell the franchise to a buyer who wanted to move the team to Washington D.C. However, a "white knight" emerged in Ray Kroc, head of the McDonald's fast food empire, who purchased the team and kept it in Southern California. With aggressive marketing techniques, as well as the acquisition of fine athletes such as Tony Gwynn and Kevin McReynolds, the Padres' attendance improved, and the team appeared in the 1984 World Series. However, following the death of Kroc, the team was sold to new owners in 1990, and the Padres have been unable to retain their niche in the hearts of Southern Californians. Failing to attract either the fans or the radio-television contracts available to the neighboring Dodgers, the Padres have sold or traded outstanding young players such as Fred McGriff and Gary Sheffield. Operating on a shoestring budget for the major leagues, the Padres in 1994 fielded a team that many critics thought was more befitting the Pacific Coast League franchise that the National League had displaced in 1969. Today, they are a much-improved ball club.

In Seattle, the 1969 American League expansion team fared even worse than the Padres. The Seattle Pilots played their home games in the refurbished minor league Sick's Stadium, finishing last and drawing fewer than 700,000 spectators. Following this disastrous inaugural campaign, the underside of which has been well chronicled by Jim Bouton's infamous *Ball Four*, the Pilots moved to Milwaukee and became the Brewers. After an eight-year absence and threats of legal action, the American League returned to the Pacific Northwest with the Mariners in 1977. Despite having a domed stadium to prevent costly rain-outs and the emergence of a superstar in Ken Griffey, Jr., the Mariners have struggled both on and off the field. With a troubled financial picture, the future of major league baseball in the Pacific Northwest remains somewhat clouded, even with a Division title in 1995 and improving attendance. Municipal support for a new stadium is uncertain.

The failure of the San Diego and Seattle markets to materialize did not discourage Bob Short from moving his Washington Senators (a 1961 expansion team that had replaced the original Senators, who moved to Minnesota) to Arlington, Texas, midway between Fort Worth and Dallas. A bitter Senators broadcaster, Shelby Whitfield, blasted Short for the transfer, stating that Arlington Stadium was inadequate, parking was poor, the press was unreceptive, and football was king. Whitfield acidly remarked, "All the seats were out in the open, directly under the sun or exposed to showers, and the stadium was notorious in the area for its toilet facilities. In Texas they like their baseball with plenty of beer, and beer and baseball don't quite go well together if you don't have a handy 'john.'" Perhaps there was something to the sour grapes of Whitfield as the Rangers, despite a traditional Western frontier image and logo, failed to provide much excitement either on the field or at the box office. Nevertheless, a group of investors headed by George W. Bush purchased the team in 1989, and their signing of free agent Nolan Ryan brought considerable interest to the franchise. The 1994 opening of a new ballpark in Arlington with plenty of facilities also rekindled fan appreciation. Even though the Rangers have produced a divisional winner in 1996, they remain second cousins to the Dallas Cowboys.

The El Dorado sought in the West by baseball owners after the initial successful strike in Los Angeles was finally found in 1991 with the awarding of a National League franchise to Denver. Expecting to draw approximately two million paying customers, the Colorado Rockies, in the Denver metropolitan area of two million, drew over four-and-one-half million fans to their inaugural season in 1993. The unexpected bonanza was attributed to geography, demographics, pent-up demand, and a solid history in Denver of supporting big league sports franchises, as well as minor league baseball. Bob Howsam, a former major league general manager with Cincinnati, played a key role in bringing major league baseball to Denver after many years with the minor league Denver Bears. Howsam knew Denver would be successful, but he believed the phenomenal attendance figures owed something to luck and timing. Howsam observed, "It just happened to come along at the right time, and the stadium was large enough, and this region is prospering economically right now. People in the mountain region have some dollars in their pockets to spend on entertainment." Frank Haraway, a retired *Denver Post* sportswriter who served as the Rockies' official scorer in 1993, simply believed the Eastern establishment of baseball had underestimated the potential of the region. Haraway quipped, "I always felt that major league sports people back east pretty much looked down the groove of their nose at us, and imagined that all we did out here was dodge behind trees and shoot Indians." While the staggering attendance figures at Mile High Stadium (also home of the Denver Broncos football team) were a most pleasant surprise for the Eastern establishment, they also surpassed the estimates of Denver baseball officials, who scrambled to add additional seating capacity to Coors Field for the Rockies' 1995 season.

Having found a Western gold mine in Denver, baseball owners, even in the midst of their long winter of discontent during the 1994–1995 strike, in which the 1994 World Series was cancelled, voted to add the Arizona Diamondbacks and the Tampa Bay Devil Rays to the ranks of major league baseball for the 1998 campaign. Boston Red Sox executive John Harrington, chairman of the expansion committee, admitted that announcing expansion plans during the prolonged labor negotiations of 1994–1995 was probably not the ideal time. However, in defense of the committee's decision to expand to Arizona and Tampa, Harrington explained, "But if you understand the pressure brought on us by Congress to expand—especially by the Florida and Arizona delegations—you would know why. They wanted teams and we would have lost Phoenix as a viable candidate if we had waited past April 1." The Phoenix group of investors had until that date to benefit from a tax approved by Maricopa County (Phoenix) voters that will raise $253 million of the $280 million price tag for a retractable-roof stadium. Thus, baseball announced expansion once again to avoid Congressional threats of antitrust legislation and to fill coffers with an estimated three million annual ticket sales in Arizona. These were similar to the reasons that had been given for baseball's initial Westward movement in 1958.

Even supposing that Phoenix proves to be a rich vein to tap like the Dodgers and Rockies, what conclusions are we to draw about the long-term ramifications of the major league baseball shift to the West? First, this brief survey of baseball in the West suggests, as Larry Gerlach eloquently argued in a recent article on baseball historiography, that much research remains to be done on baseball in the region. Nevertheless, perhaps some tentative conclusions are worthy of consideration. To place baseball within the historiographical debate between the traditionalists and New Western historians, it is obvious that the major league baseball shift has not brought unqualified growth and progress. To use the phrase coined by Patricia Limerick, the legacy of conquest has been ambiguous. The expansion of the major league baseball frontier to the West did democratize the game by bringing the major leagues into a better balance with the demographic alignment of America in the late 20th century. But this expansion brought with it the destruction of distinguished minor league traditions such as that of the old Pacific Coast League as well as the extinction of baseball loyalties in Eastern cities such as Brooklyn and Washington DC. In addition, expansion of baseball in the search for lucrative new markets and to avoid Congressional antitrust actions has encouraged baseball management to seek a safety valve in frontier expansion and to avoid dealing with its problems. Accordingly, expansionism has only accelerated the greed factor in professional baseball deplored by Robert Lipsyte in his piece for the *New York Times Magazine*.

In *Lords of the Realm: The Real History of Baseball*, John Helyar argues that to baseball executives expansion was "always a response to a problem," spreading the talent pool thinner, increasing upward pressures in salaries, while removing the scarcity that had undergirded the value of franchises. Helyar writes that all of this changed in 1993 when attendance surged past 70 million, smashing the old attendance mark by 24 percent. The new franchises in Colorado and Florida accounted for over 7½ million of this increase. However, these figures have just increased the greed in baseball that Helyar deplores. He concludes,

The Lords and the agents, the lawyers and the czars, had done their best to kill baseball. There was something about the nation's pastime that made the people in it behave badly. They were, perhaps, blinded by the light of what it represented—a growing distillate of America. Men fought to control it as though they could own it. They wallowed in dubious battle, locked in ugly trench warfare for dominion over the green fields. The money poured into the game and men gorged and gorged over it—made damned fools of themselves over it.

Major league baseball's paradigm shift to the West is part of the portrait of greed painted by Helyar. Rich baseball veins have been found in Los Angeles and Colorado, and possibly will be in Arizona, but the picture and future of baseball in Anaheim, Seattle, San Diego, Oakland, San Francisco, Arlington, and Houston remain unclear. For baseball to reach its promise as the American game, more than Westward expansion—albeit with its democratic elements—is needed. The game must be willing to reach negotiated settlements with politicians, agents, players, and umpires that will establish a solid, affordable foundation for the game and that will still place baseball within the financial grasp of the American family. Until these issues are resolved, expansion will only be a panacea, and the ambiguous legacy of conquest will persist.

DANIEL R. MARBURGER

15. Whatever Happened to the "Good Ol' Days"? The Evolution of Baseball's Labor-Management Relations

If, as the saying goes, baseball is too much a business to be a sport and too much a sport to be a business, nowhere has this been more true than in the area of player-management relations. From nearly the beginning of the professional game club owners sought to profit by controlling their costs, chief of which was player salaries. As long as players could sell their talent on an open market, bidding for their services would drive up salaries at the cost of owners' profits. In 1879 the National League established the "reserve clause," which allowed each club to reserve the services of its players and prevented other clubs from bidding for them. Although originally applied to only five players on each club, it eventually came to be imposed on all. For nearly a century the resulting reserve system dominated player-management relations and often sparked bitter confrontations. Although the owners frequently justified the system as essential to the maintenance of competitive balance, in fact they recognized that its preeminent value rested in containing salaries. The reserve clause made players the property of the club for life, or at least until the club decided to trade, sell, or "dump" them. Only when threatened by outside forces—the creation of a rival league (such as the Federal League) or challenges in court (as in federal courts leading up to the 1922 Supreme Court ruling)—did owners modify their approach. When such threats receded—competing leagues always folded or were co-opted and the courts usually sided with the owners—it became business as usual. Through the decades many notorious player-owner salary confrontations occurred, but the playing field always tilted unevenly in favor of the owners, who often resorted to outlandish tactics and abuses to keep down salaries. Probably no situation bred as much bitterness and hostility among the players as did their condition of semi-serfdom, as their contracts reminded them annually.

The turbulent 1960s affected professional baseball just as they did most segments of society. Better informed and defiant players, less inclined to accept the status quo, began to rebel against such lopsided contractual arrangements and began to organize themselves more effectively. With the guidance of experienced labor organizer Marvin Miller, they exhibited remarkable solidarity and created a strong union that gradually, with the aid of owner shortsightedness, transformed the unequal player-owner relationship. In 1975 a successful grievance ended the reserve clause, and the next year a free agency system was negotiated that forever changed the business of baseball.

Daniel R. Marburger weaves his way through the thicket of complicated issues, negotiations, and strikes that have dominated professional baseball's last three decades. Not only has the game outside the lines been profoundly affected, but some would say that play on the field has been influenced as well. In reviewing these complicated developments, Marburger makes clear that baseball has at once been the beneficiary as well as the victim of its own history.

From its poetic beginning firmly rooted in the myth of Abner Doubleday, professional baseball positioned itself as a staple of American life. As unfailing as the American Stars and Stripes flying over Fort McHenry, baseball showed its resiliency in weathering two World Wars, the Great Depression, and even a San Francisco earthquake. Baseball had even proven impervious to the Black Sox scandal in 1919. And despite the many predictions of impending doom by amateur soothsayers over the years, interest in baseball never faltered. Record attendance at games had been the rule rather than the exception. Burgeoning interest in cable television allowed fans in the remotest regions of the country to track their favorite team. For all practical purposes, baseball was invincible.

Perhaps it is all too fitting that the Titanic and the Hindenburg were also once considered models of perfection—for in 1994 the national pastime came to a grinding halt. Of course, it was not an economic recession that had caused the season to end, for baseball had withstood many of those. And it was not the perils of war that interrupted the game, for baseball can claim veterans from all but the earliest American conflicts. The single disaster that baseball was ill-prepared to endure, that ended its season prematurely and endangered its future was, of all things, a collective bargaining impasse.

A collective bargaining impasse! How could a sport that suited up players three months after the bombing of Pearl Harbor jeopardize its long-standing love affair with the American public over a collective bargaining disagreement? Work stoppages had become as commonplace as bubblegum cards in recent decades, but few aficionados of the game would have ever predicted the cancellation of a season. With the average baseball salary well over $1 million and franchise values skyrocketing at a mind-boggling pace, fans wonder if baseball is nearing the straw that will break the camel's back.

Of course, the more-seasoned fans of the game are quick to point out that baseball was not always this way. There was a time when baseball was not threatened with strikes and lockouts and when the business of baseball was behind-the-scenes activity not easily evidenced by its spectators. In reflecting upon baseball's "good ol' days," however, one should note that the peaceful coexistence of labor and management was hardly synonymous with harmony.

Throughout most of its history, major league baseball was dominated by the reserve clause. In the game's early days, bidding wars among competing teams for stars drove up player salaries at the expense of the clubs' profits. To counter these bidding wars, the reserve clause was established. Under the reserve system, no player was permitted to shop his wares to competing clubs. In effect, the reserve clause made the players the property of their clubs for life. Further, if the player's contract was traded or sold to another team, the individual became the property of the new team, subject to the same rigid rules of enforcement. Unlike most American workers, who take for granted the right to seek out alternative job opportunities, baseball players had to play for their current teams indefinitely or retire from the game.

For years, the clubs successfully defended the reserve clause as necessary to preserve competitive balance in the game. Perhaps the best summation of the necessity of the reserve clause came from Justice Smyth in the U.S. Supreme Court case of *Federal Baseball Club of Baltimore v. National League, et al.* Presenting the majority opinion, Smyth wrote: "If the reserve clause did not exist, the highly skillful players would be absorbed by the more wealthy clubs, and thus some clubs in the league would so far outstrip others in playing ability that the contests between the superior and the inferior clubs would be uninteresting and the public would refuse to patronize them."

Chief Justice Smyth's opinion did more than rationalize the need for the reserve clause. The Supreme Court decision effectively exempted baseball from federal antitrust legislation, an exemption that has only recently come under serious fire.

Thus, with the deck heavily stacked in favor of the clubs' owners, it is no wonder that baseball continued to be played year after year without interruption. Individually, players could protest the state of affairs by threatening to withhold their services, but because baseball salaries tended to exceed compensation outside of baseball, it was only a matter of time before the holdouts came scurrying back to sign their contracts.

Among the more legendary battles between players and management was the alleged exchange between Pittsburgh Pirates slugger Ralph Kiner and Branch Rickey, the team's general manager. In refusing Kiner a raise, Rickey remarked, "We finished last with you; we could have finished last without you." Of course, the comment was a vast oversimplification of the situation, because as one of the game's premier home run hitters, Kiner was the only drawing card on a losing team. Last place or not, Kiner's presence in the lineup was essential to attract crowds on game days. In reflection, the celebrated quote is more an indication of the power of the reserve clause than it is about the value of Ralph Kiner. The Kiner affair, and the many more that preceded and followed, made the case clear that absent a union and with the reserve clause intact, there was no incentive for any player to expect to receive meaningful concessions from management.

Despite the fact that the reserve clause deprived baseball players of leverage in contract negotiations, players acceded to the reserve system as an unfortunate but necessary component of the game. Throughout most of baseball's history the system went unchallenged. In 1946 outfielder Danny Gardella challenged the reserve clause, when after a stint with the Mexican League, he returned to the States only to find himself blacklisted by major league baseball's elite. The clubs avoided a federal ruling on the legality of the reserve clause, however, by settling out of court. A second challenge came a few years later when farmhand George Toolson sued after being reassigned to the minors by the Yankees. The reserve clause escaped doom when the Supreme Court ruled that a reversal of baseball's antitrust exemption was a legislative matter not a judicial one.

The reserve system's most recent threat came when St. Louis Cardinal outfielder Curt Flood filed suit against Major League Baseball in response to his trade to the Philadelphia Phillies. The case eventually went before the Supreme Court in *Flood v. Kuhn* in 1972. In his suit, Flood challenged the constitutionality of the reserve clause, which he likened to slavery. However, when the Supreme Court handed down the decision in favor of the clubs, the legality of the reserve clause, as well as its apparent acceptability, was reaffirmed.

Although the reserve clause dictated labor relations in baseball's first 100 years, the winds of change began to blow when Marvin Miller was selected by the players as the Major League Baseball Players' Association's (MLBPA) executive director in 1966. Interestingly the MLBPA was initially conceived with the blessing of the club owners, who even offered to finance the Association with proceeds from the All-Star game. Miller, however, was a product of the United States Steelworkers of America, one of the nation's largest and most powerful labor unions, and the thought of a union professional butting heads with baseball management was unpalatable to the owners at best. Even some of the players were wary of their new executive director, fearing that Miller might bring racketeering into the industry.

In the end Marvin Miller was the best thing that ever happened to major league baseball players. And for his ample achievements he was also the owners' worst nightmare.

Prior to Miller's arrival, baseball's minimum salary was $6,000, and the average baseball salary was $19,000. Multiyear contracts were virtually unheard of, and the reserve clause bound players to their clubs for life. There was no salary arbitration, no free agency, and no grievance arbitration. Topps, the baseball card company, complemented the players' salaries with a meager $125 payment to each player. In sharp contrast, by the end of 1982, Miller's last year in the official capacity of executive director, the minimum salary in baseball was $33,500, and the average salary exceeded $240,000. The reserve clause now applied to only a percentage of players, with the rest having the ability to choose their own employers or have their salary determined by an independent arbitrator. Grievance arbitration allowed for the enforcement of the collective bargaining agreement by permitting an independent third party to interpret the terms of the contract. Further, the Players' Association now negotiates licensing agreements with Topps, Fleer, and other baseball card manufacturers to the tune of tens of millions of dollars annually.

Because most of these gains entailed a direct transfer of revenues from the pockets of the owners to those of the players, Miller's legacy continued well beyond his retirement. Many of the issues at stake today are remnants of the former executive director's accomplishments.

Whether Marvin Miller was a true genius in his repeated triumphs over baseball management or just the right person in the right place at the right time is subject to analysis and debate. What may be less controversial is the simple notion that his entanglements with baseball brass were a gross mismatch. Miller had been schooled in labor negotiations by the Steelworkers' Union, which had 1.25 million members and 3,000 locals in nearly every state. Advancing through the ranks, Miller knew that the secret to any union's success was to simultaneously increase the size of the pie and then to take the largest slice.

Banging heads with the Steelworkers' Union protégé were baseball's owners, none of whom had any real experience in jawing with a labor professional over a collective bargaining agreement. Many of the owners had been around the game for years, and many firmly believed that Miller was driving a wedge between them and the cozy, cooperative relationship they'd had with their players. Some truly believed that the paychecks and perks they gave their players were acts of benevolence.

In a perverse way, the owners were right on all counts. Baseball was a different industry—different inasmuch as the reserve clause, coupled with the exemption from antitrust legislation, made each team immune from competition. The antitrust exemption granted baseball the right to protect its teams' territorial rights against encroachment. In stark contrast, the lack of similar protection in the National Football League (NFL) permitted Oakland Raiders owner Al Davis to pack his team's helmets and jerseys and invade turf that was supposed to belong to the Los Angeles Rams. The same lack of an antitrust exemption left Los Angeles without *any* NFL team 10 years later.

If the antitrust exemption turned the lock, the reserve clause threw away the key. Not only did the clubs not have to fear a fellow competitor setting up shop next door, the reserve system ensured that other teams could not pick their pockets for their most precious resource, the players. In this regard, paying and rewarding the players for their services was, in fact, an act of generosity. Most of the players had been snatched from the womb as teenagers and relatively few had college degrees. Further, disciplined instruction on the fine art of sliding or hitting the cutoff man had little marketability outside of baseball. For this reason it would have been perfectly feasible for the Branch Rickeys of the baseball kingdom to promote a player to the major leagues and refuse him a raise for the entirety of his career with minimal fear of losing him to another occupation.

In squaring off against the owners in his earliest years, Miller sought to win the easiest victories: raising baseball's minimum salary (which had been raised only once—by $1,000—in 20 years), increasing the pension fund, and establishing a formal grievance procedure. Quite possibly the most important achievement in Miller's early years was that of obtaining impartial grievance arbitration in the interpretation of the collective bargaining agreement in 1970. Ironically, as monumental as the attainment of grievance arbitration was, it is quite possibly the most understated accomplishment of the Players' Association. Ultimately it was grievance arbitration that ended the reserve clause, and it was grievance arbitration that resulted in baseball's collusion rulings and damages in the mid-1980s.

In 1973 the Players' Association bargained for salary arbitration. Actually, "bargained for" is a misrepresentation of fact. "Handed on a silver platter" is a more fitting description. Miller made no secret that the number one item on his wish list was an upheaval of the reserve clause. For this reason, the owners offered the players salary arbitration in much the same way that one might offer table scraps to a pack of hungry wolves. Salary arbitration was by no means a substitute for the free market. It might, however, present the illusion that the owners sympathized with the inequities inherent in reserve clause restrictions and, in so doing, soothe the savage beast.

Prior to baseball, interest arbitration (where an independent arbitrator determines the terms of a new contract) existed primarily in public sector occupations such as law enforcement and firefighting. In those industries, arbitration served as the substitute for a strike. In baseball, however, salary arbitration was offered as a means of living within the restrictions of the reserve clause; that arbitration would eliminate the inequities in salaries across (or within) clubs. Under salary arbitration, each side would submit an offer to an independent arbitrator. The arbitrator would then determine which of the two offers would be binding.

Miller also bargained for the "10-and-5" rule in the 1973 negotiations. This allowed players with at least 10 years of major league service (the last five years with the same club) the right to veto any trade.

The most significant event during Marvin Miller's tenure did not come during collective bargaining negotiations, however. Miller was convinced that Paragraph 10a of the Uniform Player's Contract limited the powers of the reserve clause. This section read: "On or before January 15 . . . the Club may tender to the Player a contract for the term of that year by mailing the same to the Player. If prior to the March 1 next succeeding said January 15, the Player and the Club have not agreed upon the terms of such contract, then on or before 10 days after said March 1, the Club shall have the right . . . to renew this contract for the period of one year.

According to Miller, the reserve clause did not give the club the right to the player indefinitely; it only gave the club a one-year option on a player's services after the expiration of his contract. Thus, if the parties were unable to agree upon a contract, the club could renew the old contract for one additional year only. After that, the player would be free to negotiate with any club.

Although he eyeballed dissolving the reserve system not unlike a dog surveys a steak hanging from a butcher's window, Miller stashed Paragraph 10a in his back pocket, to be wielded at the proper time. Prior to 1970, any disagreement over the interpretation of the clause would likely have been resolved by the commissioner of baseball. Miller viewed the commissioner as a puppet whose strings were pulled by the owners; he was hired by the owners, paid by the owners, and therefore was bound to represent the best interests of the owners.

After the 1970 negotiations had been completed, however, the scenario had changed. Now, an impartial arbitrator would resolve any disputes regarding the language of the Basic Agreement. Miller was convinced that a nonpartisan observer would agree that the reserve clause was only valid for one season beyond the expiration of the current contract. In professional basketball in 1967, Rick Barry left the National Basketball Association (NBA) to join the American Basketball Association. When Barry's NBA team, the San Francisco Warriors, sued to keep their star from jumping leagues, a federal judge ruled that Barry was bound to the Warriors for one year subsequent to the expiration of the contract. The relevant section of Barry's NBA contract from which the judge's decision was based was practically verbatim the same as baseball's.

While awaiting the ideal test case for which to place the interpretation of Paragraph 10a to the scrutiny of an arbitrator, Miller made repeated attempts to relax the reserve clause via negotiations. John Gaherin, who headed the owners' Player Relations Committee, secretly believed that Miller's interpretation of the contract was correct, and he implored the owners to retain some control over their own fate by negotiating modifications to the reserve clause, rather than to risk losing it all at the hands of an arbitrator. No such modifications were made.

At the end of 1974 Jim "Catfish" Hunter was to demonstrate the almighty power inherent in free agency. Hunter was one of the premier starting pitchers in the game and an eventual Hall of Famer. Having signed a two-year contract in 1974 with the Oakland A's, the team was obliged to pay half of his salary into a fund for the eventual purchase of an annuity. In fact, however, no such annuity had been purchased. The Players' Association filed a grievance on behalf of Hunter, claiming that Charlie Finley, the owner of the A's, had breached Hunter's contract, and that the pitcher should, therefore, be declared a free agent. On December 13, 1974, arbitrator Peter Seitz ruled in favor of Hunter. In the weeks that followed, a parade of suitors trekked to Hunter's North Carolina home to pitch their offers. Interestingly, whereas the terminated contract called for a total payment to Hunter of $100,000 for the 1974 season, the competitive bidding war that ensued resulted in a five-year $3.5 million contract with the New York Yankees.

With the power of free agency to increase player salaries in full evidence, Marvin Miller anxiously awaited his test case. In recent years the number of players entering into a season without a contract had been increasing. By and by, the players eventually signed contracts, however, putting the test of Paragraph 10a to rest. The test case finally came through in 1975, when pitcher Andy Messersmith played the entire season without a contract. At dispute was Messersmith's insistence upon a no-trade clause in his contract—a notion staunchly refused by Messersmith's Dodger management. Although Miller was chomping at the bit to use Messersmith as the test case, he recognized that Messersmith was less interested in filing a grievance than he was in getting the no-trade provision. Sifting through his files, Miller came upon pitcher Dave McNally as a backup in the event Messersmith were to sign. McNally was once an outstanding pitcher for the Baltimore Orioles. After many years of service, he was traded to the Montreal Expos. Feeling he had been misled by Expo management and frustrated by his own performance, McNally retired from baseball in midseason and returned to his home in Montana. Because he was an unsigned player at the time of his retirement, Miller requested that he file a grievance at the season's end.

The two grievances were filed in October of 1975. The arbitration panel was to consist of one management representative, John Gaherin; one player representative, Marvin Miller; and a neutral chair, Peter Seitz, the same arbitrator who had declared Catfish Hunter a free agent only a year earlier. Of course, the opinions of Gaherin and Miller were known to all even before the opening arguments had begun. Seitz was to determine the fate of the reserve clause.

Unfortunately for Seitz, presiding over this particular grievance hearing was akin to attending one's own funeral. The stakes were high, and Seitz's career as an arbitrator would likely be over regardless of his decision. He desperately wanted to avoid casting the deciding vote. He begged the two sides to wash his hands of the affair and come to their own settlement. When the owners refused to negotiate, the decision went to Seitz. Seitz ruled in favor of the players: Messersmith and McNally were free agents. Before the ink on the decision had even dried, Gaherin handed Seitz his walking papers.

The Seitz decision registered 8.0 on baseball's Richter scale. As of that moment, all players need do is suit up without a contract for one season and they would be fair game for competitive bidding. The owners feared anarchy and bankruptcy, not necessarily in that order. In an act of defiance, the owners locked the players out of spring training, demanding that less drastic reforms to the reserve clause be implemented.

Ironically, no one was more anxious to moderate Seitz's decision than Marvin Miller. Miller had seen the result of the Catfish Hunter ruling: one player available for hire, and 24 teams knocking at his door. The executive director viewed this type of setting as the most favorable for escalating salaries. He wanted the clubs to compete for players, and not the reverse.

Eventually, baseball commissioner Bowie Kuhn ended the lockout, and negotiations over how to implement free agency continued. The owners wanted to limit free agency. Secretly so did Marvin Miller. The "compromise" the two sides eventually agreed upon was roughly the equivalent of handing the Players' Association a blank copy of the Basic Agreement and asking them to fill in their desired free agency eligibility standard. Eligibility for free agency was granted after the player had attained six years of major league service, just at the time the players perceived the stars of the game would be at the peaks of their careers.

The competitive bidding wars that soon took place were beyond the wildest dreams of any of the players involved. Players who had hoped free agency would double their money were aghast to find themselves being offered multiyear guaranteed contracts in the multimillion dollar range. Wayne Garland signed a 10-year contract with the Cleveland Indians for $1 million. Ditto for outfielder Richie Zisk, whose 10-year contract was to earn him pocket change totaling $3 million. These were not just baseball's thoroughbreds that were cashing in their chips; along with the stars of the game were the hasbeens and Hall of Fame wannabes. Move over Babe Ruth: The Padres just signed Oscar Gamble for $2.85 million over six years. Thirty-five-year-old Bert Campaneris was signed for $950,000, guaranteeing that he could play for no other team but the Texas Rangers until he was 40 years young. Claudell Washington, whose invitation to Cooperstown must be accompanied by the price of admission, was signed by Ted Turner's Atlanta Braves to a $3.5 million, five-year contract.

In their zeal to get something for nothing, the owners repeatedly found themselves in the position of getting nothing for something. At the end of the 10 years, Wayne Garland was to log only a few more innings than the team batboy. Campaneris was paid to play baseball during the first two years of his contract, and then paid to watch it the final three. To avoid such distasteful scenarios, the owners resorted to buyout clauses. Here, if the player's ability deteriorated to the point where he was no longer a welcome member of the 25-man roster, the team could dodge the remainder of his contract by simply paying the player not to show up for spring training.

Prior to free agency the average salary was $51,501. One year later the average salary had risen to $76,066. By 1980 the average baseball player could expect to bring home $143,756.

One should not be surprised that the owners increasingly became frustrated by baseball's state of affairs. They cursed the free market, they cursed baseball's biggest spenders, and most of all, they cursed Marvin Miller. The Seitz decision was to be the apex of the executive director's career. The remainder was spent protecting his gains from the owners, who desperately sought to roll back the system to better days.

As the owners plotted to beat the horror they'd helped to create, another surprise crept into their pocketbooks. Prior to the establishment of free agency, the owners had offered salary arbitration as a means of placating the players. Although the players could use salary arbitration as a means of reducing inequities in salary scales, there was little reason to believe arbitration could play a significant role in escalating pay. Now, however, the game had changed. Players who were not eligible for free agency, who were still the personal property of their clubs, began submitting the salaries of the free agents as evidence of their value.

The landmark case came at the hands of pitcher Bruce Sutter in 1980. By the end of 1979 Sutter was arguably the game's best relief pitcher. In 1979 Sutter racked up 37 saves and was named the National League's Cy Young Award winner. Unable to come to terms with his Chicago Cubs, Sutter filed for arbitration. The Cubs submitted an offer of $350,000—the highest offer ever submitted in an arbitration hearing. Had he signed for that figure, Sutter would likely have been a hero to his relief pitcher brethren. But Sutter countered with an offer of $700,000. Among pitchers, only Nolan Ryan earned more money. Several other players, none of them pitchers, also earned salaries in the $700,000 range or better. However, the common thread among baseball's salaried elite was that they had earned their pay as free agents. Free agent salaries were a privilege, not a right. Arbitration-eligible players simply were not entitled to earn that kind of money.

The owners were convinced that the Cubs would win the arbitration case. Other top relievers were paid more in line with the Cubs' offer, not Sutter's. Further, the relevant salary comparison for Sutter was with other players with three years of major league service. Comparisons with 10-year veterans was apples and oranges. Sutter's representative at the hearing, attorney Jim Bronner, argued that Sutter had emerged as one of the game's top pitchers and therefore was entitled to be paid as one. The arbitrator hearing the case was New York University law professor Tom Christenson. Like Peter Seitz before him, Christenson knew that in filling the "appropriate" figure into Sutter's contract, he was preparing his own epitaph. Like the Seitz decision, Christenson's choice of Sutter's offer sent shock waves throughout baseball. When future arbitration decisions, most notably in the cases of Steve Kemp and Fernando Valenzuela, echoed that of Sutter, players increasingly seized upon the opportunity to use arbitration as a means of increasing their take-home pay. "Pay me what the free agents get paid," the message was clear, "or an arbitrator will force you to."

Until now the changes that Marvin Miller brought into baseball have been referred to in this chapter as "achievements," "accomplishments," and "gains." Clearly, such wording emanates from the perspective of the user. In this case the verbiage is intended to reflect Miller's role: As executive director of the Players' Association, his job was to bring home the bacon for the rank and file. From this angle, Marvin Miller's changes were an unmitigated success. From the viewpoint of the owners, however, "achievements" and "accomplishments" are the most inappropriate choice of words. To them, Miller was the devil incarnate. He pulled baseball's balance of power out from under the owners' feet. The changes he initiated were the equivalent of taking a blank check from the owners' pocketbook and marking it "payable to the players."

The incessant power struggles that existed between management and the Players' Association during these times, as well as today, were hardly confined to smoke-filled boardrooms. From the perspective of average baseball fans, who had come to view spring training, opening day, and the Fall Classic as guaranteed constants in their lives, the reality of collective bargaining brought with it the unwanted baggage of work stoppages. In baseball, such things became the rule rather than the exception.

For any union, its sole source of bargaining power is the threat of a strike. Absent a union, an individual is always free to protest his or her pay or working conditions by threatening to withhold services. Because individuals are relatively easy to replace, however, personalized strikes are unlikely to result in meaningful concessions by management. Plantwide or industrywide strikes orchestrated by a well-organized union, on the other hand, are quite another story. An entire fleet of employees is difficult for any employer to replace, and for this reason, it may be less costly for the firm to concede to some of the union's demands than it is to weather the losses incurred during a strike.

Baseball's first-ever strike occurred in 1972. At issue were the players' health care plan and retirement benefits. The Players' Association requested increases in the funding of both to reflect rising inflation over the course of the current agreement. To persuade the owners that the request was reasonable, Miller noted a surplus in the existing pension fund. The surplus, he suggested, could be applied to the increased pensions. The owners countered with a proposal for a smaller increase in health care benefits and no change in pensions.

In his more tenuous days as executive director, Marvin Miller worked overtime trying to instill the same sense of unity that was deeply ingrained within the psyche of the Steelworkers' Union's rank and file. To say that the players were green to the union mentality was a gross understatement. By 1972, however, the players were staunchly pro-union and anxious to exercise their right to strike. As the players' enthusiasm for striking grew, Miller's attitude toward orchestrating the walkout began to wane. The players had no experience in strikes, they had no strike fund built up, and they hadn't been paid since October. If the players went on strike and later scurried back to resume playing on management's terms, the damage to the Players' Association could be irreparable. Now, thought Miller, was not the time to strike.

In fact, the executive director seriously underestimated the sense of solidarity that he had cultivated among the players. They were eager to take the opportunity to stand up to the owners. The vote in favor of a strike was unanimous.

As the strike moved into its second week, the owners suddenly backed off their hard-line "Take it or leave it" stance and offered to add $500,000 to health care benefits plus a cost-of-living increase in pension benefits. Just as Miller and Gaherin thought they had come to a settlement, some of the owners threw a monkey wrench into the negotiations: The players would have to make up the lost games without pay. Not surprisingly, the proposal was patently unacceptable to Miller, and the strike continued several more days before management relented. The 86 games lost during the strike were never made up, nor were the players paid during the work stoppage. The players did, however, receive credit for major league service days during the walkout: the key component in determining player pensions.

The next work stoppage occurred in 1976. This time, however, it was the owners who initiated the action. The off-season had produced the dreaded Seitz decision, and the owners wanted to nip free agency in the bud. They had seen the Catfish Hunter affair as a precursor of things to come, and they wanted no part of it. Inevitably, dozens, maybe hundreds of players would play out their options and place themselves on the auction block. Management was quickly running out of options. They appealed the Seitz decision to the federal district court and then the federal circuit court of appeals. When the decision to uphold the Seitz ruling came down from the courts, the owners realized that their only hope of limiting free agency would be at the bargaining table. They promptly made the decision to lock the players out of spring training until a collective bargaining agreement had been reached.

An employer lockout has essentially the same impact as an employee strike. The adage "Everyone loses in a strike" was never a position taken by the AFL-CIO. Although both sides do lose money during a strike, a walkout is timed in such a way as to gain leverage. Hence, a more proper representation of the union credo is "He who stands to lose the most concedes the most."

Employers scheduling lockouts rely on the same philosophy. In this case, the owners believed that they could starve the players out. The players had no strike fund and hadn't been paid in several months. True, the exact same scenario had existed four years earlier, but in 1972 there was no real reason for the owners to prolong the strike. Relatively little was at stake. They were the ones who had given in. But this time was different. Now it was free agency, already upheld by the courts; status quo meant bidding wars and the specter of declining profits, rising losses, and even bankruptcy. This time the rallying cry belonged to them. The players were no longer *requesting* free agency, they *had* it—handed to them on a silver platter by a man who had never had to worry about making payroll. It was the owners' responsibility to hold it at bay.

The approach taken by the owners was to pretend that the Seitz decision was simply a pipe dream; that it was their own unilateral act of magnanimity in suggesting a relaxation of the reserve clause. In drafting their strategies to derail free agency, the owners assumed that Marvin Miller envisioned himself as a champion over slavery, that in affixing his name to the Seitz ruling he was a modern-day Abraham Lincoln signing the Emancipation Proclamation.

In fact, Miller was hardly the free-marketeer he was often thought to be. As executive director, his assignment was to bring home the most attractive package to those who paid him their union dues. If free agency could deliver the goods, so be it. If the owners were to offer the players 90 percent of their revenues and keys to the executive washroom in exchange for a return to the reserve clause and its involuntary servitude, Miller would likely have shipped the proposal off to the players for rapid-fire ratification. (In the next round of negotiations, of course, he would likely have bargained to have the reserve clause revoked.)

In short, both camps were brainstorming on how to limit free agency. On the players' side, there were chinks in the armor. In 1972 they knew from Miller's consultations how much money they ought to receive in health care and pension benefits and how much they were being offered by management. The difference was something they could measure. But free agency had never existed before, and its benefits were intangible. Much to the chagrin of Miller, hundreds of players flooded Florida and Arizona, organizing their own workouts and, in the mind of Miller, giving the owners ample reason to believe a lockout would eventually cause the players to crack. Then, on March 17, on a godsend from union heaven, Bowie Kuhn unbarred the gates of spring training. Let the games begin. Whether Kuhn was acting for the best interest of baseball or at the request of influential owners who stood to profit with or without free agency is subject to debate. What is relevant is that the players began receiving paychecks, and paychecks do not a successful lockout make.

In baseball, management-labor negotiators come and go as frequently as baseball managers, and in 1978 Ray Grebey came and John Gaherin went. By 1980 free agency had helped to raise the average player salary to over $140,000. With legal challenges to free agency long a moot point and a change of heart by the players as to the merits of the reserve clause about as likely as snowfall in Barbados, the owners now argued for free agency compensation.

Free agent compensation meant that a team losing a free agent would be compensated for the loss by selecting a player from the signing team's roster. In effect, compensation schemes turned free agent signings into trades. From a management point of view, free agent compensation had worked quite well in the National Football League. In a nutshell, the NFL system was the equivalent to a rule that states if Team A decides to take $10 from Team B, then Team A must compensate Team B by giving it $15. Not surprisingly, football teams had little interest in signing free agents.

Baseball's version of free agent compensation was a softer sell than football's hard-line approach. In comparison, baseball's compensation formula was set up in such a way that if Team A takes $10 from Team B, it must compensate Team B by giving Team B $5. Thus, contrary to football's compensation scheme, baseball's version was less likely to impede the movement of free agents between teams. Nonetheless, Marvin Miller understood the full ramifications of the plan. If A had to give B $5 in exchange for the $10 it received, then A's $10 was actually worth only $5, the net value after the exchange was complete. Compensation may not hinder the movement of free agents, but it could hold down their salaries.

Persuading the players to turn their noses up at compensation schemes was easy. By now, the philosophy Miller had conveyed to the players since the Seitz ruling was simply this: Everything management has done, is doing, and will do has, as its sole intent, the dismantling of free agency.

Early in the 1980 negotiations, free agent compensation was clearly going to hold up progress toward reaching an agreement. Eventually, the negotiators decided to table the compensation issue until 1981 and salvage the 1980 season without a strike by settling other issues. The two sides would assign a joint committee to study the compensation issue.

Before continuing, readers need to understand just how joint committees in collective bargaining operate. In the typical scenario, management assigns members to the committee to demonstrate why their perspective should be adopted in the collective bargaining agreement. The union handpicks persons whose sworn duty is to substantiate the reverse. In other words—joint committees represent an agreement to waste each other's time. In the case of baseball's compensation issue, the committee fulfilled its purpose with flying colors.

In early 1981 the owners made a stunning announcement: They had agreed to institute free agent compensation. Perhaps something needs to be clarified here. The announcement was that the owners had agreed to institute compensation. The Players' Association was still vehemently opposed to the idea. The feeling of déjà vu prevailed when the players set a strike date in late May.

The compensation scheme "enacted" by the owners was as follows: Players would be ranked according to position, and the top 50 percent were subject to some form of compensation. If a team signed a player who ranked in the top third of his position, the team could protect 15 members of the major league roster. The team that had lost the player could select one of the remaining 10 players as compensation. Thus, the system implied a trade whereby the signing team acquires a player in the top third of his profession and in doing so must forego the services of a player in the bottom 40 percent. For a player in the top 50 percent at his position (but not the top third), the signing team could protect 18 players on its roster. Again, although it is true that the signing team would always emerge as the winner in the transaction, compensation reduced the value of the free agent, which would almost certainly slow the free agent bidding wars.

Although the owners insisted that the compensation proposal was aimed at promoting competitive balance within baseball, Miller was convinced that its real purpose was to stunt salary growth. His response to the issue had not been altered by the passage of time. Either compensation goes or the players go.

That Miller had not embraced free agent compensation over the off-season did not surprise the owners. In anticipation of a showdown, the owners purchased strike insurance from Lloyd's of London.

The walkout began on June 12. Unlike the strike of 1972, which merely delayed the start of the season, this was the first time that a season had been interrupted in midstream by a work stoppage. Over the next several weeks, enormous strides had been made to bridge the gap in negotiations. The owners, through Ray Grebey, made it painfully clear that compensation must exist in baseball, and the players, through Marvin Miller, announced to the world that free agent compensation was unacceptable. Some progress!

Suddenly, after weeks of impasse, Marvin Miller received an unexpected phone call from Lee MacPhail, now pinch-hitting for Ray Grebey. The owners clearly were anxious to settle. Undoubtedly, their collective resolve to resume the season was attributable to their love of the game and their desire to resurrect baseball as an American institution. It bore no relationship to the fact that the strike-insurance pack with Lloyd's of London was about to expire. MacPhail soon scheduled a meeting with Miller at which he resolutely announced the owners' intent to settle immediately. Miller, with a long career as a labor negotiator behind him, correctly inferred the owners' stance as "You tell us what you want and we will agree." Miller's settlement outlined a pooled compensation scheme he had devised. Clubs that signed free agents could protect 24 players from their 40-player roster (nonsigning teams could protect 26 players). Unprotected players became part of a compensation pool. If a team lost a free agent who ranked in the top 20 percent of his position, that team could select from any of the players in the compensation pool. In this manner, the signing club was not assured of losing a player. Oh, and another thing. Although the players did not play any games over the past six weeks, they were to receive credit for major league service days as if they had. (To this day, the owners have failed to grasp the leverage inherent in this bargaining chip.)

In the aftermath of the settlement came the damage assessment. The players lost nearly $34 million in salaries, or about $52,000 a player. The owners' losses totaled $72 million, although they recovered $44 million courtesy of Lloyd's of London. Baseball lost 50 days of the season and a total of 713 games. And Ray Grebey lost his job.

Labor relations in baseball were fairly peaceful over the next couple of years. That is to say, relations between labor and management were peaceful; labor-labor relations were in an uproar. Marvin Miller announced his retirement as executive director of the Players' Association. His replacement was Ken Moffett. Moffett had served as federal mediator during the 1981 strike and had become quite friendly with some of the player reps. Unlike Miller, Moffett was not a career union man. Moffett's pronouncements of his labor philosophy reeked of status quo, preaching labor peace and advocating a more cooperative relationship with management. To Miller, this was treason. Retired or not, the Players' Association was his baby. He had nurtured it to maturity from its earliest days; he had staged the revolution against the robber baron industrialists; he had given the Association leadership, solidarity, and a who-o-ole lot of money; and he was not about to let it slip away. To him, handing the union baton over to Moffett was like George Bailey giving Mr. Potter the keys to the Bailey Savings & Loan, only to watch helplessly as Bedford Falls was leveled and replaced with the amoral corporate Pottersville.

Moffett had barely begun settling into his new office before Miller initiated a coup d'état. He wrote a memo to the players warning them about Moffett. The memo was dictated to Miller's former secretary (who was now Moffett's secretary) and was to be mailed on Players' Association letterhead. Needless to say, using the union office to issue warnings about its current director did not win the former director brownie points with Moffett. The locks on the office were changed (an employer lockout with a new twist), and Moffett issued a strong memo effectively banning Miller from active participation in the Players' Association unless it came at his (Moffett's) request. Several months later, Moffett and his appointees were fired. Miller served as interim director until Don Fehr, who had sat alongside Miller as legal counsel for several years, took over as executive director.

As the 1981 collective bargaining agreement approached expiration, the Players' Association began to eyeball baseball's skyrocketing television revenues. Historically, management funded the players' pension, life insurance, and health care plan with one-third of the money from national broadcast revenues. In the early 1970s, when the players struck for the first time, national media revenues averaged roughly $20 million. By the mid-1980s, annual broadcasting revenues were nearly 10 times higher. It didn't take a financial wizard to know that this was serious money, and the Players' Association let it be known that they were entitled to their share.

Not surprisingly, the owners backed off the customary one-third formula. If the players wanted more money, they would have to bargain for it. The owners also countered the players' demands with a claim that the industry was in dire financial straits. This claim had been made before, and the owners' cries of hysteria were usually met with yawns by the Players'

Association. This time, however, the owners supported their assertions by opening their financial statements. The Association turned the books over to economist Roger Noll, who accused the owners of concocting the losses through creative bookkeeping.

In any case, the scenario was ripe for another work stoppage. Turnover among Players' Association executive directors was not the only factor that could influence negotiations. Baseball player careers are finite in length, and usually very short. Few of the players who had been around in the union struggles of the 1970s were still active. Most duespayers to the Association in 1985 had been handed free agency, salary arbitration, and ample compensation without a struggle. The veteran players believed that they had already paid their dues, and they were more willing to sacrifice the earnings of their less-experienced underlings than they were to forego their own money during a strike. In short, Don Fehr found little of the solidarity that had united the players to weather the first two strikes.

As the strike deadline neared, the promise of another midseason interruption appeared imminent. In addition to holding the line on handing the players one-third of their broadcasting revenues, the owners wanted caps on salary arbitration awards and demanded that the requirement for arbitration eligibility be raised from two years to three years.

In the course of the negotiations, the owners unilaterally conceded the compensation pool that had interrupted the 1981 season for 50 days. The compensation pool had seemed like a reasonable compromise in 1981. The owners believed it to have some potential for slowing salary growth, and the losers of key free agents could receive bona fide players as compensation. What the owners did not consider was the fact that their own contributions to the player pool might be selected as compensation. Dissatisfaction with the system mushroomed quickly, and the owners were anxious to dispose of it.

The players easily saw through management's "concession" but were happy to oust the procedure nonetheless. This did not bring the two sides any closer to an agreement. The players walked out on August 6.

Just as the Players' Association had a new executive director leading the walkout, baseball had a new commissioner, Peter Ueberroth. Ueberroth was not about to erode fan support for the game by allowing for another strike. He called the negotiators and gave them an ultimatum. Either they come to an agreement or he would put the issues to binding arbitration. Naturally, the thought of an independent third party imposing a collective bargaining agreement sent chills up the spines of the negotiators. In rapid fashion, they designed a mutually acceptable agreement, halting the work stoppage after only two days. There would be no cap on arbitration salaries, an increase in the arbitration eligibility service standard to three years, and the two sides compromised on pension funding. Under the new contract, the players would receive less than their customary third of broadcasting revenues. Nevertheless, their take of $32.7 million was nearly double their share from the previous contract.

This chapter began with a statement that the lack of a work stoppage in baseball's first century was not to be inferred as an indication of labor harmony. Nothing could be more true of the three years that followed the 1985 negotiations; this was a period that would forever be remembered as "The Collusion Years."

Bowie Kuhn was never well suited for collective bargaining. He was hired to be the commissioner of baseball, a figurehead to preside over the integrity of the game in the shadow of Kenesaw Mountain Landis. His role was never intended to extend into intense negotiations between a pair of labor pros.

In contrast, Peter Ueberroth had been tapped as the successor to baseball's throne owing to his much-publicized stint as director of the 1984 Olympic Games in Los Angeles. The Games were long considered a death blow to the finances of the hosting city. Ueberroth, however, turned the 1984 Olympics into a tribute to Adam Smith: the first capitalistic Olympics. The most basic tenet of the laws of supply and demand were applied: Charge each patron and each sponsor the highest price the market can bear. As a result, the Ueberroth Olympic Games turned a $222 million profit.

Such a track record was of obvious significance to baseball owners, who selected Ueberroth to lead them out of their financial abyss. Ueberroth's approach was to centralize the process. He increased the authority of the commissioner to fine individual owners who were not in sync with the New Order. At meetings, he assumed totalitarian control; the owners could not speak unless they were spoken to. The owners were unaccustomed to such condescension; after all, Ueberroth worked for them, not the reverse. Nonetheless, with the Players' Association having put a permanent dent in the clubs' collective finances, the dictatorial approach of Ueberroth was tolerated.

Ueberroth made it painfully clear to the owners whom he thought the enemy to be: It was not Marvin Miller, it was not Don Fehr, and it was not Peter Seitz. The real enemies were seated at the meetings, and they bore the name "owners." Free agent mania did not bring world championships, he asserted, it only pushed players into higher tax brackets. To support his contention, he circulated some startling statistics on the fiscal irresponsibility of clubs: Nearly $50 million in salaries were owed to players who were no longer in baseball. Players with long-term contracts spent considerably more time on the disabled list than those on single-year contracts. Players with multiyear contracts exhibited deteriorating performances throughout the duration of their agreements.

In the end, Ueberroth's admonitions against fiscal waste worked only too well. Since the Seitz decision, the owners complained loudly about free agency but then rushed to the winter meetings with deep pocketbooks, anxious to deliver a Messiah to the home-town crowd at any price. When the free agent didn't pan out, or the team didn't win, or the club lost money, another Messiah was called upon to do the job. This was standard operating procedure until the arrival of Ueberroth. Ueberroth whipped the owners into submission, browbeating them into accepting his point of view. In lieu of the speeches, the statistics, the public humiliation, only a fool would have subjected himself to the wrath of the groupthink by signing a free agent.

The first player to experience the free agent drought was Detroit Tiger outfielder Kirk Gibson. Gibson, a former football star at the collegiate level, played baseball with the same reckless abandon that he did on the gridiron. To the highest bidder, he promised power, speed, and a fiercely competitive spirit. In an abrupt and unexpected change in environs, he meandered through baseball's free agent signing period as a man without a team. Defeated in his attempts to solicit bids from other teams, Gibson returned to Detroit. The other premium free agents fared no better. In fact, of the 33 players who declared free agency that year, 29 re-signed with their old teams, having received no offers from competing clubs.

Going into the 1986 free agency period, the new commissioner had created a monster operating on automatic pilot. For the first time since free agency began, the increase in the average salary showed signs of slowing to single digits. The owners discovered that the key to fiscal sanity was to turn their backs on free agency. Had an individual owner or two opted to turn their nose up at free agency, few eyebrows would have been raised. The marketplace ultimately would have determined whether such behavior was laudable or foolish. Now, however, there *was* no marketplace; by refusing to bid on free agents and not having to fear one's own stars being bid away, the teams' profits had nowhere to go but up.

The curious disinterest in the game's free agents did not get past the watchful eye of the Players' Association. Its office had been inundated with complaints from players and their agents. The Association filed grievances for each of the 1985–1986, 1986–1987, and 1987–1988 periods. The Basic Agreement plainly forbade clubs from acting in concert in the bidding for free agents, and it was just as plain that the clubs were doing exactly that. In the first two hearings, the arbitrators, Tom Roberts and George Nicolau, sided with the Players' Association and ruled that the clubs were guilty of collusion. In addition to damages, which would be settled at a later date, free agents during this period would be granted the opportunity to shop the market again if they chose to do so. Ironically, Kirk Gibson took the opportunity to jump to the Los Angeles Dodgers, leading them to the World Series and winning the National League's Most Valuable Player award. It is also somewhat poetic that his dramatic ninth-inning limp-hit home run trot remains indelibly laced into baseball folklore. The third collusion ruling, also by Nicolau, came about after the owners concocted a scheme to skirt the charges of collusion. Free agent bidding was fine, but each bidder must submit his or her bid to an information bank. Unlike the free agent bidding of the 1970s or early 1980s, when player agents would play clubs off each other to set off a bidding war, each club would now know exactly what its competitors had bid. Theoretically, then, a club could win a free agent's services by bidding the highest existing bid plus one dollar. The Players' Association filed a grievance against the information bank, and once again, the arbitrator sided against the owners. Eventually, the opposing sides settled on collusion damages totaling $280 million. As the expiration of the 1985 Basic Agreement drew near, there were murmurs of another work stoppage. Of course, by now, contract expirations and work stoppages had become synonymous; one simply couldn't exist without the other. The only relevant issue was over which side would initiate the attack.

Baseball's collusion years, hardly relegated to nasty rumors, were now a matter of public record. The owners had earned a pretty penny over the temporary throwback to the "good ol' days," and now it was about to enter payback time. Don Fehr was not about to enter the negotiations on congenial terms. Unlike his predecessor, he'd been burned by the owners. Fehr had also been publicly scorched by Marvin Miller for giving up a year of eligibility for salary arbitration, and the executive director was certain to place it at the top of his agenda. To head off the possibility of a midseason strike, the owners decided to launch the first missile. Absent an agreement, the gates at spring training would be locked. Chuck O'Connor (who succeeded Barry Rona, who had succeeded Lee MacPhail, who had succeeded Ray Grebey, who had succeeded John Gaherin) was now management's chief negotiator and the messenger of the owners' hard-line.

With big money gleefully being tossed around to free agents once again, the owners decided to take the offensive. They presented Fehr with a request for a salary cap, accompanied by a pay-for-performance formula to replace arbitration. Baseball's new commissioner was Fay Vincent. Like for his predecessors, work stoppages fell well within the scope of the "interests of baseball" of which the commissioner was to be the guardian. Convinced that Fehr would never buy the package, Vincent unilaterally pulled it from the bargaining table and replaced it with his own proposal. Shortly thereafter, O'Connor received word that Vincent had seized the chief negotiator hat for himself and was privately negotiating with Fehr at the request of no one. In the events that were to haunt Vincent over the coming year, his unsolicited involvement in labor negotiations could be referred to as "strike one."

Almost as if scripted, Fehr entered the negotiations determined to win back the year of arbitration eligibility he had given away four years earlier. Much to his chagrin, however, there was much division within the ranks. The most vocal dissenter among the rank and file was veteran catcher Bob Boone, who surprisingly had been a key player in the 1981 strike. Boone was unwilling to sacrifice salary to enhance the financial welfare of a handful of younger players, and he'd uncovered quite a few other veterans who felt the same. Fehr lured Marvin Miller out of retirement to cut off the tongue of the union's loose cannon. Boone became angered by the union brass and accused them of directing a top-down rather than grass-roots operation. Fehr and Miller worked feverishly to patch up the dissent and restore unity in the players.

Fehr's latest proposal included a flat-out compromise on the arbitration issue: Half of the players with between two and three years of service would become eligible. Fay Vincent's hands-on dealings during the negotiations had hardly endeared him to his employers, and their silent contempt for the commissioner ran high when he beckoned them to accept Fehr's offer. Before the weekend came to an end, an agreement had been reached. Baseball's minimum salary would jump to $100,000, and the salary arbitration eligibility issue, which had stalemated the negotiations, had achieved a compromise (if one were to define "compromise" as getting less than initially desired). In fact, the new terms of the agreement consisted entirely of management concessions to the players. Baseball negotiations were back to normal.

The Players' Association had already gone through its internal squabbles in the early 1980s. Now it was management's turn. The new chief negotiator for the owners, Dick Ravitch (who had succeeded Chuck O'Connor, who had succeeded . . . well, you know) was wary over Commissioner Vincent's involvement in labor negotiations during the lockout. He pushed to have Vincent's duties as commissioner redefined so as to keep his nose away from the bargaining table. Vincent steadfastly refused. The Major League

Agreement had a rule that forbade the clubs from diminishing the powers of the commissioner while he was in office, and Vincent waved it like a flag. He agreed verbally to adhere to some of the owners' requests, but an amendment to the Major League Agreement was out of the question.

"Strike two" came about over the National League's decision to add two expansion clubs. Historically, the fees charged to newcomers were somewhat nominal ($7 million per team in 1977), and the revenues were split among the clubs in the new team's league. The 1993 expansion was different. The price for membership in the Club had now risen to $95 million. The notion that a windfall this large should be distributed among National League teams only was unconscionable to the American League clubs, who demanded their fair share. After a tug-of-war between the leagues failed to achieve a resolution, the issue fell in the lap of Fay Vincent. The case had all the trimmings of the Messersmith decision: No matter what the split, one of the leagues would walk away miffed. Vincent decided to award 22 percent of the fees to the American League. The result: *Both* leagues got miffed.

"Strike three" was a spitball tossed by the Tribune Company, owners of the Chicago Cubs. The National League was preparing for realignment. Chicago and St. Louis had been in the Eastern Division since 1969, despite the fact that they were geographically west of Western Division teams Cincinnati and Atlanta. The logical move was for the four teams to swap divisions. Chicago balked. Chicago Cub baseball was a cash cow for the Tribune Company, which beamed its games nationwide on superstation WGN. A move to the Western Division would mean more games with San Francisco, Los Angeles, and San Diego, and the late starting times would certainly cut into the TV station's advertising revenue. Vincent came down from the mountaintop and ordered the move as "in the best interests of baseball." Though the rest of the clubs agreed that the Tribune Company had been rather pigheaded in this matter, they did not regard it as one to be resolved by "executive order." Fay Vincent's fate had been sealed.

Unable to fire the commissioner, the clubs gathered together to draft a statement of no confidence. Vincent dug in his heels and vowed a legal battle. The events had constituted a holy war to Vincent, and he saw himself as the sole protector of a religious shrine. He would not be removed from office without a fight. When the no-confidence vote passed by a two-thirds majority, the owners prepared for Vincent to make his first move toward litigation. To their surprise, the commissioner resigned.

One by-product of the 1990 lockout was the creation of a joint committee to report on the economic status of baseball. Like most committees of this sort, the owners and players each selected their own appointees, which included former Chairman of the Federal Reserve System Paul Volcker.

In 1992 the committee completed its report. The group pointed to the growing disparities in the revenues of the large- and small-market clubs as a cause for concern. Because national broadcasting revenue, which had become the lifeblood of smaller markets, was likely to decline, the committee urged the owners to adopt a more aggressive means of sharing revenues between teams. This, they argued, would preserve not only the financial stability of smaller-market clubs but also competitive balance within the league.

Regarding the proposal of salary caps, which would tie player salaries to a fixed percentage of league revenues, the committee did not commit itself to a position. Reflecting perhaps the partisanship of the owners and players who had appointed them, the committee limited its comments to a discussion of the pros and cons of having caps.

Unfortunately, like most joint committee work, the time spent developing the analysis was largely for naught. The two sides scoured the report for conclusions that supported their contentions and casually ignored the rest. The next showdown was to be resolved by owner and player reps at the bargaining table, not by a group of preeminent economists.

With major league baseball commissionerless following the ousting of Fay Vincent, the owners prepared for their next confrontation with labor. The collective bargaining agreement negotiated in 1990 had a reopener clause, which allowed either side to reopen the agreement after 1992. At the urging of Ravitch, the owners did so. By reopening the agreement prior to its expiration, the owners freed either side to enact yet another work stoppage.

The negotiations that ensued were probably the most intense confrontations witnessed in 20 years. Each side took extreme positions and stubbornly refused to budge. Never before had such obstinacy threatened to derail any hope of productive bargaining. Only something was missing from the negotiations: the Players' Association. This round of bargaining had nothing to do with negotiations between labor and management. This time it was management against management.

Baseball had always been characterized by large- and small-market teams. The New York, Chicago, and Los Angeles clubs had a greater drawing base than clubs like Kansas City or Seattle. In recent years, however, the gap had become substantially larger, due primarily to growing disparities in local broadcasting revenues.

As recently as 1985, the difference in broadcast dollars between the high-revenue club (the Yankees) and the low-revenue club (the Mariners) was barely $12 million. By 1990, on the other hand, the Yankees were drawing $55.6 million in local broadcast revenues, compared with the paltry $3 million pulled in by Seattle.

The wide disparity between the financial resources of the large- and small-market clubs had begun to infiltrate the field in a way not quite witnessed previously. The small-market Pittsburgh Pirates, through astute trades for major league prospects and player development within its own farm system, suffered through several years of growing pains awaiting harvest time. Eventually its crop of youngsters developed into stars and led the team to three consecutive division titles. Then, as if torn apart by a hurricane, the dynasty was instantly dismantled, as its core of stars were bid away by large-market dollars.

Even more pathetic was the plight of the San Diego Padres. The Padres, also bearing the scarlet letter "S," had finished the 1992 season in second place. Presumed by its fans to be a contender in 1993, the club promptly shed itself of anyone whose salary totaled seven digits. Fred McGriff, who had pieced together more consecutive 30-plus home run seasons than any player in the game, was dealt to the Atlanta Braves in exchange for a host of no-names for whom baseball cards had to be hastily manufactured. Likewise for Gary Sheffield, who flirted with baseball's Triple Crown only a year before. The flood of players exiting San Diego could have stocked an All-Star team. The incoming players, on the other hand, could only be identified with the aid of a high school yearbook.

The small-market clubs were not about to let this trend continue. Decreased national broadcasting revenues were on the horizon, which would only increase the imbalance. They demanded more aggressive revenue-sharing from the larger-market teams. Suddenly, Dick Ravitch, who had been hired to lock horns with Don Fehr, found himself refereeing a battle between the owners.

With no hope of a revenue-sharing agreement in sight, Ravitch had to come to grips with the double-edged sword inherent in reopener clauses. The players could organize a strike in midseason. Hoping to stave off such a possibility, Ravitch promised a no-lockout pledge from the owners in exchange for a reciprocal no-strike guarantee from the players. Fehr agreed, and baseball was spared a midseason impasse.

For the better part of the year, the owners ferociously debated revenue-sharing. The reluctance of large-market clubs to share their revenues with small-market teams was only natural. Owners are in business to make money, and agreeing to increased revenue-sharing is like the Sheriff of Nottingham handing Robin Hood his wallet.

There was more to it than just the money. The owners also like to field winning teams. Given their druthers, they would prefer to see their own team in the World Series over someone else's. Revenue imbalances improved the odds for large-market teams. Market-related revenue differentials, for example, allowed the New York Mets to bid Bobby Bonilla away from small-market rival Pittsburgh. The Mets knew they could outbid the Pirates and stay in the black, and they liked having it that way. (The fact that the Mets' bevy of high-priced free agents wound up being big-time losers is another story.) Thus, not only did revenue-sharing cut into the larger teams' profits, it also meant handing over money to competitors, who could then use it to try to bid away the large-market teams' players. Why would any sane large-market owner be agreeable to this?

Eventually, the two sides agreed to a system of revenue-sharing. It came, however, with a catch. The large-market teams would agree to revenue-sharing only if it were tied to a salary cap. In other words, the large clubs would only give up money if the players made up the difference. To no one's surprise, the players were not amenable to such a deal. They walked out on August 12, 1994.

The 1994 season had been a dandy. Both Matt Williams and Ken Griffey, Jr. were chasing after Roger Maris's non-asterisked home run record. Tony Gwynn's batting average was hovering around .400. Cal Ripken, Jr.'s consecutive game streak was now within sight of Lou Gehrig's. Perpetual loser Cleveland was one game behind the division leader. Yet all would be for naught if the season were not to resume.

The Players' Association had been preparing for this showdown for some time. It had stockpiled $175 million of licensing revenue to be used as a strike fund. The average player would lose nearly $7,000 per day during a strike. If the Association were to disburse the fund to the players at the same daily rate, it would not be depleted for a month. If the players had been prudent enough to stash away some of their own pay, they could easily last through the remainder of the season.

Salary caps had existed in professional basketball and football, the owners argued, so why not baseball? (Of course, the fact that both basketball and football players bemoaned their respective caps was beside the point.) The deal the owners laid out on the bargaining table called for all revenues in baseball to be split 50/50 between the clubs and the players. In fact, the players already earned 58 percent of the revenues. If the 50 percent was not acceptable, said Ravitch, give us your figure.

Don Fehr stated unequivocally that no salary cap would ever be acceptable and that the strike would continue as long as a cap was on the table. Fehr believed that baseball's woes could be traced solely to revenue imbalances and that the industry's problems could be resolved simply by sharing revenues on a more equitable basis. In other words—it was unacceptable for the clubs to expect the players to give up some of their money to help out Pittsburgh and San Diego; it was perfectly OK, however, for the New York Mets and Los Angeles Dodgers to give up some of theirs.

And so the gridlock continued. In between press conferences, the two sides managed to squeeze in some time at the bargaining table. No negotiations actually took place, nor were any compromises discussed. Rather, the opposing sides would get together to reiterate their stances on the issues, apparently in the event the other side had forgotten.

The Players' Association was certain that the owners would blink first. Unlike the small-market teams, for whom the status quo was patently unacceptable, there were plenty of teams that would be profitable with or without the current proposal. To them, a show of solidarity came at an enormous cost. Prior to the strike, however, the owners had adopted a new rule: No settlement could be approved without a three-fourths majority. This placed the larger-market teams in the minority and put the small- and medium-market teams in charge. The impasse continued.

On September 14, 1994, the remainder of the season was officially canceled. The announcement came without fanfare. Bud Selig, the un-commissioner, disseminated the edict in a four-paragraph fax.

The cancellation did not bring the two sides any closer together. Congress toyed with the notion of lifting baseball's antitrust exemption as a means of ending the strike. The owners offered to drop the salary cap and replace it with a luxury tax, which would punish teams with excessive payrolls. To the Players' Association, however, a luxury tax was simply a salary cap in subtitles.

On December 22 the owners finally declared an impasse and unilaterally imposed the same salary cap that had begun the negotiations. Along with the establishment of payrolls and benefits equal to 50 percent of the previous year's revenues, each team's payroll would be constrained to being within 84 percent and 110 percent of the average payroll.

The new system also implemented changes in the free agency and salary arbitration. Arbitration, long regarded as a thorn in the owners' side, was discarded. In its stead, players with between four and six years of major league service would be restricted free agents, meaning that they would be bound to their current clubs only if the team matched an outside offer for the player's services. Unrestricted free agency for players with at least six years of experience would continue.

The response of the Players' Association was to move away from the bargaining table and into the legal arena. The Association filed a charge with the National Labor Relations Board (NLRB), alleging that the owners failed to bargain in good faith when they unilaterally implemented the salary cap. If the NLRB were to file a complaint against the owners, it could move for an injunction, which would prevent the owners from implementing their plan.

In early February of 1995 the Board hinted that it would, in fact, file a complaint against management. In rapid fashion, the owners dropped the salary cap and replaced it with a proposal calling for a luxury tax, which would impose a series of penalties for payrolls existing above a predetermined threshold.

After the salary cap was removed, the Players' Association dropped its self-imposed ban on player signings. Ironically, however, management moved just as quickly to impose its own ban, arguing that issues such as free agency- and salary arbitration-eligibility were unresolved and made meaningful salary negotiations impossible. In response, the Players' Association filed another charge of unfair labor practices against management.

The Players' Association was also busy politicking for the lifting of baseball's antitrust exemption. Removing the exemption would allow the union to sue major league baseball for antitrust violations, giving it additional leverage in bargaining. Earlier in the fall, the players pledged that the strike would end if the exemption were repealed. Members of Congress, seeing a chance to take credit for ending the dreaded baseball strike, looked favorably toward removing the exemption, but then agreed to table the discussion until the start of the new year.

Although Congress's interest in lifting the exemption appeared to wane since the September hearings, President Clinton initiated his own involvement. Having already assigned William Usery as mediator to the disputes several months earlier, the President beckoned the two sides to come to an agreement before the scheduled start of spring training. In fact, he proposed a deadline of February 6, Babe Ruth's 100th birthday, for a settlement. Although the executive office has no legal power to intervene in the negotiations, he hinted that a failure of the two sides to come to an agreement by the deadline could lead to legislation calling for binding arbitration. He also suggested that Usery propose his own nonbinding solution if the parties were still at impasse at the deadline.

The players and owners doggedly tried to come to an agreement in the days that followed. Nonetheless, it was no secret that the President's threat lacked teeth. Baseball's impact on the gross domestic product is so small that it can only be detected with a magnifying glass. The industry generates little income, few jobs, and does not impact national security. Direct government intervention in an industry that generates little more than civic pride and entertainment would have been unprecedented.

In the meantime, the owners began their own offensive. They publicly discussed the possible use of replacement players should the strike continue into spring training. The National Football League had made effective use of scab players several years earlier when the players struck to obtain free agency. The crowds were smaller, but the game went on, and in time the players crossed the picket lines in droves.

As the prospect of an opening day with replacement players drew nearer, the momentum favored the owners. Productive bargaining had come to a grinding halt. If the clubs could draw enough fans to cover their game costs, it would just be a matter of time before the players cracked; hence, there was no reason for the owners to negotiate.

Then, suddenly, the bargaining leverage shifted gears as abruptly as the swirling wind changes directions at Candlestick Park (or 3Com Park to nonpurists). In late March the National Labor Relations Board ruled that the owners had not bargained in good faith when they banned player signings in early February. In seeking an injunction, the Board ruled that the two sides must continue to bargain under the rules of the previous agreement. For the players, whose only demand was to preserve the status quo, the Board's action ventured well beyond establishing a level playing field for negotiations: It essentially awarded the players an unconditional victory for the 1995 season.

Management had little time to react to the decision. U.S. Circuit Court Judge Sonia Sotomayor was to rule on the injunction the following Friday, and the season was officially scheduled to begin before the weekend was through. The owners promptly announced their "willingness" to play the 1995 season under the old set of rules (a generous act of magnanimity, given the court's power to enforce the NLRB injunction) and offered the players essentially the same luxury tax deal that had been on the table previously for the 1996 season and beyond. The players countered with their own illusion of compromise. No deal was reached, and the two sides remained miles apart.

When Judge Sotomayor sided with the NLRB's decision on March 31, the owners ran out of options. A lockout of the players was potentially illegal, and the damages resulting from a suit could add up to $5.5 million per day in back pay. They had no choice but to allow the games to begin (albeit three weeks behind schedule).

As baseball prepared to enter into the 1995 season without a collective bargaining agreement, the only view shared by the two sides throughout the strike was that baseball was impervious to permanent and irreparable damage. They had learned through all of the threats, all of the lockouts, and all of the strikes that a baseball fan's love and devotion to the game were unshakable, and that the psyche of baseball's loyal following could be summarized by a reconstructed line from the movie *Field of Dreams*: "If you play it, they will come."

Unfortunately, both sides faced a rude reality once the season got under way. Having spent the entire winter arguing over how to split the pie, they returned to the game only to discover that the pie had shrunk. Despite slashing ticket prices, despite offering giveaways, and despite taking great pains to restore the image of the game (there were even unconfirmed reports of players tipping their caps to the fans at some ballparks), the fans they had so dutifully alienated over the past several months stayed home. Attendance declined by 20 percent despite the reductions in ticket prices, national broadcasting revenues dropped by 20 percent, and local broadcasting revenues and cable advertising were down 30 percent. Baseball was damaged goods.

The diminished interest in baseball had ill effects on the players as well. The average player salary fell from $1.26 million to $1.07 million. The decline was the first decrease in player salaries since the collusion period. If the collusion period is ignored, the 1995 decline marked the first drop in player salaries since baseball became unionized.

One might have thought that the 1994–1995 strike, which cost both sides dearly and whose aftershocks carried into the 1995 season, would have caused everyone to rethink their priorities, but alas not. The bargaining table gathered dust as the owners once again appealed the NLRB decision. Don Fehr hinted at the possibility of a midseason strike unless the owners pledged not to lock out the players in 1996. Both sides spoke eloquently about the need for a new labor agreement to restore America's faith in the game, but no meaningful negotiations took place over the course of the season. Was the new agreement expected to come about through osmosis? Or were the two sides jockeying for position, trying to develop a strategy that would gain the advantage at the bargaining table? Then, in August 1996, in the midst of the second year of the automatic-pilot labor agreement, came news of a divine intervention. Randy Levine (management's labor-negotiator-of-the-week) was close to an agreement with Don Fehr. The proposed deal included provisions for a luxury tax in the first three years of the agreement. It also returned the service days lost during the 1994–1995 strike to the players in exchange for a promise to drop litigation charges against the owners for their unfair labor practices. Acceptance of the deal would pave the way for a new-and-improved revenue-sharing scheme, the beginning of interleague play, and most importantly, a five-year period of relief for the fans.

The optimistic reports brought a glow to the faces of baseball fans who were too young to know better. Twenty-three owners had to vote in favor of the proposal to complete the agreement. Sports reporters took straw votes as to how many owners would support the deal. Preliminary reports suggested that as many as eight owners opposed the agreement. Periodic updates fluctuated between eight and 12 "No" votes. Interim Commissioner Bud Selig refused to tip his hand on which direction he was leaning.

On Wednesday, November 6, the owners delivered the bad news. Eighteen of the 30 owners voted against the deal. Baseball appeared to be back to square one.

But then, three weeks later, on November 26, common sense accomplished what the gods could not. The owners reversed their previous stance and overwhelmingly voted to accept the deal by a lop-sided 26–4 margin.

What was responsible for the change of heart? Why would an agreement that was patently unacceptable to 60 percent of baseball's brass suddenly be fine and dandy only three weeks later? Could it be that the owners recognized the importance of preserving the integrity of the national pastime? Doubtful, unless one believes that canceling a World Series and preparing to suit up replacement players had similar appeal to the fans of Mudville.

To the contrary, the evidence suggests that a series of events that transpired shortly after the initial vote may have caused the tides to turn. Two weeks after the "No" vote promised yet another year of a court-ordered status quo, the Chicago White Sox signed Albert Belle to a reported $55 million five-year contract. The signing turned more heads than Madonna's announcement that she was pregnant. Belle, whose explosive bat was matched only by his explosive temper, was to become baseball's first player to sport an eight-figure annual salary. The $11 million per year salary easily dwarfed the $9 million figure pulled in by Cecil Fielder in 1996.

The Belle signing was not an aberration. John Smoltz re-signed with the Braves and became the game's highest-paid pitcher. Bobby Bonilla, who was heavily criticized in New York for being baseball's least-worthy $6 million player, signed on with the Florida Marlins for a hefty raise. The owners, it appeared, were preparing for a spending binge—and without the benefit of extra revenues from interleague play or expansion fees.

Moreover, not all of the clubs were preparing to empty their pocketbooks. The Pittsburgh Pirates made a tactical decision to make a bad team worse, and were in the process of dumping any player whose salary totaled seven figures. The Pirates' total payroll in 1996 was already less than what Albert Belle and Frank Thomas stood to earn in combined salaries in 1997, and Pittsburgh seemed hellbent on lowering it by even more.

By voting to accept the deal, the owners might halt the trend. If the recent signings were any indication, the $51 million tax threshold specified in the proposed labor agreement for 1997 would affect more than just a small handful of clubs. Only four clubs reported payrolls exceeding $51 million in 1996. A luxury tax would not only discourage teams from paying Belle-like salaries to other free agents, it would also serve as a source of much-needed revenue for small-market teams such as Pittsburgh and Milwaukee. Further, approving the deal would also allow baseball to enact its revenue-sharing plan, begin interleague play, and expand the league to include the Arizona Diamondbacks and Tampa Bay Devil Rays—after all, if the owners are going to pay eight-figure salaries, they're going to need some money! In short, the owners believed that perhaps the deal was better than they had previously thought—in any case, it sure looked better than the status quo. Peace was at hand!

As the 1997 baseball season proceeds, guided by the terms of the new collective bargaining contract, the scars from the 1994–1996 skirmishes will gradually heal. As they do, it will become easy for us baseball fans to be lulled into complacency and to adopt the belief that perhaps baseball will finally begin to resemble the fond days of yesteryear—when "strike" referred to a pitch. Let us be reminded, however, that baseball has not had a collective bargaining agreement expire without a work stoppage in over twenty years. And let it not be forgotten that it was Hall of Fame catcher Yogi Berra, and not Thoreau or Emerson, that was credited with saying "It isn't over until it's over." Are baseball's labor problems finally over? Only time will tell.

Part 4: The International Game

An autographed photo of the American and Japanese all-star teams prior to the 1934 series in Japan. Reprinted from Louis Kaufman, Barbara Fitzgerald, and Tom Sewell, *Moe Berg: Athlete, Scholar, Spy* (Mattituck NY, 1990).

DONALD RODEN

16. Baseball and the Quest for National Dignity in Meiji Japan

Conscious American attempts to export the benefits of baseball to the rest of the world date back at least to 1874, when Harry Wright and Albert Spalding, two of the game's earliest "promoters" traveled to England to introduce the game there. Although their effort ended in failure, Spalding subsequently led his highly publicized six-month world tour of all-stars in 1888–89 to promote the game overseas. He unabashedly touted baseball's incorporation of "all those essentials of manliness, courage, nerve, pluck and endurance, characteristic of the Anglo-Saxon race." Spalding failed to win many converts, although Mark Twain applauded the tour as symbolic of the "drive and push and rush and struggle of the raging, tearing, booming nineteenth century." More important than Spalding's efforts, however, were the less visible, more persistent activities of American missionaries, soldiers, businessmen, and students who, like the British and their cricket, took their pastime with them and introduced it to the indigenous populations as they followed the flag. Indeed, the parts of the world that embraced America's game the earliest were those where the physical presence of the United States was most dominant.

Ironically, Japan was not one of those places. In fact, Spalding's tour had shunned that traditionally closed society. Yet it was the Japanese who came closest to America's commitment to the game, even going so far as to adopt it as their national sport. As great borrowers and adapters of culture, they developed a national enthusiasm for *besubōru* that often bordered on fanaticism. The puzzling question that inevitably arises is why a country like Japan, whose culture and traditions differed so much from those of the United States, would adopt the latter's game? The game was introduced in Japan as early as 1873, only twenty years after Commodore Matthew C. Perry forced the opening of the Japanese treaty ports in 1853–54. Taught to college students at what would eventually become Tokyo University by a visiting American professor, Horace Wilson, the game languished for the next couple of decades despite several visitations by American college teams. Yet during the decade leading up to the turn of the century, a baseball mania infected the country's elites and spectators alike.

Donald Roden explores the broad context in which baseball swept Japan in the 1890s, examining the underlying cultural, social, and political forces of the time. In the process, he finds baseball to be a manifestation of a confluence of the competitive spirit of Social Darwinism and nationalistic determination to break out of the bonds of Western-imposed unequal treaties. It reflected a new national pride designed to instill a regimented obedience to the state, as well as to foster physical stamina and the desired values of order, loyalty, honor, and self-discipline, which would produce a new age of manliness for Japan just as it had for its Western rivals. Roden also draws attention to the inherent contradictions attendant to the spread of the American pastime to such far away places. Baseball could expand American cultural influence around the world, but if the Japanese became too proficient in our sport and became too imbued with all its professed competitive attributes, would Japan become a rival to American cultural, economic, and political dominance to the detriment of good will across the Pacific? In other words, was there a direct line from the playing fields of Yokohama and to killing fields of the war in the Pacific fifty years later?

The surge of interest in athletics and gymnastics that overtook parts of Europe and the United States at the end of the nineteenth century has begun to receive the scholarly attention it deserves as a remarkable manifestation of the spirit of the times. Despite Johan Huizinga's characterization of the sporting world as "illusionary" and "standing quite consciously outside 'ordinary' life," it is apparent that the defenders of outdoor games in Victorian England and America "quite consciously" used the playing field for very real political and social ends. For Thomas Hughes, cricket and football superseded book learning in the cultivation of Christian "manliness"; for

Edward Thring, athletic contests were a "priceless boon" in helping the English become "such an adventurous race"; for Herbert Spencer, "sportive activities," free from gymnastic regimentation and peer-group coercion, were "divinely appointed means" to human welfare and development; and, for Theodore Roosevelt, "the strenuous life" of physical strife and challenge was a key to "true national greatness." Underlying the views of these and other spokesmen for "the life of manly vigor" is the attempt to link sport, first, to the ideal social character of a governing elite and, second, to the strength of the nation.

Presumably, the recognition of the social and political value of sport was rooted in the Social Darwinist perception of "civilization" generated by what Spencer called "a persistence of force." But along with the notion of the rectitude of might was a corresponding fear that the mechanization of power in an industrializing state spawns moral lassitude. Routine, convenience, docility, and protruding stomachs were all alarming signs that, as Roosevelt declared in 1894, "a peaceful and commercial civilization" was on the verge of forfeiting those "virile fighting qualities" that were the source of its rise. Thus, participation in athletics became a moral imperative to counteract the sloth that progress brings and to keep the fires of adventure burning among those who occupy the highest offices of state. In an age when many assumed that only the fittest nations could survive and flourish in a hostile world, athletics, patriotism, and the ideology of manliness were inseparable.

While sport was gaining recognition as a symbol of national strength and elitist pretension in late nineteenth-century England and America, the absence of sport in any foreign land could be interpreted, conversely, as a sure signal of cultural weakness and even racial inferiority. According to the logic of Rudyard Kipling and Thomas Hughes, lands not inhabited by Stalkies, Tom Browns, or Dink Stovers were not "civilized" and, hence, deserved to be colonized by the bold and the athletic. William Mathews, professor at the University of Chicago, wrote in his popular, late-century handbook for "young America," "that the splendid empires which England has founded in every quarter of the globe have had their origin largely in the football contests at Eton, the boat-races on the Thames, and the cricket-matches on her downs and heaths, who can doubt? The race so widely dominant . . . is dominant because its institutions cultivate self-reliance, and its breeding develops endurance, courage, and pluck." Destitute of these hearty attributes, the "lesser races" had little hope of rising above a feeble state of subjugation. It is little wonder, then, that colonial settlements from Shanghai to Algiers had their share of sportsmen whose conspicuous club activities could be construed as evidence of superior "breeding" and vindication of imperialism. The athletic subculture in the coastal treaty ports of Japan was no exception.

In the mid–nineteenth century Japan was, like the rest of Asia, vulnerable to imperialist incursion. The "unequal" treaties negotiated among the Western powers and the Tokugawa *bakufu* in the 1850s opened six coastal ports for preferential trade and granted Americans and Europeans living in those ports complete extraterritorial authority in all criminal and civil matters. Foreign garrisons backed up by men-of-war, which used the ports as coaling stations, helped guarantee trading and residential privileges during the turbulent years of the Meiji Restoration. As a consequence of the treaties, the foreign residents, visitors, and military personnel, whose combined numbers soared to over fifteen thousand during the 1860s, were free to transform the settlements into distinct cultural enclaves. And, once the initial problems of accommodation and security were overcome, the leaders of the settlements devoted much of their civic energies to enhancing the amenities of colonial life with "international clubs" staffed by major domos in white jackets, "public parks" interlaced by sidewalks for Sunday morning strolls, spacious lawns for afternoon teas and games of croquet, and gymnasiums and playing fields for local sportsmen.

From the early years of Japanese treaty ports athletics was at the center of the male-dominated social and recreational life of the foreign community. Writing about the largest settlement in Yokohama during the 1880s, John Morris noted that "sport is pursued in all its branches with that ardour which distinguishes the Anglo-Saxon race wherever met with." Among the sports that Morris witnessed were cricket, tennis, crew, and rifle-shooting— all performed with "a zest that amazes the native population." Other early visitors to the foreign settlement in Yokohama were similarly impressed by the "zest" for athletics that accentuated the cultural disparity between "the rough and aggressive Anglo-Saxons" and "a nation whose men flew kites, studied flower arrangement, enjoyed toy gardens, carried fans, and manifested other effeminate customs and behaviors." Despite a fascination for "old samurai tales" and an awareness of the "enlightened" policies of the Meiji government, popular stereotypes of the Japanese as being "essentially feeble"—and most certainly wanting in the virtues of the athletic field— continued to influence the attitudes of resident Westerners in the 1870s and 1880s.

The cultural lag that allowed foreign citizens in the treaty ports to foist the image of effeminacy and unmanliness on the Japanese would not, of course, stand up against the overwhelming realities of the *fin de siècle*. The development of a strong constitutional government, the triumph in the

Sino-Japanese War, the growth of the textile industry for foreign export, and, finally, the negotiations to abrogate the "unequal" treaties all combined in the 1890s to make old stereotypes untenable. Suddenly, "Japan the exotic" became "Japan the competitor" in war, diplomacy, commerce, and, one may add, baseball.

Of the outdoor games that attracted Japanese youth at the turn of the century, none rivaled baseball in igniting enthusiasm among players, spectators, and readers of an expanding popular press. How baseball rose from oblivion to embody the Social Darwinist spirit of competition and "vigor" (*genki*) that swept Japan in the 1890s, how it heralded a new chapter in Japanese-American relations, and how it ultimately enhanced both the social image of a student elite and the geopolitical image of a nation that was just breaking free from the shackles of "unequal" treaties are the subject of this essay.

It is unlikely that anyone attending college in the 1870s in Japan could have predicted that athletics in general and baseball in particular would figure in the quest for national dignity at the end of the century. As it was, most students and their teachers had only the foggiest conception of Western sports, let alone a plan for an extracurricular athletic program under institutional sponsorship. In fact, early Meiji educators were not at all convinced of the need for physical education in any form. The preamble to the Educational Code of 1872, the document that gave shape and purpose to the post-Restoration school system, made no mention of physical fitness; the code's articles assigned the lowest priority to physical exercise in the primary schools and ignored the subject entirely in establishing academic guidelines for secondary schools. Behind this unhesitating dismissal was a widespread sense of urgency among educators that "practical knowledge" in the form of "Western studies" must be disseminated as quickly and as efficiently as possible. To interrupt the study of geography, basic science, or foreign languages with extended recesses for students to hoist dumbbells or skip rope seemed like a luxury the nation could ill afford. Besides, on a philosophic level, it was generally assumed in the early 1870s that a "civilized man" was someone of intellectual, and not necessarily physical, prowess.

Among the first to voice concern over the lopsided academic demands imposed upon early Meiji students were foreign teachers who had been employed by the government to facilitate the transmission of Western learning. Reflecting upon his four years of service at a commercial school in Tokyo between 1876 and 1880, W. Gray Dixon noted that "the frequency of sickness among the students and their generally delicate physique demanded greater attention to out-of-door exercise." Indeed, "a passion for intellectual development," he continued, "seemed to blind them to the necessity of an accompanying development of the body." Dixon's critique of the "narrow intellectualism" in the early Meiji school system was echoed by other Western teachers at the time, including William E. Griffis, who contrasted the scholarly aptitude of his advanced students with their "docile" dispositions and their lack of "fire, energy, and manly independence." Nor was his assessment unique: "The experience of foreign teachers on this point is almost unanimous." And, Griffis asserted in 1874, "native officials have no clear idea, often none at all, of the absolute necessity of exercise, in the open air and sunshine, for young persons of both sexes." Like Dixon, Griffis believed that Japan's development as a modern civilization would depend as much upon the building of physical character as it would upon the mastery of science and foreign languages.

Responding in large part to the opinions of American educators, the Ministry of Education decided in 1878 to establish a special Gymnastics Institute (*Taisō Denshūjo*), the purpose of which was to train physical education instructors for the primary schools. Selected as the first director of the institute was Dr. George A. Leland, a recent graduate of the Department of Hygiene and Physical Education at Amherst College and a student of Edward Hitchcock, one of the pioneers in the development of physical education in the United States. While in Japan, Leland concentrated on developing a regimen of "light calisthenics" (*kei taisō*) or group setting-up exercises that could easily be institutionalized in the primary schools. "Heavy exercise" that required more than bean bags or hoops for equipment and organized athletics were of less interest to Leland for two reasons. First, his own sense of cultural relativism, supported by "scientific" studies of Japanese stature and mores, led him to consider the Japanese psychologically and physically incapable of excelling in rigorous team sports like baseball or football. (He was more sanguine about Japanese capabilities in "softer" sports, such as tennis or croquet.) And, second, Leland probably feared that the encouragement of competitive sports might foster a resurgence of a small athletic elite that would continue the samurai legacy of using physical training as a status privilege, while the rest of the population languished in a state of obsequious indolence. Naturally, such a possibility would have undermined the goal of developing a national program of physical fitness in which every student took part.

Leland's hope for a universal and compulsory program of physical education was realized soon after his return to the United States in 1881, although not exactly in the manner he had envisioned. Beginning in the same year with the issuance of the Principles of Primary School Instruction (*Shōgakkō kyōsoku kōryō*), twenty minutes of each school day were set aside for light calisthenics. The exclusive reliance on Leland's methods was short-lived, however, as the new Primary School Ordinance of 1886 prescribed a more elaborate program of physical education that included infantry-style exercises in rank and file. The appearance of "military calisthenics" (*heishiki taisō*) in the primary, middle, and normal schools must be attributed to the influence of Mori Arinori, the minister of education from 1885 to 1889. Even before assuming office, Mori had spoken out on the need for a tightly regimented program of paramilitary drills that could supplement the less demanding routine at the Gymnastics Institute. Through this expanded regimen, he hoped not only to build stronger bodies but also to instill the nation's children with the virtues of unquestioning obedience to the state. The interlocking of body, mind, and nation was made explicit in officially sanctioned slogans and "physical education songs" that called upon the young to exercise faithfully every day "for the sake of the country."

While group calisthenics were quickly institutionalized for the rudimentary grades, the physical fitness program in the advanced higher schools and at the university was slower in developing. The underexercised student elite continued to attract unfavorable attention in the 1880s, as it had during the previous decade; only now Japanese educators led the attack. The depth of concern was reflected in an essay by one of Leland's assistants at the Gymnastics Institute, Hiraiwa Nobuo, who criticized the contemporary college students for their distorted academic "mania." "They are contemptuous of their bodies," Hiraiwa claimed, "as if strength of physique were tantamount to savagery or animalistic power." Therefore, he continued, "they just sit at their desks absorbed in their studies, failing to realize that their brains might expire with the oil in their lamps." What especially worried Hiraiwa—and a number of his colleagues—was the potential for discrepancy in a school system that forced students at the lower levels to exercise vigorously, while students in the higher schools and at the university were left alone to study or, worse yet, philander in the streets of Tokyo as their muscles grew flabby and their complexions paled. Was it not the obligation of an academic elite to be strong of body as well as of mind? Most educators thought that it was, but they were still reluctant to impose the same routine of daily exercise on the student elite that was becoming universal in the primary schools. As one higher school headmaster explained in 1888, the advanced academic institution should not be run like a military academy.

So the question arose: how could the higher school and university administrators promote physical training without turning their students into mindless followers who were stripped of all leadership capability? The best resolution was to require only minimal doses of group calisthenics and military exercises while compensating for any slack in physical fitness that might result by encouraging students to participate in "outdoor games" (*kogai yūgi*). Initially, the games were limited to occasional field days (*undōkai*), highlighted by obstacle races, tug-of-wars, and capture-the-flag contests. Unfortunately, these events failed to inspire students with a serious appreciation of physical culture. Popular literature of the 1880s tells of students entering field-day competitions solely to attract the attention of onlooking courtesans—not exactly what administrators had in mind. By the early 1890s, it was clear that, in order for "outdoor games" to have the desired effect of fostering stamina and self-discipline, they would have to be integrated into a program of extracurricular athletics. In contrast to the haphazardness and spontaneity of the field days, the new program would be devoted to organizing athletic clubs, requiring a total commitment from their members to train for intercollegiate competition in which the reputation of the school would be at stake. "Outdoor games" that had been viewed as simple fun by the students were replaced by Western team sports characterized by formal organization, rigorous training, strict rules, and the presence of officials at all matches. Although the first sport to gain popularity on the campuses was crew, which had the obvious advantage of being relatively simple as well as fiercely competitive, baseball was the sport that ultimately won the hearts of the student community in the 1890s and early 1900s.

The rise of baseball in Japan cannot, of course, be separated from the origins and development of the sport in the United States. By 1870, when cultural and diplomatic exchanges between the two countries were commencing in earnest, baseball was already widely played across the United States and was heralded by many as "the national game." In part, the soaring popularity of the sport was tied to the belief that baseball was, as Henry Chadwick so quickly pointed out, "in every way . . . suited to the American character." This particularist view was echoed by other early promoters of the sport, notably Albert G. Spalding, who summarized his long-standing feelings in one of the first histories of baseball, which was written in 1911. Baseball, said Spalding, had "all the attributes of American origin [and] American character"; indeed, it was "the exponent of American Courage, Confidence, Combativeness; American Dash, Discipline, Determination; American

Energy, Eagerness, Enthusiasm . . . ; American Vim, Vigor, Virility." To play baseball, in other words, was to exude those manly virtues that were singularly appropriate to the United States.

Accepting baseball as the incarnation of the Yankee spirit, Spalding and his colleagues had an ambiguous attitude toward the spread of the sport to other parts of the world. On the one hand, the laws of cultural relativism stipulated that baseball was created for Americans to be played by Americans, leaving little opportunity for the foreigner to learn to play. At the same time, the promoters insisted that baseball, to use Spalding's expression, "follow the flag around the world," and they made elaborate efforts, beginning with Spalding's celebrated mission to England in 1874, to introduce America's "national game" to peoples in distant lands. Even if the primary motivation behind such missionary zeal was to put American manliness on display, there was an implicit assumption that, if British, French, or Egyptian youth could begin to experiment with baseball on their own, they would also come to appreciate the depth of American ingenuity and determination. In this sense, baseball could enlarge the American cultural sphere of influence and bring greater respect for the nation around the world.

Among the American sailors and businessmen in Yokohama, who were undoubtedly the first to play baseball on Japanese soil, the game was the means of preserving a frontier spirit of daring and adventure that had brought them to this curious and distant land in the first place. By smashing home runs, a young bachelor from the Midwest compensated for the demoralizing effects of settlement brothels and grog shops while safeguarding the integrity of his national identity. Such activity was important in order to maintain social and cultural distance from the Japanese and, to a lesser extent, from the British, who outnumbered the Americans in Yokohama by as much as three to one. Owing to their superior numbers, the British initially dominated social and recreational life, including the Yokohama Athletic Club, whose cricket enthusiasts made greatest use of the one playing field in the settlement. The situation changed during the 1880s, however, when Americans joined the club in sufficient numbers to gain equal access to the field, thus paving the way for baseball to eclipse cricket as the most popular spectator sport in Yokohama. At any event, the Yokohama Athletic Club, as the sponsoring organization for all major sporting activities in the settlement and as an enduring bastion of wealth and privilege, upheld strict regulations, which lasted into the early 1890s, that forbade Japanese from entering the park where the playing field was located. Such restrictions were not, obviously, conducive to the spread of any Western sport, including baseball, beyond the perimeter of the settlement.

While young businessmen and sailors were happy to maintain baseball as a symbol of extraterritorial privilege and unique cultural identity, a few American educators in Japan had a quite different perspective on the sport. Four teachers in particular—Horace Wilson, F. W. Strange, G. H. Mudgett, and Leroy Janes—were avowed baseball *aficionados* who arrived in Japan in the early 1870s hoping to introduce America's "national game" to their students. Although no evidence suggests the four coordinated their missionary effort, each seemed convinced that baseball could effectively break down cultural barriers. Moreover, unlike Leland and other believers in the exceptional nature of American athletics, they were optimistic that Japanese students, if properly motivated and instructed, would excel in Western team sports. Toward this end Strange wrote a special handbook in 1883, entitled *Outdoor Games,* "to induce Japanese schoolboys to take more physical exercise." Among the activities discussed, Strange devoted the most attention to baseball, which he described as "the national game of the American people" and a sport requiring "mental ability" and "manly qualities." Despite his enthusiasm, the initial campus response was less than overwhelming. Whereas isolated student groups in Tokyo, Sapporo, and Kumamoto showed some interest, baseball was generally regarded throughout the 1880s as a novelty to be played along with capture-the-flag on university field days.

The rise of baseball as a serious intercollegiate sport did not occur until the end of the century, long after America's baseball missionaries had left Japan. Certainly, the drive by faculty and students to establish extracurricular athletic programs gave impetus to the sport in the 1890s. At the same time, baseball, like other sports, appears to have been the beneficiary of a surge in nationalistic sentiment aroused by the campaign to revise the "unequal" treaties and to protect Japanese interests in Korea. Peculiar to the nationalism of the 1890s was the convergence of Social Darwinism and neo-traditionalism, as public spokesmen made conscious attempts to locate the values of manliness and strength in Japan's pre-Meiji past. By so doing, Western ideas and institutions could be assimilated, rather than adopted indiscriminately, thus facilitating the quest for a proud, yet discrete, national identity. In a similar vein, student interest in athletics coincided with the search for a "national game" (*kokugi*) that would symbolize the collectivist ideal and fighting spirit of the nation as it prepared for war against China. Although indisputably lodged in traditional culture, judo and kendo were too solitary to engender the kind of public excitement required of a "national game." Western team sports were best suited to this purpose, and baseball, in particular, seemed to emphasize precisely those values that were celebrated in the civic rituals of state: order, harmony, perseverence, and self-restraint. To focus attention, therefore, on the compatibility of the sport with Japanese sensibilities, proponents compared the skilled batter to samurai swordsmen and embellished descriptions of the game with poetic allusions to medieval warrior epics. Despite foreign provenance, baseball reputedly nourished traditional virtues of loyalty, honor, and courage and therefore symbolized the "new *bushidō*" spirit of the age. For, unlike the mindless tackling and punching that were sanctioned in American contact sports, baseball struck a harmonious balance between physical strength and mental agility. The resulting demand for concentration and finesse harkened to the cultivated martial ideals of the samurai gentleman. Thus, at the end of the century, while Americans in Yokohama played baseball to be more American, Japanese students, especially in the higher schools, turned to baseball in an effort to reify traditional values and to establish a new basis for national pride. An international confrontation on the diamond had become unavoidable.

Of the ten schools to develop reputable teams in the 1890s, the club representing the First Higher School (Ichikō) of Tokyo quickly emerged as the most formidable. Since Ichikō was one of five elite preparatory schools for the national university, the students who attended were especially sensitive about maintaining an outstanding public reputation, and their concern in this regard applied as much to the athletic field as it did to the classroom. The strength of the team was initially demonstrated in a series of victories in the fall of 1890 and the spring of 1891. Thereafter, the team compiled a near perfect record in intercollegiate competition until 1904, when Keiō and Waseda Universities became the chief contenders for the national championship. Still, for nearly fifteen years, the First Higher School held the center of attention in Japanese baseball, and for a while even their strongest rivals seemed resigned to accept the players' immodest protestation that "there are no [worthy] opponents in the land" (*tenka teki nashi*).

Once convinced of their superiority among Japanese teams, the Ichikō players sent word to the Yokohama Athletic Club of their interest in an "international match" (*kokusai shiai*). The first formal challenge was made in October 1891, and it was followed by successive challenges spaced over the next five years; but the response from Yokohama was always negative. Ostensibly, the reason for not giving the idea serious consideration was the ill feeling toward the higher school, which stemmed from an incident that took place on the Ichikō campus during a baseball game with an American missionary school in the spring of 1890. Midway through that contest, an American teacher from the opposing school, Reverend William Imbrie, was apprehended by several irate Ichikō students for scaling the school fence instead of entering the campus through the main gate. Exaggerated reports of how the "good reverend" was severely beaten and even "stabbed" by the attacking students sent shock waves through the foreign community in Yokohama, which immediately condemned First Higher as an "uncivilized" bastion of antiforeignism and samurai-style "barbarism." In actuality, Reverend Imbrie sustained a small cut on his left cheek from a flying stone or piece of tile. To his angry assailants, this injury was justified retribution for a breech of etiquette and was probably far less severe than what would have been in store for any Japanese student who dared to intrude upon the settlement playing field.

Was the "Imbrie incident" really at the root of American hostility toward First Higher, or was it merely a *casus belli* to lend credence to claims of cultural superiority? After all, to engage the Ichikō baseball team on the athletic field was to admit that the students were, in effect, cultural equals—an admission few foreign residents in Yokohama were prepared to make in 1891, three years prior to both the Aoki-Kimberley accords and the outbreak of the Sino-Japanese War. In this spirit of discrimination, the Yokohama Athletic Club took pains to describe the Ichikō students as culturally and even physically unfit for international athletic competition. The haughtiness of the club's attitude is suggested by one student chronicler, who noted, "The foreigners in Yokohama have established an athletic field in their central park into which no Japanese may enter. There, playing by themselves, they boast of their skill in baseball. When we attempt to challenge them, they refuse, saying, 'Baseball is our national game' or 'Our bodies are twice the size of yours.'" Such condescension by the Yokohama Athletic Club toward the "little Japanese" only reinforced student determination to gain the opportunity to prove themselves on the settlement playing field. In their view, the continued refusal to accept an "international match" was shocking evidence that the settlement in Yokohama clung to the illegal privileges of the "unequal" treaties. A simple game of baseball therefore began to assume the dimensions of a righteous struggle for national honor.

Ironically, the foreign residents in Yokohama were not alone in perpetuating the stereotype of the unmanly Japanese. A number of early Meiji intellectuals reacted to Western thought and institutions with a deep sense of cultural insecurity and a fatalistic acceptance of the "unequal" treaties.

Such a view was espoused by Inoue Tetsujirō, a prominent professor of philosophy, who opposed treaty revision on the grounds that the Japanese were "greatly inferior to Westerners in intelligence, financial power, physique, and all else." Any attempt, according to Inoue, to stand side by side with Europeans or Americans was a sure invitation for invidious comparisons that exposed the innate weaknesses, both physical and mental, of the Japanese. For this reason, Inoue supported the continuation of the semi-colonial settlements in Yokohama and other coastal ports as a protective guarantee against undue contact with a superior Caucasian race. Obviously, educators who shared Inoue's view would lend little encouragement to the Ichikō students' bold defiance of biological reality.

Yet the warnings from conservative educators did not deter the students from their outlandish goal to engage "the six-footed Americans" in their "national game." Finally, after five years of fruitless inquiries, the students' efforts were rewarded. With W. B. Mason, an English teacher at Ichikō and long-time resident of the settlement, acting as intermediary, a game was arranged between Ichikō and the Yokohama Athletic Club, to be held on the latter's home field on May 23, 1896. It was the first official baseball game between American and Japanese teams, and its impact reverberated far beyond the settlement playing field.

With only four days' notice from the Yokohama Athletic Club, the Ichikō players had little time to practice for their historic confrontation. Lack of preparation did not worry them, for they believed that, even if the Americans had an advantage in "form" (*keitai*), the Japanese athletes had the "spirit" (*shinki*) to win. The power of the spiritual over the physical did not apply to the weather, however, which was so miserable on May 20 and 21 that the students decided to send a telegram to Yokohama to inquire whether the field would be playable. A curt reply—interpreted to mean "Are you trying to flee from us?"—was all the students needed to prepare for their departure, rain or shine. After leaving a written "testament" (*isho*) vowing to fight to the bitter end, the team, along with a band of faithful rooters, boarded a morning train on May 23 for their rendezvous with the Yokohama Athletic Club. At the insistence of the headmaster, who wished to erase the stigma of primitivism that had haunted the students since the Imbrie incident, the players traveled in spotless school uniforms with tall white collars and polished shoes, carrying their new baseball uniforms in small satchels.

Even though the Ichikō players were intent upon behaving like gentlemen, their American hosts revealed little inclination to reciprocate. Unable to accept the sight of young Japanese using a field that had always been restricted to Westerners, many spectators greeted the Ichikō students with jeers and howls when they entered the park for the pregame warm-ups. Somewhat shaken by the uncivil welcome, the Ichikō players had their difficulties during practice, dropping easy pop-ups and stumbling over the bases. For the unruly spectators, the initial ineptitude of the visitors made them even more of a target for taunts and sneers. "Are they players?" one man shouted each time a student slipped on the wet field.

The jeering quickly dissipated once the game got under way. Except for the first inning, the Ichikō players completely dominated the contest, delivering the Yokohama Athletic Club an embarrassing defeat, 29–4. The same spectators who had been bellowing catcalls from the stands were now left in stunned disbelief as the Japanese students marched off the field to the rickshaws, drawn by their rooters, that carried them triumphantly down the main street of Yokohama to the train station. Never in the forty-year history of the treaty ports had resident sportsmen been so utterly humiliated on the playing field. In a terse statement that belied a deeper sense of wounded pride, the *Japan Weekly Mail* reported, "The baseball team of the Athletic Club was badly beaten on Saturday by nine from the Tokyo Higher School, being outmaneuvered at all points of the game." While gloom pervaded Yokohama, Ichikō athletes returned home to a rousing welcome marked by *banzai* chants, choruses from the national anthem, and overflowing cups of *sake*. Underlying the ecstasy of the moment was the awareness that the victory had transcended the playing field. As the student president proclaimed, "This great victory is more than a victory for our school; it is a victory for the Japanese people!" The captain of the team concurred, explaining how he and his comrades had realized that "the name of the country" (*kokumei*) was at stake in their competition. Since the game was covered in many newspapers around the country, the Ichikō students were suddenly national heroes.

The broader implications of the game apparently did not escape the defeated Americans. Members of the Yokohama Athletic Club had waited five years before accepting the original Ichikō challenge, but it took only two or three days for them to decide on a rematch. Again, the place was Yokohama and the date was June 5, 1896. For this game, the slightly shaken athletic club recruited additional players from the crews of two American cruisers, the *Charleston* and the *Detroit*, conveniently moored in Yokohama harbor. Nonetheless, even with reinforcements from the United States Navy, the Americans fared no better in meeting the Ichikō challenge. The game ended in another rout, with the visitors winning 32–9.

Highlighting the contest on June 5 was an unprecedented outpouring of public support for the student athletes. After receiving hundreds of telegrams from well-wishers in primary and secondary schools across the land, the Ichikō team was greeted in Yokohama by a boisterously enthusiastic crowd of native citizens, who lined the street that led from the station to the baseball park. Although the crowd was denied entrance to the spectator stands, many waited outside shouting words of encouragement while the game was in progress. The enthusiasm of local citizens was shared by the national press, led by the *Asahi Newspaper*, which gave the second game front-page coverage under the headline, "A Great Victory for Our Students." In celebrating this achievement, the paper claimed that "the superiority [of the Japanese team] is now self-evident" ("yūretsu mizukara hanzuru tokoro ari"). Similarly stirred, the newspaper *Jiji shinpō* reported that the Ichikō players made the Americans look "unspeakably clumsy."

While basking in the public's affection, the Ichikō students were not happy with the response to their victory in the foreign settlement. At the conclusion of the second game, after receiving perfunctory congratulations from their opponents, the students were brusquely ushered off the playing field as if their continued presence might violate its sanctity. Interpreting this rude behavior as a desperate attempt to reassert the privileges of extraterritorial status, they grudgingly acquiesced, not out of respect to their hosts, but, as they explained, because "the foreigner's private property" could have "contaminated our feet." "So we were willing to leave—after spitting three times." Even more upsetting to the students was the unfavorable coverage of the second game in the foreign press. English newspapers in Yokohama, Kobe, and Nagasaki registered strong protests against the "uncivilized" manners of Ichikō rooters, who were accused of hurling obscenities at the American players. (Any rowdiness at the game, First Higher School spokesmen countered, took place among the "unlearned vagrants" who stood outside the gates while the students who accompanied the team inside behaved like gentlemen.) Foreign newspapers also belittled the significance of Ichikō's victories by noting, "School-boys with their daily opportunities for practice, their constant matches, and *sparer figures* have always the advantage over a team of grown men . . . who have not played together before and besides are never in practice even in the best of times." For nearly five years the athletes in Yokohama had been rejecting the higher school challenge on the grounds that the students did not measure up to the Americans in physical stature and stamina. Now, rather suddenly, the tables were turned and the students' "sparer figures" were seen as an unfair advantage. The claim that businessmen were somehow deprived of the time they needed for practice was equally unconvincing. The working day in the settlement rarely exceeded four hours.

In the heated aftermath of the second international game, both sides were eager for a rematch, only this time the Ichikō stalwarts insisted that the contest take place on their home field. From Yokohama, a team made up exclusively of sailors from the cruiser *Detroit,* who apparently felt they were better off without the assistance of the athletic club and with the full prestige of the United States Navy at stake, accepted the challenge. On the afternoon of June 27, the team of sailors marched proudly through the gates of the First Higher School, followed by a naval band that, presumably, filled the air with "Columbia, the Gem of the Ocean." As the Americans entered the campus, they were undoubtedly surprised to discover that a throng of nearly ten thousand had already squeezed around the playing field. Indeed, every inch of standing room had been occupied since the middle of the morning, forcing police to turn away some of the overflow crowd. In addition to the thousands of Tokyo citizens, a select group of one hundred dignitaries, including representatives from the American legation and the Japanese government, sat comfortably behind home plate under a pavilion especially constructed for the occasion. As the band played and the crowd roared and reporters, both foreign and Japanese, scribbled madly, Ichikō romped over its visiting opponents by a score of 22–6. To avert a repetition of the acrimony that had followed the previous match, the Ichikō administration invited all American guests and players to a postgame reception in the teachers' lounge. No sooner had crackers and tea been served than the sailors, who Ichikō observers described as "smittened with humiliation," floated the idea of yet another rematch for July 4 in Yokohama. After considerable urging, the Ichikō team accepted.

In the wake of Ichikō's third overwhelming victory, baseball players in the settlement came under enormous pressure to redeem their athletic reputations. The situation was especially tense since the next contest with the "higher school nine" was scheduled for the Fourth of July, and the specter of another humiliating defeat on Independence Day was unconscionable. Hence, every effort was made to field an "all star team" drawn from the combined ranks of the Yokohama Athletic Club and the United States Navy. Fortunately, the potential pool was greatly augmented by the arrival in Yokohama harbor of the flagship of the Pacific fleet, the battleship *Olympia,* whose crew members were noted for their prowess in baseball. Five sailors from the *Olympia* were recruited for the Independence Day game, including one who had played shortstop professionally before entering the navy.

The irony of playing a team of Americans in their national game on Independence Day was not fully appreciated by the Ichikō students, who were quite amazed when they arrived in Yokohama on the morning of July 4 to see all of the American men-of-war in the harbor festooned with flags and blasting out twenty-one gun salutes. Whether by design or not, the reverberations of the canon-fire had a slightly unsettling effect on the students, who had just completed final examinations and were not in the best psychological condition for the game. As it turned out, the American team was able to take full advantage of the situation, eking out a 14–12 victory before a much-relieved crowd of holiday spectators. At the conclusion of the game, the American team, heeding the code of good sportsmanship, gave their Japanese opponents a rousing "Hip, Hip, Hourray!" The cheers were given "in good earnest," according to the reporter for the *Japan Weekly Mail,* for it was difficult to deny that the Japanese nine, even in defeat, had "played a neater and better game in the field than did their opponents." Perhaps the ultimate tribute to the Ichikō stalwarts was a letter received during the same summer from Yale University, inviting the team to join an intercollegiate tournament on the East Coast. Lack of funds prevented acceptance, but the First Higher School players were gratified, nonetheless, to hear that news of their achievement had crossed the Pacific.

From 1897 to 1904, there were nine more games between the Ichikō Baseball Club and American teams in Yokohama. Of these, Ichikō emerged victorious in eight contests, losing only one 6–5 squeaker." Among the victories was a 4–0 shut-out ("skunk game") against the Yokohama Athletic Club and two impressive wins (34–1, 27–0) over a team of sailors from the giant battleship *Kentucky,* which replaced the *Olympia* in the early 1900s as the flagship of the Pacific fleet. Over the entire twelve-game series, Ichikō scored 230 runs to only 64 for the American teams—a statistic that raised the question of whose "national game" baseball really was.

Since sport has virtually escaped the eye of professional historians in Japan, the task of rescuing the early history of Japanese baseball from oblivion has been left to sportswriters, university alumni, and private athletic associations. Inevitably, the year books and popular histories that have been written by these groups devote a page or two to the Ichikō Baseball Club and its "heroic" encounters with the Yokohama Athletic Club, but always the significance of the series is limited to its impact upon the development of baseball in Japan. In this truncated view, the Ichikō-Yokohama series is considered important for capturing wide public interest, hastening the introduction of new fielding and batting techniques, and paving the way for baseball to become Japan's most popular spectator sport after World War I. To be sure, the last of these achievements is no small distinction given the conspicuous lack of interest that baseball has generated outside North America, the West Indies, the Philippines, and Taiwan.

Still, the disposition to view the rise of Japanese baseball in the 1890s only in terms of the later development of the sport is both simplistic and somewhat misleading. When First Higher School students took to the playing fields, they showed little interest in securing the fate of baseball in Japan or even in introducing the sport to their less privileged contemporaries. What excited them instead was the possibility that excellence in America's "national game," demonstrated in competition with American teams, would compel Westerners to reconsider fictitious stereotypes about the unmanly Japanese. Baseball was, in this sense, an instrument for the rectification of the national image. The intensity of feeling over this issue is suggested in one of the yearly reports of the Ichikō Baseball Club submitted in the immediate aftermath of the first international games in 1896. "The Americans are proud of baseball as their national game just as we have been proud of judo and kendo," the student chronicler noted. "Now, however, in a place far removed from their native land, they have fought against a 'little people' whom they ridicule as childish, only to find themselves swept away like falling leaves. No words can describe their disgraceful conduct. The aggressive character of our national spirit is a well-established fact, demonstrated first in the Sino-Japanese War and now by our great victories in baseball."

Accepting the Social Darwinist formula that a civilization is defined by its "aggressive character" (*tekigaishin*), the Ichikō students regarded their victories on the playing field in Yokohama as a great service to the nation, ranking in importance with the military victories on the battlefields in the Korean peninsula. The bold analogy bore a striking resemblance to the Duke of Wellington's supposed adage, with which the students were quite familiar, that the Battle of Waterloo was won on the playing fields of Eton. Be this as it may, the immediate inspiration for correlating baseball with national destiny was the outpouring of public gratitude that swelled with each victory over the Americans. Typical of the letters that flooded the administration office in June 1896 was one from Yokoyama Tokujirō, an elementary school principal in Gifu, who declared the Ichikō triumph "an augury [*zenchō*] of our nation's victory over the entire world." No less carried away were the service workers and other elements of the *Lumpenproletariat* attached to the settlement. Each time the Ichikō team played in Yokohama, hundreds, and perhaps thousands, of these uprooted citizens congregated outside the ball park, waiting patiently for word of the results. Upon hearing the news that Ichikō had won, the bystanders, according to student accounts, would "jump for joy" as if their livelihood depended upon the outcome. In reacting to this social phenomenon, the students imagined they were fighting for the emancipation of their downtrodden countrymen who were "suppressed by the foreigner's monetary power."

Given the degradation of Japanese workers in the settlement and the tense international environment in which the games were played, it is not surprising that the Ichikō students assumed the role of "combatants" (*senshi*) in the struggle for national dignity or that they resorted to bellicose language in describing their athletic exploits. Although the negotiations between the Western powers and Japan to abrogate the "unequal" treaties were well under way when the international series commenced in the spring of 1896, the students believed that the humiliating legacy of the settlements could never be erased without some form of retribution. Baseball was ideally suited for this task. Winning a game against a proud foreign team produced all of the glory of a military victory with few of the risks. In a more positive vein, the Ichikō team took special satisfaction in witnessing a gradual improvement in the attitude of their American opponents, who were increasingly willing to shake hands and utter half-hearted cheers as the series progressed. Such displays of respect, they reasoned, could never have been elicited without first beating the foreigners in their own game and even suggested that the day was coming when American and Japanese teams could play without cultural bias.

Thus, baseball was heralded for both accelerating Japan's rise to equal status among the world powers and serving as a possible tool for what student leaders at Ichikō once called "the preservation of diplomatic stability" (*gaikō shusei*) across the Pacific. This idea of using the athletic field to sublimate hostilities that might otherwise be acted out on the battlefield was echoed by a number of Americans in Japan, including W. B. Mason, who was deeply committed to the notion of exchanging baseball teams in an effort to bridge the Pacific. Mason's dream was finally realized in the decade following the Russo-Japanese War (1904–05), when teams from Waseda and Keiō Universities visited America, and Wisconsin, Washington, Chicago, and Stanford sent teams to Japan. Whether or not such exchanges could ever have taken place without the initiative taken by the Ichikō players in the 1890s is doubtful. Perhaps with this in mind, Lindsay Russell, president of the Japan Society in 1914, singled out the Ichikō-Yokohama series as one of the "landmarks" in inter-Pacific relations.

By the turn of the century, student athletes in Japan were expounding the Victorian ideology of manliness and duty with the same determination as their counterparts in the West. Like the Tom Brown and Dink Stover generations, they paid homage to the "fighting life" (*sentōteki seikatsu*) or the "strenuous life" (*funtō seikatsu*) as a necessary penance to be borne by a young elite in its mission to inspire the nation and to defend against the softening influences of "materialistic civilization" (*busshitsuteki bunmei*). Nor was it uncommon for them to speak of the "sacredness of games" (*gēmu no shinsei*) in expressing a self-abnegating devotion to school and nation. "The three years spent as a member of the Ichikō Baseball Club are years of total sacrifice," exclaimed a young sportsman in 1906. "Ah, sacrifice!" he continued, "Is this not the virtue that holds our society and nation together?" Amateur sportsmen in the West would have undoubtedly agreed. The value of baseball, as H. Addington Bruce put it in 1913, was that it nurtured "courage," "self-control," and "social solidarity," all of which were "requisite . . . in the life of an individual and a nation."

While the crack of the bat sounded a common ideological theme across the Pacific, was the movement of the United States and Japan toward a shared, bilateral culture of home runs and stolen bases in the clear interest of friendly relations between the two nations? Perhaps. But the legacy of the Ichikō-Yokohama series compels approaching the question cautiously, with an awareness of the ambiguities and inconsistencies of both American and Japanese participants that defy easy generalization. Although the two sides partook of the same culture of athleticism and manliness, that culture was inherently aggressive and, therefore, virtually impossible to "share" in an atmosphere of amity and mutual respect. Cosmopolitan Social Darwinism is a contradiction in terms.

From the perspective of Americans who were familiar with Japan, there was always a tension between the goal of encouraging the spread of baseball abroad and maintaining exclusive mastery over a sport that, in the words of Albert Spalding, only "American manhood" could provide the "brain and brawn" to play *par excellence.* Within limits, of course, it could be gratifying to see, as Fred Merrifield put it, "little brown people" running the bases; such a sight made Japan seem less strange and inscrutable to the American visitor. Yet it was also extremely unsettling to see the same "little brown people" humiliating the crews from the flagships of the Pacific fleet, men-of-war that were, to borrow naval historian William Braisted's phrase, "the embodiment of the wealth and pretensions" of U.S. foreign policy in the Far East.

The ambiguous attitude had its parallel in world politics, as exemplified in the pronouncements of Theodore Roosevelt, who could, at one moment, cheer the Japanese for "playing our game" in the confrontation with Russia, only to admonish them five months later on the evils of "get[ting] the big head." In other words, the Japanese were admired for their revitalization of the fighting spirit at the end of the century and for their refusal to be lumped with the Chinese, who, according to Roosevelt, were "content to rot by inches in ignoble ease." If, however, the Japanese became overly proficient in "our game," whether on the battlefield or the baseball diamond, the hue and cry was heard that "they" were not playing by "our" rules, that they were using their "sparer figures" to undue advantage, that they were guilty of hitting and pitching "samurai style." Then, as now, cultural relativism supplied the last line of defense for ensuring the national integrity of the sport.

Vacillation between seemingly irreconcilable goals characterized the attitudes of student athletes in Japan as well. The Ichikō players spoke in one breath about retribution for past injustices and, in another, about using baseball to forge harmonious relations between the two countries. They were also torn between playing baseball to project the image of the cosmopolitan man of the world and playing to revive the stoic virtues of the feudal warrior. The confusion extended to basic nomenclature: some students used the Anglicized term "besubōru" while the majority insisted upon identifying the sport with a combination of Chinese characters (ya-kyū) that were selected by one of the first captains of the team. Hence, it was as difficult for Japanese students to admit that they were playing baseball "just like the Americans" as it was for the Americans to admit that the Japanese were playing "just like us."

If the Ichikō-Yokohama series did not contribute immediately to harmony and good will across the Pacific, it most certainly did contribute to the interrelated quest for national dignity and social status among student athletes. By overwhelming the Americans in their "national game," the students aroused considerable patriotic ferment and pride in the 1890s that extended down to the lowliest denizens of the treaty ports. While they dedicated their victories quite magnanimously to the nation, the Ichikō players were also helping themselves. In an era when the athletic field was the exclusive preserve of amateurs, baseball in Meiji Japan, like campus sport in Victorian England and America, was the "pivotal link" between nationalism and social status. Before higher school and university students were equipped with bats and balls, they had little opportunity to establish their credibility as a hard-working and public-spirited elite. As privileged students, they were largely absolved of responsibilities to serve in the military, to participate in community-assistance programs, or to add anything to the productive capacity of the economy. Uprooted from their homes and vulnerable to the hedonistic and socially leveling pleasures of the city, the students needed athletics to overcome any perception of indolence in the public mind. Through baseball, they demonstrated both that the battle for national dignity could be won on the playing field and that an academic elite could be imbued with the fighting spirit expected of future leaders of the land. Whether in the form of laudatory press coverage or of impoverished citizens "jumping for joy" on the streets of Yokohama, the more praise the students received for their achievements on the diamond, the greater was the social distance between the players and their adulators. Therefore, when examining the lyrics of Ichikō's "Baseball Club Rouser" (*Yakyūbuka*), written in 1905 in commemoration of the Yokohama series, one senses a distinct overlapping of national pride with self-interest:

I

Among literary and martial arts pursued
In the righteous air of the First Higher School
Baseball stands especially high
With its spirit of honor that refuses to die.

II

The crack of the bat echoes to the sky
On cold March mornings when we chase balls on the ice
Year in and year out, through wind and rain
Enduring all hardship, we practice our game.

III

While the years have seen many a foe
Come to our schoolyard where strong winds blow
Upon touching the sleeves of our armoured knights
We turn them away, speechless with fright.

IV

The valorous sailors from the *Detroit, Kentucky,* and *Yorktown*
Whose furious batting can intimidate a cyclone
Threw off their helmets, their energies depleted
Behold how pathetically they run away defeated.

V

Courageously, we marched twenty miles south
To fight the Americans in Yokohama
Though they boast of the game as their national sport
Behold how pathetically they run away defeated.

VI

Ah, for the glory of our Baseball Club!
Ah, for the glitter it has cast!
Pray that our martial valor never turns submissive
And that our honor will always shine far across the Pacific.

17. Canada in the Country of Baseball

Perhaps no two neighboring countries in the world have enjoyed such a close relationship as Canada and the United States. Sharing a common border of some three thousand miles, with about 85 percent of Canadians living within a hundred miles of it, the two countries have analogous historical experiences. Both endured a period of British control, enjoyed a period of westward expansion, experienced a large influx of European immigration, and during the nineteenth century developed an industrialized urban society. Moreover, with a rising standard of living and increased leisure time, both developed a fascination for sports. Nevertheless, the Canadian past has elements that distinguish it from its neighbor. Canada retained English rule long after the Americans rebelled against it, and Canadians sought an identity separate from their neighbors to the south. This mix of relationships and experiences has created a certain ambivalence in the relationship between the two nations that has carried over into their sports, including baseball.

Because of Canada's prolonged colonial link with Britain, there was a strong desire to maintain political and cultural identity with the home country and its empire. Sport was one of those functions used to establish cultural identification with Mother England and to demonstrate England's cultural superiority to the local French and Indian populations. Even after the creation of the Confederation of Canadian Provinces in 1867, the Canadian elites retained a strong cultural link with Britain, symbolized by their attachment to cricket. Yet over time the Canadians, influenced by French and Indian traditions, developed their own sports, especially lacrosse, which they adopted from the Indian population, and ice hockey, which they adapted to their northern climate. Despite attempting to establish their own sporting pastimes, Canadians could not forever resist the cultural influence of their neighbor to the south. Indeed, the increasing dominance of baseball over cricket in Canadian sporting culture reflected the gradual increase of American influence. While cricket was viewed as a bastion of privileged upper-class British loyalists, baseball became the game played by all classes and ethnic groups, including French- and English-speaking Canadians alike. By the beginning of the twentieth century it had become Canada's most popular sport, perhaps its national sport, much to the disgust of those who bemoaned the fact as one more nail in the coffin of Canadian national identity.

Canadians might well have been present at the creation of the game. Certainly they had been playing a variety of bat and ball games other than cricket well before the formalization of the American game in the 1840s. From early games in Ontario, baseball spread east and west across Canada. By the 1880s it had gained a strong hold on the country. There were professional and amateur teams and leagues, and players moved freely back and forth between Canada and the United States. The Canadian game has mirrored many of the same peaks and valleys of popularity and similar issues of race, commercialization, and challenges from other sports as the game in the United States. But the one issue that remained unique to Canada has been whether the game represents too much of an intrusion into Canada's cultural identity. William Humber traces the history of the game's success north of the border, placing it in its proper context of Canadian culture and argues that far from being a victim of American cultural imperialism, Canada could be considered no less than a junior partner in the development of baseball.

There are supreme moments in Canada's infatuation with baseball such as those following Joe Carter's ninth-inning home run in the sixth game of the 1993 World Series that gave the Toronto Blue Jays their second successive baseball title. The streets of the country overflowed with unrestricted joy from Vancouver's Robson Street to downtown Saskatoon where local police had to be called out; from Pond Inlet on the northern edge of

Baffin Island where the baseball season begins as it ends in –10 degree weather and Inuit children play baseball during recess imagining themselves to be Roberto Alomar, to the lower end of Ontario's several thousand kilometre long Highway 11; from the outport of Butlerville, Newfoundland, where they cheered the next thing to a native son and even to many Québécois households in the baseball strongholds of Trois-Rivières and St-Hyacinthe—though the pleasure was tempered by memory of the Montreal Expos' failures of the early 1980s.

At other times, however, baseball pains Canadians. They wrestle awkwardly with their support for the game. It is a kind of guilt associated with a love for what is after all the national game of their neighbours to the south. The Japanese feel no such remorse, having imbued baseball with characteristics peculiar to their culture. Cubans, who have reason to be suspect of anything so symbolically American, revel in their ability to beat the Yanks at annual amateur tournaments.

In Canada successive journalists from Goldwin Smith, the country's 19th-century man of letters, to author Lawrence Martin in his 1993 book *Pledge of Allegiance* on the Americanization of Canada in the Mulroney years, have bemoaned the intrusive nature of American culture on Canadian life and used baseball as their symbol. "A national game cannot fail to exercise a great influence on character," Smith wrote in August 1880:

> What is the national game of Canada to be—Cricket, Lacrosse, or Base Ball? . . . Base Ball has now gained a strong hold upon this Continent, and all the circumstances are in its favour. It can be played through the spring, summer, and fall; it does not require much of a lawn; and what is a greater advantage still, it is quickly played, so that the game is commonly finished in an afternoon. . . . The loyal Englishman [in Canada] who regards with pensive regret the adoption of a Yankee game may console himself with the thought that Cricket and Base Ball have apparently evolved out of the same infantine British sport.

Over a hundred years later, writing in *The Toronto Star* (25 April 1993) about the symbolism of U.S. President George Bush attending a ballgame in Toronto's SkyDome in 1990, Lawrence Martin said, "The fantastic success of baseball north of the U.S. border was yet another sign of the times. Major league ball now enjoyed charter membership in English Canada's new continentalist culture. In sports, as in music, film, and books, it was a culture less conscious of borders."

This attitude is at least somewhat peculiar in that baseball was adopted in Canada while still in its primitive stage and long before it could be an agent of cultural imperialism. This is a claim that no other country outside the United States can make. The English, after all, who were responsible for bringing rounders to the new world had consigned this particular bat and ball sport to the rubbish heap of failed games, leaving it to be played by small children while adults got on with the most serious game of cricket. Canadians from Victoria, British Columbia, through to Halifax, Nova Scotia, were effectively regional participants in the game's evolution, playing what might be thought of as experimental forms of baseball from which the modern game emerged.

Until at least 1860 the game flourished as a significant regional variation in southwestern Ontario alongside other local interpretations in Philadelphia, New York, and New England. Even after the popular New York game was adopted in Canada around the time of the American Civil War, until 1876 slight rule variations still existed. This is a game with a significant heritage in Canada though one undeniably connected at a very early stage to events in the United States. Far from being victims of American taste in the matter of baseball Canadians were at the very least junior partners in the game's development. Such involvement was significant in that it showed an emerging Canadian interest in new, North American traditions rather than inherited British ones.

There was baseball of a type in Canada at least 30 years before Canadian Confederation in 1867. The absence of national direction to develop the sport in Canada was compounded by the powerful regional character of the game as reflected in local rules in the United States and Canada. Baseball in Canada has always had a pronounced north-south orientation. Maritimers played against east-coasters from Massachusetts and Maine, Québécois moved among the baseball circles of Vermont and New Hampshire and only occasionally eastern Ontario, Ontarians competed in Michigan, Ohio, Pennsylvania, and New York states. Manitobans joined leagues in Minnesota and the Dakotas, Alberta and Saskatchewan welcomed itinerant ball clubs from the American Plains states, and in British Columbia games were played along the American Pacific Coast.

Lacking a national identity, competition sought symbols other than those for national honours. In 1863 funds were solicited for a Silver Ball competition, based on an American model, to be contended for by teams in southwestern Ontario, by far the most advanced baseball region in any of the areas that now make up Canada. Likewise baseball in Canada was following the commercial path taken by the game in the United States. Culturally and politically this connection had its roots in the 1837 Upper and Lower Canadian Rebellions which borrowed democratic ideas and active help from American sources (Upper Canada Rebellion leader William Lyon Mackenzie fled to the United States after the uprising failed.) From its earliest stages baseball in Canada as in the United States was played by a wide variety of social classes and supported by a small business entrepreneurial class. As such it was part of the populist commercial entertainment favoured by the American public and gradually adopted by working-class Canadians. More privileged classes in Canada, argue Richard Gruneau and David Whitson (1993), "were drawn primarily towards the model of British 'gentlemanly' amateurism."

American-based associations representing the different regional varia-tions of baseball had been established in the United States in the 1850s, but Canadian teams were much too primitive to take part in these activities. By the time baseball in Canada had sufficiently matured, Americans were at war with themselves and baseball was slowly assuming an American identity following the triumph of the New York game. Baseball was no longer a folk game of quaint local initiative, and Canadians took tentative steps to form a Canadian Association of Base Ball Players at the time of the Provincial Exhibition in Hamilton in late September 1864. It was an early recognition of an emerging Canadian national identity at a time when the Fathers of Confederation were still debating the form of the new country. Significantly this Canadian Association was made up solely of teams from southern Ontario, a nomenclature at least excusable in 1864 as the territory of Canada West and East included only present-day Ontario and Quebec and there was little evidence of baseball activity in Canada East.

The Silver Ball championship lasted through 1876. In the 1860s it involved towns and cities from Woodstock and Ingersoll in the west to the village of Newcastle in the east, and reached its farthest extension in 1873 with teams from Ottawa and Kingston. A distinct Canadian nationalism did not infuse these competitions as it would do so later in lacrosse, hockey and football. Baseball's allegiance to commercial interests had already made it the perfect vehicle for touting the economic prospects of newly emerging urban centres. For men like Guelph brewer George Sleeman a baseball team was a means of promoting his business and his town in both the immediate hinterland and potential markets many miles away. The regional nature of competition also reflected the available means of transportation.

The first significant international event, that of the great Base Ball Tournament in Detroit in August 1867, included teams from Michigan and Ontario. Little notice was taken of national origins until the Victorias of Ingersoll were asked to allow a rival team to use a substitute for a late-arriving player, "the Canadians refusing to allow Porter to play in his place." There was little bitterness in the comment and no further reference to their Canadian background though the Detroit *Free Press* did say that "the hard-fisted laboring men" of Ingersoll should have participated in a higher class of the tournament.

William Bryce's 78-page 1876 *Canadian Base Ball Guide* was the first significant Canadian publication on the sport. It is notable for the total absence of any reference to baseball outside Ontario, a lapse inexcusable by that year though well in keeping with a popular misconception of Ontarians that they spoke for the rest of the country. Bryce was a publisher, bookseller, and sporting goods distributor whose Ontario Game Emporium was based on Richmond Street in London, Ontario. He was entirely conscious of baseball's national character, noting "The organization of a Canadian Association of Base Ball Players [at Toronto's Walker House on 7 April 1876] and the adoption of a special constitution and by-laws, playing rules, and championship code, have made the publication of a Canadian Base Ball Guide a necessity." He acknowledges "the want of authentic records of the game in Canada," but gives not the shade of a hint that this want may extend beyond Ontario's borders. His historical knowledge is sparse: he comments that "Within the past six years Base Ball has made rapid strides in public favor in Canada, and in the western and northern portions of Ontario, especially, it has to a great extent displaced Cricket and Lacrosse as a favorite summer out-door recreation." His patriotism was aroused by the exploits of Guelph's Maple Leafs in the mid-1870s who "did not even rest content with Canadian conquests, but carrying the Maple Leaf across the border gained decisive victories over the best of the American so-called amateurs. Professionals, too, have had in one or two instances to lower their banner to the Canadian champions."

The gradual importation of American professionals into Canadian base-ball ranks in the early 1870s culminating in Kingston securing "almost an entire nine from over the border," created little public concern. Indeed, by 1876 Bryce says "The impetus given to base ball by the greatly improved style of play resulting from the introduction of foreign talent, is manifesting itself in the increased patronage bestowed upon the game by the public in all parts of Canada." Concern about the importing of pro ballplayers almost always reflected the increased costs they brought to local entrepreneurs and the unsavoury association of such players with known gamblers. George Sleeman was notably guided by his pocketbook, alternately cursing imports one year and hiring them the next.

The import issue was not unique to Canada. Residents of many American cities also decried, though obviously not in national terms, the replacement of the locally born ballplayer representing his town by the itinerant mercenary who played today and was gone tomorrow. In the final analysis the majority of fans, or kranks as they were then known, supported the system because it improved the quality of local play. More of them then attended this popular form of entertainment and this in turn encouraged entrepreneurs to hire even better players to improve their chances of winning. It was a simple equation, well understood by William Bryce. He realized in 1876 that, in the same year as the National League's formation in the United States, a Canadian response was natural. "Base Ball," he said, "has not reached such a stage of perfection in Canada that its leading clubs are able to cope successfully with the best of the same class in the United States."

Significantly for many Canadians in Ontario and, in a less pronounced but nevertheless evolving sense elsewhere, baseball was becoming part of everyday life. Casual play was common. The obituary of Joseph Gibson of Ingersoll, one of that town's "hard-fisted" players, recorded that some of his happiest moments were playing baseball with his six boys in the park adjacent to their home. Likewise Tom Gillean, born in London in 1855, played the game so well as a youth that he was one of the few Canadians to play on the champion London Tecumsehs of 1877, a participation, said the *London Free Press,* that "pleased those who believe imports are not necessary, when good locals are available."

The decision of the Tecumsehs not to join the National League for the 1878 season probably had little discernible impact on baseball's future in Canada; their tenure, in those turbulent times for baseball teams, likely would have been short-lived. Still it was an opportunity that would not come again until the Montreal Expos joined the National League for the 1969 season. As the quality of professional play improved so did the desire of entrepreneurs to limit this success to a few specialized and larger centres. The reserve clause introduced in the early 1880s allowed National League teams to restrict the free movement of players and in time made possible the establishment of baseball's Minor Leagues, classified from Triple "A" to "D" by levels of play and to some extent by urban size. Smaller centres unable to compete with the major leagues for baseball talent were protected in a structure of major and minor leagues termed "Organized Baseball." The territorial markets and player contracts of local entrepreneurs were respected, allowing many of them to prosper. As this "organized" structure slowly took shape in the last two decades of the 19th century it created a mixture of resentment and resignation among hold-outs. The nominally independent and Ontario-based Canadian League of 1885 collapsed after one year when Toronto and Hamilton joined the American-run International League, one acknowledging its subservience to the major leagues. In the process William Southam's *Hamilton Spectator* bluntly declared, "Baseball is a pure matter of business and can't survive on the friendship of Guelph." Baseball's civic connections were now in a more complex commercial entertainment structure. Hamilton and Toronto might declare their economic dominance over a surrounding region but they were also being swallowed within a structure subservient to the interests of baseball's major leagues.

The present-day structure of organized baseball was realized in 1902 when the National Association of Professional Baseball Leagues was established to oversee the minor leagues' relationship with the major leagues. Under a National Agreement in place before 1902, Spalding's 1900 *Guide* noted, "the National League of the United States [was] the power that rules the whole professional base ball business of the great republic." Cal Davis, president of the Canadian League, made the case for Canadian subservience.

> The question of the relation of the minor base ball leagues to the National Board, and of the National Agreement to the game of base ball, is one which opens a very wide field for discussion. . . . from the standpoint of the Canadian League . . . the league has had a continuous existence almost since the old International League disbanded eight or nine years ago, but that only during the years 1897, 1898, and 1899 was the league a member of the National Agreement. It is my personal experience, and that of every manager in the league, that the condition of the game in Canada has been so vastly superior under the protection of the National Agreement to what it was as an independent organization that the league would sooner pass out of existence than return to the old ranks again.

Davis then mentioned the adjudication by the National Board on matters regarding disputes between his league and others of higher gradings, between clubs of different leagues, and between individual players and clubs.

Davis's response was that of a pragmatic businessman anxious to survive in the complex world of organized baseball but it shouldn't surprise that a few years later Samuel Moffett's report *The Americanization of Canada* slammed these apparent intrusions into Canadian affairs. Moffett's comments on baseball, however, were too narrowly concerned with the effects on British traditions and missed the larger implications implicit in Davis's rationalization. "It is not a trivial matter," Moffett wrote, "that baseball is becoming the national game of Canada instead of cricket. It has very deep significance, as has the fact that the native game of lacrosse is not able to hold its own against the southern intruder." Among Moffett's telling points were the Ontario Legislature's cutting short its session so that the provincial premier could throw out the first ball of Toronto's 1905 Eastern League season, and the Mayor of St Thomas's declaration of a holiday after three o'clock on the first day of the Western Ontario League season. "The Canadian newspapers," Moffett fulminated, "print fuller telegraphic accounts of the great baseball contests of the National, the American and the Eastern Leagues than they do of the proceedings of the British Parliament," and furthermore, "The American baseball language, which would be entirely unintelligible to an English reader, is fully acclimated in the Canadian press."

One of the first attempts to counter baseball's north-south axis by forming a truly nationwide baseball organization appeared in Spalding's 1914 *Canadian Base Ball Guide*. "From the east to the west the game has advanced to that extent that one can readily expect to see within a very short period of time a Canadian League that will in all probability be composed of a circuit embracing the following cities: London, Hamilton, Ottawa, Toronto, Montreal, Quebec, Saint John, and Halifax." Only excessive mileage, the writer argued, prevented extension of such a league to western Canada. The vision conformed to similar developments tying Canadian hockey and football together from coast to coast. In baseball's case, however, it was not realized, partly because the First World War intervened. More importantly, such a league in Spalding's vision would have to exist within the structure of organized baseball, and that being the case the north-south orientation made better business sense.

Historian Alan Metcalfe argues that by 1914 "baseball was truly Canada's national sport. No other sports were played across the country and exhibited such steady and sometimes spectacular growth." Cricket had declined to an inconsequential status; its clubs were often made up of older men like William Southam and Thomas Goldie, who played baseball as youths, but opted in their later years for cricket's social status. Field lacrosse had grown from a minor status in the last century after George Beers promoted it as a proper national game for the new Canadian nation. In making his case for lacrosse Beers acknowledged he had to work fast since baseball, "that American game," was gaining in popularity. A game can grow only so far on patriotic claims and by the time of the First World War lacrosse also was in decline. Its downfall is often attributed to its brutality but a more convincing argument was the game's failure to usurp baseball's successful integration into so many aspects of Canadian life. Baseball was played by men and women of all ages and social classes, a claim lacrosse could not make. As the skill level of baseball improved and threatened to chase away the casual player the game proved incredibly adaptable. Softball was gradually introduced between the First and Second World Wars and it expanded the participant base for baseball-type games. The slow pitch variation would have similar effect in the 1970s and 80s. Though purists might object, the two variations have much in common with baseball of the 1860s period. Lacrosse also tried to adapt by introducing the game of box lacrosse in indoor arenas but in the process killed the field game as an outdoor summer sport.

Some sense of baseball's popularity in this period is the level of newspaper coverage. In 1915 it was the most reported sport in Halifax (37.6%), Montreal (18.6%), Winnipeg (21.2%), and Edmonton (32%). In Toronto its 23.5% coverage made it the second most reported sport. A study by Evelyn Waters for the period 1926 through 1935 ranked baseball and hockey as almost even in newspaper coverage from coast to coast. Baseball ranked first in Toronto and Vancouver, and second in Montreal, to hockey while both sports were about even in Halifax and Winnipeg.

The game had completely surpassed all other summer games and was arguably the most popular game in Canada. Hockey was still growing and in the absence of large numbers of indoor ice rinks was limited in many parts of Canada by weather conditions ranging from January thaws to chinook winds. Yet even as baseball reached levels of popular support it was dogged by its American connection. In a 1920 essay Archibald MacMechan attacked the Americanization of Canadian sport: "Our native game, lacrosse, is dead. Cricket, which flourishes in Australia, is here a sickly exotic. But baseball is everywhere." One of the characters in New Brunswick writer George Clarke's 1926 novel *The Best One Thing* expressed the contempt of at least some Canadian critics: ". . . baseball was demoralising the youth of the land. If it was only cricket, now; a gentleman's game; a moulder of character. . . ." The cultural complaint had at least some justification from a social context. In the case of Dick Brookins, an alleged black player in the Western Canada League in 1910, league officials cowardly sought guidance from the National Association on whether he should be allowed to play.

At least in this case it could be argued that as a member of the Association the League was obliged to consult American officials. The same could not be said of an incident recalled by London newspaperman and historian Les Bronson. "A baseball team protested the use of a negro player, by, I believe, Ingersoll in the Ontario Baseball Association playoffs in the early twenties. It would be after Landis was named commissioner for I believe a letter was sent to his office to secure a ruling whether the player was eligible or not." As a Canadian amateur organization with no affiliation to organized baseball the Ontario association's resort to an American authority was a damning indictment of the game's subservience to foreign control.

This example may explain at least in part the game's somewhat troubled state in the late twenties when for several years only one Canadian-born player appeared on a major league roster and Toronto was the only city with a team in organized baseball. The only comparable period in the 20th century was the late 1960s.

Through several generations of play baseball had become a highly specialized game requiring superior bat and ball skills. Increasingly major league ballplayers were being drawn from parts of the United States where the game could be played year round. In the first decade of the 20th century there were over 500 ballplayers from the states of New York, Pennsylvania, and Ohio (which shared much in common with nearby Canadian centres) as opposed to fewer than 60 from Texas and California. The three northeastern American states retained and even slightly increased their major league participation between 1910 and 1919 (due partially to the Federal League's brief existence which for a time created an additional 200 major league jobs). California and Texas, however, contributed over 150 players. In the twenties contribution from the three northeastern states had fallen to just over 350 while Texas and California surpassed 200. The New York, Pennsylvania and Ohio total of major leaguers fell below 300 in the thirties, barely ahead of the number from the two southern states. Adding to this territorial shift in ballplayer birthplaces was the challenge of other sports. Many skilled athletes in Canada were now focusing their major league ambitions on hockey.

The period between the wars also saw the gradual spread of what were then simpler bat and ball games like softball. Softball's rapid spread drew potential players away from baseball. The earliest forms of softball were in fact indoor, winter variations of baseball played in the 1880s. Following the 1885 season members of Hamilton's professional teams, the Clippers and Primroses, had played baseball on roller skates at the Royal Roller Rink at Main and Catharine. (Among the Primroses was J. H. Barnfather who later played baseball in Winnipeg.) At the turn of the century the Toronto Garrison Officers' Indoor Baseball League met at the old University Avenue Armories; Sir Henry Pellatt was one of the directors. Experiments such as these in many North American cities led to refinements like the underhand pitching motion, a larger, less lively ball, and shorter distances between bases. These common sense responses to the playing environment were eventually taken outdoors. Softball's development was a sign that ordinary folks were simply trying to find an accessible means of connecting to the sport. As in time softball developed all of the professionalism and skill refinement of baseball, non-pros evolved the game of slow pitch.

Softball's popularity opened the doors to greater participation in bat and ball games. "Women," says Cohn Howell, "could be more easily integrated into [softball] as players," and women were attracted to softball in large numbers. From Toronto's Sunnyside to the playgrounds of Saskatchewan, a generation of women developed bat and ball skills which some of them later used in the All-American Girls Professional Baseball League. Within the native communities of north-eastern North America softball was even more attractive than baseball because gloves were not always required.

At the national level, baseball's interests were largely subsumed within the Amateur Athletic Union of Canada. Given that so much of the game was controlled by local amateur sandlot and commercial interests the game's lack of authority on the national stage was not a serious hindrance to the game's growth. In April 1937, however, the Canadian Amateur Hockey Association broke away from the Amateur Union, and was followed by secessionists from a number of other sports including baseball. Though the effect wasn't immediate, the way was paved for the eventual development of a meaningful national organization.

Though the 1940s and 50s were in fact boom years for minor league baseball in Canada, at the grass-roots level the game was faced with significant competition from other forms of recreation including automotive travel, television, summer cottages, and other spectator sports. Significantly all of these pastimes signalled an increasing privatization of life in which the simple public joy of playing or watching baseball with friends was giving way to more individual personal pursuits. Writing about baseball in Nova Scotia between 1946 and 1972, author Burton Russell described the common refrain of the day: "Some people with myopic vision or short memories tend to pass off baseball. They point out that the game is dying and that drag racing and skiing have captured the wallets, and the fancy, of the young people." While disputing their claim Russell nevertheless gave it credence in his observation that "Spectator interest in Nova Scotia senior baseball has declined drastically during the last several years. How unlike the tremendous enthusiasm displayed for the game back in the thirties, forties, and early fifties when thousands of fans poured through the gates to witness senior baseball at its best."

Interest in senior baseball in Nova Scotia reached such a low point that in 1968 the province's senior baseball league folded, and senior ball suffered the same fate in Cape Breton. Only one senior club, playing in a junior league during the season, registered for playoff action. Baseball's long minor league reign in Toronto had ended the year before. Even in the United States the sport had been replaced by football as the dominant national pastime. Theories accounting for baseball's decline referred to its slower pace, though such arguments failed to account for the game's internal logic and the role of pace in creating necessary dramatic moments. More reasoned points of view suggested that the game's delicate balance between offence and defence had become weighted in the pitcher's favour, citing the 1968 major league season in which Denny McLain of the Detroit Tigers won over 30 games and Bob Gibson of the St. Louis Cardinals had a scintillating earned run average of 1.12 runs per game.

The response at the major league level was to lower the pitcher's mound from 15 to ten inches and create a smaller strike zone. The most effective remedy, however, was that sure cure for too much good pitching—expansion. Among the new teams brought into the majors was the National League's first foreign entry, the Montreal Expos. In creating conditions for baseball's reinvigoration on the field, major league owners also encouraged the gradual resurgence of baseball interest throughout Canada.

The chief cause of baseball's apparent decline in the sixties had little if anything to do with the game itself. The post-war North American economy was expanding exponentially as virtually all of its competitors from Japan to Germany to Great Britain were forced to rebuild their industrial infrastructure. As the dominant North American summer sport baseball was the first entertainment to take advantage of this affluence. By the early fifties the game had dangerously overexpanded; its hundreds of markets would be incapable of supporting professional baseball at the slightest downturn. The same could be said of much senior baseball like Nova Scotia's Halifax and District League, which had a quasi semi-professional character. As the 1950s progressed the public began to use its new wealth to indulge in a variety of other private amusements. Not surprisingly baseball was forced to retrench but in doing so appeared to be in decline. In an affluent society appearance counts for much, and many supporters turned away from baseball rather than be identified with a public loser. Compounding this problem was the baby boomers' rejection in the 1960s of much of their parents' culture, of which there was no better symbol than baseball.

However, the game's problems had the positive benefit of forcing its amateur organizers in Canada to take remedial action. Attempts to give the sport some form of national direction dated back to the formation of the Canadian Baseball Association in 1864, again in 1876, and sporadically thereafter. These were largely regional initiatives, and short-lived. Baseball was a game dominated by commercial interests whose decisions were based on business considerations not those of national organization. The Canadian Amateur Baseball Association had been formed in 1919 but even at the amateur level regional interests dominated. In response to threats to the game's very existence an organization that today is the Canadian Federation of Amateur Baseball (CFAB) was incorporated in 1964.

The formative years of the CFAB were difficult ones. David Shury of North Battleford, Saskatchewan, secretary of the organization, was given responsibility for putting together a national team to represent Canada in the 1967 Pan-American Games in Winnipeg. Recalls Shury, "Bob Lacoursiere of Saskatoon and I had taken over earlier that year and had inherited a very sorry organization. It was broke, the provinces were in open revolt and the national organization was in difficulties with Ottawa. The Federal Government refused to let us have any funds with which to form a team."

Nevertheless, under coach Gerry MacKay from Manitoba a team was cobbled together which included a few players with past professional connections in Quebec and Ontario. Though reinstated as an amateur, pitcher Ron Stead was known to Toronto sportswriters from his try-outs with the Toronto Maple Leafs a decade before. At the time he had been profiled in a CBC documentary. The Olympic code, which applied to the Pan Am games, strictly forbade the participation of anyone who had past professional connections and news of the Canadian transgression broke during the competition. Shury later blamed Toronto sportswriters eager for a story. None of the other teams complained, he said, because they were all in the same boat. Four Canadians were sent home and the demoralized team did not win a game until their final match with undefeated Cuba. Canada's 10–9 win forced Cuba to play the United States for the gold and the Americans scored an unexpected upset.

The glimmerings of national direction for the game of baseball outside the structure of organized baseball almost immediately suffered another blow. In 1968 the federal government commissioned a study of amateur sport. The resulting report applauded the role of sports in fostering national unity and recommended federal involvement based on a sports priority standing. Priority one sports would receive favourable funding and services but as David Shury learned in early 1970 baseball was not among them, primarily because it lacked Olympic standing. Baseball officials launched an immediate public relations campaign that included support from New Brunswick Premier Louis Robichaud and former Prime Minister Lester Pearson, then honorary President of the new Montreal Expos. When the Minister of National Health and Welfare John Munro made his announcement of designated sports in April 1970, 21 sports had been designated as priority one and baseball was among them. As Shury says, "[Munro] had also mentioned that he did not realize so many people were interested in baseball."

The 1970s were kinder to baseball. The Montreal Expos began play in a converted amateur stadium, Jarry Park, in 1969. The endearing charm of that park, the team's roster of colourful players (a characterization that in fairness is applied to all expansion teams), and their national television exposure had immediate impact. In Montreal in 1968 there were only 222 amateur teams at all levels of play. That number jumped to 430 within a year. Torontonians in a burst of civic pride were doubly miffed by the award of the 1976 Olympic Games to their rival. Led by Metro Toronto Chairman Paul Godfrey and a number of commercial interests, most notably Labatt Breweries, Toronto's pursuit of a major league baseball franchise began in earnest. Baseball's long decline through the 1960s was ending. The game was simply too popular and too historically engrained to fade away and its stabilization corresponded to an era of new stars and great moments—like Carlton Fisk's home run in the sixth game of the 1975 World Series, which is often mentioned as being symbolic of the game's more adventurous offensive style. Writers—from the *New Yorker*'s Roger Angell to the novelist stylings in Roger Kahn's remembrances of the old Brooklyn Dodgers, Jim Bouton's off-the-wall observations from a player's perspective, and the statistical imagination of Bill James—were presenting the game in a fresh manner to a new generation of fans and renewing the faith for the jaded former follower. The Toronto Blue Jays, who entered the American League in 1977, were an immediate sensation, drawing nearly two million fans including over 40,000 who attended their inaugural match in, what else, a Canadian snowstorm.

Figures released by the CFAB indicated that in 1979 there were over 160,000 registered baseball players in Canada including 50,000 in Quebec and 31,000 in British Columbia. Little League, Babe Ruth, and Connie Mack associations were not included but CFAB Executive Director Paul

Lavigne suggested they accounted for another 25,000 players. CFAB figures showed only 12,000 registrants in Ontario, a number that actually shrank to under 11,000 in 1981. In fact CFAB figures also showed decline in Quebec (down to 43,000) and British Columbia (29,035). With the exception of Prince Edward Island all Maritime provinces had shown growth. The most feasible explanation for this apparent decline in registrations is a natural stabilization in participation after the initial excitement surrounding major league baseball's arrival in Canada. By 1988 the game's popularity and participation rates were less subject to the first blush of expansion. In that year participation, including Little League, Babe Ruth leagues, and regular amateur baseball affiliated with CFAB, totalled over 200,000.

Between 1990 and 1993 participation exploded at all levels except the senior (slipping from 6,700 to 5,800) where it is possible many were drawn into house league teams, softball, or slow pitch. In CFAB's affiliated recorded ranks at the youngest level, Mosquito baseball grew from 42,000 in 1990 to 74,000 a year later, and 96,000 by 1993. Pee Wee grew from 25,000 in 1990 to 41,000 three years later, Bantam grew slowly from 17,000 in the same period to nearly 25,000 by 1993, while Midget slumped from 10,000 after 1990 but recovered with 12,000 participants in 1993. Junior baseball accounted for only 3,200 in 1990 and 4,600 in 1993. (Many of these figures are misleadingly low because they do not include local house leagues in which most children play.) This participation was rewarded in 1991 when Canada's national youth team (18 and under) won the country's first-ever amateur Gold Medal at the World Youth Championship in Brandon, Manitoba. One of the team's pitchers, Joe Young from Fort McMurray, Alberta, was drafted by the Toronto Blue Jays in 1993.

Orleans in the east end of Ottawa's National Capital Region offers an example of baseball's explosive growth in Canada. Orleans is a relatively new community but one that sought to put down roots by developing a youth sports program. Formed in 1983 with about 150 players, the Orleans Little League grew within a decade to 730 players, a maximum dictated by the limited number of ball diamonds. Players range in age from 8 to 18 and are drawn from an area that includes the eastern part of Gloucester and the western part of Cumberland township. Coaching and umpiring have improved over time and all-star teams compete as far away as Montreal and northern New York state. The impact of the Expos, the Blue Jays, and in 1993 the Triple A Ottawa Lynx has caused many children to rethink their decision to devote all their dreams to a hockey career. Junior hockey players with the Ottawa 67s keep their options open by playing baseball in the Orleans system.

The number of participants in fast and slow pitch softball is astounding. In 1988 Robert Barney noted that perhaps as many as two million Canadians played some version of the underhand game; just over 10 per cent were registered in some form of league play leading to recognized championships. These participants were split almost evenly between males and females. Barney notes by way of contrast that hockey including its connected forms of girls' ringette and, largely, men's ball hockey accounts for about half a million players.

In 1994 the Canadian Parliament confirmed hockey as Canada's winter game and lacrosse as the country's summer sport. If participation and national enthusiasm, such as that which followed Joe Carter's home run mean anything, there can be little doubt that the real national pastime of Canada has always been baseball.

SAMUEL O. REGALADO

18. Viva Baseball!
The Beginnings of Latin American Baseball

When one thinks of the internationalization of the American pastime, the Latin game immediately comes to mind. Clearly no other area of the world has had as much influence on the North American game in the last half of the twentieth century. The reverse is also true. The result has been an intense rivalry between the two regions. Often subjected to intervention by the "Colossus of the North," Latin Americans have sporadically sought to display their independence from such neocolonial intrusion. Baseball has frequently mirrored this peculiar relationship. The game has been a catalyst for positive as well as negative developments: it has been the source of great wealth for some but exploitation for others; it has stimulated great nationalistic pride for some Hispanics but humiliation for others; it has provided outstanding examples of racial tolerance for some but bigotry for others. Baseball has been a source of foreign cultural hegemony and influence, but it has also provided a tool for local political tyranny. Whatever its manifestations, however, for most of the game's existence baseball has been used as a way of adopting as well as resisting American culture and has therefore become more than a game in many Latin American countries.

By the end of the twentieth century more than five hundred Latin American–born players had donned major league uniforms, including players from Cuba, the Dominican Republic, Mexico, Venezuela, and even Curaçao. Seven Hispanic players had been inducted into baseball's Hall of Fame, and numerous major league awards had been won by Hispanic players. What began as a trickle of players in 1911, with the signing of two players by the Cincinnati Reds, became a stream in the period following the integration of baseball in 1947, which allowed black Hispanics to play, and became a flood by the end of the century. Although most of the early Latin players came from Cuba, when that country began to dry up as a source after Castro's revolution, other countries, especially the Dominican Republic, Puerto Rico, and Venezuela took up the slack. Yet throughout the history of player exchanges between Latin America and the United States, it has been far from one way. As early as the 1920s, all-black American teams, as well as all-white teams, toured the region, and American white players played alongside American and Hispanic blacks on winter league teams. By the 1920s, the newly organized Negro League teams traveled freely back and forth. Many of the most prominent American black players like Satchel Paige, Josh Gibson, and Buck Leonard spent parts of their peripatetic careers playing for Latin American teams that promised higher salaries than they could earn in the United States. Moreover, it should be recalled that in order to ease Jackie Robinson's integration of the game in 1947, the Dodgers held spring training in Cuba that year.

Clearly the path for such vigorous exchanges and player development was well prepared by the game's early groundbreakers in Latin America. In the following essay by Samuel O. Regalado, drawn from his larger study of the Dominican Republic's contribution to major league baseball, the author seeks to determine the causes of baseball's diffusion to Latin America, especially to the Caribbean area, and he seeks to account for its growth and passionate following in the context of broader United States–Latin American relations.

Dodger Stadium reverberated with excitement on the warm evening of May 14, 1981. Dodgers fans had come to see a young pitcher's attempt to establish a major league record for the most consecutive wins by a rookie at the start of a season. Moreover, they came just to see him. None of the 56,000 seats was empty as patrons sat impatiently in the ballpark awaiting their hero's attempt to capture his eighth straight victory. As the Dodgers took the field, the roar of the crowd reached a crescendo when Fernando Valenzuela, the twenty-year-old Mexican star, popped out of the dugout on his way to the mound. Throughout the stadium fans shouted encouragement in both Spanish and English as Helen Dell, the Dodger Stadium organist, used the

"El Toro" theme instead of the more familiar "Charge" for that evening's battle cry.

In the press box, journalists from around the nation jockeyed for space as they sought to cover the phenomenon dubbed "Fernandomania." Behind their microphones, Dodgers broadcaster Vin Scully prefaced the contest with a dramatic analysis of Valenzuela while Jaime Jarrín, the "other voice of the Dodgers," did the same for his Spanish-speaking listeners, which numbered well into the millions. Indeed, in the next several weeks similar scenes occurred in other National League cities when Valenzuela pitched. The native of Etchohuaquila in Sonora, Mexico, had captured national attention. Fans clamored to get his autograph; reporters groped for new information on him. English-speaking baseball followers were captivated by the young man from a humble background who seemed to spin magic on the pitcher's mound. Their Spanish-speaking counterparts saw him—and the surrounding delirium—as symbolic of Latin influence in the United States. Latins had arrived.

Clearly, the attention directed toward Valenzuela was a watershed in the history of Latins in America's national sport. Although prior to 1981 Latins had never received such nationwide acclaim, Fernando Valenzuela was nonetheless simply the most celebrated representative of a distinguished group of athletes who have helped shape major league baseball and American culture. Talented stars such as the Alou brothers, Luis Aparicio, Jorge "George" Bell, Orlando Cepeda, Roberto Clemente, Adolfo Luque, Juan Marichal, Dennis Martínez, Orestes "Minnie" Miñoso, and Rubén Sierra were prominent during their respective years of play. Most were driven by a desperate desire to succeed—what Octavio "Cookie" Rojas described as that "special hunger." "I knew it was going to take a lot of hard work, desire, and determination [to succeed]," reflected Dominican Manny Mota in 1982. "When I came to the United States to play professional baseball, I wanted something that nobody was going to give me. I had to go and get it myself."

As these baseball pioneers explored their frontiers in search of stardom and the financial rewards often denied them in their native lands, they expanded the American national pastime into a truly international sport. Latin ballplayers coming to the United States entered a sporting institution that personified the American dream of opportunity, upward social mobility, and success. They brought to major and minor league baseball not only their remarkable skills but also flair and charisma that enhanced the game's spectator appeal. Ultimately, their achievements motivated clubs and the American media to modify their infrastructures, such as expanding scouting regions and employing bilingual personnel.

The importance of the Latin contingent in American baseball, however, transcended the sport. Players often bridged gaps between Latin America and the United States—and their distinct and often conflicting cultures. Throughout most of the twentieth century, major league rosters included those from Cuba, the Dominican Republic, Mexico, the Commonwealth of Puerto Rico, and other Central and South American countries. Brothers joined brothers and sons followed fathers as generations of Latin players gave America's national pastime an international composition. Often heroes in their own lands, they sought to exhibit their national pride on the diamond. Most Latin players saw themselves as "ambassadors" representing their respective countries and frowned at the stereotypes that homogenized all Latins. At the same time, their Spanish-speaking tongue was a crucial bond between players in spite of their varied nationalities. Their language both shielded them from criticisms and served as an impediment in their quest for recognition.

Moreover, the language barrier highlighted the difficulties of Latin acculturation into the United States. Separated from family and home, players struggled daily with loneliness and the pitfalls of a foreign cuisine. For many, such problems were sometimes complicated by the starting points of their American careers. While some Latins landed in areas with large Hispanic enclaves, others were less fortunate. Rico Carty traveled to Yakima, Washington; Juan Marichal went to tiny Michigan City, Indiana; and Zoilo Versalles was a seventeen-year-old in Elmira, New York, places with almost no Latin residents. In addition, political tensions all too often disrupted the lives of Latin players. In 1961 broken diplomatic ties virtually eliminated recruiting in Cuba, which up to that point had been an important source of talent.

But according to Latin American baseball players, their most troubling encounter was with racism. Brought to the United States because of their skills, most Latin players believed in the great American dream. And they assumed that success came by virtue of merit. Too often, however, they learned otherwise. Professional baseball in the United States mirrored the larger American society. The major leagues had excluded African American players from the late nineteenth century until 1947. After the color barrier was breached, the turbulence created by the civil rights movement in the ensuing decades proved unsettling for Latin players on and off the field. Often singled out because of their background, Latins repeatedly felt the stings of American racial prejudice and discrimination. Finally, while Latins and American blacks confronted racism together, Latins alone dealt with the additional trauma of acculturation.

Yet for many players from Spanish-speaking countries, their negative experiences faded into the background when compared with the poverty found in their own countries. Baseball for many was clearly the only way out. Furthermore, it embodied the Latin virtues of individualism, personal honor, and integrity.

Starting in 1911 Latin players came to the United States with growing regularity, and with each wave their impact in the major leagues enlarged. From 1911 to 1947, they entered the majors almost exclusively via the rosters of the Cincinnati Reds and the Washington Senators, who fostered scouting efforts to recruit low-cost talent, primarily from Cuba. But after Jackie Robinson joined the major leagues, black Latins poured into the United States during the integration years of the 1950s and 1960s. The influx reflected expanded scouting efforts that drew players from Latin regions well beyond Cuba. By the 1970s and 1980s, as incoming talent from Cuba diminished, major league programs, such as those found in the small Dominican town of San Pedro de Macorís, were created to develop talent and orient players to U.S. culture. Early Latin pioneers such as Felipe Alou, Santos Alomar, Tony Oliva, and Manny Mota served within the major league framework to help coach the future stars seeking the gold and glory that their predecessors had achieved. Moreover, Roberto Clemente's legacy proved to be an important inspiration.

Like their African American counterparts, Latins played magnificently. From Roberto "Beto" Avila in 1954 to José Canseco in 1988, Latin players captured the Most Valuable Player award six times, in addition to seven Rookie of the Year titles, three Cy Young trophies, and seventeen batting championships. By the end of the early 1990s the Baseball Hall of Fame inducted five Latins: Luis Aparicio, Roberto Clemente, Juan Marichal, and Rod Carew were honored for their outstanding careers in the major leagues while Martín Dihigo, a Cuban player, represented the American black leagues.

The expansion of baseball's Latin contingent mirrored the growing importance of Latin cultures in the United States. Victims of racial and cultural stereotypes prior to World War II, Spanish speakers struggled to gain a foothold in mainstream U.S. culture. As the Hispanic population increased, social and political organizations developed to address a variety of urban and rural issues. Benefiting from the gains of the activism of the 1960s, a greater number of second- and third-generation Latins, armed with education and advanced skills, entered the larger corporate and media markets. Many were determined, however, to maintain their cultural heritage. Most certainly the successes of Latins gave rise to optimistic thinking; one Latin leader eagerly announced that the 1980s would be the "Decade for Hispanics."

The achievements and turmoil faced by Latin players coincided with major developments in the larger Spanish-speaking world. Other Latins sought to maintain cultural ties in an unfamiliar and arbitrary environment. The struggle to achieve recognition and parity in the major leagues was part of the larger Latin quest for equality in the United States. Indeed, the experiences of Latin players in the major leagues provided a unique perspective and often brought into clearer focus the larger Hispanic experience.

Paradoxically, however, Latin ballplayers were the most visible Latins in the United States but the most invisible players in the major leagues. American baseball aficionados could cite their names and statistics, but knew little else about them. At the same time, writers of American twentieth-century cultural history, particularly the experts who delineated the contributions of Spanish-speaking groups in the United States, failed to acknowledge the Latin impact on one of America's most cherished institutions—baseball. Yet, clearly the Latin path that led to baseball's "promised land" was a paradigm of the larger Latin historical experience in the United States. By 1981, patterns apparent both in the baseball world and in the broader Hispanic universe came together in an explosion called Fernandomania. But to understand that special hunger and the long and difficult path culminating in the Valenzuela euphoria, we must begin a century earlier.

Esteban Enrique Bellán probably had little idea of his significance in American baseball history. His 1871 membership on the Troy Haymakers of the National Association of Professional Base Ball Players distinguished him as the first Latin American player in the major leagues. Bellán's trailblazing inaugurated a movement of Latin players to the United States. Most were Cubans until the midtwentieth century, when increasing numbers from all over Latin America had a growing impact. During the pre-integration period, however, Latin players were rarely taken seriously. Their limited arsenal of skills coupled with the difficulty in communicating with them led some managers to feel that they were more trouble than they were worth. Baseball observers in the United States, of course, were not exempt from the large-scale and historical arrogance that most Americans held toward their Latin neighbors. This attitude, compounded by ignorance about Spanish-speaking cultures and racial biases, often polarized the two regions and hindered opportunities to strengthen their common interests.

Baseball carried the potential to close the gap. Instead, the prevailing attitudes toward Latins not only forestalled any expansive migration of them into the big leagues but also deprived American fans of enjoying their skills to a greater degree for a half century. Latins, to the surprise of many, were quite passionate when it came to baseball. Indeed, baseball's development in the United States predated the game's emergence in Latin America by only twenty years. Yet, between 1871 and 1911 the big leagues extended an invitation to only one Latin. And invitations on a larger scale were not soon forthcoming.

Between 1871 and 1946 Latins trickled into the major leagues with no great fanfare. Although all of them were considered white, some were deemed a novelty and others became targets of journalistic humor. Their experiences with the press and teammates, moreover, laid the groundwork for American perceptions and stereotypes of Latin players that lasted for decades. Because Latin American players came from cultures that also revered baseball, they were anxious to exhibit their talents in a game that many Americans placed on a pedestal.

Since the end of Spanish rule in the 1820s (save the Caribbean in 1898), sports on the whole in Latin America held varied implications. Similar to the growth of organized sports in the United States, athletics in Latin America reflected class lines, both in cultural and financial terms. The rigid social stratification, which was the centerpiece of life during the more than three hundred years of Spanish rule, remained intact. And the development of sporting competitions throughout Latin America served as a microcosm of that tradition. Late-nineteenth-century sports clubs, for instance, emerged not from families of mixed ancestry or from the still-oppressed Indians or from black Latins. They came from the ranks of the urban Creole elite and their European counterparts. Like the status communities found in the United States, the Latin sports clubs were a means of closing ranks to protect cherished positions in the traditional social hierarchy. But the athletic activities that emerged were not distinctively Latin American.

Indeed, Latin America's high profile sports stemmed from what cultural, socioeconomic, and political elites viewed as "progressive" civilizations abroad. As historian Steve Stein pointed out with respect to Peru, its "elite, increasingly integrated into the international economic system, was quick to imitate the cultural patterns of [outside] elites. As with other European imports, soccer arrived in Peru in the 1880s aboard an English ship." Nineteenth-century Latin aristocrats "readily understood what was happening in Europe and ably discussed the latest ideas radiating from the

Old World, which they welcomed to the New," according to E. Bradford Burns, until "civilization and the progress that led to it became identified with Europe." Not surprisingly, cricket, polo, cycling, and, by the 1890s, soccer, were reserved exclusively for people of means. "The typical 'sport-man,'" claimed Stein in his discussion about Peruvian competitors, "was energetic, athletic, carefree, and the member of a wealthy and prominent family." As for traditional culture, "European thought . . . proved to be an ideological flood, which swept before it most American originality." Native sports were so victimized that by the late twentieth century, argued Latin historian Joseph L. Arbena, "the most popular sports . . . have little connection with traditional society, not much with colonial society, and even less with pre-Columbian civilizations." However, as soccer and other European sports satisfied the urban elite, baseball developed prominence among the other classes.

While the bulk of southern Latin America fancied European sports, U.S. influences penetrated the Caribbean region, Central America, and parts of Mexico. Throughout the mid- to late nineteenth century, U.S. capitalists and speculators poured into these areas in search of profit. Cornelius Vanderbilt opened his overland transit route through Nicaragua in 1850. The Boston Fruit Company, later the powerful United Fruit Company, started shipping bananas out of Guatemala in 1885. And by the 1890s, Americans had heavily invested in Mexican mines and railroads. As these revenues grew so, too, did American interest in acquiring territory. Manifest Destiny had already victimized Mexico, resulting in the loss of nearly half of its territory to the United States by 1848. And American greed in the Caribbean and Panama continued throughout the nineteenth century. To that end, U.S. diplomats made repeated efforts to purchase such areas as the Virgin Islands and Santo Domingo in 1867 and 1879, respectively. In 1850, the Clayton-Bulwer Treaty between Great Britain and the United States decreed that neither would attempt to acquire exclusive rights to a canal in Central America. In 1901, through careful maneuvering, the United States pressured the British to abrogate the treaty, which ultimately paved the way for the Panama Canal. By then, the United States had defeated Spain and had acquired greater territory and influence in the Caribbean.

Through it all, American arrogance was clear. "We are Americans," proclaimed Secretary of State William Seward in 1869, a chief architect of expansion. "We are charged with the responsibilities of establishing on the American continent a higher condition of civilization and freedom" than seen elsewhere in the world. As American interests expanded, contact between the English- and Spanish-speaking peoples inevitably grew. And within this framework, America's national pastime became an export item.

Several interpretations have been offered to explain baseball's emergence in the Caribbean, Mexico, and South America. Like other Latin American sports that appeared during the nationalistic period of the midnineteenth century, baseball filtered in from outside. As to who imported it—American sailors on leave, Caribbean students home from the United States—remains a cloudy issue. This much, however, is clear: Cuba was baseball's epicenter in the region. Indeed, baseball's development in Cuba was an indirect link to the history of the sport on the other islands. "It's much the same as that which happened with Christianity," claimed Dominican Pedro Julio Santana. "Jesus could be compared to the North Americans, but the apostles were the ones that spread the faith, and the apostles of baseball were the Cubans. Even though the Dominican Republic and Puerto Rico were occupied by the North Americans, the Cubans first brought baseball here."

Although no one is sure who introduced baseball to Cuba, according to Cuban historian Luis Hernández a student named Nemesio Guillot returned home in 1864 with a ball and bat after he had completed his studies in the United States. Two years later, Latin America's romance with baseball reportedly began when a group of American sailors, whose ship was stationed in Havana, invited a few Cubans to participate in a game. At Palmar de Junco the sailors designed a baseball diamond and shortly thereafter games commenced. While there exists no conclusive evidence as to which style of baseball—the New York or Massachusetts game—the Cubans initially adopted, Esteban Bellán's familiarity with the New York brand is suggestive. Although only those of privilege initially competed, various U.S. companies—particularly those in the sugar industry both in Cuba and later in the Dominican Republic—as well as strategically placed American troops helped baseball transcend class and racial lines until it became the sport of choice in Cuba's poorer rural sectors. In 1868, Cuba ushered in professional baseball when a team from Havana defeated a rival from Matanzas 51–9. Interest in baseball spread rapidly in the 1870s and 1880s throughout the Caribbean and eventually onto the Central and South American mainland. The bastion of Latin baseball, however, remained in Cuba, which for nearly one hundred years provided the American big leagues with the bulk of Latin baseball talent.

Known during his career as the "Cuba Sylph," Esteban Bellán was born in 1849 in Havana. In 1866 he came to the United States to attend Fordham

University. Already knowledgeable about baseball from his encounters with American sailors in Cuba, Bellán joined the amateur Rose Hill College Baseball Club as a catcher. In 1868 he played with another amateur team until his debut with the Troy Haymakers. During his two-year tenure in the major leagues, first with Troy then with the New York Mutuals, Bellán developed a reputation as a good third baseman. The *Troy Daily Whig*, which appeared to set a precedent in Americanizing Latin names, wrote that " 'Steve' has courage and activity, laces the hottest 'liners' [and] 'grounders,' " and was an "accurate thrower to the bases." He fueled further Cuban interest in baseball when he returned home. Bellán, who participated in Cuba's first professional contest, continued as a player-manager until 1886, promoting and teaching the game at every available opportunity. By the late 1880s, Cuban writer and former player Wenceslao Gálvez y Delmonte wrote that "baseball . . . had rooted itself so strongly in this land as proven by the hundreds of clubs in almost all parts of the island." Furthermore, he correctly predicted that the "baseball fields of Cuba will persist longer than the cockfight and the bullring."

As early as 1878, Emilio Sabourín helped to establish that island's first organized league, the Liga de Béisbol Profesional Cubana, in which regional teams competed and intense rivalries formed. The most popular was between Havana and Almendares—teams that fielded the best talent on the island. Other clubs representing towns such as Cienfuegos, Fe, Marianao, and Santa Clara also became part of Cuba's rich professional baseball heritage. Early stars like hitter Wenceslao Gálvez y Delmonte of Almendares and pitcher Adolfo Luján of Havana added to the excitement on that island. Sabourín managed the Havana club to nine championships between 1878 and 1892 before his death at the hand of the Spanish government in 1897. Like Sabourín, many affiliated with baseball garnered praise not only for their skills but also for their patriotism, as monies earned at the gate sometimes ended up in the coffers of the Cuba Libre movement that fought against Spanish oppression.

Cuban players became so skilled that, following the Spanish-American War in 1898, American big league clubs and individual stars visited the island with increasing frequency. The warm weather during winter months, proximity, and an opportunity for added revenue all made Cuba an attractive spot to visit. While Ty Cobb and Christy Mathewson were among the first white American stars to play in Cuba, American black professionals eventually competed in Cuba to enhance their finances and gain a needed reprieve from the torrent of racial abuse in the United States. Cuba was clearly the hub of baseball activity in Latin America. Indeed, one American writer described the Pearl of the Antilles as "stark raving dottily crazy over baseball."

Baseball also expanded into other Caribbean regions. But it did so during an era when many islanders resented U.S. hegemony. By the turn of the century, the military and economic power of the Great Colossus of the North affected all realms of Caribbean life. Encroachment by the United States, had, of course, concerned Latins long before 1900. Seward's 1869 enunciation of prevailing American attitudes brought great discomfort to Latin intellectuals, who readily understood the ramifications of Manifest Destiny. Indeed, as early as 1811 a Cuban writer characterized the United States as "a colossus which has been constructed of all castes and languages and which threatens to swallow up, if not all our America, at least the northern portion of it." Latin nationalists understandably squirmed as North American investments poured into their countries, sometimes by invitation, as was the case in Mexico under Porfirio Díaz in the latter part of the nineteenth century. During the last years of Spanish rule in the Caribbean, the Puerto Rican press corps sharply debated the U.S. presence in the region. Some admired Americans' willingness to intervene on Cuba's behalf for "moral" reasons, while others warned of an impending "Yankee peril."

Those who were uncomfortable with a seemingly unchecked United States could hardly turn to historical precedent to ease their minds. Since 1822, when the United States sent Joel Poinsett to develop diplomatic relations with the court of Mexico's Augustín de Iturbide, Latin observers were already apprehensive about their northern neighbor's appetite for expansion. Throughout most of the nineteenth century, as the United States competed with other neocolonial powers, such as Great Britain and France, American influence into Latin America grew more intense. Perhaps anticipating the inevitable, Cuban patriot José Martí warned, "Once the United States is in Cuba, who will get it out?"

As a result of the Spanish-American War, the United States by the end of the nineteenth century was, indeed, in Cuba as well as in Puerto Rico. Unable to extricate themselves from American militarization or capitalism, Latins learned and used baseball as a means of expression and took great pleasure in beating the "gringos" at their own game. After 1900, baseball continued to blossom in Puerto Rico and, soon thereafter, those serious about the sport formed professional clubs. Though the first Puerto Rican to enter the big leagues—Hiram Bithorn—did not make his appearance until 1942, baseball was already well-entrenched in the new American commonwealth. As islanders gained a reputation for providing formidable competition, visiting clubs from Cuba and the United States began to routinely dock at San Juan to test Puerto Rican talent. American black stars such as Satchel Paige, Josh Gibson, and Buck Leonard also competed there against some of the island's legendary players, including Chato Rivera, Liborio Caballero, Pancho Coimbre, and Perucho Cepeda. Indeed, the Puerto Rican Winter League, founded in 1938, became one of the most popular off-season havens for American big leaguers.

Baseball had already found a home in the Dominican Republic by the time of the Spanish-American War. Cubans who fled the brutality of the Ten Years' War (1868–78) brought baseball with them. The Dominicans learned the game rapidly so that by 1907 they had professional clubs, including a Santo Domingo team called Licey, for which most of that island's best athletes competed. Later other clubs, such as Escogido, rose to challenge Licey's dominance. As the appeal of baseball fanned Santo Domingo's sportive fires, Licey and its rivals drew thousands to their games. More than just sporting rituals, the games crossed class lines as they provided entertainment for both high society and those of lesser income. By 1910 the Dominicans also competed against clubs from neighboring islands.

Like their counterparts in Puerto Rico, many Dominican baseball aficionados viewed their adopted sport as a symbolic show of pride and defiance against U.S. imperialism. During the frequent American occupations following 1916, games with U.S. military personnel provided Dominicans with "a chance . . . to measure themselves against their occupiers." Dominican Manuel Joaquín Báez Vargas claimed with pride that "these games with North American sailors and marines were very important. There was a certain kind of patriotic enthusiasm in beating them." In 1914, for instance, when the popular Enrique Hernández pitched a no-hitter against an American navy team, baseball became a symbol of resistance. Another pitcher, Fellito Guerra, however, reached even greater heights in Dominican lore. According to the story, big league scouts chased the standout pitcher in the early 1920s, and one eventually offered him a contract. But Guerra, in protest of an American military presence in his country, refused the invitation to sign with the "occupiers." Given that the first Dominican to reach the big leagues—Ossie Virgil—did not do so until 1956, it is difficult to fathom that the majors showed the type of interest that accompanied the fable. But to an extent the symbolic nature of the story exhibited the degree of Dominican nationalism seen through baseball.

Juan Bosch, the former president whose path to regain office was blocked in 1965 by American marines sent to restore order, later offered an embittered analysis of early twentieth-century North American baseball influence over his country. Baseball contests between American servicemen and Dominicans, he contended, had little to do with goodwill. "These games manifested a form of the peoples' distaste of the occupation. They were a repudiation of it," he claimed. Contests were fueled with the incentive to go and "beat the North Americans."

Apart from the political connotations, however, baseball was popular in its own right. From the smallest villages to the largest cities, baseball often overshadowed such traditional pastimes as horse racing and cockfighting. Dominican sports historian Tirso Valdez claimed that baseball was a vital part of community life. "Through [baseball] the village experiences moments of happiness, when its team realizes its desires and wins, or passing moments of dejection if a defeat becomes a rout . . . but above all, the village experiences the hope that always prevails in baseball of coming from behind or winning the next game." The passion in the hearts of the Latins for this adopted sport was apparent during the early years of the twentieth century and grew in subsequent decades.

Baseball, in fact, was underscored by its popularity even in moments of revolutionary crisis. In August 1933, for example, during a revolt against the Cuban tyrant Gerardo Machado, the island lost communication with the outside world for a week. When contact was restored, the *San Juan El Mundo,* the country's leading newspaper, wanted to know, above all else, the American baseball scores of the previous week. The *Sporting News* reasoned that "cutting [the Cubans] off from the scores was like sitting them down in a desert." In fact, "they were as happy to hear how the ball games came out as they were in the restoration of peace in their country." In later years, when Fidel Castro conducted his own revolution from the mountains of Cuba, he listened regularly to Spanish-speaking baseball announcer Buck Canel broadcast the 1958 World Series. Shortly thereafter, when Canel tried to interview Castro about the revolution, the Cuban leader wanted to know "why [Milwaukee Braves manager Fred] Haney pitched [Warren] Spahn instead of [Lou] Burdette in the sixth game [of the World Series]." In the Dominican Republic, during the unstable period following the 1961 assassination of Rafael Trujillo, an armed rebel cornered an American journalist to learn how Juan Marichal had fared in the recent All-Star Game. Baseball's hold on Dominicans was such that some claimed "there will never be any political trouble during the . . . season, only afterwards."

Fueling this excitement about baseball were the regular visits made by major league teams to the Caribbean to compete against Latin all-star teams. Between 1890 and 1911, the Cincinnati Reds, Detroit Tigers, New

York Giants, Philadelphia Athletics, and Philadelphia Phillies visited the islands but did not always leave unscathed. American League president Ban Johnson, in 1911, however, temporarily halted the Caribbean barnstorming trips after several Cuban clubs defeated their American counterparts. "We want no makeshift club calling themselves the Athletics to go to Cuba to be beaten by colored teams," he remarked. National League teams, however, continued to march into the Caribbean. The 1936 Cincinnati Reds faced formidable competition in a Dominican all-star squad before finally winning 4–2. However, when the Reds traveled to Puerto Rico that year to face the Cuban Almendares squad, Cincinnati lost. The front-page story in Puerto Rico's leading newspaper the next day was the defeat of the American team. For their part, Latins viewed their passion for the game as not solely based on financial gain, but as a labor of love, whereas "the Yankee baseball players came . . . always for speculation, since they do not understand baseball in any other way."

Unlike in the Caribbean, baseball's beginnings in Mexico were not grounded on the notion of humiliating the imperialists. Nor were Americans directly responsible for introducing baseball into the country. In the Yucatán Peninsula, for instance, evidence suggests that Cuban workers introduced the sport as early as the 1860s. If this is true, it is hard to fathom that the game was readily understood by any of the participants, as the Cubans themselves had only just been introduced to it. Baseball, nonetheless, subsequently captured the interest of those in the working- and middle-class communities. There, "boys in their early teens," claimed the historian Gilbert M. Joseph, "spilled into the plazuelas of Santiago and San Juan near the center of Mérida and played ball well into the evening." But baseball during the 1880s and 1890s also grew to be the sport of the elite, for it "fit nicely into the oligarch's roseate turn-of-the-century vision of a grander, more modern Yucatán founded upon the virtues of physical vigor and competition." El Sporting Club, a team of young men who learned the game while attending schools in the United States, was the most competitive in the region. Games in which they participated "ranked among Mérida's important social events."

Interestingly, baseball also gained great prominence as a political tool during Mexico's 1910 revolution. Carrillo Puerto, the region's socialist leader, encouraged baseball activities because it "seemed singularly appropriate to the social transition that the [revolutionary] party would carry out in the Yucatán." Joseph argues that, as Puerto's followers saw it, "the individual [in a baseball game] was only part of a larger entity, whose success depended upon the transformation of individualism into collective conscience." Though Puerto's "New Yucatán" did not entirely come to pass, baseball survived, and there, amidst the ghosts of the old Mayan deities, diamonds graced the land. Ironically, and perhaps justifiably, almost a century after baseball took hold of the Yucatán region, Mexico's greatest sports product, Fernando Valenzuela, donned the uniform of the Mérida Leones on the eve of his move into the U.S. professional ranks and almost immediate stardom.

In the northern and central flanks of Mexico, baseball's entry came in a more traditional manner—American influence. Made convenient by what William H. Beezley called "The Porfirian Persuasion," baseball appeared when "Mexicans saw their country zooming into modernization, hence they rushed to adopt the styles, attitudes, and amusements of other modernized western nations." Though records indicate that citizens of Mexico City did not see their first baseball game until the early 1880s, new American arrivals, baseball fans undoubtedly among them, manufactured a tale in which Abner Doubleday, who served as an American officer in the war with Mexico, promoted his game to troops stationed at the old Aztec capital. That an Illinois volunteer used Antonio López de Santa Anna's captured wooden leg for a baseball bat made the story even more outrageous.

Realistically, a combination of factors led to baseball's emergence in the areas beyond the Yucatán: the Mexican elite's familiarity with cricket, previously introduced by the British; the daily contact between Mexican industrial and railway workers and their American counterparts, particularly in Mexico's northern frontier cities like Monterrey and Chihuahua; and Mexican intrigue with all aspects of modernization, a direct result of the positivist ideology during the Porfiriato that emphasized order and progress.

As the game developed throughout the countryside, amateur and semiprofessional leagues formed. In 1906 El Record, Mexico's most popular club, played a Chicago White Sox team that had come to Mexico City for training and added revenues. Though the Americans easily won, Mexican baseball continued to grow. Following the revolutionary period, teams reestablished league play. The Mexican Baseball League, formed in 1925, was the most prominent of these institutions. Mexican baseball, in subsequent years, blossomed and, as a result, came to threaten the more established American big leagues.

Despite the popular notion that baseball in North America greatly predated its spread elsewhere, Latins were playing baseball less than twenty years after Alexander Joy Cartwright established its basic rules in 1845. Cuba's first professional league began operations only two years after the 1876

inauguration of the National League in the United States. And by the
1880s, baseball was nearly twenty years old in Mexico's Yucatán Peninsula.
Indeed, even the distant Japanese were playing the game before the end of
the 1880s. Clearly, the roots of baseball in the United States were not much
deeper than where it was later adopted. One might presume that ballplayers
whose countries were so close to the United States, and whose people were
"stark raving dottily crazy over baseball," might warrant attention from
the American professional clubs. Ironically, American capitalists paid little
attention to the notion of incorporating Latins into American professional
baseball. Consequently, by the end of 1910 the presence of Latins in the big
leagues was sparse.

Bibliographical Essay

Perhaps a sure sign of baseball's continuing health and vitality is reflected in the flood of books and articles that appears each year and shows no sign of abating. Because it was the earliest team game to develop and because of its designation as America's pastime, baseball has been the game that received the earliest and most persistent attention from all manner of scholar, journalist, and enthusiast. It is not possible, therefore, to give justice to the many fine works that have predated this anthology and have provided the basic groundwork upon which many of these selections are based. The intent of this essay is simply to provide readers with a sampling of materials that are available should they wish to pursue further the topics, ideas, and interpretations suggested by the authors. In keeping with the volume's intent to focus on the most recent scholarship in this field, with a few notable exceptions, the following titles represent the best scholarship of the last two decades of the twentieth century. This decision is also based upon the belief that it has been during that time period that the field of baseball history has established its credibility as a scholarly field of inquiry and has therefore attracted some of the most thoughtful and best researched studies of the game.

The first place to start when considering the best of baseball's recent histories is Larry R. Gerlach's fine essay, "Not Quite Ready for Prime Time: Baseball History, 1983–1993," *Journal of Sport History* 21 (summer 1994): 103–37, in which he reviews with the careful scholar's eye the key works of the period, including monographs, biographies, anthologies, and team histories covering the full course of the history of baseball, while also identifying areas needing further research. Paul J. Zingg's article, "Diamonds in the Rough: Baseball and the Study of American Sports History," *The History Teacher* 19 (May 1986): 385–403, takes a similar, though less comprehensive, approach. The best complete bibliography is *Baseball: A Comprehensive Bibliography* (Jefferson NC, 1986), with two supplements published in 1993 and 1998, compiled by Myron J. Smith; it includes a comprehensive compendium of books, articles, bibliographies, and guides. See also Marion Fornier, et al., *The Baseball File:*

A Comprehensive Bibliography of America's National Pastime (Gloucester, Ontario, 1992). For the latest listings, the Society for American Baseball Research (SABR) publishes many monthlies, annuals, and special studies.

Solid scholarly and thoroughly researched general histories of the game have been written that provide useful syntheses. Two multivolume histories paved the way. One was Harold Seymour's meticulously researched two volumes, *Baseball: The Early Years* (New York, 1960), and *Baseball: The Golden Years* (New York, 1970), about the development up to 1930 of the game's organization, which the author regards as an example of modern capitalism. The other was David Q. Voigt's trilogy, *American Baseball* (Norman OK, 1966–71, and University Park PA, 1983), which takes the story to the 1980s with an emphasis on baseball's culture. Two scholarly single-volume histories are Benjamin G. Rader's beautifully written *Baseball: America's Game* (Urbana IL, 1992), a thoughtful analysis of the game in the broader context of baseball's relationship with American society, and Charles C. Alexander's *Our Game: An American Baseball History* (New York, 1991), an engagingly written volume that spends less time on the external influences on the game and more on the game itself, its personalities, pennant races, and highlights. Two single-volume studies that deserve mention because of their unique approaches are *Diamonds in the Rough: The Untold History of Baseball,* by Joel Zoss and John Bowman (Chicago, 1996), and *Koppett's Concise History of Major League Baseball,* by veteran sportswriter Leonard Koppett (Philadelphia, 1998). The former is a fascinating series of anecdotal essays, almost offbeat, that give the reader a sense of the popular culture of the game. Koppett's volume has an unusual, if somewhat awkward, arrangement of chronologies interspersed with period surveys and analytical sections, and it includes a wealth of information and statistical data.

NATIONAL PASTIME

Baseball's early development has recently attracted many historians, who have filled gaps in our knowledge of the amateur era. Three important studies about the early game and its participants have provided an analytical framework for our understanding of the game's early development: Melvin L. Adelman, *A Sporting Time: New York City and the Rise of Modern Athletics 1820–1870* (Urbana IL, 1986); George B. Kirsch, *The Creation of American Team Sports: Baseball and Cricket, 1838–72* (Urbana IL, 1989); and Warren Goldstein, *Playing for Keeps: A History of Early Baseball* (Ithaca NY, 1990). Together they paint a complete picture of how baseball became the urban-industrial middle-class pastime. Adelman's imaginative study, based on an analysis of the socioeconomic backgrounds of the organized club members, places the game's origins clearly on the doorstep of the urban middle class, while identifying the game's attributes that proved so attractive as to make it the national pastime. Kirsch explores the reasons why baseball won out over cricket as America's game within the context of larger cultural and societal issues of the period. Goldstein analyzes the influences on and off the field that account for the evolution of baseball from a middle-class amateur game to that of a professional game supported by the urban working class and why the game began to be played "for keeps." Steven A. Riess, *City Games: The Evolution of American Society and the Rise of Sports* (Urbana IL, 1986), studies the roles of demographic change and urban politics in the development of the game. Riess's *Touching Base: Professional Baseball in American Culture in the Progressive Era* (Westport CT, 1980) focuses on baseball's status during the Progressive Era, emphasizing that its popularity stemmed from the fact that it touched base with more themes in American culture and society than any other sport. In a study of the same period, Donald Mrozek in *Sport and American Mentality: The Rise of Respectability, 1880–1910* (Knoxville TN, 1983) examines the role of the sons of eastern elites who sought to prove their manhood by their vigorous athletic pursuits, including baseball. For a recent study of the immediate post–Civil War era, see William J. Ryczek, *When Johnny Came Sliding Home: The Post–Civil War Baseball Boom, 1865–1870* (Jefferson NC, 1998). Robert F. Burk, *Never Just a Game: Players, Owners, and American Baseball to 1920* (Chapel Hill, 1994), is especially good at describing the stresses on the game and the nation caused by World War I. For the crisis caused by the Federal League, see Marc Okkonen, *The Federal League of 1914–1915: Baseball's Third Major League* (Garrett Park MD, 1989).

For important articles about baseball and the urban working class, see Steven Gelber, "Working at Playing: The Culture of the Workplace and the Rise of Baseball," *Journal of Social History* 16 (summer 1983): 3–22; Steven Gelber, "Their Hands Are All Out Playing: Business and Amateur Baseball, 1845–1917," *Journal of Sport History* 11 (spring 1984): 5–27; and Melvin L. Adelman, "Baseball, Business and the Work Place: Gelber's Thesis Reexamined," *Journal of Social History* 23 (winter 1989): 285–301.

Several important biographies are Peter Levine, *A. G. Spalding and the Rise of Baseball: The Promise of American Sport* (New York, 1985); David Stevens, *Baseball's Radical for All Seasons: A Biography of John Montgomery Ward* (Lanham MD, 1998); Eugene C. Murdock, *Ben Johnson: Czar of Baseball* (Westport CT, 1982); Paul J. Zingg, *Harry Hooper: An American Baseball Life* (Urbana IL, 1993); Charles C. Alexander, *John McGraw* (New York, 1988); Henry W. Thomas, *Walter Johnson: Baseball's Big Train* (Lincoln NE, 1995); Dennis DeValeria and Jeanne Burke DeValeria, *Honus Wagner: A Biography* (Pittsburgh, 1998); and Charles Creamer, *Matty: An American Hero* (New York, 1993).

THE GOLDEN ERA

Books abound covering various aspects of the period between World War I and the end of World War II. Perhaps the best attempt to describe baseball's larger social significance is by Richard Crepeau, *Baseball: America's Diamond Mind, 1914–1941* (Orlando FL, 1980), which studies the cultural images of the game as depicted in the popular periodical literature of the times, especially *The Sporting News*. Consult Riess, *Touching Base* (cited above), for the urban context of baseball's ideology during the early years of the period.

A fascinating array of volumes covers a wide range of topics for the period. Lawrence Ritter has written a model of oral history that has been widely emulated. His edited collection of oral testimonies, *The Glory of Their Times: The Story of the Early Days of Baseball Told by the Men Who Played It* (New York, 1966, 1984), stimulated similar works by Donald Honig, *Baseball: When the Grass Was Real* (New York, 1975); Rich Wescott, *Diamond Greats: Profiles and Interviews with 65 of Baseball's History Makers* (Westport CT, 1988); Eugene Murdock, ed. *Baseball Players and Their Times: Oral Histories of the Game, 1920–1940* (Westport CT, 1991), and *Baseball between the Wars: Memories of the Game by the Men Who Played It* (Westport CT, 1992); and Walter M. Langford, ed., *Legends of Baseball: An Oral History of the Game's Golden Age* (South Bend IN, 1987). Richard Bak, *Cobb Would Have Caught It* (Detroit, 1991), combines interviews with a first-rate history of the Tigers from 1920 to 1950. For a somewhat later cohort of players, see Cynthia Wilber's interviews in *For Love of the Game: Baseball Memories from the Men Who Were There* (New York, 1992); Mike Bryan, *Baseball Lives: Men and Women of the Game Talk about Their Jobs, Their Lives, and the National Pastime* (New York, 1989); and Lee Heiman, Dave Deiner, and Bill Gutman, *When the Cheering Stops: Ex-Major Leaguers Talk about Their Game and Their Lives* (New York, 1990). With due caveats about the inherent shortcomings of such testimonies, an impressive amount of raw material has been preserved for future researchers in the field.

For the events of the post–World War I period examined in this anthology, see Elliot Asinof's well-researched and eminently readable *Eight Men Out: The Black Sox and the 1919 World Series* (New York, 1963), which has become the standard treatment of the 1919 World Series fix and Black Sox scandal. Nothing of recent vintage can top it, including Robert I. Goler's "Black Sox," *Chicago History* 17 (fall-winter 1988–89): 42–69. For the role played by the scandal's most prominent player, see Donald Gropman, *Say It Ain't So, Joe!: The Story of Shoeless Joe Jackson* (2d rev. ed.; Secaucus NJ, 1999). Kenesaw Mountain Landis and his reign as czar of baseball can be studied in David Pietrusza, *Judge and Jury: The Life and Times of Judge Kenesaw Mountain Landis* (South Bend IN, 1998), and Clark Nardinelli, "Judge Kenesaw Mountain Landis and the Art of Cartel Enforcement," in Peter Levine, ed., *Baseball History* (New York, 1989). On the batting revolution of the 1920s, see William Curran, *Big Sticks: The Batting Revolution of the Twenties* (New York, 1990). A sense of the nature of the postwar game can be gotten from Mike Sowell, *The Pitch That Killed* (New York, 1987).

The study of black baseball prior to the integration of the game has generated considerable interest and substantial writing during the past twenty years. The trailblazer in such studies was Robert Peterson's *Only the Ball Was White* (Englewood Cliffs NJ, 1970). Several important works have appeared since then that have filled in the picture. See Mark Ribowsky, *A Complete History of the Negro Leagues, 1884–1955* (New York, 1995); John B. Holway, *Blackball Stars: Negro-League Pioneers* (Westport CT, 1988); Donn Rogosin, *Invisible Men: Life in Baseball's Negro Leagues* (Boston, 1983). For specific Negro League teams, see Janet Bruce, *The Kansas City Monarchs* (Lawrence KS, 1985); Rob Ruck, *Sandlot Seasons: Sport in Black Pittsburgh* (Urbana IL, 1987); Richard Bak, *Turkey Stearns and the Detroit Stars: The Negro Leagues in Detroit, 1919–1939* (Detroit, 1994); Paul Debono, *The Indianapolis ABCs: History of a Premier Team in the Negro Leagues* (Jefferson NC, 1997); and James Bankes, *The Pittsburgh Crawfords: The Lives and Times of Black Baseball's Most Exciting Team* (Dubuque IA, 1991). Two studies of key black players are John B. Holway, *Josh and Satch: The Life and Times of Josh Gibson and Satchel Paige* (Westport CT, 1891), and William Brasher, *Josh Gibson: A Life in the Negro Leagues* (New York, 1978). Three books give a glimpse inside the business and entrepreneurial world of black baseball: James Overmyer, *Queen of the Negro Leagues: Effa Manley and the Newark Eagles* (Lanham MD, 1998); Charles Whitehead, *A Man and His Diamonds* (New York, 1980), on Rube Foster; and Sol White, *Sol White's Official Base Ball Guide, 1905,* reprinted with a fine introduction by Jerry Malloy (Lincoln NE, 1994).

Jewish participation in the game can be appreciated in Peter Levine's outstanding study, *Ellis Island to Ebbets Field: Sport and the American Jewish Experience* (New York, 1992), and Walter Harrison's brief but valuable essay, "Six Pointed Diamond: Baseball and American Jews," *Journal of Popular Culture* (winter 1981): 112–18.

For the World War II era, see three books for the general audience that make up the brief list: Richard Goldstein, *Spartan Seasons: How Baseball Survived the Second World War* (New York, 1980); Bill Gilbert, *They Also Served: Baseball and the Home Front, 1941–1945* (New York, 1992); and a reissue of *Even the Browns* (Chicago, 1978), retitled *Baseball Goes to War,* by William B. Mead (Washington DC, 1985). A different perspective can be gained from David M. Jordan, *A Tiger in His Time: Hal Newhouser and the Burden of Wartime Baseball* (South Bend IN, 1990). For the spectacular events of the last season before America's entry into the war, see Michael Seidel, *Joe DiMaggio and the Summer of '41* (New York, 1988), and Robert Creamer, *Baseball in '41: A Celebration of the Best Baseball Season Ever—In the Year America Went to War* (New York, 1991).

Studies of baseball during the period at the local, amateur level, along the lines of Pendleton's "Jim Crow Strikes Out," have been slow to arrive. Some of the better ones include Gary Ross Mormino, "The Playing Fields of St. Louis: Italian Immigrants and Sports, 1925–1941," *Journal of Sport History* 9 (summer 1982): 5–19, and Michael E. Lomax, "Black Entrepreneurship in the National Pastime: The Rise of Semiprofessional Baseball in Black Chicago, 1890–1915," *Journal of Sport History* 25 (spring 1998): 43–64.

Among the better biographies for the period are George De Gregorio's *Joe DiMaggio: An Informal Biography* (New York, 1981); Michael Seidel, *Ted Williams: A Baseball Life* (Chicago, 1991); Ray Robinson, *Iron Horse: Lou Gehrig in His Time* (New York, 1990); Ira Berkow, *Hank Greenberg* (New York, 1989); Charles C. Alexander: *Ty Cobb* (New York, 1984), and *Rogers Hornsby: A Biography* (New York, 1995); Marshall Smelser, *The Life That Ruth Built* (New York, 1975; Lincoln NE, 1993); and Robert Creamer, *Babe: The Legend Comes to Life* (New York, 1974).

THE NATIONAL GAME

The plethora of written materials for the most recent era is nearly overwhelming, so what follows is necessarily a highly selective list focusing on the relationship of baseball to social and cultural forces of the period. The integration of professional baseball has received great attention. The fiftieth anniversary in 1997 of Jackie Robinson's breakthrough with the Dodgers presented an opportunity to undertake retrospective analyses of his achievement and subsequent events. The benchmark study of postwar baseball integration within the context of American race relations remains Jules Tygiel, *Baseball's Great Experiment: Jackie Robinson and His Legacy* (expanded ed.; New York, 1997). Among the more recent biographies is an excellent study by Arnold Rampersad, *Jackie Robinson: A Biography* (New York, 1997). See also David Falkner, *Great Time Coming: The Life of Jackie Robinson from Baseball to Birmingham* (New York, 1995), which places Robinson's life in the broad context of social forces of the era and his significant role in the civil rights movement of the late 1950s and 1960s. Robinson's own story is recounted in *Breakthrough to the Big Leagues: The Story of Jackie Robinson* (New York, 1985), and *I Never Had It Made* (New York, 1972; repr. Hopewell NJ, 1995). Rachel Robinson's vantage point is told in her volume, *Jackie Robinson: An Intimate Portrait* (New York, 1996). Unfortunately no worthy study focusing on Branch Rickey has yet emerged, leaving much room for speculation about his role and motivations. The second person to accomplish an historic feat is usually overlooked, and this has been the case with Larry Doby, who became the second black player to play in the major leagues, only a few months after Robinson. This has been corrected by a fine study by Joseph T. Moore, *Pride against Prejudice: The Biography of Larry Doby* (Westport CT, 1988). See also Mark Ribowsky, *Don't Look Back: Satchel Paige in the Shadows of Baseball* (New York, 1994), for a biography of the legendary black pitcher.

Although the literature about women in sports is growing rapidly, the role of women in baseball has been neglected compared to their participation in other sports. Perhaps sparked by the film *A League of Their Own,* there has been a renewed interest in the subject, although overemphasizing the All-American Girls Professional Baseball League. Lois Browne's *Girls of Summer: The Real Story of the All-American Girls Professional Baseball League* (New York, 1992) is a highly popularistic account. More analytically based and serious studies can be found in Diane Helmer, *Belles of the Park* (Bookfield CT, 1993), about the Racine Belles. Barbara Gregorich, *Women at Play: The Story of Women in Baseball* (New York, 1993), pulls together a series of biographical sketches of women in all phases of the game. See also Gai Berlage, *Women in Baseball: The Forgotten History* (Westport CT, 1994) for the nineteenth century.

The issues of franchise history, movement, and expansion have generated much journalistic heat, although little scholarly light. Unlike the older genre of team histories that focused upon exploits on the field, two of the best recent studies of baseball franchises, one highly successful and one ultimately failing, deal with the broader issues of baseball's political and economic relationships with franchise cities, social and cultural connections with the surrounding communities, and team business operations. See James Miller, *The Baseball Business: Pursuing Pennants and Profits in Baltimore* (Chapel Hill, 1990), and Bruce Kuklick, *To Everything a Season: Shibe Park and Urban Philadelphia, 1909–1976* (Princeton, 1991). Patrick Harrigan, *The Detroit Tigers: Club and Community, 1945–1995* (Toronto, 1997), uses a similar formula. Such studies, along with a boom of new stadium construction, have stimulated an interest in some of the game's historic stadiums. These studies of latter-day cathedrals give a perspective about the evolution of the game, the communities, and the owners of their day. Among others, see Rich Wescott, *Philadelphia's Old Ballparks* (Philadelphia, 1996); Philip J. Lowrey, *Green Cathedrals* (rev. ed., Reading MA, 1992); Michael Gershman, *Diamonds: The Evolution of the Ballpark* (Boston, 1993); Lawrence R. Ritter, *Lost Ballparks: A Celebration of Baseball's Legendary Fields* (New York, 1992). A nice juxtaposition can be gained from Michael Betzold and Ethan Casey, *Queen of Diamonds: The Tiger Stadium Story* (Bloomfield MI, 1992), about the most recent victim of the wrecking ball, and Peter Richmond, *Ballpark: Camden Yards and the Building of an American Dream* (New York, 1993), about the stadium that sparked the current wave of building fan-friendly ballparks.

The issues of franchise movement and expansion necessarily confront the issue of baseball and entrepreneurship, and the literature in this area is rapidly growing, although with uneven results. For a study of the move that shocked the baseball world as well as society at large and opened the door for the subsequent deluge of franchise mobility, see Neil J. Sullivan, *The Dodgers Move West* (New York, 1987). A broader treatment of the politics and economics of such movements is found in Charles C. Euchner, *Playing the Field: Why Sports Teams Move and Cities Fight to Keep Them* (Baltimore, 1993), and James Quirk and Rodney Fort, *Hard Ball: The*

Abuse of Power in Pro Team Sports (Princeton, 1999). Economists have weighed in with their perspectives and models in seeking to understand the arcane world of baseball finance and business practices. See Gerald S. Scully, *The Business of Major League Baseball* (Chicago, 1989); Daniel R. Marburger, ed., *Stee-Rike Four: What's Wrong with the Business of Baseball* (Westport CT, 1997); and especially Andrew Zimbalist, *Baseball and Billions: A Probing Look Inside the Big Business of Our National Pastime* (New York, 1992), which is a nicely researched, jargon-free study, in historical context, of the dynamics that drive the business of baseball. See also Kenneth Jennings, *Balls and Strikes: The Money Game in Professional Baseball* (New York, 1990), and Paul M. Summers, ed., *Diamonds Are Forever* (Washington DC, 1992).

For baseball's labor-management relations, there has been an outpouring of studies. The best place to start is with Lee Lowenfish and Tony Lupien, *The Imperfect Diamond: The Story of Baseball's Reserve Clause and the Men Who Fought to Change It* (New York, 1980, 1991). Other more technical studies are Kenneth Jennings, *Swings and Misses: Moribund Labor Relations in Professional Baseball* (Westport CT, 1997), and Paul D. Staudohar, *Playing for Dollars: Labor Relations and the Business of Sports* (Ithaca NY, 1996). Highly readable but lacking documentation are John Helyar, *Lords of the Realm: The Real History of Baseball* (New York, 1994), and John Feinstein, *Play Ball: The Life and Troubled Times of Major League Baseball* (New York, 1993). Both reveal the shortsightedness and pomposity of the owners. In a similar vein, see also Neil J. Sullivan, *The Diamond Revolution: The Prospects for Baseball after the Collapse of Its Ruling Class* (New York, 1992), and Peter Gammons and Jack Sands, *Coming Apart at the Seams* (New York, 1993). An important autobiography by the players' hero and the owners' nemesis is Marvin Miller's *A Whole Different Ball Game: The Sport and Business of Baseball* (New York, 1991).

THE INTERNATIONAL GAME

A small but growing body of literature exists concerning the game as it has spread overseas, although it remains a fertile area for additional research. The best coverage extends to baseball in Latin America. The best of the general studies of the region is Peter C. Bjarkman, *Baseball with a Latin Beat: A History of the Latin American Game* (Jefferson NC, 1994). A bit too thin and focused on individual players is Michael M. Oleksak and Mary Adams Oleksak, *Latin Americans and the Grand Old Game* (Grand Rapids MI, 1991). The foremost studies of baseball south of the border are Alan M. Klein, *Sugarball: The American Game, the Dominican Dream* (New Haven, 1991), and Rob Ruck, *The Tropic of Baseball: Baseball and the Dominican Republic* (Westport CT, 1991; repr. Lincoln NE, 1998). Both focus on the unique flavor and features of baseball in the Dominican Republic, especially the impact of the sugar mills; both are well researched and heavily reliant on personal interviews; and each author—Klein a sociologist and Ruck an historian—brings his own disciplinary approach to bear. A recent well-researched study of Cuban baseball that attempts to correct American views about Cuban baseball is by Roberto Gonzalez Echevarría, *The Pride of Havana: A History of Cuban Baseball* (New York, 1999). Samuel O. Regalado, *Viva Baseball!: Latin Major Leaguers and Their Special Hunger* (Urbana IL, 1998), provides an outstanding example of research possibilities as he traces the struggles with racism and cultural isolation that Latin American players have faced in professional baseball in the United States. See also Regalado's study, "The Minor League Experience of Latin American Baseball Players in Western Communities," *Journal of the West* 16 (January 1987): 65–70. For an interesting study of the unique status of baseball along the United States–Mexican border, see Alan M. Klein, *Baseball on the Border: A Tale of Two Laredos* (Princeton, 1999). Biographies of varying value have been written about Roberto Clemente, Juan Marichal, Minnie Minoso, Orlando Cepeda, Luis Tiant, and Fernando Valenzuela, among others.

Japanese baseball has received two studies by Robert Whiting, *You Gotta Have Wa* (New York, 1989), and *The Chrysanthemum and the Bat: Baseball Samurai Style* (New York, 1977). On the struggles and opportunities for American players who seek to penetrate the unique cultural world of Japanese baseball, see Warren Cromartie and Robert Whiting, *Slugging It Out in Japan: An American Major Leaguer and the Tokyo Outfield* (New York, 1991). For a biography of Japan's legendary slugger Sadaharu Oh, see Sadaharu Oh and David Falkner, *A Zen Way of Baseball* (New York, 1984).

Canadian baseball has been surprisingly neglected considering the long relationship that it has enjoyed with the American game. Two recent studies by William Humber, *Diamonds of the North: A Concise History of Baseball in Canada* (Toronto, 1995), and Colin Howell, *Northern Sandlots: A Social History of Maritime Baseball* (Toronto, 1995), give hope that interest in the game will spark further serious study of its roots, development, and character.

Serious studies have yet to be written about baseball in the non-Caribbean areas of Latin America, as well as the burgeoning game in the Far East, Europe, and Australia. For an insightful survey of baseball overseas, see "The International Game," in Joel Zoss and John Bowman, *Diamonds in the Rough: The Untold History of Baseball* (Chicago, 1996), pp. 384–417.

Source Acknowledgments

THE NATIONAL PASTIME

Chapter 1: Reprinted from Warren Goldstein, "The Base Ball Fraternity," chapter 1 of *Playing for Keeps: A History of Early Baseball* (Ithaca NY: Cornell University Press, 1989), pp. 17–31. Copyright © 1989 by Cornell University. Used by permission of the publisher.

Chapter 2: Ronald Story, "The Country of the Young: The Meaning of Baseball in Early American Culture," in *Cooperstown Symposium on Baseball*, ed. Alvin Hall (Westport CT: Meckler, 1991), pp 324–42.

Chapter 3: Steven A. Riess, "Professional Baseball and Social Mobility," *Journal of Interdisciplinary History* 11, no. 2 (autumn 1980): 235–50. © 1980 by the Massachusetts Institute of Technology and the editors of the *Journal of Interdisciplinary History*.

Chapter 4: Michael S. Kimmel, "Baseball and the Reconstitution of American Masculinity, 1880–1920," *Baseball History* 3 (1990): 98–112.

Chapter 5: Jerry Malloy, "Sol White and the Origin of African American Baseball," reprinted from *Sol White's History of Colored Baseball, with other Documents on the Early Black Game, 1886–1936*, introduction by Jerry Malloy by permission of the University of Nebraska Press. © 1995 by the University of Nebraska Press.

THE GOLDEN ERA

Chapter 6: David Q. Voigt, "The Chicago Black Sox and the Myth of Baseball's Single Sin," chapter 5 of *America through Baseball* (Chicago: Nelson Hall, 1976), pp. 65–76.

Chapter 7: Norman L. Rosenberg, "Here Comes the Judge! The Origins of Baseball's Commissioner System and American Legal Culture," *Journal of Popular Culture* 20 (spring 1987): 129–46.

Chapter 8: Leverett T. Smith Jr., "The Changing Style of Play: Cobb vs. Ruth," in *The American Dream and the National Game* (Bowling Green OH: Bowling Green University Popular Press, 1975), pp. 188–207.

Chapter 9: Jason Pendleton, "Jim Crow Strikes Out: Interracial Baseball in Wichita, Kansas, 1920–1935," *Kansas History* 20 (summer 1997): 86–101.

Chapter 10: William M. Simons, "The Athlete as Jewish Standard Bearer: Media Images of Hank Greenberg," *Jewish Social Studies* 44 (spring 1982): 95–112. Published by Indiana University Press.

THE NATIONAL GAME

Chapter 11: Jules Tygiel, "A Spectacular Season: Jackie Robinson Breaks Through," introduction to *The Jackie Robinson Reader: Perspectives on an American Hero*, ed. Jules Tygiel, pp. 1–14. Copyright © 1997 by Jules Tygiel. Originally published by Dutton. Reprinted by permission of Curtis Brown, Ltd.

Chapter 12: Debra Shattuck, "Playing a Man's Game: Women and Baseball in the United States, 1866–1954," *Baseball History* 2 (1989): 57–77.

Chapter 13: Bruce Kuklick, "The Demise of the Philadelphia Athletics," *Baseball History* 3 (1990): 33–48.

Chapter 14: Ron Briley, "More Legacy of Conquest: Long-Term Ramifications of the Major League Baseball Shift to the West," *Journal of the West* 36 (April 1997): 68–78.

Chapter 15: Daniel R. Marburger, "Whatever Happened to the 'Good Ol' Days'?," chapter 1 of *Stee-Rike Four! What's Wrong with the Business of Baseball*, ed. Daniel R. Marburger (Westport CT: Praeger, 1997), pp. 7–36. Copyright © 1997 by Daniel R. Marburger. Reproduced with permission of Greenwood Publishing Group, Inc., Westport CT.

THE INTERNATIONAL GAME

Chapter 16: Donald Roden, "Baseball and the Quest for National Dignity in Meiji Japan," *American Historical Review* 85 (June 1980): 511–34.

Chapter 17: William Humber, "Canada in the Country of Baseball," from *Diamonds of the North: A Concise History of Baseball in Canada*, by William Humber (Toronto: Oxford University Press, 1995), pp. 3–14. Copyright © Oxford University Press Canada 1995. Reprinted by permission of Oxford University Press Canada.

Chapter 18: Samuel O. Regalado, "That Special Hunger" and "Beginnings," chapters 1 and 2 in *Viva Baseball! Latin Major Leaguers and Their Special Hunger* (Urbana: University of Illinois Press, 1998), pp. 1–18. Copyright 1998 by the Board of Trustees of the University of Illinois. Used with permission of the University of Illinois Press.

Index